Religious and National Discourses

Diskursmuster
Discourse Patterns

Edited by
Beatrix Busse and Ingo H. Warnke

Volume 33

Religious and National Discourses

Contradictory Belonging, Minorities, Marginality and Centrality

Edited by
Hanna Acke, Silvia Bonacchi, Charlotta Seiler Brylla and Ingo H. Warnke

DE GRUYTER

Free access to the e-book version of this publication was made possible by the 40 academic libraries and initiatives that supported the open access transformation project in German Linguistics.

ISBN 978-3-11-221491-6
e-ISBN (PDF) 978-3-11-103963-3
e-ISBN (EPUB) 978-3-11-104020-2
DOI https://doi.org/10.1515/9783111039633

This work is licensed under the Creative Commons Attribution 4.0 International License. For details go to http://creativecommons.org/licenses/by/4.0/.

Creative Commons license terms for re-use do not apply to any content (such as graphs, figures, photos, excerpts, etc.) that is not part of the Open Access publication. These may require obtaining further permission from the rights holder. The obligation to research and clear permission lies solely with the party re-using the material.

Library of Congress Control Number: 2023938634

Bibliographic information published by the Deutsche Nationalbibliothek
The Deutsche Nationalbibliothek lists this publication in the Deutsche Nationalbibliografie; detailed bibliographic data are available on the Internet at http://dnb.dnb.de.

© 2025 the author(s), published by Walter de Gruyter GmbH, Berlin/Boston
This volume is text- and page-identical with the hardback published in 2023.
The book is published open access at www.degruyter.com.

Printing and binding: CPI books GmbH, Leck

www.degruyter.com

Open-Access-Transformation in Linguistics

Open Access for excellent academic publications in the field of German Linguistics: Thanks to the support of 40 academic libraries and initiatives, 9 frontlist publications from 2023 can be published as gold open access, without any costs to the authors.

The following institutions and initiatives have contributed to the funding and thus promote the open access transformation in German linguistics and ensure free availability for everyone:

Dachinitiative „Hochschule.digital Niedersachsen" des Landes Niedersachsen
Universitätsbibliothek Augsburg
Freie Universität Berlin
Staatsbibliothek zu Berlin – Preußischer Kulturbesitz
Technische Universität Berlin / Universitätsbibliothek
Universitätsbibliothek der Humboldt-Universität zu Berlin
Universität Bern
Universitätsbibliothek Bielefeld
Universitätsbibliothek Bochum
Universitäts- und Landesbibliothek Bonn
Staats- und Universitätsbibliothek Bremen
Universitäts- und Landesbibliothek Darmstadt
Sächsische Landesbibliothek – Staats- und Universitätsbibliothek Dresden
Universitätsbibliothek Duisburg-Essen
Universitäts- und Landesbibliothek Düsseldorf
Universitätsbibliothek Eichstätt-Ingolstadt
Universitätsbibliothek Johann Christian Senckenberg, Frankfurt a. M.
Albert-Ludwigs-Universität Freiburg - Universitätsbibliothek
Niedersächsische Staats- und Universitätsbibliothek Göttingen
Fernuniversität Hagen, Universitätsbibliothek
Gottfried Wilhelm Leibniz Bibliothek – Niedersächsische Landesbibliothek, Hannover
Technische Informationsbibliothek (TIB) Hannover
Universitätsbibliothek Hildesheim
Universitätsbibliothek Kassel – Landesbibliothek und Murhardsche Bibliothek der Stadt Kassel
Universitäts- und Stadtbibliothek Köln
Université de Lausanne
Zentral- und Hochschulbibliothek Luzern
Bibliothek des Leibniz-Instituts für Deutsche Sprache, Mannheim
Universitätsbibliothek Marburg
Universitätsbibliothek der Ludwig-Maximilians-Universität München
Universitäts- und Landesbibliothek Münster
Bibliotheks- und Informationssystem (BIS) der Carl von Ossietzky Universität Oldenburg
Universitätsbibliothek Osnabrück
Universität Potsdam
Universitätsbibliothek Trier
Universitätsbibliothek Vechta
Herzog August Bibliothek Wolfenbüttel
Universitätsbibliothek Wuppertal
ZHAW Zürcher Hochschule für Angewandte Wissenschaften, Hochschulbibliothek
Zentralbibliothek Zürich

Contents

Hanna Acke, Silvia Bonacchi, Carsten Junker, Charlotta Seiler Brylla and
Ingo H. Warnke
Minorities and Majorities, Marginality and Centrality. An Introduction —— 1

Part I: **Marginalising and Centralising Discursive Practices**

Gábor Egry
Unlikely Brothers? Entangled Székely and Moți Peripheries in a Contested Province: Transylvania 1900–1944 —— 11

Svante Lindberg
Francophone Calvinists in 18th Century German-Speaking Europe. On Charles Étienne Jordan, Mathurin Veyssière La Croze and Éléazar de Mauvillon —— 37

Hanna Acke
"To the End of the World". Legitimising Strategies in Protestant Missionary Discourses around 1900 —— 57

Part II: **Intersections of National and Religious Belonging**

Esther Jahns
Positioning in the Community. The Interplay of Language, Nationality and Religion for Jewish Speakers in Berlin —— 83

Mercédesz Czimbalmos
Masculine Disposition and Cantonist Ancestry. Symbolic Capital within the Jewish Community of Helsinki —— 103

Maya Hadar
Together we Stand? Exploring National Identification Among Israeli Arabs, Jews and Immigrants Following Israeli Military Successes —— 127

Herbert Rostand Ngouo
Religion Weaponised. An Analysis of the Deployment of Religious Themes in the Discourse of Anglophone Nationalist and Secessionist Leaders and Activists in Cameroon —— 155

Part III: Contradictory Operations of Marginalisation and Centralisation

Christopher M. Schmidt
Shaping Identity through the Use of Language. The Finland Swedish Paradox —— 189

Diana Hitzke
Contradictory Narratives in Sorbian Literature. The Concept of a 'Sorbian Island' and Discourses of Hybridity —— 213

Katharina Bock
The Pressure to Convert. Literary Perspectives on Jewishness in the Era of Jewish Emancipation in Denmark —— 227

Index —— 247

List of Contributors —— 253

Hanna Acke, Silvia Bonacchi, Carsten Junker, Charlotta Seiler Brylla and Ingo H. Warnke
Minorities and Majorities, Marginality and Centrality

An Introduction

The volume you hold in your hands (or have opened on your screen) is a result of the editors' observations and perhaps initially also only of the assumption of a current shift in societal understandings of majorities and minorities. Groups we had so far thought of as part of the majority, as part of what in German is labelled the *Mehrheitsgesellschaft*, have recently positioned themselves as threatened minorities to claim rights. We are well aware that the *we* of the observer's position is of special importance in such a statement and that such statements are fundamentally bound to one's own affiliations. This is certainly also true for William Davies, whom we cite here as an example, because he makes similar observations quite accurately and rightly refers to debates about recognition: "The struggle for recognition has turned into an arms race, in which majority cultural identities deploy the language of minority rights in their defence. In contexts such as Brexit, liberals have also engaged in demands for identity recognition, with street protests, flags and claims of cultural marginalization." (Davies 2021: 85)

Societal liberalisation, an increasing equality and successful politics of recognition of certain minority groups have led to a situation in which it seems much more difficult to determine who belongs to the *Mehrheitsgesellschaft* – and thus is located at the metaphorical centre of society – and who is not. To make it clear: it has never been easy to distinguish between majorities and minorities. It only seemed easier for two reasons: first, the predominance of white, heterosexual, cis-gendered, able-bodied individuals was not questioned as widely, and they were often seen as representing the broader or even whole society. Second, reducing individuals to only one group identity made the categorisation into minority and majority seem more obvious before. Only preferring one categorisation over another

---

Note: The editors would like to thank the Research Council at the Faculty of Arts, Psychology and Theology, Research Services and the Strategic Research Profile Minority Studies at Åbo Akademi University for their financial support for this volume and the libraries that fund De Gruyter's Open Access Transformation Packages programme for the possibility of publishing open access.

makes it possible to count and to determine numbers which are transparent indicators of majority and minority belonging. We can, for example, clearly say that when only 287.933 inhabitants of Finland were Swedish speakers in 2021 while 4.800.243 were Finnish speakers, the Swedish speakers formed a minority group (see Statistikcentralen 2022). We also know that most of these 287.933 individuals identified as either men or women and by that group categorisation were neither a majority nor a minority in the Finnish context. Furthermore, we can assume that most of them identified as Finns, which made them a self-evident part of the *Mehrheitsgesellschaft* in Finland. But even the language question is complicated by political categorisations: to start with, who is counted as a Swedish speaker and why? For example, the statistics do not take bilingual individuals into account. Furthermore, Swedish – regardless of its actual low number of speakers – is not officially considered a minority language in Finland. It is one of the two national languages by law (see Institutet för de inhemska språken n.d.).

It is the pluralisation of heterogeneous societies that calls for a shift in the gaze from minority/majority towards marginality/centrality or even to marginalisation/centralisation. Terms like *majority*, *minority*, or especially the *Mehrheitsgesellschaft*, are powerful concepts that can be used to assert and to enforce privileges and rights. The democratic logic of majority voting systems supports the kinds of claims which lend rights to majorities and positions them in the centre. This becomes clear in the following examples: the majority of the population in Germany supports the introduction of a speed limit on the motorways. Then politics should consider the introduction of a speed limit, shouldn't it? If the majority of a population supports the idea that a certain religion should be privileged over others, should politics consider privileging that religion? While democratic rule is by far the most advantageous political system for minorities as the protection of minority rights is seen as one cornerstone of liberal democracy, this logic also leads to contradictory frictions within democratic societies. Thus, the importance of minority rights in democracy also makes it possible to claim rights by asserting minority status for one's own group.

A shift from minority/majority towards marginality/centrality might thus disentangle the idea of democratic majorities from questions of justice and equality. Of course, marginality/centrality are always situationally bound; they are not understood by us as stable localities. It is precisely for this reason that we believe this shift will support a more nuanced perspective on fragile, multiple, and partial belongings of individuals to groups as it suggests less of a binary categorisation. Minorities and majorities are seen as distinct entities while marginality and centrality form a spectrum. Thus, the latter categorisations cannot be quantified as easily. Quantifications carry an aura of truth and are thus much more difficult to question. A shift from minority/majority towards marginalisation/centralisation, furthermore, emphasises the importance of the processes by which belonging to a majority or to a minority is negotiated and thus reflects the instability of categorisations and belongings.

One of the goals of our cooperation, which brings together the expertise in minority research from Åbo Akademi University with the innovative interdisciplinary work on contradiction in the framework of *Contradiction Studies* at the University of Bremen as well as the research network *Language and Power* at Stockholm University, the research centre at the University of Warsaw on intercultural pragmatics and interdisciplinary studies, and a research focus on diversity studies at the TU Dresden, is to foster interdisciplinary discussions of these concepts and thereby to further an understanding of marginalising and centralising discourses and processes. As many of us come from linguistics, the role of language – the discursive and symbolic arenas – are of special interest to us and we believe that especially naming, i.e., linguistically categorising a group or a phenomenon, is part of giving it an existence in the social world. Nevertheless, we also consider the materiality of bodies and the materialisations of discursive categorisations. We are interested in the (strategic) use of a metaphorical spatial order of society – across national borders and throughout history: who has been imagined as being at the centre as well as at the margins? On what grounds? How is this displayed in the way groups in societies represent themselves? What consequences does this have for individuals' and groups' influence in society as well as for the allocation of rights, assets, and resources?

To even begin to ask these questions, analysing them empirically and in detail, as well as theorising them can also shed light on current discussions on identity politics. Is identity politics about showing that one's own group is the marginalised group that needs to be compensated for past and present injustices? Or is it about using one's own group as an example to show the effects of marginalising discourses and to oppose these kinds of processes in general? Or might it be both? Historically speaking, the second option seems to be more accurate. The first use, or one of the first, of the term *identity politics* comes from the 1977 *Combahee River Collective Statement* in which the authors write:

> This focusing upon our own oppression is embodied in the concept of identity politics. We believe that the most profound and potentially most radical politics come directly out of our own identity, as opposed to working to end somebody else's oppression. In the case of Black women this is a particularly repugnant, dangerous, threatening, and therefore revolutionary concept because it is obvious from looking at all the political movements that have preceded us that anyone is more worthy of liberation than ourselves. We reject pedestals, queenhood, and walking ten paces behind. To be recognized as human, levelly human, is enough. (Combahee River Collective 2017: 19)

Starting from their own multiple or intersectional oppression (see also Crenshaw 1989), these women asked to be recognised as human and as equals. They speak of *recognition* here, possibly forming one of the starting points of something that Nancy Fraser (2000: 109), with reference to Georg Wilhelm Friedrich Hegel and Charles Taylor, has discussed as the *politics of recognition*. She warns against a politics of recognition replacing struggles for redistribution, but the *Combahee River Collective Statement* resonates well with Fraser's call for a status model instead of an identity model of recognition that would serve to avoid replacing redistribution:

> I shall consequently propose an alternative approach: that of treating recognition as a question of social status. From this perspective, what requires recognition is not group-specific identity but the status of individual group members as full partners in social interaction. Misrecognition, accordingly, does not mean the depreciation and deformation of group identity, but social subordination—in the sense of being prevented from participating as a peer in social life. To redress this injustice still requires a politics of recognition, but in the 'status model' this is no longer reduced to a question of identity: rather, it means a politics aimed at overcoming subordination by establishing the misrecognized party as a full member of society, capable of participating on a par with the rest. (Fraser 2000: 113)

Research on marginalising and centralising discourses, which is correspondingly dynamic, will enable us to understand if claims for recognition are aimed at overcoming subordination and what use they make of certain markers of group belonging. The larger entities within which marginalising and centralising discourses and processes are thought to take place are essential for an understanding of these discourses and processes. In the German word the *Mehrheitsgesellschaft* the larger entity is explicitly named: marginalising and centralising metaphorical ordering takes place within *society*. But what is the extend of *society*? What categorises this meta-group?

In this volume we focus on two categorisations – nationality and religion – which, often quite unnoticed, make up the context of the metaphorical spatial order, the meta-group within which individuals and groups are ordered according to race, class, gender, sexuality and ability. What we call *society* can be the nation state or it can be a religious community. Thus, we have chosen here to focus on marginality and centrality with respect to national and religious belonging. Nationality and religion are two markers of belonging with a very long and entangled history which have often been used to normalise metaphorical spatial orders. Protestant Christianity has, for example, been seen as making up the core of the Nordic nation states, thus legitimising the exclusion of individuals and groups from other religious traditions. At the same time, religions – also Protestant Christianity – were and are seen as inherently transnational.

Part of what the authors of the contributions to this volume do is to establish which understandings of nationality and religion exist and have existed in different historical and regional contexts. The authors explore similarities and differences between mechanisms of inclusion into and exclusion from, as well as centralisation and marginalisation within national and religious communities. How did these concepts get into conflict, contradict each other and also align? How did they intersect with other concepts? Here, the authors examine the interdependencies between these categorisations as well as their interdependency with other categories such as race, gender, and class. These processes of marginalisation and centralisation are often contradictory in character. We identify and describe these contradictions and ask if they are representative of inclusive and exclusive discourses.

The volume is structured into three parts. Part I *Marginalising and Centralising Discursive Practices* focuses on nationality (and related concepts such as race, peoples, ethnicity) and religion as mutually reinforcing centralisations. In the first contribution, historian Gábor Egry analyses the marginalised within two rival nation states as the most authentic and thus central part of the discursive construction of group belonging in his study on Székely and Moți in and between Hungary and Romania. Literary scholar Svante Lindberg shows that, in Prussia, the emergence of the German "nation" as Protestant against a rival Catholic French nation enabled a contradictory central-marginal positioning of exiled French Protestants in this context. In the last contribution of this part, disciplinarily located between linguistics, history, and religious studies, Hanna Acke uses the example of Swedish Protestant missions in Congo and China to point to a centralising effect that was achieved when Sweden as a marginalised nation state within Europe was inscribed and anchored in hegemonic European discourses through Christian universalist belonging and the marginalisation of other religions.

The second part has *Intersections of National and Religious Belonging* as a theme. Both Esther Jahns, a linguist, and Mercédesz Czimbalmos, a scholar of religion, discuss centrality and marginality within religious minority communities, the Jewish communities in Berlin and Helsinki, respectively. The metaphorical space within these rather different religious communities is partly ordered by national belongings and specific national groups seen as "original" maintain a central position despite their numerical minority position. Political scientist Maya Hadar points to contradictory and surprising effects when belonging to a nation state is measured quantitatively. Using Israel as an example, she shows how support for one's own nation state rises in case of violent conflicts regardless of religious belongings that might question this affiliation. All three contributions take as a starting point how the collapse of the Soviet Union as a political event has changed the discursive landscape of marginalisation. The final contribution, by linguist Herbert Rostand Ngouo, looks at the role and the use of religion in social media debates in the context of a violent struggle about national belonging when analysing the Anglophone separatist movement in Cameroon.

The third and final part of the book is dedicated to the topic of *Contradictory Operations of Marginalisation and Centralisation*. Linguist Christopher M. Schmidt asks whether the members of the Swedish-speaking minority in Finland marginalise their language and themselves in a contradictory way through their linguistic behaviour as well as their metalinguistic statements. Diana Hitzke, a scholar of literature, looks at contradictory positionings of a national minority in society through literature, using the case study of Sorbs in Germany. The last chapter, on Jewish characters in Danish literature from the nineteenth century, is also written by a literary scholar. Katharina Bock describes the contradictions that emerge when individuals seek to move through the metaphorical spatial order from the margins towards the centre.

We return here to the research foci of our own institutions. Using the example of *Contradiction Studies* (Warnke/Hornidge/Schattenberg 2021; Lossau/Schmidt-Brücken/Warnke 2019a, b; Warnke/Acke 2018; Junker/Warnke 2016), we would like to conclude by pointing out that empirical individual studies make an important contribution to the critique of models of majority and minority, and that a dynamic view of the unstable relation between centrality and marginality is empirically much more appropriate. However, we have to bear in mind that this should also be associated with a questioning of unambiguous affiliation. In case of a distinct because measurable, mapping of belonging, attention should also be paid to grey areas. These grey areas are characterised not least by tensions and contradictions. Privileges from one affiliation can at the same time be counteracted by a lack of privileges from other affiliations; the renunciation of unambiguity can clearly stand in the way of coherent perceptions of one's own positionality. Plural and heterogeneous societies produce spaces of contradiction that cannot simply be resolved and should even best be left unresolved. In other words, diversity is about contradictory belongings. This is where the actual resistance of liberal democracy to authoritative forms of questioning polyphony comes to the fore. Contradictions arising from multipositionality should be endured in order to be able to live well in complex dynamics of centrality and marginality.

And here, language comes into the picture once again: the tendency of speech to unify the world lexically or propositionally, or at least to understand language in this way, stands in the way of an acceptance of the contradictory. It is not the unambiguous naming of identities that makes contradictions livable, but their dynamisation in a society whose members perceive themselves as dynamically positioned in a mesh of centrality and marginality and thereby not least exercise their political, and that also means discursive, rights to recognition.

References

a. Research literature

Combahee River Collective (2017): "The Combahee River Collective Statement. April 1977". In: Keeanga-Yamahtta Taylor (ed.). *How We Get Free. Black Feminism and the Combahee River Collective*. Chicago: Haymarket Books, 15–27.

Crenshaw, Kimberlé (1989): "Demarginalizing the Intersection of Race and Sex. A Black Feminist Critique of Antidiscrimination Doctrine, Feminist Theory and Antiracist Politics". In: *University of Chicago Legal Forum* (1), 139-167. https://chicagounbound.uchicago.edu/uclf/vol1989/iss1/8/ (accessed 20 September 2020).

Davies, William (2021): "The Politics of Recognition in the Age of Social Media". In: *New Left Review* (128), 83–99. https://newleftreview.org/issues/ii128/articles/william-davies-the-politics-of-recognition-in-the-age-of-social-media (accessed 20 August 2021).

Fraser, Nancy (2000): "Rethinking Recognition". In: *New Left Review* (3), 107–120.

Junker, Carsten/Warnke, Ingo H. (2016): "Marguerite Stix and the Shell – Notes on Disciplinarity and Contradiction". In: *Quaderna. A Multilingual and Transdisciplinary Journal* 3. http://quaderna.org/marguerite-stix-and-the-shell-notes-on-disciplinarity-and-contradiction/, (accessed 20 August 2022).

Lossau, Julia/Schmidt-Brücken, Daniel/Warnke, Ingo H. (eds.) (2019a): *Spaces of Dissention: Towards a New Perspective on Contradiction*. Wiesbaden: Springer VS.

Lossau, Julia/Schmidt-Brücken, Daniel/Warnke, Ingo H. (2019b): "The Challenge of Contradictions: Thinking Through Spaces of Dissention." In: Julia Lossau/Daniel Schmidt-Brücken/Ingo H. Warnke (eds.): *Spaces of Dissention: Towards a New Perspective on Contradiction*. Wiesbaden: Springer VS, 1–16.

Warnke, Ingo H./Acke, Hanna (2018): "Ist Widerspruch ein sprachwissenschaftliches Objekt?" In: Alexander Ziem/Martin Wengeler (eds.): *Diskurs, Wissen, Sprache. Linguistische Annäherungen an kulturwissenschaftliche Fragen*. Berlin: De Gruyter, 319–344.

Warnke, Ingo H./Hornidge, Anna-Katharina/Schattenberg, Susanne (eds.) (2021): *Kontradiktorische Diskurse und Macht im Widerspruch*. Wiesbaden: Springer VS.

b. Online sources

Institutet för de inhemska språken (n.d.): Språk i Finland. https://www.sprakinstitutet.fi/sv/om_sprak/sprak_i_finland (accessed 20 April 2022).

Statistikcentralen (2022): 11s2 -- Finskspråkig och svenskspråkig befolkning efter åldersgrupp och kön områdesvis, 1990-2021. https://pxweb2.stat.fi/PxWeb/pxweb/sv/StatFin/StatFin__vaerak/statfin_vaerak_pxt_11s2.px/table/tableViewLayout1/ (accessed 20 April 2022).

Part I: **Marginalising and Centralising Discursive Practices**

Gábor Egry
Unlikely Brothers?
Entangled Székely and Moți Peripheries in a Contested Province: Transylvania 1900–1944

Over the course of a century, Transylvania was a hotly contested borderland that was subject to claims by both Hungarians and Romanians. Changing hands from Hungary to Romania from 1919 to 1920, divided between 1940 and 1944, and finally restored to Romania in 1947, the conflict produced images of alterity that posited Romanians and Hungarians as opponents, not only in the present, but at the origins of their common past. Thus, issues of precedence, such as whether the Hungarian conquerors around 900 A.D. had found Romanians in the province (either descendants of the Dacians or only of their Roman conquerors) or only Slavs, or the memory of armed struggles between Hungarians and Romanians, have shaped discourses on the topic of Romanianness and Hungarianness. Within these broader groups, however, regional and ethnographic varieties were acknowledged and often hailed as their most authentic, oldest and purest variety (see T. Szabó 2008). Perhaps not coincidentally, the discursive reflections of national rivals also noticed these regional groups and weaved them into their own discourse as significant others.

Two of these regional groups, the Romanian-speaking and predominantly Orthodox Moți, and the Hungarian speaking and Western Christian Székelys, figured prominently during the 19th and early 20th centuries within the respective national imageries in their dual roles, and signified the extreme opposite of Hungarianness and Romanianness. Still, starting at the beginning of the 20th century, a curious development occurred that brought them ever closer to each other and ultimately created an entanglement between Moți and Székelys. Arguments legitimating and facilitating state-led development efforts in these geographic zones were consciously created in a way that not only used customary tropes and figures to recast one's own group as deserving aid, they also did so through the deliberate use of elements that were typical for discussing the other group. Because both the Székelyland (*Székelyföld* in Hungarian, *Secuime* in Romanian) and the Țară Moților ("Mócvidék" in Hungarian) were economically underdeveloped and backward, life tended to be traditional and rural, and situated in the mountains. As a result, the above efforts targeted marginality, mobilised the centre and attempted to show why this kind of marginality was central to the nation's future.

Throughout this process, not only did political rhetoric evolve into entanglement, contemporary academic and quasi-scientific discourses followed suit and joined the political discourse in its effort to demonstrate the authenticity and centrality of marginal groups. Most of the scientific products of the pre-WWII era – in history, ethnography, historical linguistics, archaeology – were part of an ongoing effort to prove and substantiate nationalist political claims and to delegitimise rival demands. This does not mean they entirely lacked any scientific value and merit, but their context was – and this is especially true for the works cited in this text – political, and their use was politicised. Therefore, it should not surprise anyone that these academic currents within the broader national discourse also became entangled with each other across national boundaries. In this chapter, I will argue that the similar economic characteristics of the Moți and Székely regions, together with their analogous geographic and symbolic situation within the same contested region and within the respective national spaces, combined with the nationalising developmental model of the nation-state, facilitated this entanglement. In turn, the entanglement recast the respective groups, morphing the Moți and Székelys into a vaguely defined but tightly interconnected single group and challenging the usual distinction between nationalism and regionalism. In doing so, I will first briefly outline their regions and their socio-economic characteristics, describe their imagery from within and without, and, finally, analyse how the respective discourses appeared and morphed into each other during the first half of the 20th century.

1 Seclusion, remoteness, social ills vs. past heroism and purity: Țară Moților and Székelyland

Since the beginnings of modern nationalism, Transylvania was a contested territory that had been claimed by Romanian and Hungarian nation-builders. The union of Transylvania with the Kingdom of Hungary was among the famous 12 points of the 1848 Hungarian revolution, while in May of that year, a Romanian assembly in the city of Blaj/Balázsfalva demanded the recognition of Romanian as an equal nationality in the principality of Transylvania and rejected unification in any form. In the armed conflict between imperial troops and Hungarian revolutionaries, Romanians sided with the emperor, and in 1863 they were finally recognised as one of the four nations in the province (see Deák 1979, Retegan 1979).

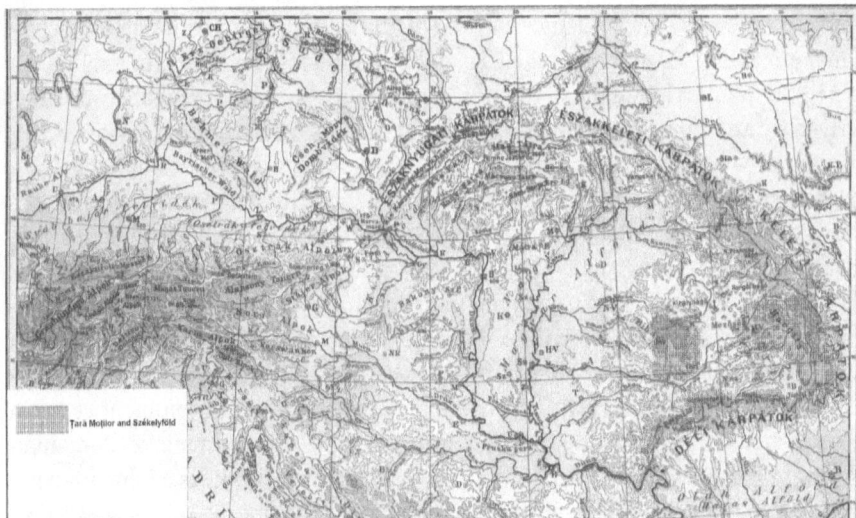

Fig. 1: Natural geography of Austria-Hungary.[1]

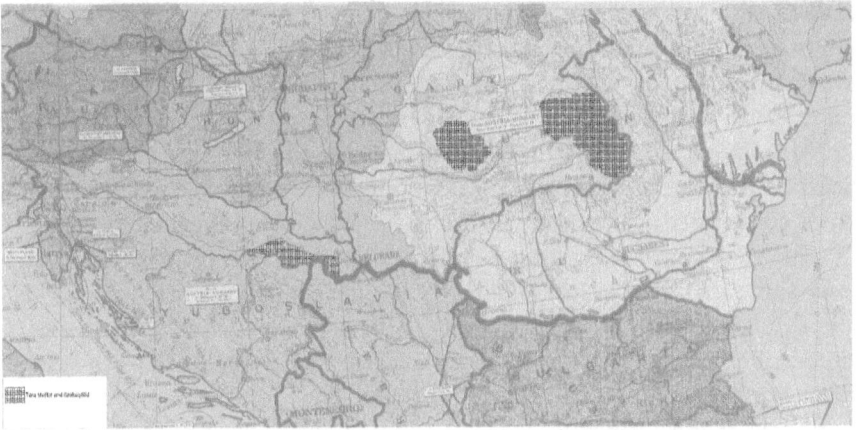

Fig. 2: Interwar Romania and Hungary.[2]

The *Ausgleich* in 1867 between the emperor and the Hungarian liberal elites again transferred the province under Hungarian rule. Within their newly independent

---

1 Kogutowicz Manó: Magyar földrajzi iskolai atlasz 1913, public domain.
2 National Library of Wales, public domain, via Wikimedia Commons.

state, Hungarian elites pursued the goal of unification, the creation of a Hungarian nation state. Even though the Law on Nationalities from 1868 granted linguistic rights and civic equality, politics increasingly became nationalist and was driven by an ethnic understanding of the nation. As a result, school policies, administrative reorganisations and cultural policies attempted to assimilate minorities, including Romanians. Magyarisation was to bring strength and unity, the creation of a homogeneous national space that included Transylvania (see Brubaker et al. 2007, 56–67).

In turn, nationalist elites among the minorities vowed to fight for the autonomy of their nation and demanded the recognition of the political subjectivity of minorities. For Romanians, it meant Transylvanian autonomy, or, as a more radical demand, unification with Romania (see Fati 2007). Their moment came in 1918, when defeated Hungary, unable to contain the advance of Romanian troops, did not want its new, democratic government to suppress a Romanian national revolution. In the ensuing period, however, Romanian politics was driven by the same ideas as the ones that had motivated Hungary prior to 1918. They envisaged an ethnically homogeneous Romania, including all of Transylvania, and pursued this goal with methods similar to the Hungarian practices. Finally, the Second Vienna Award of 30 August 1940, an act of arbitration by the foreign ministers of fascist Italy and Nazi Germany, reunified the northern parts of Transylvania with Hungary, bringing Székelyföld under Hungarian rule once again (until 1944), while leaving the Țara Moților as part of Romania (see Livezeanu 2000, Brubaker et al. 2007 68–82). As the region inhabited by both Moți and Székelys was part of these rival national projects, it was imagined and discursively constructed against the backdrop of the Hungarian-Romanian rivalry.

The most palpable common denominator of the two regions is the natural geography. That is to say, the importance of high mountains and their impact on climate, agriculture and economy. As a consequence, communication lines with the outside world were often weak, causing seclusion if not for all, then at least for most inhabitants of the area. Up through the end of World War II, the presence of mountains was a defining element for the economy and society, though with the not insignificant difference that the Székelyland was a series of smaller basins where arable land, even if it was of mediocre quality, was accessible. This contrasts with the Țară Moților, where narrow river valleys provided a small quantity of ground for raising cereals. Thus, forestry and husbandry on the mountain pastures was the almost excusive form of agriculture in Țară Moților, while in Székelyland they were only dominant. In both cases, craftwork made from wood, which was sold outside the region, figured among their most important products.

Furthermore, Țară Moților was also a region with important deposits of gold and other metals, which were mined by individuals and the crown.

The existence of some form of commons within the villages was also important, and a feature that either survived the abolishment of serfdom (Székelyland) or afterwards generated conflicts with the owners (Țară Moților). In the Székely villages and districts, common ownership of pasture and forest dominated and defined the method of exploitation. Instead of a profit-oriented production of lumber and timber, it was a matter of providing necessities (lumber, firewood, forest fruits and mushrooms, pasture for cattle, etc.) to the households, but the start of land consolidation at the end of the 19th century entailed the consolidated use of forests and enabled local farmers to own more than 100 acres. This reduced the use of land for their own lives and made it possible for them to make a profit (see Egyed 2004: 27). The ownership rights of the Țară Moților mountains, however, rested with the crown, though Maria Theresa granted free pasture rights and wood usage to the locals, who not only took advantage of the latter for household use, but for commercial purposes as well. Moti craftsmen roamed the country, sold their products and bought the food of the lowlands.

Nevertheless, both areas were among the least developed in dualist Hungary (see Demeter/Szulyovszky 2018: 15–84), and against this backdrop of traditional economy with minimal productivity and a weak capacity for food production, population growth caused serious issues. Forests were a potential source of additional revenue, but in the Székelyland, lack of capital and knowledge constrained the emergence of new methods of exploitation in the common forests (see Péter 1906, Oroszi 1989: 37–38). In the Țară Moților, the state forestry implemented new forest management methods, or leased the forest out to entrepreneurs. This gradually rescinded existing customary rights and imposed restrictions on the use of state-owned forest (holdings that previously belonged to the crown), which severely reduced access to pastures and forest. The result was the loss of resources that locals used in their household, for cattle raising and for craftsmanship. The combination of natural conditions, the limited income of families, and population growth led to steady migration that was often permanent. Székelys were roaming the streets of Bucharest and hailed as good craftsmen and reliable housemaids. They were also known to be victims of human trafficking. Moți visited the lowlands as seasonal workers and traders of their own products (see Erdélyi 1926: 5–6, Makkai 2018, Makkai 2019, Csiki székelyek nyomora 1900, Gunda 1944: 472, Etédi 1929: 249).

Thus, the living conditions in both regions were bad and poverty was widespread. However, in this regard, the Țară Moților was much worse off, with diseases spreading more broadly, and malnourishment more frequent, not least because of the most significant difference-maker in socio-economic indicators and social characteristics: education.

Although literacy rates in the Székelyland were somewhat lower than the average in the comparison of Hungarian counties, they were significantly higher than the ones in Țară Moților – as Table 1 shows:

Tab. 1: Literacy Rates and Mother Tongue in Székelyföld and Țară Moților at the Beginning of the 20th century (in percentages)[3]

Region/County	Hungarian Mother Tongue			Romanian Mother Tongue			Overall
	1880	1890	1900	1880	1890	1900	1900
Țară Moților							
Alsó-Fehér (Alba de Jos)	38.5	45.5	56.6	5.6	9.7	18.6	26.4
Kolozs (Cluj)	22.8	34	43.8	4	8.8	11.8	21.5
Hunyad (Hunedoara)	50	55.9	65.1	9	8.3	13.8	21.4
Torda-Aranyos (Turda – Arieș)	37.3	43.4	51.7	5	9.3	12.8	23.1
Székelyföld							
Csík (Ciuc)	21	32	41	3.1	6.2	12.9	37.5
Háromszék (Trei Scaune)	32.8	43.7	52.7	12.6	19.4	25.6	48.9
Maros-Torda (Mureș–Turda)	29.8	37	44.7	8.8	12.4	17.8	34.8
Udvarhely (Odorhei)	29.5	41.5	51.4	12.8	16.2	25.1	50.8

Elementary education was traditionally more efficient among Székelys, and certain historical developments, especially the separate existence of Transylvania during the Ottoman conquest of Hungary (1541–1699) and religious diversity after the reformation, led to the emergence of important educational centres (Székelyudvarhely/Odorheiu Secuiesc, Kézdivásárhely/Târgu Secuiesc, Marosvásárhely/Târgu Mureș, Székelykeresztúr/Cristuru Secuiesc, Sepsiszentgyörgy/Sfântu Gheorghe, Csíkszereda/Miercurea Ciuc) at the secondary level. These were highly respected schools that attracted pupils from afar. Given that Székelys were a privileged group enjoying collective nobility until 1848, pursuing an education was a feasible career path that was not restricted by the limitations that serfdom imposed on personal liberties. Before 1848, more than half of Székelys enjoyed

---

3 Source: Népszámlálás 1900 (1909: 162–163.)

feudal rights or counted as free peasants (see Csetri/Imreh 1990: 385. Table 9). It was true, however, that the Moți also held some form of special status, as without much arable land, the system of serfdom was impossible to implement there, and individual miners (around 15% of the population) often had a privileged status (see Csetri/Imreh 1990: 398–399). Thus, special status and special forms of ownership, or access rights, were entangled and contributed to the sense of specificity associated with these groups.

But the most important factor behind the idea that Székelys and Moți were special within their emerging nations was neither the legal peculiarity nor the specificities that emerged from the natural environment itself. For both groups, a historical narrative was constructed that claimed a different form of authenticity and was posited as a pure expression of the nation's origins and dreams. Given the conflict between Hungarians and Romanians – one that also entailed legal and social differences, as in most cases Hungarian noblemen were the overlords of Romanian serfs – it is hardly surprising that part of these historical constructs was rooted in past conflicts (see Hegedüs 2010).

Nevertheless, the key element of the Székelys alleged difference from Hungarians, and of their purity, was the tradition and legend of their direct descent from the Huns – more specifically, from King Attila's son, Csaba (see Hermann/Orbán 2018: 22 –359). Since the 18th century, a carefully crafted mythology appeared and spread among Székelys. It became more and more popular, as it seemed to reinforce their privileged status in feudal Transylvania. According to this line of argument, their privileges were the result of their Hun origins, which were acknowledged by the Hungarian kings when they began to settle in Eastern Transylvania in the 12th century.

The Moți had no special feudal privileges to retroactively "prove" their mythical origins, as was the case with the Székelys. But seclusion and the practice of endogamy, easily interpreted as purity, also enabled the invocation of legendary descent, this time from the first ancestors of Romanians. Thus, some authors claimed that the Moți were the remnants of the Dacians, or the Roman legionaries who withdrew to the mountains after Roman Dacia was abandoned by Emperor Aurelian in A.D. 271. Some authors even pointed to ethnographic similarities to prove that the Moți were connected to Illyrians (see Philippide 1923: 175).

Historical myths facilitated the assertion of privileges, but for modern nation-building, more recent armed conflicts lent both Székelys and Moți an additional significance. The Țară Moților was the core area of two Romanian uprisings. One, between 1783 and 1784, was against Hungarian landlords (led by Horea, Cloșca and Crișan); the other, between 1848 and 1849, against the unification of Transylvania with Hungary (led by Avram Iancu). Horea failed and was executed together with Cloşca and Crişan, while Iancu fought on the winning side in an alliance of Imperial and Russian troops against Hungarian revolutionaries. However, the rights provided by the neo-absolutist centralisation after 1849 fell short of the Romanian demands for political autonomy, and Iancu died in a mental asylum. On both occasions, violence was committed on a large scale and sometimes brutally, which meant that they continued to linger in social memory even in the first decades of the 20th century. Thus, the term Moţi (Hungarian for *móc*) was easy to use as shorthand for unrestrained and primitive savagery. As examples of how the Moţi and their world were imagined, the *Budapesti Hírlap* wrote that the "Moţi are the most dangerous of Romanians" (A románok kultúrája 1897, my translation), while the *Pestmegyei Hírlap* asserted that someone who was "raised in the lap of wild Moţi" also "breathed the air of hell" (21 krajcár és Kossuth Ferenc 1894, my translation).

The uprising and civil war in Hungary from 1848 to 1849, during which the Moţi mountains were only one theatre, also figured prominently in the reshaping of Székely imagery. The Székelys, with their high number of free or privileged people, and with many experienced soldiers from the imperial border regiments that had been established on this territory in 1762, used their secluded countryside to set up armed defences against a numerically and technically superior imperialist enemy. While never the scene of large battles, the area was an important recruitment base and the location of some essential arms factories up until the Hungarians were defeated. The events of these 15 months thus nicely demonstrated the alleged legendary martial capabilities of the Székelys, and even more importantly, situated the group as the core supporters of Hungarian nation-building. Their enthusiastic participation in this founding event of Hungarian nationhood, the revolution and war of liberation of 1848-1849, again proved their exceptional national characteristics and reinforced their claims for special treatment after the loss of their feudal status (see Egyed 1978; Egyed 1998). These claims were based on the myth of their Hun origins (see Egyed 1978; Egyed 1998).

But the rage of the Székelys did not spare Romanians and German-speaking Saxons, as they pillaged a series of villages, and small towns saw images of their savagery first-hand. Thus, around 1900 two regional groups lived in Transylvania whose image and meaning for the rival nation states of Hungary and Romania was surprisingly similar. The area they lived in was situated in the middle of the imagined national territory of the respective rival, which literally blocked any connections between co-nationals. The stereotypical images of the groups mirrored each other, as they were considered both the most authentic within their nations as well as the most feared among the other nation. Both were marginal in socio-economic and geographic terms, and as such, situated at the extreme opposite ends of the respective spectrums for Hungarianness and Romanianness. Being Székely or Moți was the ultimate Hungarian-Romanian antagonism: each represented the ethnically purest and most enthusiastic supporter of violent nationalism within their own kin, and as such, was the most distanced from the other.

2 State-led development efforts

The Székelyland and Țară Moților were just two of Hungary's mountainous and underdeveloped regions, and the state-led development efforts did not start with them either. The first so-called *Akció* (action plan) was introduced in the northeastern counties, where Ruthenians lived in the Carpathians. This plan fused nationalism, antisemitism and conservative modernisation ideas, as the main social ill detected by its leader, Ede Egan, was the dominance of Jewish middlemen and money-lenders (for Egan, they were simply usurers) in the region's rural communities. Egan's main goal was to improve the situation of the Ruthenian speakers – often indifferent to nationalist politics – by making them willing to assimilate and become loyal subjects (see Gyurgyák 2001: 350–359; Oroszi 1989).

But alongside its nationalist aims, the action plan disseminated knowledge in the form of brochures and lectures, and, in addition to promoting cooperatives, provided the means for better agricultural techniques and easier access to cheap credit. At its core was a reform plan for the mountain economy which was supposed to introduce new species for husbandry, advocate for a more methodical use of mountain pastures and promote household industry (see Oroszi 1989; Balaton 2017b; Balaton 2019). It also entailed investment in roads, communication, schools, dispensaries and public health services. Never fully implemented and failing to transform local communities – despite the attempted knowledge transfer – the Ruthenian Action Plan did not achieve its sweeping goals. Nonetheless, it was still the largest coordinated effort to invest in the region.

This action-plans model that was subsequently introduced to almost all of the Kingdom of Hungary's mountain regions (except the Țară Moților, see Balaton 2019) involved measures that were usually implemented elsewhere. But the intention of these actions was always ambiguous. A complete transformation towards social modernity in these more traditional communities, which would involve the upending of traditional social relations, was treated as dubious. Instead, the plans focused on promoting economic development in a more practical sense, which would preserve as much of traditional society as possible. However, the plan to modernise the state was not always just a top-down activity. The

Székely Akció (action plan) was the first to grow out of a social movement that spread all over the country, and had the aim of mobilising support and putting pressure on the government. Local elites used the symbolic weight of the Székely for the Hungarian national imagery, which was to advance their argument and frame the *Akció* as a necessary and urgent effort to save the Székelys from catastrophe, and the Hungarian nation as a whole from the loss of its easternmost bastion (see Balaton 2010; Balaton 2017a).

The so-called *Székely Kongresszus* (Székely Congress) held in 1902 at the small spa resort of Tusnád (Băile Tuşnad), demonstrated that there was a mobilisation of people and mass support for the government intervention. It was a multi-day event where delegations from several villages presented their problems and made speeches demanding immediate action. They pointed out that the best of Hungarians were in danger of disappearing, and those present were able to enjoy a series of cultural activities that was supposed to demonstrate the authentic character of all Székelys (see Balaton 2017a).

Thus, contrary to the Ruthenian case, the usual toolkit of developmental intervention aimed at preserving the alleged national authenticity of the region. It was also about the restoration of a way of life and form of community ownership that had been violated by the intrusive capitalism represented by capitalist forestry enterprises (see Oroszi 1989: 38–39; Nagy 2013). On the other hand, however, it viewed industrialisation as the only way of stopping the emigration of people who were either leaving for Hungarian cities or – a more threating action in the eyes of the Action's nationalist initiators – for Romania, where tens or even hundreds of thousands of Hungarians were living. Their feared assimilation into Romanian society was a dual threat in that not only was there net loss of Hungarians, but a net gain of the "enemy" as well (see Nagy 2017: 65–92; Nagy 2011).

The Székely Akció fostered a rare consensus among Hungary's deeply divided political factions, where that of István Tisza fought bitter battles with his opposition. However, this consensus did not yield immediate social and economic results, not to mention self-sufficient solutions. The preservation of what contemporaries saw as the first positive signs was only possible through continuous financing of the effort. Therefore, a government delegation – a branch of the Ministry of Agriculture – was established in the region, which oversaw ongoing projects and regularly reported on their progress. The action plan itself was extended year after year with significant budget subsidies (see Balaton 2019).

It was during one of the parliamentary debates on the allocated budget that the first entanglement between Țară Moților and Székelyföld emerged, at least with regard to development efforts. The Romanian nationalist MP Ștefan Cicio-Pop (see Képviselőházi Napló vol. IV 1906: 305–314) delivered a speech in which he demanded that the *Székely Akció* be extended to the Țară Moților. Given that parliament was dominated by Hungarian nationalists, one could view the Romanian politician's decision not to attack the legitimacy of advancing nationalist goals among the Székelys as nothing more than a clever tactic. This was not the case, however, as he also recognised the necessity of their effort and the legitimacy of its goals, and praised the patriotism of the Székely MPs who had managed to increase the portion of the budget allocated to the action plan (see Képviselőházi Napló vol. IV 1906: 306). At the same time, in a speech dedicated to presenting a sociographic description of the problems facing the Țară Moților, he pointed out the striking similarities in the social and economic conditions for both regions, including the detrimental effects of new forest exploitation methods (he likened them to bribery, swindle and graft) in the Székelyland. He argued that the Moți, who also dealt with these same problems, were also entitled to state support and the implementation of the same practical measures. The issue of Moți migration provided a strong analogy, though the fact that it was to the Hungarian lowlands went unmentioned. Nevertheless, it was an obvious counterpart to Székely emigration to Romania (see Képviselőházi Napló vol. IV 1906: 306–314).

Romanian deputies continued to pursue the issue from this point on, and not only Cicio-Pop, but also the leader of the Romanian National Party himself, Iuliu Maniu, participated in debates regarding the extension of the *Székely Akció* to the Moți (see Képviselőházi Napló vol. XXI 1906: 475; Képviselőházi Napló vol. VII 1910: 223 – 224, 229). Maniu became the head of Transylvania's Romanian governing body after a mass assembly declared the territory's unification with Romania on 1 December 1918. Thus, the establishment of a Government Commissariat for the Țară Moților (*Comisariat Guvernamental pentru Țară Moților*, later *Comisariat Guvernamental pentru Munți Apuseni*, *Munți Apuseni* meaning "Western Mountains" in English) as one of its first acts should not surprise anyone. The task of its leader, Laurențiu Pop, was to present a survey of the area's socio-economic conditions and propose solutions (see ANIC CD Admin. Gen. doar 10/1919 f. 102-104).

However, the action plan was not implemented, as the Ruling Council was dissolved in April 1920. But the Moți's problems did not disappear, and subsequent governments, irrespective of their political colours, regularly returned to the idea of a Moți action. Governments led by the Bucharest-based National Liberal Party (Ciupercă 1992) were initially less inclined to start development efforts, but they had to admit that the situation was hardly tolerable and needed intervention. Thus, they organised a Moți congress in 1924, where deputations from various villages presented their misfortunes and demands to government representatives who subsequently discussed possible measures with a range of local and national experts (see Rusu Abrudeanu 1928: 503–506). A Government Commissariat was re-established in 1927, then in 1929 and 1933. It survived the next change in government at the end of the latter year and throughout the 1930s operated as part of the Cluj County prefecture (see Zainea 2007). Somewhat surprisingly, the congress format had a popular appeal too. The State Security Police (*Siguranța*), among others, reported in 1928 that a delegation from various Moți villages had urged Amos Frâncu, a senator, paternal figure and long-time defender of the Moți, to convoke another congress (see ANIC DGP 17/1928 f. 16–17).

The continuous return to these kinds of institutional structures not only proves their viability, but also how little the actions achieved in the region (see *Guvernul face totul și nimic pentru Moți* 1927). In the meantime, the Székelyföld suffered not only from the discontinuation of the Hungarian *Székely Akció*, but also from a series of nationalising measures that had little to do with development (see Livezeanu 2000: 140–142, Bottoni 2013). These measures included the nationalisation of large parts of the community properties, the so-called *Csiki Magánjavak*, a public foundation that had been created from crown property dedicated to the former border guard communes on *Székelyföld* territory was used to support the Székelyföld elementary schools. Thus, the Székelys faced a new problem, one that was identical to one experienced by the Moți: the state forestry regulations caused them to lose their access to the mountains.

Because of ongoing underdevelopment and the fact that local Hungarian MPs were no longer able to influence government decisions, the roles of the dualist era were reversed. Unsurprisingly, from this point on Hungarian politicians referred to the Moți Action as a model, and requested state intervention based on the reasoning that the Székelyland suffered from the same problems and should receive similar treatment (see Szoboszlay 1928). One of the ideas that continued to resurface was the creation of a separate Moți county (the region was divided among four counties), and the Hungarian press often referenced this when discussing the creation of a separate Székely county (as this region was also shared between four counties) (see Mócmegye, székely ispánság, szász grófság 1929). However, the latter would have also potentially been the realisation of the dream of an autonomous Hungarian territorial unit, and as such would have been hard to imagine as being part of efforts to nationalise Greater Romania.

The *Székely Akció* thread was picked up again in September 1940, when the region was reunified with Hungary, leaving most of Țară Moților to Romania. The Hungarian government convened a special commission for the region's economic development (see Oláh 2008: 20–35; Ablonczy 2011: 189–194; Szavári 2011) and once again made this issue a core focus. With Țară Moților finally politically detached from Székelyföld, the political and economic entanglement between both regions loosened. Even in this peculiar moment, however, it formed part of the basis for the argument regarding possible measures in Székelyföld. These included the Romanian government's granting of transport tariff reductions to trains coming from Țară Moților (see Csak az exportálhasson tűzifát 1937; Hamarosan rendeződik 1941; Az Erdélyi Gazdasági Tanács 1941).

3 Entangled peripheries? The discursive representation of Székelyföld and Țară Moților

In their respective discourses, the Székely and Moți actions were a constant point of reference as models and arguments against the dual form centres. First of all, the idea of authenticity legitimised unconditional support for the periphery. The danger threatening the most authentic element of the nation was to a very large degree a common cause and the potential loss would have been irreplaceable. Secondly, the rival national movement's model was not only presented as a threat (its success would undermine their own nation) – it was also as an example to follow, a best practice of conscious, goal-oriented nation-building that helped remedy the problems arising from a modernisation that allegedly endangered the national way of life. Therefore, it was not only to be followed as an allegedly proven development model that was practical and efficient, but also as the logical form of both national struggle and survival.

Therefore, the developmental elements of the discourse happening around that time were entangled in multiple ways. Furthermore, their entanglement sometimes became almost physically palpable, especially when discursive acts happened within the same space: in the rooms of their respective parliaments or in the pages of monthly reviews and daily newspapers. The arguments, which usually only served to promote the case of one group and not both, could shift from 1) using the example of the other as a threat to urge the leaders of their own nation to act on 2) legitimising ideas to promote their own nation through accepting, even upholding the nationalist justification of their rivals as an example for their respective development project.

The speech that the Romanian Cicio-Pop gave in the Hungarian parliament in 1906 is a prime example of the second type of argument, and his fellow Romanian National Party MPs followed suit in subsequent years. He began by praising the minister as being highly competent over the course of many years, someone whose stewardship will benefit every inhabitant of the country. This was followed by a reference to the serious ongoing issues with regard to the forests, and again acknowledged how the ministry increased the *Székely Akció*'s budget at the behest of the Székely MPs:

> I pay tribute to those of my fellow Székelys, [fellow MPs, my translation] who moved everything for the interest of the Székely race, who keep this question on the agenda with unmatched zeal because it will make the country pay attention not only to the Székely question, but to extend this interest to other poor areas of the country. (Képviselőházi Napló vol. IV 1906: 306)

The decision to recognise the initiative's merits on its own nationalist terms instead of attacking the tenets of Hungarian nationalism was still not enough to result in a favourable solution to Cicio-Pop's request. However, it was still a way to link Székely and Moți with powerful images of poverty that were quite similar to the ones used to describe Székelyföld. Cicio-Pop went into detail regarding how locals were denied access to the forests and had to bribe the rangers (usually with physical labour, as they did not have money) in order to obtain this access. He also discussed how the industrialised enterprises provided wood of poor quality to the Moți craftsmen, who consequently lost their consumers, and how the Moți suffered from the heavy-handed application of the forestry regulations, which resulted in serious punishments for minor offences (see Képviselőházi Napló vol. IV 1906: 308–310). Descriptions of the Székelyland given before the Székely Congress took place abounded in similar themes (see Székely Kongresszus 1901: 79, 81), together with pictures of poverty, alcoholism and hunger. All of these were tropes that Cicio-Pop had mentioned (see Képviselőházi Napló vol. IV 1906: 310).

The imagery of human suffering remained constant throughout the reports of the interwar period, both from Székelyföld and Țară Moților alike (see Rusu Abrudeanu 1928; Erdélyi 1926; Bánffy 1934, 1935, 1940). Captivating as it was, even popular magazines ran reports centred around the poverty of the Moți and its effects on them. Sandru Vornea's multipart report titled "Caravanele foamei" (Caravans of hunger) was published in the magazine *Realitate Ilustrată* and described a trip featuring Moți who roamed Romania and the Balkans to earn some money. Vornea's scenes illustrate many forms of Moți misery, including one report featuring the suicide of a mother who could not bear to hear her children's cries for food (see Vornea 1931a, Vornea 1931b). Individuals who read literary representations of Székely could find counterparts of those scenes in almost all of literary works on them (see Tamási 1932), and in a less emotional form, the misery of the common people in Székelyföld was the main thread of all policy proposals (see Szoboszlay 1928; Székelyfőzés 1933; Ötszáz székely lány 1938).

Though external factors were among the main causes of Székely and Moți poverty (and continued to be throughout the interwar period, see Tamási 1932; Rusu Abrudeanu 1928), the backwardness of both groups was never disputed. Solutions were always discussed in public, at parliamentary sessions and in newspapers and journals. These were mindful of broader social developments and included obtaining better access to mountain resources in a way that would not impact the local economy. The close resemblance of these proposals was the result of similar natural and social conditions, and of their continuous referencing of one other.

The Székely Congress and *Akció* invoked by Cicio-Pop in 1906 was also invoked in 1926 by Secretary of the Commissariat, Emil Dandea. He tried to have his institution replicate their activities (see Dandea 1926).

The initial ideas, listed by Cicio-Pop in 1906 with regard to the Țară Moților, were scaled down in comparison, but still included the restoration of access to forests, the provision of cheap wood for Moti craftsmen, lower pasture fees, lower taxes and a new forestry school in the heart of the region, Câmpeni/Topánfalva (see Képviselőházi Napló vol. IV 1906: 313; Képvselőházi Napló vol. VII 1910: 224). The programs that were later created after Romanian sovereignty was established were more extensive, and involved a wholescale regional development effort with new roads, a new railway, improved Alpine pastures, the introduction of new cattle and sheep species, alimentation through cooperatives, cheaper combustibles and mining concessions, new dispensaries, hospitals and general practitioner posts, and a spree of new secondary and vocational schools (see ANIC CD Adm. Gen. 10/1919 f. 102–104; Rusu Abrudeanu 1928, 509–512; ANIC PCM 19/1933 f. 10–34; Florescu 1938).

Beyond the proposed measures, the institutional framework was also modelled on the others' solutions, starting with Cicio-Pop's and Maniu's insistence on extending the *Székely Akció*, followed by the Government Commissariat for the Moți. The most telling was the imitation of those forms that intended to demonstrate the inclusion of the people in the planning process. The Congress format was adopted by the Romanian National Liberal Brătianu government in 1923, as was the practice of consulting experts by the People's Party's Avarescu government in 1927 (see Rusu Abrudeanu 1928, 503–506). All subsequent programs, up to the Hungarian ones established for Székelyföld in 1940, were prepared using these methods that involved some form of interaction (see Szavári 2011). The significance of these solutions was that they tacitly recognised the uniqueness of the administratively divided areas. The specific development plans legitimised the idea of regional unity and also led to speculations about the need for administrative reorganisation. The frequent connections between Moți and Székely administrative reorganisation, sometimes strengthening the relationship of these two areas, again suggested something identical in their character (see Mócmegye, székely ispánság 1929).

4 Historical and ethnographic discourse

The cross-referencing of development policies and their modelling on that of the other was only one form of entanglement in Székely and Moți discourses. It was relatively straightforward with respect to Székely and Moți, and a reliance on and competition for the resources provided from the centre brought the issue of the relationship between Bucharest and Budapest to the fore, and highlighted how this relationship was the determining factor for development policy. In terms of arguments and discourse, the justification for access to those resources was at stake, and poverty and underdevelopment, accompanied by the threat posed to the nation (through the degeneration or emigration of co-ethnics) was certainly a powerful reason. But it also left Székely and Moți at the mercy of the capitals and turned the help they received into a gesture that exposed their marginality.

Other aspects of the two groups' discursive representation – one of which I will subsequently analyse in this section – aimed to counterbalance this one-sidedness and shift the relationship more in the favour of the marginal group. The threat to the nation was once again its basis, but this time Székelys and Moți were detached from the national group and positioned in relation to it. Ethnographic and historical arguments were used to point out their authenticity and their quality of being the best representatives of their nations. For these reasons, they deserved to have their lives improved unconditionally. This was in striking contrast with their actual socio-economic situation, and for the nationalists in each country, the loss of their respective group would have been significant.

Entanglement in this regard was, however, more complex, as such characterisations were not one-sided in the contested province. Discourse on Moți and Székely was not just a matter of representation within and concerning the respective national group – it was also continuously present as a discourse of alterity. Neither Székely nor Moți were secluded enough to not be noticed by intellectuals or politicians from the other group, as was exemplified by the cross-referencing of their respective development plans. Furthermore, Țară Moților and Székelyland were not simply on the margins of the national territory – they were also at the centre of the other's imagined national space (see Biharvármegyei osztály 1894; Iorga 1925; Oprișan 1925; Sándor 1894: 128; Három főtulajdonságnak 1942; Țurlea 2011). From an ethnographic, and not simply a socio-economic point of view, their existence was an aberration, as they dispelled the notion of a consolidated "Hungary" or "Romania", and made its realisation impossible. Their elimination was therefore an important goal for those striving to achieve an ethnically homogenous nation state.

Shifting ethnographic and historic discourses emerged from these complex entanglements, which bundled together both internal and external perspectives in a way that was often astonishing and that not infrequently looked for connections between Székely and Moți. But the foremost issue for situating Moți and Székely was actually more of a matter of separating them from their nations by attesting to their peculiar origins.

In a general sense, the origins of the Hungarians and Romanians were "settled" by the turn of the 20th century. Hungarians were supposed to have come from the East at the end of the 9th century as a semi-nomadic people, one that spoke a Finno-Ugric language. The origin of the Romanians went back further in time. Because they used a Romance language, they were considered descendants of the Romans, who, under the reign of the Emperor Trajan, conquered Dacia with their legions. Later scholarship, however, insisted on a direct connection with the Dacians due to the genealogical convergence of Romans and natives, and the continuous presence of Romanians in Transylvania (roughly Roman Dacia) since the Roman conquest (see Boia 2001). It was actually an issue that separated Hungarians and Romanians, as it was thought that the people who had first arrived at the contested province were the ones who had established ownership rights.

Since one of the theories that tried to explain the lack of sources regarding the Romanian presence between the evacuation of Roman Dacia in A.D. 271 and the mid-12th century claimed that the local Romanians withdrew into the mountains to emerge centuries later, the Moți had an easy way to assert their authenticity: they lived in the area where the Dacians dwelled starting in the late 3rd century. Székelys, on the other hand, settled in their region in the 12th century, as attested to by a large number of written sources. But the peculiarity of the Moți and Székely gave rise to alternative ideas concerning their origins and other ideas that occasionally brought these groups together. One author hinted at the Moți possibly having Illyrian origins based on the custom of maiden fair, which had allegedly been brought over from Dalmatia and the Dinarides (see Philippide 1923; Ajtay 1943). Another highly esteemed author, Ovidiu Densușianu, ventured to claim that they had Iranian (Alan) origins (see Revista Periodicelor 1921: 880; Rusu Abrudeanu 1928: 116–120).

The latter claim was all the more interesting due to the fact that a group of Alans (*Jász* in Hungarian) held a privileged position in Hungary before 1848 and the canonised myth of Székely origins (the one that ultimately won out) claimed direct descent from the Huns (see Hermann/Orbán 2018). Thus, the Moți could be reidentified as an Asiatic people (instead of being of Roman origin), like the Hungarians or Székelys, while both legendary ethnogeneses made one thing clear: Székelys and Moți were the oldest and purest of their nations and probably even had a shared origin (see A románok kultúrája 1897). Purity was rarely contested publicly, and politicians accepted the idea uncritically. One example was Prime Minister Alexandru Vaida Voevod, who wrote in his internal correspondence regarding the reestablishment of the Moți Commissariat. In it he made an assertion that had not been forced out of him by pressure from the public: "[The Moți are] a group of the most authentic guardians of our race, who are as brave as important in economic terms" (ANIC PCM 19/1933, f. 3., f. 8. For similar claims concerning Székelys see: Egry 2008: 125–134).

In addition to the issue of origins, the historical role of Székely and Moți was the most important factor in defining these groups, especially where military exploits were concerned (which, depending on the group, were occasionally against Romanians or Hungarians). Their heroes, Avram Iancu, Horea, Cloșca, Crișan, and Áron Gábor, just to name a few, were included in the respective national pantheons as indispensable figures in their national history, another type of leverage for arguments about material help (see Bucur 2009; Ce vrem noi? 1933; Demeter/Váry 2014).

But military prowess was not the only character trait that was recognised. Hospitality; a love of freedom, humour and teasing; an idiosyncratic way of thinking; and industriousness were also viewed positively. With their traditional way of life and economy, some of their characteristics could be seen, depending on the individual bias of the observer, as either positive or negative, or as signs of authenticity or backwardness (see Vornea 1931a; 1931b Kőváry 1853: 253–255; Sándor 1894). Poverty, and the refusal to embrace modernisation – which would have meant giving up methods that were traditional in a rural economy – were just as easy to dismiss as the laziness and stupidity associated with social health problems (alcoholism or venereal diseases) as they were to be highlighted as signs of adherence to the nation's purity. These signs included stubbornness, independence, reticence towards outsiders, honesty and sincerity (see Robul 1921). This is where outside and inside perspectives intersected the most easily, as the laziness of the Moți was easy for Hungarian observers to interpret as temperance, a life aligned with nature, while for others, including Romanians, the focus was on consumption and the destruction of resources (see Kőváry 1853: 253–255; Rusu Abrudeanu 1928: 121–124). For Romanian observers, anti-Hungarian fervour was the sign of stubborn national loyalty, in the eyes of the Hungarians, it was madness and savagery.

With their discourse of authenticity, Moți and Székelys began to view one another as the very embodiment of a most dangerous enemy. In this way they mutually reinforced their perspective of the other, which meant that recognition from their most significant enemy was also proof of exceptionality within their own nation (see Elnémult harangok 1941). In Hungarian parlance, the word "móc" not only took on a derogatory meaning, it was also almost always used for reporting on the savagery of Romanians and the violence committed against Hungarians. Between 1919 and 1920, for example, when Eastern Hungary was under Romanian occupation, Hungarian newspapers most often referred to the Romanians as "mócok", while they had a strong tendency to publish stories of abuses committed against Hungarians (see Szabolcs fölszabadított földjén 1920, Az oláhok ki akarták rabolni a Magyar Nemzeti Múzeumot 1919). For Romanians, the threat from Székelys was much less direct – even though fear of a Székely revolt did occasionally surface (see Planuri de revoluție săcuiești descoperite 1920, Români care se magharizează în România Mare 1923) – but this didn't make it any less serious. The Székelyland, being at the geographic centre of the new Greater Romania, was considered its most alien region, and was mourned as the cemetery of hundreds of thousands of Magyarised Romanians. According to Nicolae Iorga, who became Greater Romania's preeminent historian "Székelyland was a totally different territory: different outlook of the soil, different outline of the villages, different type of houses and their different decorations, different type of the inhabitants themselves, who wore a Romanian costume and spoke Hungarian, without being either completely Hungarians nor Romanians" (Iorga 1925). Others, who calculated and listed their nation's losses, were much more belligerent in their complaints (see Oprișan 1925), even asserting that after 1920, Romanians in the region continued to suffer from oppression.

Thus, the relationship between Romanians and Székelys was not simply one of extreme opposition. The appropriation of the latter group by the Romanians was also possible, and was actually a mainstream effort in interwar Romania. As Iorga's words may suggest, Romanians typically asserted that Székelys were originally of Romanian origin and had been Magyarised throughout the centuries (see Popa-Lisseanu 1932). Authors such as Iorga found proof for this claim in historical documents, family names in 16th and 17th century registers, and geographical names. Since the late 19th century, the Hungarians had also utilised this method to a certain extent. Given that there was a scarcity of historical documents relating to most of the early history of the Țara Moților, they based their arguments on ethnography, linguistics and legal history, which was more of a history of customs. It was all the more important for them to use these types of sources, as historical documents rarely revealed meaningful encounters between Székely and Moți. Ethnography, or more precisely, the description of the rural world in these areas, including local dialects, enabled researchers on both sides to find a series of overlaps and identical elements. The appearance and structure of houses, folk costumes, popular character, legal customs of inheriting along the female line of succession, allegedly borrowed words, music and songs, and similar labour practices were among the "proofs" (see Székely 1894; Moldován 1894; Oprișan 1925; Iorga 1925; Gunda 1940; Sebestyén 1941; Ajtay 1943) that enabled them to postulate a different origin for the other, or at least a part of that group.

The most extreme variant of these claims was also the most modern in terms of the science of the period: blood group analyses conducted among the Székelys came to the conclusion that their genetic origins were Romanian (see Malán 1943: 621, 659; Turda 2007). Such results legitimised extreme nationalist policies, including the introduction of monolingual Romanian education in the region (see Livezeanu 2000: 140–142). This policy enhanced the latter's backwardness, especially through its debilitating effects on literacy. Paradoxically, integrating a group that represented the extreme opposite of the Romanian nation into the nation itself did not reduce this group's marginality – it increased it.

5 Politics of centrality and marginality

Appropriation attempts, regardless of the degree of scholarly conviction that underpinned them, obviously belonged to the realm of politics. Their manifest political implications, however, could not hide the fact that all elements of the parallel and entangled discourses regarding the Székely and Moți were easily politicised beyond nationalism's self-evident political aspects. As soon as the stakes were high enough, symbolic issues were transposed to material politics, and used to advance local and regional goals.

This form of argumentation, which brought the marginal groups closer to the centre of national efforts and to the heart of the symbolic nation, was the most palpable effort to discursively manage real marginality. It involved reducing distance between marginal and central parts of the nation by positing the former in the centre. In extreme cases, it even subverted the existing asymmetry, as, due to their lack of authenticity, the parts of the nation outside the marginal group became second-class members. If accepted, authenticity made it almost impossible for the government to refuse action, as salvaging the most valuable elements of the nation was imperative for nationalists (see Balaton 2002; Zainea 2007; Oláh 2008) and ensured priority over many other underdeveloped regions where the inhabitants also desperately needed large-scale development programs, but were not capable of demonstrating their extraordinary value for the nation.

The complementary, more academic currents of the discourses easily served the same purpose, but their deployment created a complex web of entanglements. The simplest form of entanglement was the referencing of the Moți or Székely development programs and the borrowing of knowledge from those efforts. The mutual images of alterity could play a similar role, although within these efforts, Moți and Székely were rarely directly connected, and, without any hint of a relationship, they served as the most emblematic figures among the "others" who were significant in shaping their respective identities. Most intriguing of all – especially given that the identification of Székelys and Moți through an ethnographic approach was the most frequent argument in the above cases – was appropriation, attempts to demonstrate that the most authentic Romanians are those with Hungarian origins and vice versa.

The reason for the emergence of this intricate set of entanglements was the multiple centralities and marginalities at play in Transylvania. There was a geographic and a socio-economic entanglement that situated both mountain zones and both ethnic groups at the margins, irrespective of the political framework or whether the country in question was Hungary or Romania. As much as politics was significant in this regard, the question was which type of nationalism was dominating state politics at that time. This was because the state provided access to resources and the regional group that could claim authenticity within the dominant nation had a more realistic chance of receiving support. But it was the Hungarian and Romanian nations and not the states that had their own structures of centrality and marginality. They were not only symbolic, but existed in material terms too, overlapping, interfering with each other, reflecting each other, and creating interactions. One result of this was the cross-referencing of development efforts, another was appropriation. The latter was one way to resolve the discontinuity of the national space that had been caused by a large area in its centre, one that was inhabited by a group from another nation. With this "unification" one could erase one form of marginality – the ethnic other, which was usually discriminated against by the state while still living in a central geographical location – from the map. At the price of switching one's allegiance, the promise of emancipation was also inherent in this logic.

However, the least expected result of this discursive framework was the discursive loosening of boundaries for these groups, and with them, the nation. Appropriation efforts made explicit what was already implied in the frequent cross-referencing of the developmental discourse: a strange connection between or identification of the two groups, which were otherwise the extreme symbolic opposites of Hungarianess and Romanianness. Their similar socio-economic conditions, along with the identical logic of state-driven development in both Hungary and Romania, which, in its interplay with ethnographic discourses, transformed realigned boundaries and brought them to the centre of both national imaginations. At the same time, the boundaries between the two were blurred.

References

a. Research literature

Ablonczy, Balázs (2011): *A visszatért Erdély* [Transylvania reannexed]. Budapest: Jaffa Kiadó.
Balaton, Petra (2002): "A székely akció előzménye és története" [A history of the Székely action and its preparations] *Székelyföld*, 6, 62–91.
Balaton, Petra (2017b): "A háziipar „felfedezése" és jelentősége a Székelyföldön, a 19 – 20. század fordulóján" ['Discovery' of the household industry and its significance in Székelyland at the run of the 19th and 20th centuries]. *Orpheus Noster*, 1, 7–19.
Balaton, Petra (2010): A székely társadalom önszerveződése: a székely társaságok (I–II), *Korunk*, 1. 78–85, 2. 71–77.
Balaton, Petra (2017): The Székely Action (1902–1914) The Example of Regional Economic Development in Austro-Hungarian Monarchy. *Ungarn Jahrbuch. Zeitschrift für interdisziplinäre Hungarologie* 33, 223–236.
Balaton, Petra (2019): The Role of the Hungarian Government in the Development of Peripheries in the Austro-Hungarian Monarchy Focusing the Policy of the Ministry of Agriculture (1897–1914). In: Viktória Semsey/Petra Balaton/Csaba Horváth/José Antonio Sánchez Román (eds.): *National Identity and Modernity 1870–1945. Latin America, Southern Europe, East Central Europe*. Budapest/Paris: Károli Gáspár Református Egyetem, L'Harmattan 241–254.
Boia, Lucian (2001): *History and Myth in Romanian Consciousness*. Budapest/New York: CEU Press.
Bottoni, Stefano (2013): National Projects, Regional Identities, Everyday Compromises: Szeklerland in Greater Romania (1919–1940). *Hungarian Historical Review* 2 (3) 477–511.
Brubaker, Rogers/Feischmidt, Margit/Fox, Jon/Grancea, Liana (2007): *Nationalist Politics and Everyday Ethnicity in a Transylvanian Town*. Princeton/Oxford: Princeton University Press.
Bucur, Maria (2009): *Heroes and Victims. Remembering War in Twentieth-Century Romania*. Bloomington: Indiana University Press.
Ciupercă, Ion (1992): *Opoziția și putere în România între anii 1922 și 1928*. Iași, Universității Al. I. Cuză.
Csetri, Elek/Imreh, István (1990): „Erdély társadalmi rétegződéséről" [Of Transylvanian social stratification]. In Szabad György (ed.): *A polgárosodás útján. Tanulmányok a magyar reformkorról* [On the way towards embourgeoisement. Studies on the Hungarian reform era]. Budapest: Tankönyvkiadó, 377–414.
Deák, István (1979): *The Lawful Revolution: Louis Kossuth and the Hungarians, 1848–1849*. New York: Columbia University Press.

Demeter, Gábor/Szulovszky, János (eds.) (2018): *Területi egyenlőtlenségek nyomában a történeti Magyarországon. Módszerek és megközelítések.* [Territorial Inequalities in Historical Hungary. Methods and Approaches.] Budapest/Debrecen.

Demeter, Lajos /Váry, O. Péter (2014): A székely nemzet hőse – Gábor Áron élete és emlékezete Háromszéken [The Hero of the Székely Nation – The Life and Memory of Áron Gábor]. Sepsiszentgyörgy: Háromszék Vármegye Kiadó.

Egry, Gábor (2008): *Az erdélyiség „színeváltozása". Kísérlet az Erdélyi Párt ideológiájának és identitáspolitikájának elemzésére, 1940–1944.* [The Transfiguration of Transylvanism. An Attempt to Analyse the Ideology and Politics of Identity of the Transylvanian Party, 1940–1944.] Budapest: Napvilág Kiadó.

Egyed, Ákos (1978): *Háromszék 1848–1849* [Háromszék in 1848–1849]. Bukarest: Kriterion.

Egyed, Ákos (1998): *Erdély 1848–1849 I–II* [Transylvania in 1848–1849]. Csíkszereda: Palas-Akadémia.

Egyed, Ákos (2004): „A Székelyföld 1848–1918 között" [The Székelyland between 1848 and 1918]. In: *Limes* 17 (1), 21–28.

Etédi (1929): "A földbirtokreform a megszállt magyar területeken" [Agrarian reform in the occupied Hungarian territories]. In: *Magyar Gazdák Szemléje* 34 (5–6), 227–265.

Fati, Sabina (2007): *Transilvania, O Provincie in Cautarea Unui Centru: Centru si Periferie in Discursul Politic Al Elitelor Din Transilvania, 1892–1918.* Cluj-Napoca: EDRC.

Gunda, Béla (1944): „Magyar hatás az erdélyi román műveltségre" [Hungarian influence on Transylvanian Romanian folk culture]. Deér József /Gáldi László (eds.) Magyarok és románok [Hungarians and Romanians]. Vol. II. Budapest: Gróf Teleki Pál Tudományos Intézet, 458–490.

Gyurgyák, János (2001): *A zsidókérdés Magyarországon* [The Jewish Question in Hungary]. Budapest: Osiris.

Hegedüs, Nicoleta (2010): *Imaginea magharilor în cultura Românească din Transilvania (1867–1918).* Doctoral thesis. Universitatea Babeş-Bolyai, Cluj-Napoca.

Hermann, Gusztáv Mihály/Orbán, Zsolt (2018): *Csillagösvény és göröngyös út. Mítosz és történelem a székelység tudatában* [Starpath and rough road. Myth and history in Székely self-image]. Kolozsvár: Erdélyi Múzeum Egyesület.

Livezeanu, Irina (2000): *Cultural Politics in Greater Romania. Regionalism, Nation-Building and Ethnic Struggle 1918–1930,* Ithaca, NY/London: Cornell University Press.

Makkai, Béla (2018): "Kivándorló magyarok és integrációjuk Szlavóniában és a Regátban (1867–1918)" [The integration of Hungarian Emigrants in Slavonai and the Romanian Old Kingdom (1867–1918)]. In: Penka Peykovska/Gábor Demeter (eds.): *Migracii na hora i idei v Bylgaria i Ungaria (XIX-XXIvek) == Emberek és eszmék migrációja Bulgáriában és Magyarországon (19-21. század) == Migrations of People and Ideas in Bulgaria and Hungary, 19th-21st Centuries.* Sofia: Izdatelstvo Paradigma, 236–255.

Makkai, Béla (2019): "Changes in National Self-Image and the Image of Neighbourhood of Expatriate Hungarians in the Romanian Old-Kingdom." In: Viktória Semsey/Petra Balaton/Csaba Horváth/José Antonio Sánchez Román (eds.): *National Identity and Modernity 1870–1945. Latin America, Southern Europe, East Central Europe.* Budapest/Paris: Károli Gáspár Református Egyetem, L'Harmattan, 201–219.

Malán, Mihály (1943): "Erdélyi magyarok és románok az embertan tükrében" [Transylvanian Hungarians and Romanians in the light of physical anthropology]. In: József Deér/László Gáldi (eds.): *A Magyar Történettudományi Intézet Évkönyve, 1943 – Magyarok és románok*

I. kötet [Yearbook of the Hungarian Institute for Historical Sciences – Hungarians and Romanians I.] Budapest: Atheneum Könyvnyomda, 600–667.

Nagy, Botond (2011): "Székely kivándorlás és hivatalnoki magatartás Háromszéken" [Székely emigration and the official's behavior in Háromszék]. In: *Acta Siculica* 5, 297–306.

Nagy, Botond (2013): "Erdővagyon-újraelosztás és faipari nagyvállalatok megjelenése Háromszéken" [Redistribution of forested property and the appearance of large forestry entreprises in Háromszék]. In: Emese Egyed/László Pakó/Attila Weisz (eds.): *Certamen I. Előadások a Magyar Tudomány Napján az Erdélyi Múzeum Egyesület I. szakosztályában* [Certamen I. Lectures presented in the I. Section of the Transylvanian Museum Association at the Day of Hungarian Science]. Kolozsvár: Erdélyi Múzeum Egyesület, 335–352.

Nagy, Botond (2017): "Közteherviselés és fejlesztéspolitika a dualizmus kori Háromszéken (Gazdaságtörténeti vázlat)" [Public burdens and development policies during the dual monarchy of Austria-Hungary in Háromszék County]. In: *Magyar Kisebbség* 22 (3–4), 7–95.

Oláh, Sándor (2008): *Kivizsgálás. Írások az állam és a társadalom viszonyáról a Székelyföldön* [Investigation. Studies on state-society relationship in the Székelyland]. Csíkszereda: Pro-Print.

Oroszi, Sándor (1989): "A magyar kormány havasgazdálkodási programjának gazdaságpolitikai háttere (1898–1918)" [Economic background of the Hungarian government's Alpine economic program]. In: *Agrártörténeti Szemle* 32 (1–4), 27–55.

Philippide, Alexandru (1923): *Originea românilor. Ce spun izvoarele istorice?* [Orgins of the Romanians. What do the historical sources say?]. Vol. I. Iași: Tipografia Românească.

Popa-Lisseanu, Gheorghe (1932): *Secuii și secuizarea românilor* [The Székelys and the assimilation of Romanians into Székelys]. București: Tipografia ziarului Universul.

Retegan, Simion (1979): *Dieta românească a Transilvaniei (1863–1864)*, Cluj-Napoca: Editura Dacia.

Rusu Abrudeanu, Ioan (1928): *Moți. Calvarul unui popor eroic, dar nedreptățit* [Moti. Unjust calvary of a heroic people]. Bucuresti: Cartea Românească.

Szabó, Levente T. (2008): "Erdélyiség képzetek (és regionális történetek) a 19. század közepén" [Ideas of Transylvania (and regional stories) at the mid-18th century]. In: Levente T. Szabó (ed.): *A tér képei. Tér, irodalom, társadalom* [Images of the space. Space, literature, society]. Kolozsvár: Komp-Press-Korunk, 13–98.

Szavári, Attila (2011): "Teleki Pál Erdély-politikájáról: értekezletek Erdélyben" [Pál Teleki's Transylvania-policy: conferences in Transylvania]. In: *Magyar Kisebbség* 41 (2–3), 191–282.

Turda, Marius (2007): Nations as an Object. Race, Blood, and Biopolitics in Interwar Romania. In: *Slavic Review* 66 (3), 413–441.

Țurlea, Petre (2011): "Un memoriu despre importanța Congresului Secuiesc, ținut în anul 1902 la Tușnad din punct de vedere românesc, dezbătut în ședința Consiliului de Miniștri din mai 1941" [An Aide Memoire on the importance of the 1902 Tușnad Székely Congress from Romanian perspective, discussed at the session of the Government in May 1941]. In: Vilică Munteanu/Ioan Lăcătușu (eds.): *Românii în dezbaterile Congresului secuiesc din 1902. Premise, deziderate și reverberații.* [Romanians in the debates of the 1902 Székely Congress. Premises, demands and reverberations.] Onești: Editura Magic Print, 115–120.

Zainea, Ion (2007): The Commisary of the Apuseni Mountain and its plan for economic recovery of the region (1934–1936). In: *Cumidava* XXX, 104–115.

b. Empirical sources

Arhivele Naționale (ANIC), București
Fond Consiliul Dirigent (CD)
Administrația Generală (Amdin. Gen.)
Fond Direcția Generală a Poliției (DGP)
Fond Presedinția Consiliului de Miniștri (PCM)

21 krajcár és Kossuth Ferenc (1894): In: *Pestmegyei Hírlap* VII (56) October 14., 1.
A románok kultúrája II (1897): In: *Budapesti Hírlap* 17 (233) August 22., 4.
Az Erdélyi Gazdasági Tanács a tanoncotthonok kérdésének intézményes megoldását kéri [The Ecoomic Council for Transylvania requests the permanetn soultion of the problem of apprentice homes] (1941): 62 (70.) March 27., 7.
Az oláhok ki akarták rabolni a Magyar Nemzeti Múzeumot [Vlachs wanted to pillage the Hungarian National Museum] (1919): In: *Magyar Jövő* 1 (38.) November 18., 5.
Ajtay, József (1943): Erdély őslakói [The first inhabitants of Transylvania]. In: *Pesti Hírlap* 65 (278.) December 8., 5.
Bánffy, Miklós (1934): *Megszámláltattál* [You are counted]. Kolozsvár: Erdélyi Szépmíves Céh.
Bánffy, Miklós (1935): *És híjával találtattál* [And you are found wanting]. Kolozsvár: Erdélyi Szépmíves Céh.
Bánffy, Miklós (1940): *Darabokra szaggattatol* [You are torn to pieces]. Kolozsvár: Erdélyi Szépmíves Céh.
Biharvármegyei osztály [Bihar County section] (1894) In: *Erdély* III. (4), 111–112.
Ce vrem noi? (1933) In: *Zărandul* I (1) February 15, 1.
Csak az exportálhasson tűzifát, aki arányos mennyiséget a belföldi piacon is elad [Export permits should only be given to those who sell a proportional amount of goods inland too] (1937) In: *Brassói Lapok* 43 (176) August 28, 6.
Csiki székelyek nyomora. In: *Magyar Polgár* 23. (216) September 21, 1900. 7.
Dandea, Emil (1926): Chestiunea Moților [The Moți question] In: *Societatea de Mâine* 3 (19) May 9, 356–358.
Elnémult harangok. Felújítás a Nemzeti Színházban [Silenced Bells. Rerun in the National Theater]. In: *Új Magyarság* 8 (45) February 23., 13.
Erdélyi, Viktor (1926): A mócok földje [The land of the Moți]. In: *A jövő társadalma* 2 (2), 2–10.
Florescu, Florea (1938): "Vidra. Vănzătorii și meșteșugarii ambulanți," [Vidra. Wandering salesmen and craftsmen] In: *Sociologie Românească*, 4–6, 248–255.
Gunda, Béla (1940): "Kárpát-Európa vándorai" [The wanderers of Carpathian Europe]. In: *Magyar Nemzet* 3 (138.) June 10., 9.
Guvernul face totul și nimic pentru Moți [The government does everything and nothing for the Moți] (1927). In: *Adevărul* 40 (13444) October 15, 2.
Hamarosan rendeződik a székelyföldi munkaalkalmak teremtésének kérdése [The issue of creating Székely employment possibilities will soon be resolved] (1941) In: *Reggeli Újság* 11 (72) March 29., 2.
Három főtulajdonságnak köszönhetjük a történelmi Magyarországot [Historic Hungary was the result of three main characteristics] (1942) In: *Székely Nép* 60 (264) November 21, 3.
Iorga, Nicolae (1925): "În Secuime" [In the Székelyand]. In: *Universul Literar* XLI (30) July 26, 2–3.

Képviselőházi Napló (1906): *Az 1906. évi május hó 19-ére hirdetett Országgyűlés Képviselőházának Naplója.*
Képviselőházi Napló (1910): *Az 1910. évi június hó 21-ére hirdetett Országgyűlés Képviselőházának Naplója.*
Kőváry, László (1853): *Erdély földe ritkaságai* [Rarities from Trasylvania]. Kolozsvár.
Mócmegye, székely ispánság, szász grófság [Moți prefecture, Székely district, Saxon county] (1929) In: *Ellenzék* 50 (266) November 21.
Moldován, Gergely (1894): "Székelyek-e a mócok?" [Are the Moți Székely]. In: *Erdélyi Múzeum* XI (6), 403–416.
Népszámlálás (1909): A *Magyar Korona országainak 1900. évi népszámlálása. A végeredmények összefoglalása* [The 1900 census in the land of the Hungarian crown. Summary of the results]. Vol. 10. In: *Magyar Statisztikai Közlemények* 27.
Oprișan, Nicolae (1925): La marginea Românismului [On the margins of Romanianism]. In: *Societate de Mâine* II (34–35), 602 –603.
Ötszáz székely lány tűnik el évente a romániai leánykereskedők hálójában [Five hundred Székely maidens a year disappear in the net of Romanian traffickers] (1938) In: *Esti Újság* 8. 28. 3. (194), 9.
Péter, Lajos (1906): *Háromszéki erdőpanamák* [Forest swindles in Háromszék]. Sepsiszentgyörgy: Kossuth Nyomda.
Planuri de revoluție săcuiești descoperite [Plans of the Székely revolution were discovered] (1920) In: *Gazeta poporului* 2 (40), 3.
Revista Periodicelor (1921): *Dacoromania. Buletinul „Muzeului Limbei Române" Universității din Cluj.* 880.
Robul, Constantin (1921): Pe Arieș, în sus. (Scrisorile unui răzeș) [Down the Arieș. (Writings of a Moldovan)]. In: *Gândirea* 1 (15), 273–274.
Români care se magharizează în România Mare [Romanians, who are become Magyars in Greater Romania] (1923) In: *Gazeta Transilvaniei* LXXXXVI (159) December 26., 3.
Sándor, József (1894): Skerisorai kirándulás [Excursion to Scărișoara] In: *Erdély* III (5), 126–130.
Sebestyén, Károly Cs. (1941): *A székely ház eredete* [Origins of the Székely house]. Budapest.
Szabolcs felszabadított földjén [On the liberated fields of Szabolcs county] (1920) In: *Reggeli Hírlap* XXIX (49) February 28, 2.
Székely, Béla (1894): "Az oláh kérdés" [The Vlach Question]. In: *Pesti Napló* 45. (155) June 6, 3–4.
Székely kongresszus [Székely Congress]. (1901) In: *Erdély*, 10 (8–10) August 1. 74–84.
Székelyfőzés [Winning over Székelys]. (1933) In: *Brassói Lapok* 39 (285) December 11. 6.
Szoboszlay, László (1928): "A faji kisebbségek helyzete." [The situation of racial minorities] In: *Székely Nép* 46 (9.) January 29., 2.
Tamási, Áron (1932): *Ábel a rengetegben* [Ábel in the Wilderness]. Kolozsvár: Erdélyi Szépmíves Céh
Vornea, Sandu (1931a): "Caravanele foamei" [Hunger Caravans] In: *Realitatea Ilustrată* V (239) August 21. 23–25.
Vornea, Sandu (1931b): "Caravanele foamei. Care femeea s-a spânzurat" [Hunger Caravans. The woman who strangulated herself] In: *Realitatea Ilustrată* V (240) September 2. 21–22.

Svante Lindberg
Francophone Calvinists in 18th Century German-Speaking Europe
On Charles Étienne Jordan, Mathurin Veyssière la Croze and Éléazar de Mauvillon

In 2017, the 500th anniversary of the Reformation was celebrated. Its transformative effects on European society were recognised in a variety of ways, both in the tourism industry and in academic life. In this study, I will focus on Calvinism in 18th century Europe, especially with regard to the question of French-speaking Huguenots – many of whom were exiled to the German-speaking region of Europe as a result of religious persecution in France[1] – as well as the phenomenon of cosmopolitanism. Furthermore, the study is to be seen as part of the ongoing discussion on world literatures, as the three authors in question – Charles Étienne Jordan (1700–1745), Mathurin Veyssière la Croze (1661–1739) and Éléazar de Mauvillon (1712–1779) – wrote literature for audiences beyond the borders of their country of residence. Jordan was born in Prussia, whereas La Croze, his teacher in Berlin, was born in the French city of Nantes. The latter would later become an important member of the Prussian capital's French-speaking intelligentsia. De Mauvillon was born in France, but emigrated to Prussia and later moved to Kassel and Braunschweig. The decision to study these intellectuals was based on my aim of discussing first and second-generation immigrants in the German-speaking region, as well as that of providing an opportunity to examine the French language as both an immigrant (minority) language and the cosmopolitan language of this period. This is why the writers examined in this article can also be regarded as examples of cultural agents who participated in contradictory discourses. These discourses are the voices of minority and majority groups, and in the intersection

---

[1] In 1598 Henry IV had inaugurated a period of relative religious toleration in France. The Edict of Nantes guaranteed the protection of Protestants in different ways: "With the beginning of a new era of toleration, the minority population of French Protestants was granted the basic rights to follow the teachings of Calvin and to worship in Reformed temples, along with the right to participate in professions, be admitted to schools and public hospitals without prejudice, and hold public office" (Sample Wilson 2011: 10). This changed during the reign of Louis XVI, and in 1685 Protestants "were forced to abjure their Calvinist faith and unite with the Catholic church" (Sample Wilson 2011: 11).

ට Open Access. © 2023 the author(s), published by De Gruyter. This work is licensed under the Creative Commons Attribution 4.0 International License.
https://doi.org/10.1515/9783111039633-003

between margin, cosmopolis and nation, they express different ways of cultural belonging. Having said this, it is also important to examine the cultural reality and the ways that ideas and books were circulated in 18th century Europe. Contrary to the idea of a "national" book market that is often assumed to have existed at that time, the situation as far as intellectual and linguistic circulation was concerned was in fact somewhat different. As Jeffrey Friedman (2012: 1) states, "books have not been as respectful to national borders as the historians who study them [...]" And as far as the movement of books is concerned, Friedman says that their distribution "cannot be folded neatly into the geography of nations, let alone that of states" (Friedman 2012: 1). He also describes a situation in Germany "where international and national typographical styles and French and German literature mingled promiscuously in the bookshops" (Friedman 2012: 2). As for the role of the French language during this period, the vehicle of cosmopolitanism was central to book publishing: "With the aid of Huguenot refugees, who had taken up residence in many of the Protestant states of Europe following the revocation of the Edict of Nantes, French-language publishing firms flourished along the borders of the French kingdom, from Amsterdam to Geneva" (Friedman 2012: 5).

This means that studying the relationship between languages (French and German) during this period also needs to be done from an "archaeological" perspective, and not only from the point of view of cultural or political power relations. The latter perspective is something that we are used to adopting in contemporary postcolonial studies, whereas the former relies more on a Foucauldian point of view. In this context, it is appropriate to remember Foucault's distinction between archaeology and genealogy:

> [...] if archaeology addresses a level at which differences and similarities are determined, a level where things are simply organized to produce manageable forms of knowledge, the stakes are much higher for genealogy. Genealogy deals with precisely the same substrata of knowledge and culture, but Foucault now describes it as a level where the grounds of the true and the false come to be distinguished via mechanisms of power (O'Farrell 2007–2021).

Jean Bessière (2012: 34) adopts a Foucauldian archaeological way of examining French writing in Europe during this period and describes this writing as one of many *writing practices* that coexisted with other European writing practices. The authors studied in this article are thus part of an already existing pattern of cultural and literary circulation. However, this is a research area that has in many ways remained unexplored. According to Gretchanaia, Stroev and Viollet (2012: 13), French writing in Europe is a research field that is, in many ways, a new or revitalised one. It is also a topic of particular importance in today's European reality: "La littérature européenne d'expression française offre une image de l'Europe perçue en tant que fondatrice d'une société qui, depuis le XVIIIe siècle, s'établit au-delà des barrières nationales" [French-language European literature presents an image of Europe as the founder of a society that, since the 18th century, has extended beyond national barriers.] (Gretchanaia/Stroev/Viollet 2012: 13).[2]

This writing is also characterised by its diversity: "Les écrits en question concernent plusieurs domaines de la production écrite: poésie, romans, théâtre, mémoires, journaux personnels, correspondences, ouvrages philosophiques et historiques, périodiques" [The writings in question concern several areas of written production: poetry, novels, theatre, memoirs, diaries, correspondence, philosophical and historical works, periodicals.] (Gretchanaia/Stroev/Viollet 2012: 13). By also adopting a more contemporary literary theoretical point of view, I will nevertheless argue that some contemporary literary theories on migration can shed light on the 18th century cosmopolites studied here. In *Les passages obligés de l'écriture migrante* (2005), Simon Harel talks about post-exile in his studies on contemporary immigrant literature. This is seen as a condition that ensues after the actual exile phase, when the migrant has adapted and established themselves in the new country. Cultural elements from the old country blend together with the culture of the new country, enriching the latter, and the two cultures exist side by side.

Another point of view is the one represented by Bertrand Van Ruymbeke (2016) in his discussion of the terms diaspora and *refuge* (haven). Van Ruymbeke noted that the latter is the most relevant term for describing French Huguenots in exile. This is because the notion refers to a kind of fresh start in a location defined by a strong sense of "here and now", rather than to a position within a diaspora, i.e. a location on the outskirts of a centre – in this case the old homeland of France. Van Ruymbeke emphasises that it is the new country (North America in his studies), one that has offered shelter to refugees, that will be regarded as the motherland, and not the old one. Both Harel's concept of *post-exile* and Van Ruymbeke's use of *refuge* underscore the new country at the expense of a nostalgic retrospective envisioning of the old one. The first concept signals a temporal distancing whereas the second one refers to a spatial distancing, to *another* space. While both theories deal with time and space, it is crucial to bring in a third dimension, i.e. the subjective agent. Here it is relevant to refer to the notion of *cultural go-betweens* proposed by the Franco-Indian cultural studies researcher, Kapil Raj (2009). These are individuals who are culturally competent on several levels and who serve as translators of culture. Cultural power relations can be

---

2 All translations from French to English are made by the author of the article.

studied in many ways, one of which is the point of view of "cultural ecology", a subject that Alexander Beecroft discusses in *An Ecology of World Literature* (2015) in connection with the research field of world literature. This book studies the systems of cultural balance, or the ecology of literary expression in different cultural and historical surroundings, and identifies a number of types of conditions, i.e. epichoric, panchoric cosmopolitan, vernacular, national and global literatures. As far as cosmopolitan literatures are concerned, Beecroft (2015: 34) states: "Cosmopolitan ecologies are found wherever a single literary language is used over a large territorial range and through long periods of time. Cosmopolitan literatures, almost by definition, represent themselves as universal, and yet their very reach often brings them in touch with rival cosmopolitanisms." On the other side, there are national literatures, a sort of opposite pole:

> The national literary ecology emerges out of the vernacular literary ecology of Europe, together with the emergence of nationalism per se. Since the notion of the nation-state rests on the claim (only loosely connected with reality) that each nation speaks a single language, and is represented by a single polity, the national-literature ecology does the same. (Beecroft 2015: 35).

The authors examined here can be found in this border zone between cosmopolis and nation, between universal French and emerging German. They are subjective agents in positions that are unstable and dynamic, and they "situate and navigate *themselves*" within a fluid literary system (McDonald & Suleiman Rubin, 2010b, x).

My focus will be on cultural mediation, on the way the examined texts take part in this mediation and on the authors as cultural go-betweens. In fact, the text material itself bears witness to this mediation. In the part dedicated to Jordan, I rely to a great extent on Jens Häseler's book on this author, *Ein Wanderer zwischen den Welten Charles Étienne Jordan* (1993). The most important source of my comments on La Croze is Jordan's book about him, *Histoire de la vie et des ouvrages de Monsieur La Croze* (1741). The third part of my study deals with de Mauvillon's biography *Histoire de Gustave-Adolphe Roi de Suède* (1764), where I analyse the author's own comments about cultural differences between the Nordic countries and continental Europe, and about Protestantism. On the one hand, I will consider the extent to which this mediation can be seen as both a power relationship and as an act of negotiation between a minority and a majority. This type of focus is often not only used in colonial/postcolonial studies, but also in the study of migration and minority literatures. In his book on minority literature, François Paré (1972) writes about literatures of exiguity, a sort of writing from a distance. However, this condition is often still seen in a hierarchical and territorial context in relationship with a centre. Lise Gauvin (2003: 38) describes this condition in the following way:

> On pourrait dire de ces littératures qu'elles voyagent peu, que leur importance à l'échelle mondiale est inversement proportionnelle à leur impact dans leur société d'origine. Mais là encore, l'exiguïté suppose un comparant plus large, plus étendu, plus expansionniste. Ces littératures sont encore nommées par référence à une hiérarchie. Aussi séduisant qu'il soit, ce modèle me semble risqué, puisqu'il repose sur une conception territoriale de la littérature.
> [One could say of these literatures that they travel little, that their importance on a global scale is inversely proportional to their impact in their society of origin. But here again, smallness presupposes a broader, more extensive, more expansionist comparison. These literatures are still named by reference to a hierarchy. As attractive as it is, this model seems risky to me, since it is based on a territorial conception of literature.]

The other way of looking upon French-language writing in Europe is to study it from a culturally archaeological perspective, i.e. as the expression of the coexistence of languages and cultures within a given cultural context. Jean Bessière (2012: 29-35) points out that there is French-language European writing that does not easily fit into an analysis that studies it from a genealogical and power-related perspective. Instead, this writing should be viewed as archaeological evidence of a cultural expression in different European countries that are not necessarily regarded as "Francophone". This Francophone writing is part of a specific "plurality" of History and has its own (often little-explored) archives (Bessière 2012: 34). The main question under consideration here is if the examined authors and the texts are suitable for a modern, colonial/postcolonial, migrant literature analysis or if it is more appropriate to examine them from the cultural-archaeological analysis proposed by Bessière. Do the texts provide material for genealogical and/or archaeological study?

1 Cultural contextualisation

In order to provide a framework of religious history and the history of mentalities, I will start by referring to an article by the German historian Gerlinde Strohmeier-Wiederanders (2017: 35–41) concerning conflicts of faith in Berlin and Brandenburg in the 17th century. The Brandenburg electorate had been a supporter of Calvinism since Johan Sigismund came to power in 1608 and subsequently converted to Calvinism in 1613. His successor George Wilhelm also advocated a form of neutrality policy, while the successor Crown Prince Frederick Wilhelm (1620–1688), sometimes referred to as the Great Elector, represented a type of tolerant but centralised absolutism. He ruled over a multifaceted kingdom that not only included Brandenburg, but also areas such as Westphalia and Niederrhein. Here, many different variants of the Christian religion were practiced, which is why tolerance out of practical necessity became a key concept. Although peaceful religious coexistence was a central political issue, there were other issues to consider during this period in history, in particular the problem of Brandenburg-Prussia's depopulation as a result of the Thirty Years' War. Thus, Frederick Wilhelm issued a number of "tolerance edicts" that encouraged immigration. In 1671, Brandenburg-Prussia received 50 Jewish families who had been expelled from Vienna. Later on, the Edict of Potsdam (1685) enabled the reception of 20,000 French Huguenots who had suffered severe persecution in France after the revocation of the Edict of Nantes that same year. The French Protestant immigrants who arrived in Berlin and Prussia brought with them their education and professional knowledge, which contributed significantly to Prussia's rapid development and prosperity. At Frederick the Great's court, French was spoken and the prince himself, having received his education in this language, spoke it better than German. He also preferred French literature to German literature. All this transformed Prussia into a region that was in many ways prepared for the French-speaking immigration. According to Strohmeier-Wiederanders (2017: 41), one can talk about a significant cultural transfer from France to Brandenburg-Prussia. This consisted, among other things, of new types of craftsmanship, trade, scientific activities and culinary knowledge being introduced into the German-speaking region. The domain of science is particularly interesting, and out of 37 members of the Academy of Sciences in Berlin (founded in 1700), eight had their origins in the French-speaking colony. According to Strohmeier-Wiederanders, although the 17th century had been characterised by religious conflict, a new trend towards greater tolerance emerged, one that coexisted with the centralisation of state power. Two additional forces contributed to reinforcing this smooth process towards cohabitation. The first was the spread of the religious movement of Pietism. This version of Christianity emphasised the importance of emotion in religious experience. In his book on early German Pietism, F. Ernest Stoeffler (1973) describes this movement's motivation as having been characterised by:

> [t]he need for, and the possibility of, an authentic and vitally significant experience of God on the part of individual Christians (the religious life as a life of love for God and man, which is marked by social sensitivity and ethical concern [...]. Morever, the church is looked upon "as a community of God's people, which must ever be renewed through the transformation of individuals, and which necessarily transcends all organizationally required boundaries [...]. (Stoeffler 1973: ix).

If individualism and social awareness are central to Pietism, a second factor that led to increased tolerance was the European Enlightenment. Though a French phenomenon, this movement quickly became a European mission. Ira Wade (1971: xiii) describes the content and dynamics of these ideas and refers to certain typical aspects: "their romantic tendencies; the foreign influences, particularly England, upon them, and their influence in Europe as a whole". Wade continues: "[...] the desire to pass from the factual, positivistic level to a higher synthesis, in short, from the analytic to the organic, is everywhere visible" (Wade 1971: xiii).

In the scholarship of the time there is also a wish to "give to the movement a European, even a 'Western Civilization' scope, rather than a French perspective" (Wade 1971: xiii). According to Strohmeier-Wiederanders (2017), the combined presence of Pietism and Enlightenment ideas caused one to question the strength of both reason and revelation. The author argues that a process was set in motion whereby reason and tolerance were to gain in importance at the expense of religious orthodoxy, which paved the way for a more pluralistic openness.

The role of the Huguenots in Berlin-Brandenburg can be examined in the light of recent theories on the spread of science and scientific knowledge. This question has been studied by, among others, Kapil Raj (2013), who identified two trends that represent the distinction between power relation and archaeology that I brought up at the beginning of this article. On the one hand, there is the binary centre/periphery model, or the rift between metropolitan versus colonial realities. On the other hand, one can identify a more irregular means of transfer. Raj (2013: 343) argues that the way we view the transmission of knowledge and the very notion of science itself should be reconsidered so "that by science we understand not free-floating ideas, but the production of knowledge, practices, instruments, techniques and services; and by circulation we understand not the 'dissemination', 'transmission' or 'communication' of ideas, but the processes of encounter, power and resistance, negotiation, and reconfiguration that occur in cross-cultural interaction[...]." As one can see, Raj emphasises the transformative dimension of circulation in his study of cultural transfer, at the expense of a model that underscores the hierarchy of knowledge that exists between a centre and a periphery.

2 Charles Étienne Jordan's life and works

Charles Étienne Jordan can be seen as an illuminating example of a person who took part in the kind of transformative cultural exchange that Raj refers to in his study. An interesting insight into Jordan's life and into the Berlin of the first half of the 18th century, a time of transition, is provided by Jens Häseler in *Ein Wanderer zwischen den Welten. Charles Étienne Jordan* (1993). The following part of my study describes Jordan's life and work, and is mainly based on Häseler's book. Häseler describes Jordan, a prominent Huguenot in Berlin, as a transgressor of frontiers, not only between the worlds of French and German, but also between different French-speaking environments in Berlin. This was especially the case in, on the one hand, the French-speaking Huguenot colony, and on the other, the court of Frederick the Great. As a result, Jordan performed in several cultural arenas within Prussia. Born in Berlin as the son of the merchant Charles Jordan, an immigrant French Huguenot, he enrolled as a student at the University of Geneva, one of the leading Calvinist universities of the time, in 1718. He was to stay there for only two years before returning to Berlin, where he gradually gained access to the highest theological circles of his time. After graduating in theology, he became a pastor in the Uckermark region north of the German capital, an area characterised by the religious practice of the Huguenots. Living a fairly isolated life in the Prussian countryside, he was obliged to pursue his spiritual and intellectual development in his spare time. According to Häseler (1993), this was typical of this generation of theologians who served in the country. Correspondence was a way of promoting intellectual development, and Jordan devoted a large amount of time to this activity. The contact between Jordan and reformed scholars in Berlin, as well as his international correspondence, were crucial for the theologian's intellectual development. One of his contacts was the French writer Jean-Pierre Nicéron, with whom he planned to write a European history of science. He wanted to include a wide range of knowledge in the planned volume, i.e. encyclopaedic knowledge in the fields of science, book publishing, philosophy and church history. According to Häseler (1993), Jordan can be inserted into a Protestant tradition with a strong historiographic focus. Häseler also sees Jordan and his works as an example of a tendency in the evolution of European intellectual life where language and nation (in the case of French) were gradually separated. This movement led from a strictly France-centred focal point towards a more pluralistic, cosmopolitan worldview that nevertheless continued to use the French language as its tool for expression. This view is confirmed by other researchers working on the phenomenon of French Enlightenment thought in Europe (see Wade 1971).

Jordan was to write two kinds of work: philological and textual bibliographies, and biographies of historical personalities. One of his aims was to show how the style of French humanist poets in the 16th century, especially those belonging to the group known as *la Pléiade* (e.g. Pierre de Ronsard and Joachim Du Bellay) continued to have a far-reaching influence, 200 years later, on both the French language and on the literary style and tastes of many Huguenots living as far away as Berlin. He thus wanted to show how the stylistic principles of the 16th century survived in the Berlin of the 18th century. In 1741, Jordan published his biography of his former teacher in Berlin, Mathurin Veyssière La Croze. From his location of exile in Berlin, this Huguenot had written a French literary history that had become a sort of standard reference. Through his literary and biographical works, and through his good contacts among the reformed theologians in Berlin, Jordan gradually became an important person, not only in Berlin's Calvinistic circles, but also in the European *République des lettres*. His career expanded and transformed itself, and he went from being a theologian to becoming an educated humanist.

After his wife's death in 1732, Jordan undertook a European educational journey that had Paris as its main destination. Examining this from the point of view of the ideas of refuge and diaspora developed by Bertrand Van Ruymbeke (see *supra*), some interesting observations can be made. The journey had as its destination the country where Jordan's "native language" was spoken. France, however, was a country that he had never visited before. After arriving in the French capital, he met with scholars such as Voltaire, and visited theatres and museums. It is very interesting to observe Jordan's experience of alienation in Catholic France. Although he was impressed and influenced by the cultural and intellectual life, he did not feel at home in what should have been his "native" land. Häseler (1993) is not writing a story of a homecoming, but rather a story of cultural and religious self-understanding. Jordan's reactions were quite different in the next country he visited, England. His encounter with the country across the channel made him write that he was happy to feel stable Protestant soil under his feet once again (Häseler 1993: 84). During his visit to Oxford, he was also impressed by the teaching methods at the university, especially by the fact that the country's own language was used in teaching and in the dialogue between students and teachers. For Jordan, the previously discussed trip "back" to France did not work as a return from a state of diaspora to an abandoned centre. His encounter with France should be seen in the context of the resistance, negotiation and reconfiguration that Raj (1993) referred to rather than as a return to a place of origin. It also illustrates a condition beyond that of dominated and dominating cultures, as described by Pascale Casanova in her influential book *The World Republic of Letters* (2004 [1999]).[3] McDonald and Suleiman Rubin (2010b: xvii) refer to Casanova's idea in their discussion of the transnational dimension of writing:

---

3 Pascale Casanova (1999): La république mondiale des lettres. Paris: Seuil (The World Republic of Letters [2004]. Translated by M.B. Debevoise. Cambridge, Mass.: Harvard University Press).

> Expanding Bourdieu's views about "dominant" and "dominated" poles in the literary field to the world stage, Casanova proposes what she calls a "dual historicization": a writer's work, in her view, must be seen both in terms of the place it occupies in its "native" (national) literary space and in terms of the space occupied by the native's native literature in a larger world system. (McDonald/Suleiman Rubin 2010b: xvii)

Viewed through this dual historical perspective, Jordan is both a representative of a German literary condition where the coexistence of French and German was a natural thing at the time, and an example of French writing "in exile" in Germany (if seen from the French point of view).

The trip to France and England was a turning point in Jordan's life and confirmed his transformation from theologian to educated humanist. But this career change was not accomplished without friction and effort. He initially made a living as a private teacher while he completed and published an account of his trip to France and England, *Histoire d'un voyage littéraire, fait en 1733 en France, en Angleterre, et en Hollande* in 1735. Furthermore, he was in contact with La Croze until the latter died in 1739. It was when Jordan became *homme de compagnie* [companion, conversational partner] and later secretary to Crown Prince Frederick (later Frederick the Great) that his career gathered fresh momentum. One of his first assignments was to translate moral philosophy texts into French that had been written by the German philosopher Christian Wolff. In addition, Jordan's new employer assigned him two other main tasks: engaging in cultivated conversation in French and acquiring books. The latter task meant searching for and buying French literary texts and bringing them to Prussia for the purpose of informing his patron's taste. When it came to questions concerning French literature, there was one writer above all others who had a great influence on Frederick: Voltaire. The French philosopher's stay as Frederick's guest from 1751 to 1753, in Berlin and at Sanssouci in Potsdam, is well-known.

As previously discussed, Jordan's role as a border crosser is complex. His function as a cultural and literary mediator does not only apply to French and German cultures, but can also be seen in his contacts among different French-speaking groups in Berlin. He belonged to both the city's learned francophone circles and the court's French-speaking milieu.

For example, the second part of Jens Häseler's book presents Jordan as an intercultural contact person within the court. Häseler describes his role as a mediator between Voltaire and Frederick, his participation in the reorganisation of the Berlin Academy of Sciences, which was carried out according to the French model, and his lack of enthusiasm for Frederick's war project. Jordan's efforts were made possible by his familiarity with the spiritual and intellectual life in Prussia at the beginning of Frederick the Great's reign. However, the next phase of Jordan's development was characterised by a certain degree of distance from court activities. He eventually switched his focus towards his own studies and to expanding his own library, and also devoted himself to strengthening contacts with Berlin's French-speaking colony. Furthermore, he wanted to spend more time in the scholarly French-speaking circles outside the court. His educational background in the field of theology again came to the fore in his farewell letter to Frederick, where he addressed religion's importance for culture. According to Häseler (1993), Jordan's contribution to early Prussian cultural life was of great value. It was to his credit that the Protestant educational ideal was introduced at the Prussian court.

According to Häseler's biography, one can conclude that Jordan is a clear example of the French cultural influence of the Huguenots in Prussia and of a person who started something new in the country that his parents had emigrated to. He is also an example of the transformation at work in cultural exchange, since his French origin was a way of enriching the cultural life of his new country, and because Jordan managed to be accepted into several circles in the Prussian capital. This process of transformation is closely linked to subjective agency. Jordan is someone who produces knowledge of and for Prussia's French-language Huguenots. He is also someone who is in a position of negotiation between French and German, as well as between different levels of Frenchness in Berlin. If Jordan is in many respects a mediator, the question of the hierarchies of language and the fact that there is a discrepancy between language and territory (he is a French speaker living outside of France) adds to this complexity. This is a question that can be examined from the "Global French" perspective introduced by McDonald & Suleiman Rubin (2010a). If one regards Jordan through the lens of world literature, he should be seen as an individual participating in a dual historicisation rather than as an example of the close relationship between literature/language and nation. In his case the territorial/hierarchical point of view is less important, whereas Kapil Raj's idea of cultural expression as the result of encounters and reconfiguration (in an already plurilingual environment) provides a more relevant point of view.

3 Mathurin Veyssière La Croze as seen by Charles Étienne Jordan

In the following section, which deals with Jordan's teacher Mathurin Veyssière La Croze, the idea of reconfiguration will be illustrated further. The written documentation of the life and works of an intellectual can be seen as examples of reconfiguration/reformulation in the process of cultural transfer and cultural implementation as described by Raj. Jordan's book on the French-Prussian intellectual La Croze is an example of the deterritorialisation of French erudition in circumstances similar to those found in the literature of exiguity developed by Francois Paré (1972). I will focus on some aspects of La Croze's life and work as they appear in Jordan's book *Histoire de la vie et des ouvrages de Monsieur La Croze* (1741) and also consider the text as a way of establishing La Croze as a significant cultural personality in his new home country. In this biography, a Jordan often adopts the I perspective, which gives the text the form of an autobiography – this is spite of the fact that it should really be regarded as a "biography."[4] Jordan starts out by saying that La Croze is "un des membres les plus distingués de la République des Lettres que le siècle ait produit" [(...) one of the most distinguished members of the Republic of Letters that the century has produced.] (Jordan 1741: 2), thus commencing his mission of not only situating his protagonist within the local cultural life, but also within a cosmopolitan context. As far as reconfiguration is concerned, one can say that La Croze's life is an example of this, as he was someone who reconfigured, who changed his religious affiliation and transformed himself into an important intellectual in his new country. Jordan's biography is another example of reconfiguration, as it reformulates La Croze's life in written form.

Jordan's book informs us that La Croze was born in Nantes in 1661 and had started his career as a French Benedictine historian and orientalist, though he later converted to Protestantism. He showed an interest in learning early on and eventually became an avid scholar. Travel was another one of his interests, and he visited the French Antilles in his youth. From La Croze's native Nantes, the reader can follow the protagonist's relocations: first to the learned centre of the Abbaye de St.-Germain-des-Prés in Paris and then to Basel, as well as his meeting in the latter with several prominent Protestant personalities. This led to La Croze's conversion to the Reformed religion. As mentioned above, the book is in many parts written in the style of a conventional autobiography. However, it also seems to have educational and pedagogical ambitions, since it often presents the

---

[4] Jordan's book was written before the emergence of what is sometimes called formal autobiography. At this time, the border between fiction and reality was not so strict as we know it to be today. Jordan's book can be regarded as a "biography" in the same way as, for example, Voltaire's biography of Charles XII. One interesting thing is that Jordan's book contains parts that were written in the third-person singular and others that were written in the first-person singular. See for example Murray Kendall 2000.

main character as a sort of learned role model. Jordan talks about how La Croze then proceeded from Basel to Berlin, where he became Royal Librarian and a specialist in Armenian languages at the University of Berlin. La Croze completed his dictionary of Latin and Slavonic languages, and later went on to write a dictionary of these languages in Egypt. The reader also learns a great deal about another important book written by La Croze, his history of Christianity in India (1724), and about the positive reception of this book by learned critics. It was written in French but later translated into German. As Jordan's book on La Croze has a didactic strain, the reader is also provided with in-depth details on La Croze's research.[5] For example, in the chapter called *Remarques de Mr La Croze*, we learn how the protagonists reflected on different ways of thinking, a sort of meditation on mentalities and how they change over time. The goal was to demonstrate cultural relativism, and this part of the text ends with a sentence about tolerance: "Le plus dangereux de tous les préjugez est de croire qu'on n'en a point" [The most dangerous of all the prejudices is to believe that one has none.] (Jordan 1741: 337). Jordan's book has a mediating and a culturally consolidating function. In writing his text, he reconfigured the life and work of an important agent from that time in the arena of Prussian cultural life. The text also provides documentation on the life of a first generation member of learned Calvinists in Berlin, which also talks about his participation in inclusive discourse.

4 On Éléazar de Mauvillon

As far as Éléazar de Mauvillon – the third author that this article examines – is concerned, the topics of mediation and cultural transfer are also important. Active mainly in Braunschweig and Kassel, he was a cultural mediator in several ways. To start, he was a teacher of French, which meant that he mediated between this language and German. Another thing that qualifies him as a cultural mediator was his contact with the Finland-Swedish politician and intellectual Johan Arckenholtz (1695–1777). After a political career in Sweden, Arckenholtz made extensive journeys throughout continental Europe and lived there for long periods of time (see Jacobson). The Protestant point of view appears in de Mauvillon's writing, as is also the case in his biography of the Swedish king Gustavus

---

[5] On Page 155, the reader is informed about La Croze's philosophical explanations of concepts, such as "Définitions", "Demandes" and "Axiomes". Another example is the chapter "Remarques de Mr La Croze", where Jordan has La Croze reflect on changes in mentality over the centuries, which is a form of cultural relativism.

II Adolphus. The contact between de Mauvillon and Arckenholtz mainly concerned de Mauvillon's preparation for and writing of this biography, which was completed in 1764. The choice to write about the Protestant monarch is already telling, but one can also see indirect references to Protestantism in the footnotes. Here, if we regard Arckenholtz as a fellow Protestant in the North, it is interesting to see that there are many references to this Nordic colleague. Arckenholtz appears to have provided the Franco-German author with facts and cultural knowledge about Swedish, and more generally, Nordic societies, as when reading the text we witness examples of concrete cultural transfer.

The reading also provides insight into the cultural differences and intercultural attitudes of the era in question. De Mauvillon often regarded Gustavus II Adolphus as a role model and a moral example. In the eyes of de Mauvillon, the king represented Christian, presumably Protestant, virtues: "Gustave se comporte en Prince chrétien [...]." [Gustavus behaves like a Christian king] (de Mauvillon 1764: 246). The sovereign is sometimes also given a symbolic function, as he is seen as someone who to a certain degree advocates for equality, and is also enlightened, liberated and peace-loving. He is both a king and philosopher, as well as a person who enters into open and honest dialogue with his friends and subjects. Furthermore, he is someone who sees war as an evil (de Mauvillon 1764: 213), and can also be credited with bringing Sweden closer to continental Europe. According to de Mauvillon, this is a political endeavour that can be achieved with a certain type of leadership, and the Swedish king is able to fulfil this role. It is through the moral and political genius of its sovereign that Sweden becomes more European. According to the author, the king's very being has great influence on the Swedish people and his role as a pedagogical role model is unquestioned. De Mauvillon writes, among other things, that the king knows how to unite his own genius and strategic talent with the notorious courage of the Swedish people, which means that the country can make the most of its potential and achieve the same level of civilisation as other European countries (de Mauvillon 1764: 280).

It is interesting to consider the combination of religious and strategic motivation that de Mauvillon includes in his description of the king's personality, a complexity that continues to interest contemporary researchers. Thus, Clark A. Fredrickson (2011: 2) writes about the Swedish king: "A farewell speech at Stockholm on May 30, 1630 indicates that Gustavus Adolphus wanted to defend Protestantism, and although a deeply religious man, some scholars have questioned his underlying motives. The three primary motives often studied are: political, economic and military". In de Mauvillon's book, the king's religiosity is underscored over and over again; he is a man who has a strong connection with the great truths of religion, one who puts his trust in God and respects the commandments of the Christian faith (de Mauvillon 1764: 304).

In addition to reproducing historical events, de Mauvillon also goes into some detail about the Swedes' experiences in the German-speaking region during the Thirty Years' War. As previously mentioned, his depiction of the king is often idealised. There is also a similar tendency to simplify the portrayal of the Swedish soldiers, who are, for example, portrayed as hardened and fearless Northerners accustomed to cold climates (de Mauvillon 1764: 415). As we can see, the complexity of the king's goals and the role of religion are also discussed in recent research. One example is Pärtel Piirimäe (2002: 500, referred to by Fredrickson [2011: 3]), who claims that Sweden did not wage war in a traditional way, i.e. for reasons of self-defence or aggression, for example, but used a theological justification that was meant to gain public support. As a result, Gustavus Adolphus was able to present a religious case for going to war that helped establish his strong military and public support.[6]

Whereas Jordan and La Croze can be seen as mediators between French and German, and between several levels within these cultural spheres, de Mauvillon's importance in this context can be regarded as an example of an international cosmopolite whose writing contains a considerable religious undertone. In his work on the Swedish king, he writes in French about international political issues, but also about a Protestant hero who is characterised by his high degree of tolerance. He also gives us a practical example of cultural transfer between the Nordic countries and continental Europe. His contact with Arckenholtz provides examples of two migrants who actively participated in cultural exchange in the cosmopolitan cultural arena.

5 Final remarks

The main purpose of this article was to investigate the life and work of three Francophone cultural mediators in 18th century Prussia in order to see if a selection of texts on and by them were suitable for genealogical or archaeological readings. Could the examined writing be regarded as the expression of cultural/linguistic power relations in the sense that we are used to examining things from a

---

[6] Piirimäe Pärtel (2002), "Just War in Theory and Practice: The Legitimation of Swedish Intervention in the Thirty Years War." In: The Historical Journal, 45 (3), 500. Referred to by Fredrickson (2011: 3).

contemporary postcolonial or migrant literature point of view, or was it rather to be understood as the expression of a natural coexistence of languages, one where the frictional aspects played a minor role? The aspect of cosmopolitanism also played an important role in the investigation, as the French language was a powerful means of cultural communication during the European 18th century.

The topics of marginalisation and centralisation provided an important framework for the discussion, since the authors that were studied can be seen as belonging to marginal groups that, over the same period, became increasingly important as cultural agents in their new countries. However, this marginal condition has little visibility in the texts that were studied. When one examines them from the point of view of contemporary literary studies, where exile, migration and multilingualism are important issues, one is struck by the effortless use of the French language and by the lack of comments about the X. This is something that needs to take the cultural reality of that period into consideration in order to be understood.

Rebecca L. Walkowitz (2015: 12) writes about the coexistence of languages and the phenomenon of pre-emptive translation: "Preemptive translation, or the division of writing and speaking languages, was the expectation until the late eighteenth century, which inaugurates the era of national languages and literary traditions." This seems to be relevant for each of the authors that were the focus of this study. Language seems to be used as a means of communication, and little is said about language barriers or cultural differences. Jordan and La Croze are examples of cultural go-betweens in Kapil Raj's sense, while at the same time they contributed to the Prussian nation's emergence, as the state also sought to strengthen itself through cultural means. Here they serve as important mediators, which one can see, for example, in the case of Jordan, who had an active role in the renewal of Berlin's scientific institutions.

If one considers Bertrand van Ruymbeke's terminology of *refuge* and *diaspora*, these authors lived their lives in what should be regarded as a *refuge* rather than in a diasporic condition, as both identified with their new country. These immigrants were certainly part of a minority group, but through the French language they became representatives of a cosmopolitan relationship with the world and formed part of a greater whole. Their cultural deeds were of an eminently practical nature. Jordan contributed through his work at Frederick's court and within the Berlin colony to the internationalisation and cultural strengthening of Prussia. La Croze, who wrote a large number of dictionaries and who had had a brilliant academic career in Berlin, contributed in a very practical way to scientific development and scholarship in his new country. The encyclopaedic ideals that we recognise from the Renaissance seem to live on in their work. De

Mauvillon, being a linguist and a writer of historic texts, represented the same evolution from a minority position into that of a cosmopolitan erudite.

The documents that were used for this study provided information on the cultural mediation that the authors took part in and showed how they were involved in the emerging Prussian state's inclusive discourse. Again, on the textual level, little could be found with regard to cultural conflict or any tensions in the use of French and German. There is also little evidence of the competing (cultural) cosmopolitanisms that Alexander Beecroft (2015) referred to. In Häseler's text on Jordan, little is said about the German language and its relationship with French. On the other hand, Jordan's command of French is a qualification that opens doors for him, both at the national and international level. In the same way, language proficiency is given little attention in Jordan's book on La Croze, who seems to be moving effortlessly between France, Switzerland and Germany without being hindered by any linguistic borders. De Mauvillon's biography is the text that shows a certain degree of intercultural awareness, as the author refers to and reflects upon differences between Nordic and other European cultures. If there are different cosmopolitanisms, then they are more of a religious nature than of a linguistic/cultural one. The adherence to Protestantism is a recurrent topic, whereas linguistic belonging is much less talked about. This means that the texts that were the focus of this study are better suited for being examined as cultural practices that could be analysed from an archaeological point of view, than as evidence of cultural power relations.

References

a. Research literature

Beecroft, Alexander (2015): An Ecology of World Literature. From Antiquity to the present day. London: Verso.

Bessière, Jean (2012). "Notes sur les études francophones. Pour dire la diaspora de l'usage du français et le pouvoir foucauldien des expressions en français hors de France". In: Elena Gretchanaia/Alexandre Stroev,/Catherine Viollet (eds.): La francophonie européenne aux XVIIe-XIXe siècles. Perspectives littéraires, historiques et culturelles. Brussels: P.I.E. Peter Lang, 29–36.

Fredrickson, Clark A. (2011): Building an Empire: How Gustavus Adolphus Carried Sweden to the Forefront of European Politics. Madison: University of Wisconsin Eau Claire. Bachelor's thesis.

Freedman, Jeffrey (2012): Books Without Borders in Enlightenment Europe: French Cosmopolitanism and German Literary Markets. University of Pennsylvania Press.

Gretchanaia, Elena/Stroev, Alexandre/Viollet, Catherine (2012) (eds.): La francophonie européenne aux XVIIe-XIXe siècles. Perspectives littéraires, historiques et culturelles. Brussels: P.I.E. Peter Lang.
Harel, Simon (2005): Les passages obligés de l'écriture migrante, Montréal: XYZ.
Gauvin, Lise (2003): "Autour du concept de littérature mineure. Variations sur un thème majeur". In: Jean-Pierre Bertrand/Lise Gauvin (eds.): Littérature mineure en langue majeur. Montréal: Presses de l'Université de Montréal, Peter Lang, 9–40.
McDonald, Christie/Rubin Suleiman, Susan (eds.) (2010a): French Global. A New Approach to Literary History. New York: Columbia University Press.
McDonald, Christie/Rubin Suleiman, Susan (2010b): "Introduction. The National and the Global". In: Christie McDonald/Susan Rubin Suleiman: French Global. A New Approach to Literary History. New York: Columbia University Press, ix–xxi.
Paré, François (1972): Les littératures de l'exiguïté. Hearst: Le Nordir.
Raj, Kapil (2009): "Mapping Knowledge Go-betweens in Calcutta, 1770–1820". In: Simon Schaffer et al. (eds.): The Brokered World. Go-Betweens and Global Intelligence, 1770–1820. Uppsala Studies in the History of Science, Vol. 35. Sagamore Beach: Science History Publications.
Raj, Kapil (2013): "Beyond Postcolonialism...and Postpositivism. Circulation and the Global History of Science". In: ISIS 104 (2), 337–347.
Ruymbeke, Bertrand van (2016): "Une nouvelle contrée, un nouveau roi. Le rêve Anglican des Huguenots en Amérique". Lecture at the colloquium Protestantism and Political Rebellion in Early Modernity, University of Granada, 1–2 December.
Sample Wilson, Christie (2011): Beyond Belief: Surviving the Revocation of the Edict of Nantes in France. Bethlehem (US): Lehigh University Press.
Stoeffler, F. Ernest (2018 [1973]): German Pietism During the Eighteenth Century. Leiden: E. J. Brill. E-book version.
Strohmeier-Wiederanders, Gerlinde (2017): "Glaubenskonflikte und Toleranz im Berlin des 17. Jahrhunderts". In: Berliner Geschichte 2017 (8), 35-41.
Wade, Ira O. (1971): Intellectual Origins of the French Enlightenment. Princeton University Press.
Walkowitz, Rebecca L. (2015): Born Translated. The Contemporary Novel in an Age of World Literature. New York: Columbia University Press.

b. Empirical sources

Häseler, Jens (1993): Ein Wanderer zwischen den Welten. Charles Étienne Jordan (1700–1745). Sigmaringen: Jan Thorbeke Verlag.
Jordan, Charles Étienne (1735): Histoire d'un voyage littéraire, fait en 1733 en France, en Angleterre, et en Hollande. La Haye: Adrien Moetjens.
Jordan, Charles Étienne (1741): Histoire de la vie et des ouvrages de M:r La Croze, avec des remarques de cet auteur sur divers sujets. Amsterdam: François Changuion.
Mauvillon, Éléazar de (1764): Histoire de Gustave-Adolphe Roi de Suède: composé sur tout ce qui a paru de plus curieux, & sur un grand nombre de manuscrits, & principalement sur ceux de Mr. Arckenholtz. Vol. 1–4. Amsterdam: Chatelain.

c. Online references

Jacobson, G. (no year) Entry: »Johan Arckenholtz«. In: *Svenskt biografiskt lexikon [Swedish Biographical Dictionary]*. *National Archives* https://sok.riksarkivet.se/sbl/Presentation.aspx?id=18766 (accessed 22 February 2017).

Murray Kendall, Paul (2000): Entry: »Biography Narrative genre«. In: *Encyclopedia Britannica* (online version). https://www.britannica.com/art/biography-narrative-genre (accessed 2 July 2021).

O'Farrell, Clare (2007–2021). Entry: »Michel Foucault: key concepts«. In: *Foucault News*. https://michel-foucault.com/key-concepts (accessed 5 July 2021).

Hanna Acke
"To the End of the World"

Legitimising Strategies in Protestant Missionary Discourses around 1900

"[T]o the end of the world" – this biblical phrase from the Acts of the Apostles (Acts 1:8) was a common quote in missionary publications from the 19th and early 20th centuries.[1] It expresses the spatial perspective of the world and the people living on it that was an inherent part of missionary discourses of that time. The members of the missionary organisations placed themselves at the centre. From here they wanted to go out to the assumed margins and spread Christianity. They shared this view – which constructed Europe as the centre from which its inhabitants should penetrate other parts of the world – with contemporary discourses that can be described as colonial. A clear-cut distinction between a centre and a margin was a fundamental part of how European and North American missionary organisations legitimated their efforts to spread Christianity in Africa, Asia and Oceania during the colonial era.

Although a temporal interpretation of the phrase does not arise from Jesus' biblical statement, the context of the missionary publications offered this understanding alongside the spatial one. It was detached from the original context and mixed with similar biblical allusions in missionary writings, and thus reproduced the idea of purposefulness and world history having a specific course. In particular, it was blended with Jesus' promise to the disciples that he would be with them "always, to the end of the age" (Matthew 28:20) in the Great Commission of Matthew's Gospel. This view of a target-oriented progression of world history was consistent with the contemporary colonial and racist assumption of different successive stages of development for "peoples". It was a temporal interpretation of the biblical phrase that reconciles the idea of a common humanity with racist ideas, thus resolving a contradiction – at least on the surface: the people categorised as "heathens" were humans, but from the perspective of European Christians, they had not come as far on the path towards progress and/or salvation as they themselves had. In both the spatial and the temporal interpretations of the quote, colonial and missionary patterns of thought were

---

[1] For this contribution, I have used the English Standard Version for Biblical quotes in English. Although it is a modern but not contemporary translation, it is similar in style to the Biblical quotes used in the Swedish missionary publications that form my main sources.

thus combined. As this example shows, missionary discourses coincided in many ways with colonial bodies of knowledge. Through this parallelisation with the Bible, colonial discourses were even legitimised.

The historical research literature on modern Christian missions has time and again debated the relationship between Christian missions and European colonialism and partly used it as an explanatory model for missionary activities (see for example Hammer 1978; Gründer 1982; Stanley 1990; Porter 2004; Klein 2010). European countries like Sweden which – at least at that time – were not involved in colonial activities, stand out in this context as research objects of particular interest. The Kingdom of Sweden did not take an active part in colonial endeavours in other parts of the world since it had sold its only overseas possession – the island of St. Barthélemy – in 1878. Compared to countries like the Netherlands or Great Britain, it had always been "a small player" in colonialism. At the same time, a comparatively large number of Swedish missionaries travelled to other regions of the world to spread the gospel.[2] Several questions arise from this constellation: how was the relationship between missions and colonialism in a national context, one in which the State had no plans for colonial activities? What role did Christian missions in other parts of the world play in Sweden, the country that financed the missionaries and sent them abroad? And finally: how were missionary bodies of knowledge and the commitment to this work legitimised in this national context?

To answer these questions, I have analysed the publications issued by one of the three large, trans-regional missionary organisations in Sweden. Thus, I am examining the knowledge produced in this particular case and how it was interconnected with other, especially colonial, bodies of knowledge. Furthermore, my work contributes to an analysis of linguistic and discursive strategies for the legitimisation of knowledge and how these make use of narratives of centralisation and marginalisation.

Processes of the production of knowledge – or discourses – are closely entangled with negotiations of power. In this view, power is not understood as something that one group or person possesses or does not possess, i.e. as a contrast between power and powerlessness (see Foucault 2008: 1004–1005). Instead – as the term negotiation suggests – power is understood as the power of interpretation, of how knowledge is produced as valid. Power is thus also about legitimisation. This broad understanding of legitimisation, the presenta-

---

[2] According to Marianne Gullestad, during this period the Scandinavian countries sent out the largest number of missionaries to other countries in relation to their respective populations (see Gullestad 2007: 2).

tion of a certain knowledge as the only valid knowledge, is informed by the legitimising function of language usage described by Peter Berger and Thomas Luckmann (see Berger/Luckmann 1991: 112). In a narrower understanding, legitimisation can be understood as the justification of calls to action (see van Leeuwen 2008: 105).

In the following, I will briefly introduce my sources and contextualise them. The missionary organisation that forms the basis of this study is the *Swedish Missionary Covenant* or *Svenska Missionsförbundet* (in the following: SMF). It was founded in 1878 as a community of Christians inspired by Pietism, who denied the State *Church of Sweden* the legitimacy to represent what were in there view true believers. From the beginning, SMF advocated for its members to be actively committed to missionary work within and beyond Sweden. Congo – or more precisely, the Bakongo who lived along the southern course of the River Congo – and China – or more precisely, the inhabitants of several cities in the province of Hubei – were the most important targets of the SMF's missionary efforts. Therefore, these regions as well as reports on Protestant missions in all parts of the world are the focus of my analysis. SMF's publications, especially the periodical *Missionförbundet*, the society's official organ, form the main sources for my discourse linguistic analysis.

In this contribution, I will summarise my findings by elaborating on the three main legitimisation strategies for Christian missions and missionary knowledge:[3]
– the authorisation of speakers and speaker positions,
– the construction of a community (of knowledge),
– the reduction of complexity.

1 The authorisation of speakers and speaker positions

The authorisation of those who expressed knowledge was one way of legitimising this knowledge. I use the term authorisation to describe the process in which the speakers achieved credibility and integrity.[4] I use the *speaker* label for per-

---

[3] For a more detailed analysis of the materials, see my monograph on the topic (see Acke 2015b).
[4] Not only were the speakers authorised, the media they used was too. As an example, the missionary organisation established its periodical *Missionsförbundet* as a credible and familiar

sons who were also the authors of the statements uttered in the written form of the periodical. The speakers were in most cases the missionaries sent to Congo and China by SMF. The portraits and other photographs printed in the periodical were one way of authorising the missionaries and presenting them as trustworthy and credible individuals; another was the fact that they regularly addressed the readers directly through their letters printed in *Missionsförbundet*.

Fig. 1: Portraits of missionaries in the periodical *Missionsförbundet*. I am grateful to *Equmeniakyrkan* for the permission to reproduce the images in figures 1 and 2.

Most of the pictures that were printed in the periodical showed the society's missionaries, either in the form of portraits or in the form of photographs that presented them together with converts. The portraits especially, which were detailed wood engravings in the first volumes of the journal, contributed to an authorisation of the missionaries. As Julia Voss has shown using the example of Charles Darwin portraits (see Voss 2008: 232, 238), being able to look at or even own a portrait of a person whose texts one reads can strengthen that person's authority.

---

medium by publishing it regularly in the same printed form or one that was only selectively modified (see Acke 2013; Acke 2015b).

Emma och Wilhelm Sjöholm.

Fig. 2: Wilhelm Sjöholm, Hilda, Mafuta and Emma Sjöholm.

The pictures in *Missionsförbundet* also contributed to the categorisation of different people into hierarchically ordered groups. There were numerous portraits of Swedish missionaries, but very few portraits of Congolese or Chinese converts. In the photographs from Congo and China, the missionaries stood in focus in the images themselves, but even more so in the captions. Often, the Congolese and Chinese people who could be seen in the pictures were not mentioned at all or did not have their names in the captions. Images typically showed the white missionaries in the foreground or at the centre of the picture with the converts in the background. This determined their respective importance for the missionary cause from the perspective of the society: the missionaries stood at the centre; the converts remained at the margins. It also – together with similar strategies in the texts – presented Christian white people as individuals and challenged the individuality or even the humanity of black and brown people.[5]

This visual representation contributed to creating the special position held by the missionaries within the organisation and granted their statements a persuasive power. SMF sent them abroad to represent the organisation and all of its members. Thus, the members believed that they were fulfilling the tasks that God had assigned them in the name of the *Swedish Missionary Covenant*. Their personal experiences also strengthened their credibility: the missionaries were the only members who were actually located in the regions in which SMF carried out missionary work. They had first-hand experience in the areas that had been combined into "the heathen world" and with the alleged "heathens", which was viewed as enabling them to report credibly about both.

Letters by the missionaries made up more than half of the periodical's contents (see Kussak 1982: 10). Because missionaries rarely visited Sweden, letters were the main form of contact between the society and those they had sent out to spread the Gospel. Editing and printing their letters to publish them was an efficient way to inform the members about how their donations were being used. Furthermore, letters demonstrated communicative functions that were useful for authorising missionary knowledge. In contrast to (missionary) narratives or reports, letters are generally characterised by direct address (see Robert 2002: 77). Thus, they have characteristics that lend them a very high degree of authenticity and notable immediacy and directness. Because of this, the readership could receive them as immediate and authentic reports from the "mission fields", which bridged the spatial and temporal distance separating the "friends" from the missionaries.

Their position and staging as eyewitnesses were important factors in the authorisation of speakers. In research literature, immediate spatial and temporal vicinity to the events is discussed as a prerequisite for successful witnessing (see Hutchby 2001; Peters 2001; Zelizer 2007). Nevertheless, this was not sufficient. The missionaries' power of persuasion depended on whether they managed to let themselves as individuals disappear behind their descriptions, which gave them an impression of objectivity. At the same time, they had to be credible as individuals by seeming familiar to the readers. Sybille Krämer has

---

[5] For a detailed analysis of the images in the periodical, see Acke 2015b: 84–101, for a discussion of the individuality of converts, see Acke 2015a.

termed this contradiction the *dilemma of witnessing* (Krämer 2009: 89). The missionaries tried to resolve this by using a narrative style that gave readers the feeling of being able to join them. Missionary Sofi Karlsson wrote about the situation of women in Congo in a free-standing publication issued in 1897. This is how she introduced her narrative:

> Så följen mig nu till en by i Kongo. Vi måste gå öfver den där grässlätten, där det höga gräset, hvars strån äro så grova som en vanlig bamburörskäppp [sic], når oss öfver huvudet. Se, där uppe på kullen ligger byn! (Karlsson 1897: 5)[6]
> [Follow me now to a village in Congo. We must cross this grassy plain where the tall gras, whose blades are as coarse as a normal bamboo cane, reaches above our heads. See, up there on the hill lies the village!]

The missionaries addressed the readership directly and integrated them into their we-group. At the same time, they stressed their role as eyewitnesses: "Skada bara, att I ej kunnen se, hvad vi sågo, och höra, hvad vi hörde. Edra hjärtan skulle då stämmas till mera tacksamhet mot Herren" [What a shame that you cannot see what we have seen and hear what we have heard. Your hearts would be moved to more thankfulness for the Lord] (Holm 1902: 5). Just as missionary Albert Holm did in this letter extract, they acknowledged that it made a difference whether they themselves were in Congo or China or whether one had to trust the reports of the missionaries. At the same time, the missionaries made a plea to their readers to retrace their narratives and thus not only to trust them, but to also replicate their feelings within themselves. The joint perspective that missionaries and their readers adopted with respect to non-Christian people lent their testimonies credibility and urgency.

In this context, it is important to mention that it was almost exclusively the Swedish members of the missionary organisation who had the opportunity to make their voices heard in the publications. There was – to use Foucault's phrase – "a rarefaction [...] of the speaking subjects" (Foucault 1981: 61–62). Congolese or Chinese Christians, or potential converts, could rarely express themselves in the publications. This is noteworthy as their conversion to Christianity was the overarching goal of the missionary endeavour. Their statements in the publications – or rather, statements that were attributed to them – only became valid when missionaries shared and interpreted them. Quoting Congolese, Chinese or other persons, or *letting them speak* in the letters and articles did not serve the purpose of representing their voices. Instead, the authors of

---

[6] For more examples, see Flodén 1911; Sjöholm 1896. All translations from Swedish and German in this article are mine.

the texts demonstrated the alleged need for Christian missions through recipients or even through opponents of missions. The most striking example of this was a parallel that was drawn between a contemporary situation and a biblical scene in which Paul the Apostle dreams of a man in Macedonia calling him there to help (Acts 16:9). In her analysis of Norwegian Christian missions to Cameroon, Marianne Gullestad has shown that the biblical quote "Come over [into Macedonia], and help us" was of great importance for the Protestant missionary endeavour (Gullestad 2007: 75–97). Also, in SMF's publications, the missionaries let the people in the so-called mission fields speak this sentence:

> Från hednavärlden höres allt högljuddare ropet: Kom öfver och hjälp oss! [...] Särskilt från Kongo hafva genom våra bröder kommit hjärtskärande bönerop om snar hjälp, på det att de glesnade lederna snart måtte fyllas och folkets behof af evangelii predikan i någon mån tillfredsställas. Och äfven till de öfvriga missionsfälten önska de få förstärkning. Skola vi låta dessa bönerop fåfängt förklinga? (*Till missionens vänner* 1892)[7]
> [From the heathen world the cry is heard louder and louder: come over and help us! [...] Especially from the Congo, through our brethren, have come heart-rending appeals for urgent help, that the thinning ranks may soon be filled, and that the people's need for the preaching of the gospel may to some extent be satisfied. And they also wish for reinforcements in the other mission fields. Shall we let these pleas die away in vain?]

Using this strategy of *letting the Others speak*, the authors of missionary writing conveyed an impression of a multitude of voices. In a way, this belied the fact that only those voices of individuals who were seen as members of the community were authorised and could make their voices heard. Knowledge production in the missionary writings was thus closely tied to the construction of a community.

2 The construction of a community (of knowledge)

The next knowledge legitimisation strategy that I derived from my analysis is the construction of a community. The authors of letters and articles created an *imagined community* in the sense of Benedict Anderson's concept (Anderson 1991), especially by addressing the readers directly and indirectly. This appellation of the SMF members as "Älskade missionsvänner" [Beloved friends of the mission] (e.g. Engdahl 1892: 86; Walfridsson 1892: 25) and as a collective Christian *we* produced and reproduced one's sense of emotional belonging to this

---

[7] For a more detailed analysis of this quotation and the strategy of *letting the Others speak*, see Acke 2015b: 109–137.

religious community. It can be described as a community of knowledge in the sense that sharing the community's knowledge was a prerequisite for belonging to it. The missionary publications were the most important written medium in which the missionaries and other core SMF members negotiated cohesive goal(s) and shared perceptions, and thus constructed knowledge that was valid for the community.

The missionary publications constructed the evangelisation of all non-Christian people as a joint, identity-forming goal of their readership and thus as a concern for the whole community. Gathered around this goal, the community appeared almost limitless in time and space. Regarding time, the publications situated it not only as a part of the Protestant missionary movement, which originated in the 18th century, but also in direct continuity and thus in communion with the biblical apostles. This was achieved through biblical allusions, such as the *call from Macedonia* or the Great Commission mentioned above.[8] One way of imagining the contemporary community was through joint events coordinated in time, such as a shared prayer week that missionary Wilhelm Walldén described in one of his letters:

> Äfven här i Mukimbungu firade vi den [böneveckan], fastän vi icke hunnit få böneämnena; men vi hade nog böneämnen ändå. Vi erforo, att vi icke stå ensamma härute på denna aflägsna strand, utan äro förenade med alla Guds barn. Det kännes ljufligt och trosstärkande att erinra sig, att vi voro ihågkomna i bönen inför Gud af våra syskon der hemma. (Walldén 1890: 100)
> [Even here in Mukimbungu we celebrated it [the prayer week], though we had not received the prayer themes in time; but we had enough prayer themes nonetheless. We learned that we are not alone out here on this distant shore but are united with all the children of God. It is sweet and faith-strengthening to bear in mind that we are remembered in prayer before God by our brethren there at home.]

The reason why he and his fellow missionaries did not feel "alone out here", he states, was that they felt united with the *Missionary Covenant* in Sweden through a concerted prayer week. Thus, the community bridged the space between Sweden and Congo or Sweden and China. Also, with respect to space the global focus of the missionary movement, as discussed above regarding the "to

---

8 Some examples from my Swedish corpus, where the *call from Macedonia* or the Great Commission are referred to are Gån ut i hela verlden och gjören alla folk till lärjungar 1883; Hvarför skola vi bedrifva mission? 1888; Svenska Missionsförbundets 14:e årsmöte [1892] 1892; Gån ut i hela världen 1905.

the end of the world" biblical quote, contributed to a notion of limitlessness.[9] While the missionaries in Congo and China spread the Gospel, the so-called friends of the mission in Sweden donated and prayed for this goal, as the quote also shows. In addition, the community spanned space due to how the missionaries perceived of Sweden's respective relationships with Congo and China. Belonging to the we-group of all SMF missionaries in Congo was, for example, determined by belonging to a certain space, a space that from the perspective of this group was defined as where they were, i.e. "here" (in Mukimbungu, Congo, in the above quote), and yet at the same time remained peripheral: Missionary Wilhelm Walldén described his location as a "distant shore". The missionaries in both Congo and China would often use the phrase "vi/oss härute" [us out here] (e.g. Andreæ 1889: 4; Sköld 1893: 114; Svensson 1889: 39) when talking about themselves and their spatial belonging. The supporters of the mission, in contrast, were "[missions]vännerna därhemma" [the (missionary) friends there at home] (e.g. Andersson 1894; Lund 1893: 104; Walfridsson 1893: 104). The space between the missionaries and the "friends" thus had both a separating and a unifying effect. The distance was explicitly named, and the regions in which missionary work was performed were constructed as far away, peripheral and different. At the same time, Sweden was constructed as both the centre and their shared home. Although missionaries and supporters literally viewed the world from different spatial perspectives – i.e. from Africa or Asia, or from Europe – in their communication, the missionaries shared their readers' outside perspective of Africa and Asia being on the periphery.

The distinction and classification of regions was closely related to the distinction and classification of persons. Even here, a clear-cut division between the European Self and the non-European Other was made, as I will show in the following. The belonging and descent of the people in the mission's target regions were either determined by nation or, in relation to the Congo, through a classification based on *race* and the African spatial origin associated with it. For this, appellations like "Kongos folk" [the people of the Congo] (e.g. Lembke 1905: 101), "Kinas folk" [the people of China] (e.g. Tånnkvist 1901: 390), "Kinas egna söner och döttrar" [China's own sons and daughters] (e.g. Tonnér 1903: 376), "Kongos svarta söner och döttrar" [the black sons and daughters of the Congo] (e.g. Andersson 1889: 38) and "Afrikas svarta barn" [the black children of Africa] (e.g. Gauffin 1908: 50) were used.

---

9 An example from my Swedish corpus, where "the end of the world" is referred to, is *Svenska Missionsförbundets årskonferens [1884]* 1884.

The concepts of nation and *race* were not clearly distinguished from each other in the publications and the Swedish term *folk* (people) was also used for both, as can be seen from the examples mentioned. In relation to China, however, the missionaries used the term *nation*, while in relation to the Congo, *black* and *dark-skinned* were words they applied again and again to refer to the (supposed) skin colour of the people, which was generally regarded as a characteristic that they used to distinguish the different human "races". This ambiguity in the concepts of *nation* and *race* can be explained by the general flexibility of the concept of *race* in science and in the public, as described by Silke Hensel. On the one hand, it was never (and could never be) sufficiently defined, and on the other hand, it persisted on the borderline between scientific theories, everyday ideas and ideologies pertaining to social order. According to Hensel, the concepts of *race* and *peoples* were already intermingled in the work of Arthur de Gobineau, who transferred the category from natural history to the explanation of human historical development in its entirety (see Hensel 2004: 40–43).

While Swedish people were categorised mainly through their religious belonging when they were described as "God's children", the people in non-European regions, from the perspective of the missionaries, lacked a religion and were thus categorised through their belonging to a certain region in the same way that the Swedes were seen as belonging to God. A conversion changed their religious status, but the association with the peripheral region did not change and also remained obvious in the appellations used by the missionaries. The converts were hardly ever described just as "Christians", instead the missionaries wrote of "de svarta kristna" [the black Christians] (e.g. *Den evangeliska missionen i Uganda* 1894: 88), "de kinesiska kristna" [the Chinese Christians] (e.g. Tånnkvist 1901: 389) or "kristna kineser" [Christian Chinese (people)] (e.g. Engdahl 1892: 88), of "de infödda kristna" [the native Christians] (e.g. Speer 1911: 130) or of "de infödda troende" [the native believers] (e.g. Sjöholm 1895: 82). The converts' in-between status was most obvious in the appellation "hednakristna" [heathen Christians] (e.g. *Den evangeliska missionens jubelår* 1893: 162; Laman 1903: 50), which locked them in a marginal position even within the Christian community and questioned the genuineness of their conversion. The world view of SMF can thus be described with the help of concentric circles, where the centre, the innermost circle, their own community, was Christian, European, white, enlightened and "civilised". A circle further away from the centre consisted of Christian but non-European, non-white, partly knowledgeable and partly "civilised" converts, and the outer circle or margins were heathen, non-European, non-white, "uncivilised", unknowledgeable and dark. The community thus defined new Christians and those devaluated as "heathens" through alleged deficiencies as Others, and relegated them to the margins or excluded them altogether.

Thus, in the publications, the contradiction between a shared humanity, which lay at the core of Christian thinking, and a religious and racist separation, was one of the main patterns of thought that legitimised the missions:

> Hafva vi för egen del fått erfara, att det är evinnerligt lif att känna Gud och den han har sändt, Jesus Kristus, så må vi ock låta våra medmenniskor, som ännu vandra i syndens och okunnighetens mörker, få veta det samma. (*Hvarför skola vi bedrifva mission?* 1888: 85)
> [If we ourselves have come to know that it means eternal life to know God and him whom he has sent, Jesus Christ, let us also let our fellow human beings, who still walk in the darkness of sin and ignorance, know the same.]

The argument was because "we", the community of knowledge, had received knowledge of God and salvation, "we" were obliged to share this knowledge with the Others. The description of the Others as "walking in the darkness of sin and ignorance" aligned with contemporary conceptions of a lack of civilisation, which was time and again also described in the publications. The metaphorical darkness of "the heathen world" paralleled the (perceived) darkness of the bodies of the Others (see Acke 2015b: 297–299; Gullestad 2007: 4).

But even in missionary discourses, the shared humanity was sometimes called into question when racist thought patterns were reproduced explicitly. In his letter quoted above, missionary Walldén calls the converts "our black brothers". Nevertheless, it was not the community made up of converts at the mission station in Congo that fulfilled the function of reminding him that they were "united with all the children of God". Missionaries often wrote that they were alone even though it becomes clear from the context that they were just the only white people present among Congolese or other Africans (see Andreæ 1888: 110; Pettersson 1911: 135). The loneliness of white Europeans among Africans and Asians was a frequently used figure of thought. The latter were thus not only classified as racially different – since they did not count as human society, their humanity was also called into question. In the material, the racist classification differed for Congolese and Chinese (potential) converts. As mentioned above, an appellation based on skin colour usually referred to Congolese groups and individuals, while the Chinese were mostly classified based on their national belonging. The missionaries mentioned an alleged "yellow skin" only a few times and in these cases they were primarily describing Chinese children (e.g. Fredén 1905: 190). Nevertheless, a racist attitude towards Chinese people was present in the materials, such as when a group of missionaries argued that the standard period for a stay in China could not be prolonged from seven to ten years, as this would endanger the mental health of the missionaries:

En missionär kan till sin yttre människa vara frisk, men genom att dag efter dag år ut och år in vistas bland kineserna blir han till sin inre människa trött, ja, kanske sjuk. Den omgifvande hedendomen, folkets djupa andliga och lekamliga nöd utöfva dagligen sitt tryck på missionären, [...] den medfödda falska och af synden fördärfvade karaktären framträder t.o.m. hos dem, om hvilka man haft de bästa förhoppningar. [...] Det är icke utan risk för en missionärs inre hälsa, om han för en längre tid får vara ensam bland kineserna. (Sköld et al. 1905: 243)

[A missionary may be outwardly healthy, but by spending day after day, year after year among the Chinese, he becomes inwardly tired, perhaps even sick. The surrounding heathenism, the deep spiritual and bodily need of the people, exert their daily pressure on the missionary, [...] the innate false character, corrupted by sin, appears even in those for whom the best hopes were placed. [...] It is not without risk to a missionary's inner health if he is left alone among the Chinese for any length of time.]

Although the missionaries first mentioned the alleged "heathendom" of the Chinese as the reason, they then continued with a racist categorisation of the people that they used biology to justify: in their view, they had an "innate false character" that was only further corrupted by sin, i.e. by heathendom. Here, they reproduced the racist notion that innate biological differences existed between peoples. In the end, they invoked the above-mentioned figure of thought of the loneliness of whites among other peoples.

My analysis thus confirms Piotr Cap's theory that proximisation is a prerequisite of legitimisation. In order to be able to argue for a cause and to give instructions to people for taking action, this cause must be spatially, temporally and axiologically (i.e. in a value-based way) made a concern for one's group (see Cap 2010: 5–6). In the missionary publications, this was tied to the process in which the group or community was created by distinguishing between the Self and the Other. Furthermore, the Other was excluded from the production of valid knowledge in the processes of *letting them speak* described above. Because of their status as eyewitnesses, the missionaries claimed exclusive access to detailed knowledge on the living conditions, religion and ways of thinking for the people living in Congo and China. The perspectives of the people in and from these regions not only receded into the background – it was completely omitted. *Letting them speak* without actually giving them a voice thus served to provide the community with a monopoly on knowledge. The missionaries objectified the people in Congo, China and all other parts of the world that did not have a history of Christianity by excluding them from the (knowledge) community. They used them as sources of knowledge but did not see them as capable of systematising and communicating that knowledge themselves.

Through this clear separation of the Christian, white, European, "civilised", knowledgeable Self from the Other defined exclusively through negative differentiation, the missionary writings produced and reproduced a binary division of the world while creating their knowledge community. This dichotomy was by no means neutral, but implied valuations and hierarchies. Through metaphors of light and darkness, as well as war and cultivation of the soil, the authors assigned themselves positive traits, universalised their own values, and empowered the Self while devaluating the Others and degrading them to objects of their own actions. They conceptualised the relationship between themselves and the people they aimed to evangelise as parallel to their own relationship with God. While God ruled over them as a fatherly sovereign and guided them, they saw themselves as destined to teach and guide non-Christian people and converts because of their own Christian spirit, knowledge and alleged progressiveness. To construct Christianity as the solution and missions as a necessity, the absences of Christianity had to be viewed as a problem.

3 The reduction of complexity

The third strategy was the reduction of complexity. The missionary publications reduced complex circumstances to a simple equation by propagating Christianity throughout the world and thus the conversion of every individual to this religion as the only solution to the alleged savagery and "poverty and need" of "the heathen world": Christianity was good and enabled all individuals to lead a satisfied, dignified, just and "civilised" life. "Heathendom" was bad and offered undignified conditions for individuals.

Of course, this binary division of the world existed alongside more complex divisions and images – but these were marginal. For example, the missionary writings differentiated between the mission target areas of Congo and China, as I have already explained above regarding nationality and *race*, while at the same time equalising them. Congolese and Chinese people were the same from the perspective of the missionary organisations because they were all heathens and thus lacked knowledge of salvation. In the publications, not knowing about Jesus was often equated with being unknowledgeable in general. Describing the people of the mission regions with collective appellations like "heathens", "blacks", "Africans" or "Chinese" and categorising them only through deficiencies led to depriving them of their individuality. Rather, they were generally described as a homogeneous collective characterised by cultural and temporal traditions that had allegedly always been in place.

The reduction of complexity, the simple division between Christianity and heathendom, between "white" and "black", between knowledgeable and unknowledgeable, and between light and darkness, bestowed legitimacy upon the missionary endeavour. One account, which reproduced this simple justification for the necessity of the missions, was a series of conversion narratives.[10] They all followed a distinct pattern, which presented the conversion to Christianity as a positive turning point in the lives of individuals. From an arduous existence marked by inner dissatisfaction, the lives of Swedish, Chinese or Congolese young people or adults changed for the better – solely because they had found God. Through the conversion of individuals, whole societies would in turn be changed for the better. In these simple stories, Christianity appeared to be the only and effective path to a good life, a just society and the salvation of individuals after death.

Although this general pattern is the same in the narratives of (or rather about) Swedish missionaries and converts to Christianity in the mission regions, the descriptions of conversions vary significantly. The conversion narratives of the missionaries, which SMF published in greater number in the 1880s, and which later lost their significance in the periodical, were extensive and always described individual lives. They followed the pattern of typical pietistic conversion narratives that were analysed, for example, by D. Bruce Hindmarsh (2001), though they were usually written in the third person and not in the first. A conversion from what the awakened members of the missionary movement perceived as nominal Christianity to true Christianity was part of the pietistic tradition. In contrast, the conversion of Congolese, Chinese and other converts to Christianity from other traditions was hardly the topic of a whole narrative text. Instead, it was mentioned in reports from the mission field, letters or other texts. Apart from the so-called "first fruits", the conversion narratives of alleged "heathens" hardly ever described individual conversions, but those of whole families or groups of people. When narrating individual conversions, the missionaries generalised their significance, such as when they omitted the name of the convert:

> En till Kristus omvänd hedning i Kongo, Central-Afrika, yttrade vid aftonmötet här vid stationen: 'Under den tid jag vandrade främmande för den sanne Guden kommo några i vår by att lemna afgudarne och tro på Kristus. Jag hatade och begabbade dem derför. Men de talade i stället vänligt till mig och voro glade. Detta väckte oro i mitt hjerta, och jag började längta efter frid. Hade de, såsom mänge nu göra, undandragit sig försmädelsen, så hade vi ännu vandrat i mörker, ty genom dem har evangelium kommit in i oss. Låtom oss följa Jesus under lidanden och förföljelser'. (Hammarstedt 1887: 72)
> [A heathen converted to Christ in the Congo, Central Africa, said at the evening meeting here at the station: 'During the time when I wandered as a stranger to the true God, some

---

10 See Acke 2015b: 136–169 for an analysis of the conversion narratives in the materials.

in our village came to leave the idols and believe in Christ. I hated and taunted them for it. But they spoke kindly to me instead and were glad. This stirred up trouble in my heart, and I began to long for peace. If they had not endured the scorn, as many do now, we would still be walking in darkness, for through them the gospel has come into us. Let us follow Jesus in suffering and persecution'.]

This quote is another example of *letting the Other speak*. Especially because the convert is not mentioned by name, it is and was impossible to know how reliably missionary Lars Fredrik Hammarstedt recounted his words. While he introduced the convert – whom he then let speak – in a most general way by calling him "a heathen converted to Christ in the Congo" and then broadened the geographical focus even further by adding "Central Africa", he then specified the place where he had heard the man speak as exactly his own mission station (Mukimbungu). On the one hand, the man's statement was easily generalisable because it could not be traced back to a specific person, but on the other hand, Hammarstedt expressed that he had heard it himself as an eyewitness. Altogether, the differences between conversion narratives strengthened the impression of European individuality while Asians, Africans and other non-European people were imagined as collectives.

Furthermore, the previously discussed imagery added to the reduced complexity. Metaphors of war, darkness and light as well as soil cultivation were abundant in the publications.[11] All of these metaphors originated in the Bible, but the authors of the publications applied them to the contemporary context of missionary work in Africa and Asia and merged them – especially regarding the dualism of darkness and light – with enlightenment and colonial discourses to legitimate the missionary cause. The simplifying dualism between light and darkness as well as Christianity and "heathenism", which was clearly associated with a division into good and evil or right and wrong, was apparently a core idea of the missionary worldview during that the time (see Acke 2013: 236–242). The visual representation of this dualism in the metaphors of darkness and light reduced the complexity of the relationship between Christianity and "heathenism", and thus also between Christians and "heathens", to a minimum. It ensured that the boundary between the two appeared unambiguous, while at the same time ascribing a positive value to one group and devaluing the other.

Rolf Reichardt has pointed to the function of images in reducing concepts to a simple meaning, thus increasing their social impact through sensualisation, emotionalisation and popularisation (see Reichardt 1998: 139). Although Reichardt refers to actual visual representations, I would argue that this applies

---

[11] See Acke 2015b: 281–340 for an in-depth analysis of the metaphors used in the materials.

equally to metaphorical representations. While the illustrations in the missionary publications are certainly a visual representation of the symbolism of darkness and light, it was their metaphorical use that was predominant. Following the findings of research on metaphors (see Lakoff/Johnson 2003; Gibbs 2006; Ritchie 2011), I assume that this symbolism appealed to the readers' senses and evoked emotional reactions in them. "Heathenism" and everything associated with it had to appear repulsive and evil, while at the same time underlining the position of Christianity as the only remedy against evil.

The notion that the continent's inhabitants descended from Noah's cursed son Ham connected the classification of the skin colour of Africans as black with European light-darkness symbolism. This notion was formulated from the 17th century onwards and was referred to in missionary publications (see Svensson 1888: 102; Walldén 1893: 182; Werner 1898: 242). Although the Bible describes the cursing of Ham, it at no point makes any reference to his skin colour or that of his sons (see Martin 2001: 287; Nederveen Pieterse 1992: 44). As descendants of Ham, however, this figure of thought marked all Africans as cursed and thus sinful through their skin colour and associated them with darkness, which in the publications was equated with the devil, sin and heathenism.

The metaphors were also intertwined, and as a result formed a coherent metaphorical system as described by Lakoff and Johnson (2003: 7–13, 41–45). With references to the Bible, the publications presented the mission as a war that the missionary organisation fought in the name of God against the devil and the powers of evil that personified – in their view – the darkness of "heathendom".

> Äfven detta år måste för Guds folk blifva ett stridens år, ty så länge mörker öfvertäcker jorden och mörkhet folken, så få vi icke hvila på våra vapen, utan vi måste draga i härnad mot mörkrets härar. Ve oss, om vi det icke göra! (*Herrens högra hand gifver seger [1892]* 1892)
> [This year must also be a year of war for God's people, for as long as the dark covers the earth and darkness the nations, we cannot rest our arms, but must go forth in armour against the armies of darkness. Woe to us if we do not!]

This call from a theologically edifying editorial in the journal *Missionsförbundet* from the year 1892 made it clear that all members of SMF, all Christians, were expected to take part in this metaphorical war. As the publications stressed, victory in this war was assured and entailed the Second Coming of Jesus. Setbacks and sacrifices were to be expected in a war. This meant that this metaphor could even justify the deaths of missionaries. At the same time, resistance and rejection on the part of those to be converted could be interpreted as a necessary part of missionary work instead of a fundamental challenge to the endeavour. The metaphor of war legitimised an intervention into the lives of individuals – if necessary, even against their will. The figures of speech simplified complex circumstances and reduced them to a simple formula: Christianity is the solution to all the (alleged) problems of "the heathen world".

Through the metaphors, the conversion narratives and the above-mentioned appellations, the missionary publications reduced the complexity of the topics they discussed, especially when it came to the relationship between Christianity and other religions, and between the group delimited as the Self and the people constructed as Others. This relationship was simplified as one of binary opposition in which intermediate positions hardly seemed possible.

4 Discursive continuities

In the analysed materials, Christian missions were legitimised through contradictory discourses in which religion, nationality and *race* were intertwined. The explicit goal of Christian missions was religious inclusion, inviting all humans into the Christian fold in order to bring about the return of Christ. This was based on the assumption of a common humanity. But as the missionaries categorised religion, nationality and *race* as interdependent categories in their writings, they assigned their converts to a marginal position within the religious group, just as colonial efforts assigned all non-Europeans a marginal and inferior position within the world, thus legitimising colonial exploitation and undermining the idea of a common humanity.

One important finding of my analysis is that the missionary discourses were closely intertwined with other contemporary discourses. This contributed to the legitimisation of the missions, as the missionaries thus tried to present Christian missions as a natural consequence of ostensibly uncontroversial statements, such as the idea of different stages of development that different groups of people had reached. In doing so, they located missionary knowledge in more general bodies of knowledge of the time and thereby strengthened their own authoritative position and credibility. They confirmed assumptions instead of offering alternative interpretations that would have contradicted their readers' previous knowledge.

The missionaries repeatedly drew on two bodies of knowledge: biblical knowledge and colonial discourses. The references to the Bible had an almost unquestionable importance for Protestant Christians of the time who were influenced by Pietism, i.e. for the primary target group of the publications. One characteristic of pietistic thinking was that the Bible was highly significant for the life of every Christian individual.

The missionaries also included colonial and racist bodies of knowledge in their argumentation and reporting, especially by not accepting their (potential) converts as coequals. Religious Christian ideas were entangled with colonialist, racist notions of superiority. Thus, missions became colonialist and colonialism became Christian. In the discursive legitimisation of the analysed publications, evangelising work was constructed as a "Herrschaftsbeziehung zwischen Kollektiven" [relationship of domination between collectives] (Osterhammel 2003: 21). This is the wording Jürgen Osterhammel uses in his definition of colonialism. In the publications, Christians saw themselves as superior to "heathens". The authors attributed this to their alleged advantage in knowledge and insight, which they derived from their knowledge of salvation through Jesus Christ. Furthermore, they propagated a universalisation of their own ideals and, consequently, devaluated the Others with respect to the categorisations of *race* and "civilisation". From their alleged superiority, Christians derived the obligation to guide, lead and to preside over the Others.[12] The missionaries were not willing to adapt culturally and justified their claim to leadership with the help of mission-related ideological ideas of superiority, just as Osterhammel has clarified with regard to colonisers (Osterhammel 2003: 19–21). In contrast to colonial activities, however, Christian missions did not have any connection with economic interests, nor was physical violence a systematically used or legitimate means of exercising authority (see also Klein 2010: 157; Osterhammel 2003: 19–21).

For Sweden, the missionary endeavour is nevertheless to be regarded as a form of colonialism, as it enabled the country to be inscribed and anchored in European discourses of superiority. Only a few Swedes were directly involved in Sweden's official colonial projects. The missions, however, were sustained by many Swedes: they donated to the missions, read about them in different publications, heard about them during events, services and in Sunday schools, and they, their family members or acquaintances travelled to other parts of the world as missionaries.

Ulla Vuorela's concept of *colonial complicity* (see Vuorela 2009) provides an excellent description of Sweden's participation in hegemonic European discourses. Sweden contributed to the production and reproduction of European ideas of superiority and the resulting discrimination of all non-European people without implementing colonial activities itself. The country did not take centre stage in the colonial endeavour, but it did participate in it by adopting and

---

[12] That this was in practice (if at all) only possible with (potential) converts can be regarded as secondary with respect to discursive legitimisation.

shaping hegemonic bodies of knowledge. My work has shown that Christian missions played a fundamental role in Sweden's colonial complicity. Furthermore, Christian missions are still relevant today. Just as the missionary discourses reveal continuities with discourses that precede and run parallel to them in time, the structures and patterns of thought for missionary (colonial and biblical) discourses are still contained in statements today, e.g. when discussing development aid and migration.

Discursively, Swedish Protestant missions around 1900 can be interpreted as an answer to Sweden's own marginal position in Europe and in the European colonial endeavour. Participating in and further developing discourses that marginalised Africans and Asians enabled the Swedes to collectively claim a place in the contemporary centre of the world.

References

a. Research literature

Acke, Hanna (2013): "Missionary Periodicals as a Genre. Models of Writing, Horizons of Expectation". In: Felicity Jensz/Hanna Acke (eds.). *Missions and Media. The Politics of Nineteenth-Century Missionary Periodicals*. Stuttgart: Franz Steiner, 225–243.

Acke, Hanna (2015a): "Konversion als Individualisierung? Konstruktionen von Individualität in schwedischen Missionspublikationen". In: Martin Fuchs/Antje Linkenbach/Wolfgang Reinhard (eds.). *Individualisierung durch christliche Mission?* Wiesbaden: Harrassowitz, 173–186.

Acke, Hanna (2015b): *Sprachliche Legitimierung protestantischer Mission. Die Publikationen von Svenska Missionsförbundet um 1900*. Berlin/Boston: Walter de Gruyter.

Anderson, Benedict (1991): *Imagined Communities. Reflections on the Origin and Spread of Nationalism*. 2nd edn. London, New York: Verso.

Berger, Peter L./Luckmann, Thomas (1991): *The Social Construction of Reality*. London et al.: Penguin.

Cap, Piotr (2010): *Legitimisation in Political Discourse. A Cross-Disciplinary Perspective on the Modern US War Rhetoric*. 2nd edn. Newcastle upon Tyne: Cambridge Scholars.

Foucault, Michel (1981): "The Order of Discourse". In: Robert Young (ed.). *Untying the Text. A Post-Structuralist Reader*. Boston/London/Henley: Routledge & Kegan Paul, 55–78.

Foucault, Michel (2008): Der Wille zum Wissen. Sexualität und Wahrheit 1". In: Michel Foucault: Die Hauptwerke. Frankfurt am Main: Suhrkamp, 1023–1151.

Gibbs, Raymond W., Jr. (2006): "Metaphor Interpretation as Embodied Simulation". In: *Mind and Language* 21 (3), 434–458.

Gründer, Horst (1982): *Christliche Mission und deutscher Imperialismus. Eine politische Geschichte ihrer Beziehungen während der deutschen Kolonialzeit 1884–1914 unter besonderer Berücksichtigung Afrikas und Chinas*. Paderborn: Schöningh.

Gullestad, Marianne (2007): *Picturing Pity. Pitfalls and Pleasures in Cross-Cultural Communication: Image and Word in a North Cameroon Mission.* New York: Berghahn Books.
Hammer, Karl (1978): *Weltmission und Kolonialismus. Sendungsideen des 19. Jahrhunderts im Konflikt.* München: Kösel.
Hensel, Silke (2004): *Leben auf der Grenze. Diskursive Aus- und Abgrenzungen von Mexican Americans und Puertoricanern in den USA.* Frankfurt am Main: Vervuert.
Hindmarsh, D. Bruce (2001): "Patterns of Conversion in Early Evangelical History and Overseas Mission Experience". In: Brian Stanley (ed.). *Christian Missions and the Enlightenment.* Grand Rapids, MI: Eerdmans, 71–98.
Hutchby, Ian (2001): "'Witnessing'. The Use of First-Hand Knowledge in Legitimating Lay Opinions on Talk Radio". In: *Discourse Studies* 3 (4), 481–497.
Klein, Thoralf (2010): "Mission und Kolonialismus – Mission als Kolonialismus. Anmerkungen zu einer Wahlverwandtschaft". In: Claudia Kraft/Alf Lüdtke/Jürgen Martschukat (eds.). *Kolonialgeschichten. Regionale Perspektiven auf ein globales Phänomen.* Frankfurt am Main: Campus, 142–161.
Krämer, Sybille (2009): "Über Zeugnisgeben und Zeugenschaft. Wie der Glaube und das Erkennen zusammenhängen". In: *fundiert: Das Wissenschaftsmagazin der Freien Universität Berlin* (2), 84–90. https://www.fu-berlin.de/presse/publikationen/fundiert/archiv/2009_02/media/fundiert_2-2009_glauben.pdf (accessed 25 April 2023).
Kussak, Åke (1982): *Författaren som predikant. Ett frikyrkosamfunds litterära verksamhet 1910–1939.* Stockholm: Gummessons.
Lakoff, George/Johnson, Mark (2003): *Metaphors We Live By.* Chicago/London: University of Chicago Press.
Martin, Peter (2001): *Schwarze Teufel, edle Mohren. Afrikaner in Geschichte und Bewußtsein der Deutschen.* Hamburg: Hamburger Edition HIS.
Nederveen Pieterse, Jan (1992): *White on Black. Images of Africa and Blacks in Western Popular Culture.* New Haven/London: Yale University Press.
Osterhammel, Jürgen (2003): *Kolonialismus. Geschichte – Formen – Folgen.* 4th edn. München: C. H. Beck.
Peters, John Durham (2001): "Witnessing". In: *Media, Culture & Society* 23 (6), 707–723.
Porter, Andrew (2004): *Religion versus Empire? British Protestant Missionaries and Overseas Expansion, 1700–1914.* Manchester: Manchester University Press.
Reichardt, Rolf (1998): "Light against Darkness. The Visual Representations of a Central Enlightenment Concept". In: *Representations* (61), 95–148.
Ritchie, L. David (2011): "Justice is Blind. A Model for Analyzing Metaphor Transformations and Narratives in Actual Discourse". In: *Metaphor and the Social World* 1 (1), 70–89.
Robert, Valérie (2002): "Briefformen in der Presse. Versuch einer situativen und metakommunikativen Klassifizierung". In: Kirsten Adamzik (ed.). *Texte, Diskurse, Interaktionsrollen. Analysen zur Kommunikation im öffentlichen Raum.* Tübingen: Stauffenburg, 61–115.
Stanley, Brian (1990): *The Bible and the Flag. Protestant Missions and British Imperialism in the Nineteenth and Twentieth Centuries.* Leicester: Apollos.
Voss, Julia (2008): "Darwin oder Moses? Funktion und Bedeutung von Charles Darwins Porträt im 19. Jahrhundert". In: *NTM: Zeitschrift für Geschichte der Wissenschaften, Technik und Medizin* 16 (2), 213–243.
Vuorela, Ulla (2009): "Colonial Complicity. The 'Postcolonial' in a Nordic Context". In: Suvi Keskinen/Salla Tuori/Sari Inri et al. (eds.). *Complying with Colonialism. Gender, Race and Ethnicity in the Nordic Region.* Farnham: Ashgate, 19–33.

Zelizer, Barbie (2007): "On 'Having Been There'. 'Eyewitnessing' as a Journalistic Key Word".
In: *Critical Studies in Media Communication* 24 (5), 408-428.

b. Empirical sources

Andersson, Anna (1889): "Mukimbungu den 2 jan. 1889". In: *Missionsförbundet* 7 (4), 37-38.
Andersson, Karl Teod[or] (1894): "Mukimbungu, Kongo, den 28 dec. 1893". In: *Missionsförbundet* 12 (6), 83.
Andreæ, Karl Fredr[ik] (1888): "Mukimbungu den 6 aug. 1888". In: *Missionsförbundet* 6 (10), 110-111.
Andreæ, Karl Fredr[ik] (1889): "Mukimbungu den 26 oktober 1888". In: *Missionsförbundet* 7 (1), 4-5.
"Den evangeliska missionen i Uganda" (1894). In: *Missionsförbundet* 12 (6), 84-89.
"Den evangeliska missionens jubelår" (1893). In: *Missionsförbundet* 11 (11), 161-162.
Engdahl, Karl [Wilhelm] (1892): "Wu-chang den 10 jan. 1892". In: *Missionsförbundet* 10 (8), 86-88.
Flodén, S[ven] A[ugust] (1911): "I väckelsetider". In: Wilhelm Sjöholm/Jakob E. Lundahl (eds.). *Dagbräckning i Kongo*. Stockholm: Svenska Missionsförbundet, 273-276.
Fredén, Anna (1905): "Wuchang den 21 febr. 1905". In: *Missionsförbundet* 23 (12), 189-190.
Gauffin, J[ohan] B. (1908): "Missionssinne". In: *Missionsförbundet* 26 (4), 49-50.
"Gån ut i hela världen. Under året första gången utgångna missionärer" (1905). In: *Missionsförbundet* 23 (24), 370-371.
"Gån ut i hela verlden och gjören alla folk till lärjungar" (1883). In: *Svenska Missionsförbundet* 1 (1), 2-5.
Hammarstedt, Lars Fredrik (1887): "Lars Fredrik Hammarstedts dagbok". In: *Missionsförbundet* 5 (6), 67-72.
"Herrens högra hand gifver seger [1892]" (1892). In: *Missionsförbundet* 10 (1), 1.
Holm, Albert (1902): "Mukimbungu den 22 okt. 1901". In: *Missionsförbundet* 20 (1), 4-5.
"Hvarför skola vi bedrifva mission?" (1888). In: *Missionsförbundet* 6 (8), 85-86.
Karlsson, Sofi (1897): *Kongokvinnan såsom barn, hustru och änka. Skildring från verkligheten*. Stockholm: Svenska Tryckeriaktiebolaget.
Laman, K[arl] E[dvard] (1903): "Mukimbungu den 13 dec. 1902". In: *Missionsförbundet* (4), 50-51.
Lembke, C[arl] W[ilhelm] (1905): "Mukimbungu den 24 jan. 1905". In: *Missionsförbundet* 23 (7).
Lund, F[rans] Edw[ard] (1893): "De mördade kinamissionärerna. Swedish Missionary Society, Wuchang den 3 juli 1893". In: *Missionsförbundet* 11 (17), 257-259.
Pettersson, K[arl] J[ohan] (1911): "Svenska Missionsförbundets mission i Kongo före 1886". In: Wilhelm Sjöholm/Jakob E. Lundahl (eds.). *Dagbräckning i Kongo*. Stockholm: Svenska Missionsförbundet, 108-135.
Sjöholm, Wilh[elm] (1895): "Mukimbungu den 4/4 1895". In: *Missionsförbundet* 13 (11), 82-83.
Sjöholm, Wilhelm (1896): "Mukimbungu den 8 mars 1896". In: *Missionsförbundet* 14 (10), 148-151.
Sköld, Eva et al. (1905): "Till Svenska Missionsförbundets Styrelse, Stockholm". In: *Missionsförbundet* 23 (16), 242-244.
Sköld, Joh[an] (1893): "Wu-chang den 12 nov. 1892". In: *Missionsförbundet* 11 (8), 114-115.
Speer, Robert E. (1911): "Missionen och rasandan". In: *Missionsförbundet* 29 (9), 129-131.
"Svenska Missionsförbundets 14:e årsmöte [1892]" (1892). In: *Missionsförbundet* 10 (12), 133-139.

"Svenska Missionsförbundets årskonferens [1884]" (1884). In: *Svenska Missionsförbundet* 2 (6), 81–93.
Svensson, Mina (1888): "Palabala den 11 juli 1888". In: *Missionsförbundet* 6 (9), 101–102.
Svensson, Mina (1889): "Mukimbungu d. 2 februari 1889". In: *Missionsförbundet* 7 (4), 38–39.
"Till missionens vänner" (1892). In: *Missionsförbundet* 10 (23), back cover.
Tonnér, G[ustaf] (1903): "Wuchang den 2 okt. 1903". In: *Missionsförbundet* 21 (24), 374–376.
Tånnkvist, S[ven] (1901): "Wuchang den 30 okt 1900". In: *Missionsförbundet* (1), 387–390.
van Leeuwen, Theo (2008): *Discourse and Practice. New Tools for Critical Discourse Analysis*. Oxford, New York: Oxford University Press.
Walfridsson, K[arl] S[imon] (1892): "Mukimbungu den 25 nov. 1892 [sic]". In: *Missionsförbundet* 10 (3), 25–27.
Walfridsson, Ruth (1893): "Mukimbungu den 1 Dec. 1892". In: *Missionsförbundet* 11 (7), 104–105.
Walldén, W[ilhelm] (1893): "Redogörelse för verksamheten vid Mukimbungu under 1892". In: *Missionsförbundet* 11 (12), 182–184.
Walldén, Wilh[elm] (1890): "Mukimbungu den 25 jan. 1890". In: *Missionsförbundet* 8 (9), 100–101.
Werner, N. (1898): "En julhögtid i Kongo". In: N. Werner (ed.). *På hedningarnes väg. Bilder från Svenska missionsförbundets missionsfält*. Köping: J. A. Lindblads Förlag.

Part II: Intersections of National and Religious Belonging

Esther Jahns
Positioning in the Community
The Interplay of Language, Nationality and Religion for Jewish Speakers in Berlin

This article discusses how nationality and religion structure Berlin's Jewish community in the perception of its members and explains to what extent language reflects these perceived boundaries. The findings in this article are the outcome of interviews with Jewish speakers in Berlin that I conducted as part of my research project on the "distinctively Jewish linguistic repertoire" (Benor 2008: 1068) of German-speaking Jews in contemporary Berlin. The research project as a whole encompasses a description of the linguistic repertoire that Jewish speakers in Berlin have access to and make use of and an analysis of the categories that affect speakers' choices with regard to the use of lexical elements from this repertoire.

For this paper I analysed speakers' statements concerning the subdivisions of Berlin's Jewish community and their perception of linguistic reflections of this subdivision.[1]

1 Language in Jewish communities

Since the 6th century BCE, Jewish communities have been more or less permanently living in a multilingual environment. After a short period of monolingualism with Hebrew as the spoken language, forced exile and conquest led to a trilingual situation with Aramaic and Greek. Thus, around the beginning of the CE, Palestine was triglossic (see Spolsky 1983). Since then this pattern has been typical for Jewish communities and has emerged in their various exiles with clear functions for each of the respective languages: Hebrew-Aramaic remained the sacred language for religion; the territorial languages were used for communication with non-Jews; and, quite often on the basis of the territorial language, a third language developed that served as a vernacular for in-group speech (see Spolsky/Benor 2006). In linguistics, the latter are often labelled "Jewish languages",

---

[1] I would like to thank the reviewers as well as Britta Schneider and Philipp Krämer for their advice and very helpful comments on this article and the organisers of the very inspiring conference BTWS#2 in Åbo/Turku.

and since the first half of the 20th century have been researched both individually and from a comparative perspective under different denominations (see Benor 2008; Gold 1981; Wexler 1981). In the territory of today's Germany, this "Jewish language" was Yiddish, which in addition to Ladino is the most prominent "Jewish language". There are, however, also other examples from different territories where Jewish communities settled, e.g., Judeo-Arabic, Judeo-Provençal or Judeo-Tat in the Eastern Caucasus (see Hary/ Benor 2017).

Although contemporary Jewish languages are generally less distinct from their co-territorial languages than their historical ones, Benor (2011) and Klagsbrun Lebenswerd (2016) show in their respective studies about American and Swedish Jews that these communities do make use of a "distinctively Jewish linguistic repertoire", as Benor describes it (2008: 1068). This means that speakers, when speaking the territorial majority language, have access to an additional repertoire. This repertoire consists mainly of lexical loans from Hebrew and "Jewish languages" that have not only been spoken in the respective territory (e.g. Yiddish), but also might contain some distinctive grammatical features.

Research from my project on Jewish speakers in contemporary Berlin provides evidence that this is also true for the city's German-speaking Jews (see Jahns 2021). These speakers also make use of a distinctively Jewish linguistic repertoire that consists of loans from Hebrew, Yiddish, and, to a lesser extent, Aramaic, that are integrated into German, as well as a small number of German lexemes that are not used by non-Jewish German speakers. My main focus is lexical loans, and to a smaller extent, pronunciation variants as the most salient difference between the dialects of Eastern Yiddish, as well as between Eastern and Western Yiddish (with an emphasis on stressed vowels in the latter case) (see Aptroot/Gruschka 2010; Jacobs 2005). The reason for focusing on lexical items is that findings from research on other Jewish communities have shown that the speech patterns within contemporary Jewish communities differ from the majority language of the respective country, mainly concerning the lexicon (see above). As this is to my knowledge the first study on language use within a contemporary Jewish community in Germany, the lexicon seems to be an appropriate starting point.

2 Variation in the linguistic repertoire and its function

In addition to one main function of contemporary Jewish linguistic repertoires, i.e. expressing alignment towards the Jewish community, an integral part of it is the degree of variations that they allow, as their users also have the option of displaying the subtle characteristics of their Jewish identity. As Benor states, "Jews make selective use of this repertoire as they index their identities as Jews and as certain types of Jews" (Benor 2011: 141).

There are two layers of variation. One is the use of the repertoire itself, as in every utterance the speaker has the option of using an item from, in the case of the current study, the German of the majority instead of an item from the repertoire. This layer also encompasses the quantity of items used. The second layer of variation is choosing between the different variants that the repertoire offers. This means choosing from variants based on the different donor languages, Hebrew and Yiddish, between variants from Western and Eastern Yiddish, and also different dialectal variants of Eastern Yiddish. In my study, I am focusing on this second layer of variation, the choice between variants within the repertoire, as I am interested in processes of positioning and presenting oneself through stylistic choices (see Rickford/Eckert 2001). By choosing a variant and rejecting another with the same referential meaning, speakers can express a social meaning that this variant carries (see Eckert 2012; Johnstone/Andrus/Danielson 2006).

This is in line with 3rd wave sociolinguistics, which marks a dramatic change in the perspective on variation in relation to previous work, i.e. a change "[...] from a view of language as reflecting the social to a view of language as also creating the social". (Rickford/Eckert 2001:6). This means that speakers are seen as agents presenting themselves through their linguistic choices. As a consequence, linguistic variants are a means of constructing and positioning identity, as they are capable of assuming social meaning. Variants that are perceived as typical for speakers of a certain group can develop into an index for membership within this group or for characteristics that are attributed to its members. Speakers who wish to align with this group or to be linked with the respective characteristics of its members might therefore choose to integrate these variants into their personal style (see Eckert 2012: 94). Therefore, it is of interest to see how speakers perceive and interpret the language use of others, how this perception influences their linguistic choices, and to what extent the linguistic variation reflects the perceived boundaries within the community.

3 The Jewish community in Berlin

The Jewish community in Berlin is the largest in Germany. In this context, the term community does not entail a homogeneous group nor a close-knit network where every member knows each other. The term is instead used here as a blanket term for all persons of Jewish faith or ancestry. It is crucial to note that Jewishness is not only a religion but also an ancestry, and that it is necessary to keep this interweaving of religion and ancestry in mind throughout the current study, as it contrasts with other communities of faith, e.g. Christianity.

Berlin also has the biggest *Jüdische Gemeinde*, a so called *Einheitsgemeinde* ("unity-community")[2] which is the institution that acts as an umbrella organisation for most Jewish congregations in Berlin. On 31 December 2020, the unity-community had 8,702 members (see ZWST 2021). There is no official number of Jews who are not a member of the *Jüdische Gemeinde*, but their number is estimated to be much larger than that of members (see Strack 2018). The *Jüdische Gemeinde* does not have a strictly religious character, which means that Jews who regard themselves as secular are also members and take part in its cultural and social activities, as well as the services that are offered. There are also religion-specific congregations among the numerous Jewish initiatives outside the *Jüdische Gemeinde*. As a result, the *Jüdische Gemeinde* cannot be defined as a purely religious institution, yet at the same time, not all non-members or outside initiatives are of a secular character. Congregations and initiatives under the umbrella of and outside of the *Jüdische Gemeinde* offer a broad variety of religious and cultural activities, and Berlin's Jewry is highly diverse with respect to both linguistic and cultural backgrounds (see part 5) and religious denominations.

4 Method

For this paper, I analysed eleven semi-structured qualitative interviews that I conducted across 12 Jewish speakers in Berlin in 2017. The interviews were generally conducted with only one speaker, as I was aiming for an unbiased reaction from the individual speaker. However, in one case, the interviewee asked if a colleague could participate in the interview, which led to an interesting debate at some points in the interview. As an explorative pre-study I conducted expert interviews (see Meuser/Nagel 1991 on this methodology) with Jewish leaders in Berlin (e.g. rabbis, leaders of Jewish organisations, teachers at Jewish schools). In addition to the fact that these interviews revealed the existence of a "distinctive Jewish linguistic repertoire" among Jewish speakers in Berlin, the experts contributed

---

[2] The concept of the unity-community is typical for Jewish communities in Germany. It can be described as a single congregation embracing all the denominations. Its members might have a preferred synagogue they attend, but it is not uncommon to attend religious services at different locations, or to be a member of the unity-community without defining oneself as religious.

lexical elements that are part of this repertoire. This led to a collection of elements that I used as stimuli for the main interviews. These included religious items such as *Kippa* ("skullcap"), *Gabbai* ("officer of the synagogue"); *Git Schabbes*[3] (Shabbat greeting) as well as everyday items from Yiddish and Hebrew, such as *Balagan* ("mess"), *jiddische Mame* ("Jewish mother"), and *Tuches* ("buttocks"), as well as some German items that are either unfamiliar to non-Jewish German speakers or used differently, such as *Beter* ("member of congregation") or *Jahrzeit* ("anniversary of death"). Thus, the items represent a part of the distinctive repertoire of Jewish speakers in Berlin, which may overlap to some extent with the linguistic repertoires of other Jewish communities.[4]

I recruited speakers for the main interviews based on the recommendations of the experts or other interview partners. To allow for different perspectives on the community and a variety of interlocutors, I aimed for speakers from different backgrounds. In determining the different backgrounds, I considered categories that played a role in previous studies on language use in other contemporary Jewish communities (e.g. Benor 2011). Among my 12 informants, nine were women and three were men. Five of the 12 informants considered German to be their mother tongue[5], while four indicated Russian, one both German and Russian, one Polish and one Swiss German. I did not include L1 speakers of Hebrew in my sample for two reasons; firstly, they often do not speak German with other Jewish speakers, and secondly, even if they were to do so, Hebrew loan words in German might have a completely different social meaning for Hebrew L1 speakers, or even none at all due to being used also as part of the speaker's L1. The 12 speakers were born between 1959 and 1992, which means that they were between 25 and 58 years old when the interviews took place. Eight of them regarded themselves as religious (four as Orthodox, one as Masorti, one as Reform and two without further specification) and four as secular. As this study seeks to shed light on speakers' perception of Berlin's Jewish community and language use within this community, I did not apply religious or scientific definitions of Jewishness when

---

3 As both Yiddish and Hebrew are written in the Hebrew alphabet (square script) and most items from the distinctive repertoire are very seldomly written and if written mainly the Latin alphabet is used, several spelling variants exist for each item. I used spelling variants according to either Weinberg's two dictionaries (1969, 1994); the spelling the speakers themselves used (if possible); or the spelling rules of the German language.
4 To what extent these repertoires are similar and where they differ goes beyond the scope of this article and will be discussed in the larger project on this topic.
5 I deliberately asked speakers about their mother tongue – although this concept has been rejected in linguistics and is replaced by L1 – as I did expect them to be more familiar with the term of mother tongue and to interpret this term in a more emotional way.

selecting speakers. Instead, I regarded those individuals as Jewish who perceived themselves as Jewish.

All interviews were audio-recorded and had a length between 30 and 100 minutes, with most of them lasting around one hour. I transcribed the interviews with the transcribing tool f4, which I also used afterwards for the analysis. My transcription was based on HIAT, which means that I basically transcribed according to the orthographic rules of written German, but included information on laughter and self-reparation. Speakers' names have been replaced with pseudonyms to avoid drawing conclusions concerning their identities.

Each interview was divided into three parts. The first part consisted of general questions about Jewish Berlin and speakers' positioning within the community. These questions were not related to language and language use. Speakers were asked to describe Jewish Berlin, if the community can be structured into distinctive subgroups or networks, and, if so, which criteria are used for structuring it. The second part of the interview comprised a task where speakers were asked to evaluate lexical items from the distinctive Jewish linguistic repertoire. The third part was a short questionnaire on personal data including a self-evaluation on language proficiency in Hebrew and Yiddish as well as on the religious denomination that the speakers aligned with.

During the second part, it was mainly single items that were evaluated, though formulaic sequences like greetings were also included. More precisely, informants were asked to stack items written on cards according to the following three categories: (1) items they know and use themselves; (2) items they know, but would not use; or (3) items they do not know. During the task, the informants were asked about the choices they made and encouraged to comment on their decision-making. The presented lexical items were chosen from the items collected during the expert interviews. The number of elements that speakers evaluated depended on their time and how comfortable they felt with the task. Some of them were very eager to comment on more items. The minimum number of presented items was 51, the maximum, 76.

As I was looking for variation, I selected items with either existing variants within the collection, such as the Hebrew *Tallit* vs. the Yiddish *Tallis*[6] (both 'prayer shawl') or items that according to the literature were presumably only used by a certain group of speakers. Doing this task, the speakers made their own

---

6 As this is a study on speakers' perceptions, I stick with speakers' differentiations and the labels they used. Speakers generally differentiated only between Hebrew and Yiddish and did not go in more detail in for example differentiating between Eastern and Western Yiddish or mentioning that some items in Yiddish are Hebrew-derived.

language use (first category and stack) visible in contrast to the language use of others (second category and stack). The second category is therefore of special interest as it contains lexical items that the individual speaker is familiar with, but reports to not make use of for certain reasons. The aim of the overall project was to reveal speakers' explanations and justifications for the linguistic choices that they make. A possible explanation for rejecting certain items might be that speakers perceive these items as typical for a certain group that they want to distinguish themselves from.

In this study I am describing and analysing according to which criteria speakers subdivide the Jewish community in Berlin. To investigate whether this subdivision is based on a perceived linguistic difference, I will then compare the perceived subgroups with those lexical items that speakers attribute explicitly to certain groups.

5 Perceived groups

For the question about subgroups within the community, no categories were suggested, as the intent was to keep the question completely open. Even if being Jewish does not necessarily include a religious faith, I expected that the subgroups within the community would be structured along religious denominations (e.g. orthodox, traditional, progressive), or, due to the heterogeneity of the community as a whole, along much smaller local networks of which I, as an outsider, could not be aware. Interestingly, two main criteria emerged during the interviews under which my informants' answers can be subsumed: religion, as was expected, but also, surprisingly, nationality. However, my informants attributed different importance to the two criteria or interpreted them in different ways. Some speakers saw the groups' boundaries as shaped by only one of the two main criteria, while others considered it a mixture.

Concerning nationality, speakers generally divided the community into three groups:

(1) Naja es gibt halt diejenigen, die aber mittlerweile leider aussterben, natürlich, klar, die halt den Holocaust noch überlebt haben und hier geblieben sind und also ja, in Berlin geblieben sind und ähm, ja dann eben, wo sich eben die Generationen quasi weiter fortgeführt haben. Ähm, also aus so'ner Familie komm ich zum Beispiel auch. Dann gibt es ganz viele Russen. Es gibt super, super viele Russen. Und diese Familien werden eigentlich immer weniger, also, werden eigentlich übermannt von den Russen, kann man sagen. Und dann gibt's mittlerweile sehr, sehr viele Israelis auch. Aber diese Gruppen, also das ist so ganz grob so'ne Dreiteilung, sag ich jetzt mal. (Julia, 1:45)

[Well, there are those who are unfortunately dying off by now, of course, who survived the Holocaust and who have been staying here and yes, staying in Berlin and um, where the generations have been continuing. Um, me too, I am from such a family, for example. Then there are many Russians. There is a huge, huge number of Russians. There are less and less of these families, they are actually getting overpowered by the Russians, you could say. Meanwhile, there are also many, many Israelis. And these groups, so that's a sort of rough tripartition, I would say.][7]

The tripartition according to national belonging is in line with studies from other disciplines (see Kranz 2016 on the lifeworld of Jews in Berlin, Kessler 2003 for findings from a survey of *Jüdische Gemeinde Berlin* members). According to Kranz, the three biggest groups in today's Berlin are "local Jews", "Russian Jews", and Israelis. The first group encompasses German Jews and Jewish displaced persons. The "local Jews" label refers to the fact that, compared to the other groups, this group has been living in Berlin for the longest time, i.e. their members are either Holocaust survivors or their descendants, as indicated in the above quote, or displaced persons that came to Berlin after the Holocaust and their descendants. In Kessler's survey, this group is also sometimes labelled as *Einheimische* ("natives"). Both denominations, "local Jews" and *Einheimische*, suggest that the labelled groups own this place and are entitled to live there. My informants did not use these labels, but did speak of *deutsche Juden* ("German Jews", see another quote from Julia below) or of those who want to appear established. This is also forming the basis of a new debate about centrality within the community.[8]

The second group describes the immigrants from the former Soviet Union who have entered Germany since the 1990s. Despite their various countries of origin, they are labelled as "Russians" in public debates both within the Jewish community and outside of it. This group and their descendants currently represent the largest number of Germany's Jewish population. Precise numbers are difficult to obtain, but are estimated to be as high as 95% (see Belkin 2017: 10). This proportion is also true for Berlin and highlights an important change within Berlin's Jewish unity-community. On the one hand, these immigrants from the former Soviet Union, i.e. the *Commonwealth of Independent States* (CIS), in a way ensured the survival of a community that had been shrinking. On the other hand,

---

[7] As the interviews were conducted in German, I've provided my own translations of the quotes into English.

[8] Even though my speakers do not use the label "local Jews", I will make use of it as a blanket term. The reasons are a) that speakers that are subsumed under this label act similarly in this study (see below) and b) the label addresses the debate with regard to becoming established in Germany and having stayed there, which also falls under this topic (see quote (1) above).

the fact that the proportions have been completely reversed has also been perceived by speakers of the first group. This is evident in the use of the verb *übermannen* [to overpower] in Julia's quote above.

The third group refers to the increasing number of Israelis who have moved to the city of Berlin, primarily since 2000. As they rarely become official members of the unity-community, and often have dual citizenship – information that Germany's registry offices do not request – their number is difficult to determine (see Kranz 2015: 9). In public debates, especially in German newspapers, the number of Israelis is often estimated to be much higher than it actually is (see Kranz 2019).

In my data, the division of the Jewish community according to nationality emerges several times and always includes the three nationalities mentioned above. Americans are sometimes mentioned as an additional group. Some of the speakers, like Zeruya, confirmed the tripartition (replacing the label "Russian" with "migrants"), even though her answer to the question did not explicitly use the category of nationality. However, she did introduce the groups later in the interview:

(2) Ich würde mich aber... ich gehör nicht zu den Zuwanderern, also mein Vater ist Israeli, aber meine Mutter ist Deutsche. (Zeruya, 6:44)

[But, I myself would... I don't count myself among the immigrants. Well, my father is Israeli, but my mother is German.]

Interestingly, among the informants who used nationality as either the only criterion or one of the main structuring criteria of the Jewish community, all had in common that they were what Kranz refers to as "local Jews", i.e. German L1 speakers and one Polish L1 speaker, who all had been living in Germany for most of their lives. Among these speakers, some were secular and some were religious. There are several explanations for the fact that these speakers perceive the community as being structured by nationality, while speakers with Russian as their L1 did not. First of all, it is plausible that people who immigrate into another country are perceived as groups by those who already live in the country at that time, no matter whether they themselves were immigrants at an earlier time or have been living in that place for generations. Those who previously immigrated benefit from newer immigrants as the new group allows the former immigrants to become more aligned towards the local population. More evidence for this explanation is the fact that most speakers, including those who did not mainly structure the community according to nationalities, mentioned the Israelis as a distinct group. More precisely, speakers with Russian as their L1 perceived the next group of Jewish migrants as a group that was defined by nationality, namely the Israelis who entered Berlin in large numbers, which mostly occurred after immigration to Germany from the CIS came to an end.

Another explanation emerges through a more in-depth analysis of quote (1). The speaker positioned herself as part of a we-group, which contrasts with the two groups that are not part of this we-group. This is a common pattern within the context of migration (see Spieß 2018: 39). The distinction between the we-group and the other groups is reinforced by the threat that the others represent for the we-group. The speaker highlights the large number of "Russians" via replication of the adjective *super*, which is itself intensifying the quantitative word *viel* ("many"), and the large number of Israelis via replication of the adverb *sehr* ("very"), again intensifying *viel*. With regard to the group of "Russians", the sense of threat increases with the use of the verb *übermannen*, which I translated as "to overpower". Thus, this speaker felt that the arrival of Jewish immigrants from the CIS brought about a significant change not only in the power relations within the Jewish community as a whole, but also especially within Berlin's unity-community. This explanation and the labelling of the two groups is, of course, tied to the topic of language use, as the groups defined by nationality are also considered as such due to their differing language use, i.e. speaking Russian or Hebrew. The perceived change in power relations also led to an actual change to the language policy within the unity-community: the monthly magazine of the *Jüdische Gemeinde* appears today in both German and Russian, and several activities are only offered in the Russian language.[9] In quote (1), the perceived threat of the group labelled as "Russians" seemed to be stronger than the perceived threat of the Israelis, as the former group was attributed the activity of overpowering the we-group, whereas the latter group was not. This perception can be explained by the quasi absence of Israelis in the unity-community, as there is naturally a bigger need to debate the positioning between the "local Jews" and the "Russians" – the organisation's two main groups. This is supported by the following quote:

(3) Aber das ist wie gesagt, das ist natürlich ne ganz eigene Gruppe. Also ich würde noch mal... also man kann auch sagen, dass diese deutsche Juden mit den Russen, die kennen sich noch einigermaßen. [...] Wobei die Russen auch eher für sich sind, aber da gibts schon Überlappungen, sag ich jetzt mal. Aber die Israelis sind schon sehr für sich. Also, die kennen sich eigentlich kaum mit den Anderen. (Julia, 13:06)

[But that is as I said, that is of course a very distinct group. Well, I would again... well, you could say, that the German Jews and the Russians do more or less know each other. [...] Even

---

[9] See archive of the magazine *Jüdisches Berlin* at the website for the *Jüdische Gemeinde* http://www.jg-berlin.org/ueber-uns/juedisches-berlin.html.

though the Russians tend to stay among themselves, there are overlaps, I would say. But the Israelis are very much among themselves. They actually don't really know the others at all.]

Thus, the arrival of the two groups of migrants (interestingly, the Israelis are never referred to as migrants, but this issue is outside the scope of the current study) has changed the situation and position of the "local Jews". These groups are perceived the way they are due to the different L1s that their members speak, i.e. speakers refer to Jews that migrated from the CIS and their descendants as "Russians" or "Russian-speaking Jews", equating a L1 with the nationality sharing its name. This is what Irvine and Gal have labelled "erasure", i.e. the "process in which ideology, in simplifying the sociolinguistic field, renders some persons or activities (or sociolinguistic phenomena) invisible" (2000: 38). In this case the differences between languages spoken in the countries forming the former Soviet Union, such as Russian and Ukrainian, are erased, as well as the fact that people are coming from different countries even though they might all speak Russian as one of their languages. This highlights the language ideology that one language is tied to one nation which is still very prominent in Europe, especially in Germany (see e.g. Blommaert/Verschueren 1998).

An example of a speaker who does not see nationality as the main criterion for subgroup definition within the community, but nevertheless mentions the Israelis as one distinct group, leads us to the other criterion that is perceived as structuring the community: religion.

(4) Lea: Also es gibt ähm einerseits unsere Gemeinde, also die [Name der Gemeinde]. Ich weiß nicht wie, ja wie Sie das kennen auch.
Interviewer: So'n bisschen.
Lea: Ähm, da würd ich sagen [Name anderer Gemeinde], dann die insgesamt, also jüdische Gemeinde an sich, ja, vielleicht dann die ganzen Israelis, die hier sind, die ganzen jüdischen Is-, also die Israelis, die insgesamt eigentlich schon jüdisch sind. (Lea 1:20)

[Lea: Well there is, um, on one hand our congregation, that is [name of the congregation]. I don't know whether, yes if you know it also.
Interviewer: A little bit.
Lea: Um, then, I would say [name of other congregation], then the whole, well the Jüdische Gemeinde as such, yes, maybe then all the Israelis, who are here, the, the Jewish Is-, well the Israelis, who are, generally-speaking, Jewish.]

This speaker divides Jewish Berliners according to two different congregations, neither of which are part of the *Jüdische Gemeinde zu Berlin,* or the *Jüdische Gemeinde* itself. Religion as a criterion for structuring the Jewish community operates on two different layers. The first layer is the intra-religious differentiation, which divides the community according to the different religious denominations (including secularity). Boundaries are defined according to different congregations (4) or, as in the following quote, the denominations that congregations align with and that are more or less similar across countries:

(5) Also ja, es gibt die Orthodoxie, verschiedenartig, aber doch insgesamt irgendwie auch schon ein, mhm, vielleicht ein Monolith, aber man kann sie doch definieren, also s'is ne definierbare Masse. Mhm, es gibt die, immer noch die Traditionellen. [...] Äh, und es gibt natürlich noch die Liberalen. [...] Das wären vielleicht die drei größten Gruppen. (Leo, 5:31)

[Well yes, there is Orthodoxy, differentiated, but nevertheless a sort of, mhm, maybe a monolith, but you can define it, so it is a definable lot. Mhm, there are, still the traditionals. [...] Um, and there are of course the liberals. [...]. That might be the three biggest groups.]

Those speakers who differentiate Berlin's Jewish community according to religious congregations or denominations, i.e. along intra-religious boundaries, have in common that they regard themselves as Orthodox. This is plausible considering that Orthodoxy is, so to say, the most religious way of being Jewish, at least in Berlin, where no ultra-orthodox communities exist (in contrast to Jerusalem, New York and Antwerp). Therefore, the speakers whose strong religious faith and beliefs form the basis and structure of their Judaism and daily lives, perceive the Jewish community according to religious denomination.

The boundaries that the other speakers perceive who use religion as the structuring criteria divide the community, in contrast, into either a religious and a secular part or into institutionalised (religious) life and Jewish life outside the *Jüdische Gemeinde*. I subsume both of these ways of perceiving boundary divisions under an inter-religious division, as religiosity is the dividing factor, even if the *Jüdische Gemeinde* institution is not a purely religious organisation (see above). Speakers who divide the community along inter-religious or institutionalised boundaries, or mention this as an additional criterion, have in common that they define themselves as secular. One of the speakers summarises it in a nutshell with the dichotomy of "Gemeinde vs. Gemeinschaft" [congregation vs. (comm)unity] (Aliah 2:57). Another speaker experiences the boundary in a more excluding way, as his answer to my question on how Jewish Berlin could be described was:

(6) Äh. Leider oder wie soll ich sagen, leider, äh, hab ich wenig Bezug dazu. [...]. Und da ich eben ähm ein Agnostiker bin, fehlt mir der religiöse Bezug. Äh, ich habe jüdische Freunde ähm, aber das, also Jüdischsein als solches ist kein großes Thema. (Alexander 2:49)

[Um, unfortunately or how should I say, unfortunately, um, I have only a weak relationship with it. [...]. And as I am an agnostic, I lack the religious bond. Um, I have Jewish friends um, but well, Jewishness as such is not a big topic.]

So even if this speaker clearly defines himself as Jewish, he reports having hardly any relationship with the community due to his being a secular Jew. This suggests that the Jewish community in Berlin is perceived as an exclusively religious community, despite the fact that Jewishness has (as described above) both a religious and an ancestral component.

In addition to these larger categories mentioned across the whole spectrum of speakers, individual speakers also named other criteria, such as political stance or social status.

In sum, nationality and religion are perceived by my informants as the main criteria for structuring the Jewish community in Berlin. While nationality was perceived only by "local Jews", i.e. descendants of families that have been living in Germany for generations, religion as the structuring criterion, no matter which layer, seemed to not correlate with nationality or L1. Speakers who considered religion as the main criterion had different L1s, i.e. Russian, Swiss German and German (one German L1 speaker provided a mixture of both criteria, i.e. nationality and an institutional/inter-religious boundary), but viewed themselves as Orthodox when intra-religious boundaries were highlighted, or as secular when the distinction between religion/institution and secularism was emphasised.

6 Linguistic reflexes for perceived groups

As previously explained, 3rd wave sociolinguistics also understands linguistic variation as creating a social and linguistic style for positioning oneself within the social landscape. To be successful with this positioning means to be interpreted by the listener in the way that the speaker intended. Success requires distinctiveness, or more precisely, salience, evaluation and contrast (see Irvine 2001). This entails that hearers perceive features as distinct for a respective speaker or group of speakers.

Therefore, it is of interest to the current study whether the group boundaries were also perceived by my informants in linguistic terms, i.e. that listeners could clearly attribute distinct lexical items to speakers from the above-mentioned subgroups in Berlin's Jewish community. To this end, I analysed the perceived variation within the distinctive linguistic repertoire of Berlin's Jews. This means that my focus was the variation concerning the integration of different items from the repertoire into German, not the general use of different languages, such as the Hebrew spoken by Israelis. More precisely, among the lexical items and formulaic sequences that my informants were presented with, I investigated if some were perceived as shibboleths for special groups or as an index for national and/or religious belonging. Every item that was mentioned by at least one informant as being typical for a certain speaker group was considered.

First, the data was analysed for lexical items attributed to speakers from the different nationalities and religious denominations. With respect to nationalities, only very few items were explicitly mentioned as typical for speakers from these groups.

For speakers with a German heritage, two lexical items or formulaic sequences could be listed. One is the expression *die ganze Megille* ("the whole story"), which is said to be used by speakers from the "altes deutsches Judentum" ("old German Jewry") (Petra 46:25). The other is *Barches* (variant for "Shabbat bread") which, according to the informant, was used by Berlin Jews, but has since been replaced by the more frequent item *Challe*. Both speakers are from the group that could be labelled as "local Jews" and have German as their L1. However, they do not use these items themselves or at least not frequently or exclusively, but attribute them to a subgroup within the group of local or German Jews, namely older German Jewish speakers like their parents. Due to their own upbringing, they do not consider themselves part of this group, even if they are familiar with this language use. Additionally, so called *jeckische Juden* ("Jews of German heritage") were said to use pronunciation variants, e.g. *Taura* (a variant for *Tora*, "the holy book of Judaism"). Here again, the speakers who mention this pronunciation variant do not consider themselves part of the group that would make use of it.

Two items were attributed to the group of speakers labelled as "Russians" by "local Jews"; *Git Schabbes* (Yidd. dialectal variant for the Shabbat greeting) and, especially to older "Russians", *Toire* (another variant for *Tora*). No distinct items were attributed to Israelis. General statements were also made about the language knowledge of "Russians" and Israelis. "Russians" were said to know fewer items in general and, except for older generations, have no proficiency in Yiddish or Hebrew. Israelis were said to have no knowledge of Yiddish in general. A general statement about Israelis without any mention of distinct items is not surprising, as the study is about the Jewish repertoire integrated into German, and communication between Israelis and other Jews might happen less frequently in German, but in English or (if the other speaker is proficient enough) Hebrew instead. At least with concern to the interviewees of this study, however, this is often not the case. Therefore, it is less probable that speakers have been in contact with distinct items that Israeli speakers make use of in German. Furthermore, Israelis were not included in the pre-study, where items were collected, or in the main study. General statements referring to the "Russians'" lack of Yiddish and Hebrew language knowledge included neutral statements, among other sentiments, that explained the political situation in the former Soviet Union, where the use of these languages was suppressed. The quote below is from an interview with an expert and is in response to a question about whether he would use a distinct item with all Jewish speakers.

(7) Na, wenn du, sagen wir mal, mit einem von den Russen, hat doch gar keinen Wert. Die wissen's doch gar nicht. Würden dich angucken... (Michael 29:44)

[Well, if you, let's say, with one of the Russians, that wouldn't make any sense at all to them. They have no idea. They would just stare at you...]

Interestingly, this alleged general lack of knowledge concerning the items that I was asking about was not supported in the data for speakers with Russian as their L1. In fact, the orthodox Jews with Russian as their L1 whom I interviewed were those who knew most of the items, while secular Jews with Russian as their L1 knew the fewest items.

The perception of "Russians" having less knowledge of the two languages was also accompanied by the perception that they also lacked knowledge about Jewish religion:

(8) Weißte die lernen noch 'n Seminaren bei der ZWST, Zentrale Wohlfahrtsstelle, da lernen die n' bisschen Religion und hebräische Begriffe, die werden dann vielleicht auch aktiviert. Aber das ist jetzt nichts, was schon da gesessen hat. (Ruth, 19:12)

[You know they learn in seminars at ZWST, Central Welfare Board of Jews in Germany, that is where they learn a little about religion and some Hebrew items that might then be activated. But that is nothing that had existed there before.]

Thus, a group that is now numerically much larger than the group that had before the 1990s been the majority is, in a way, marginalised due to its alleged lack of knowledge concerning the identity marker language (see Blommaert/Verschueren 2010: 192) and the Jewish community's other identity marker: religion.

As mentioned above, "Americans" were explicitly mentioned by only one informant as another nationality forming a subgroup. She perceives *Jarmulke* ("skullcap") and *Schul* (variant for "synagogue") as typical for the "Americans" or would only use these items with those speakers.

In addition to the nationality groups that I previously mentioned, another nationality (or, more precisely, origin) emerged that was triggered by distinct items. Speakers with either a Polish or, more generally, Eastern European background, were said to use *Git Schabbes* ("Good Shabbat") and *Schil* (another variant for "synagogue"). Thus, on the lexical level, which was the primary focus of my study, only a small quantity of linguistic evidence could be found for the different nationality groups. However, two additional groups emerged, "Americans" and speakers of a Polish or Eastern European origin. One item (*Git Schabbes*) was mentioned as typical for both "Russians" and for speakers of Polish or Eastern European origin, which indicated a relatively broader use of the term. Interestingly, speakers with German as their L1 also indicated having used this variant.

Concerning the different religious denominations that were perceived in structuring the communities, several lexical items and formulaic sequences were perceived as mainly typical for Orthodox speakers, e.g. *Haschem* ("God"), *Sollst zajn gezunt* ("Be healthy"), *Toire* (variant of *Tora*), *pessachdig* ("acceptable for pesach"), *Git Schabbes* ("Good Shabbat") and *Schil* ("synagogue"). In the following quote, Petra takes an ironic stance when describing the exaggerated use of the noun *Haschem* or related sequences like *Baruch Haschem* 'Thank God' by Orthodox Jewish speakers, a group that she does not belong to and distinguishes herself from.

(9) Und jedes zweite Wort... du sagst irgendwie "und wie geht's?", "mmh (hohe Stimmlage) *Baruch Haschem*" und "So *Haschem* will" und "Es liegt alles bei *Haschem*" und "Wie geht's den Kindern?" "Ah ja, wenn *Haschem* will, dann geht's denen gut" (Petra, 49:50)

[And every second word... you say like "How is it?", "hum (high pitch) *Baruch Haschem*" and "If *Haschem* allows" and "It's all in *Haschem*'s hands" and "How are the children?" "Ah yes, if *Haschem* allows, then they are fine"]

For other religious denominations, speakers did not seem to perceive distinct lexical items. It was only generally stated that more religious speakers prefer Yiddish variants to Hebrew ones, which is in line with the fact that Yiddish is spoken as L1 exclusively in extremely religious communities. Yiddish variants can therefore take over the indexical meaning of religiosity. Indexical values are, however, not necessarily fixed, but rather fluid (see indexical field below).

Thus, distinctive linguistic items were mentioned only for some of the groups that were perceived when attempting to structure the community. However, several items discussed during the interviews were perceived as typical for the following groups of speakers, which are neither national nor religious groups, and were not mentioned in response to my question on subgroups within the community.

Some items were said to index either having a connection to Israel (in the sense of spending time in Israel and having a positive attitude towards the country) or a knowledge of Hebrew, e.g. *sababa* ("cool") and *Jesch* ("I have", used for affirmation). Others are categorised under the label "*Machane*-slang", as these items are typically used during *Machane* ("Jewish summer camps for children") or more generally during youth activities under the roof of the *Jüdische Gemeinde*, e.g.: *Rosch* ("head of the camp"), *Chug* ("group activity"), and *Chanich* ("camp participant"). The latter group of items could also be defined as indexing a special age group, namely younger speakers. For older speakers, there were also several items uttered, e.g. *Toire* (variant for *Tora*), *die ganze Megille* ("the whole story"), and *Sollst zajn gezunt* ("be healthy"). Interestingly, these items were also mentioned as typical for speakers of other groups, namely all of them for Orthodox Jews, *Toire* for "Russians" and *die ganze Megille* for "German Jews" (see above).

Thus, it has been shown that there are variants or items that are perceived by at least one speaker as typical for the above-mentioned groups. However, the number of typical items is small and there are overlaps with other groups, which could allow for two interpretations: either the items cannot be considered as distinct features for one single group or the indexing value varies according to the listener (and the respective speaker) and their respective backgrounds. The latter would be in line with Eckert's conception of the indexical field, where "[...] the meanings of variables are not precise or fixed but rather constitute a field of potential meanings – an indexical field" (Eckert 2008: 453). Moreover, for some of the groups, no distinct items were mentioned. Instead, only very general statements were made. The reason for the absence of typical items for these groups could lie, however, in the selection of items chosen for the task.

In sum, the data reveals a more complex picture than the very broad categories that were explicitly uttered by my informants at the beginning of each interview.

7 Conclusion and outlook

My data show that speakers perceive the Jewish community in Berlin as mainly structured by national and religious belonging. However, which criterion is more prominent or how it is defined (inter- vs intra-religious boundaries) depends on what is important for the individual speaker and her or his Jewishness. While speakers from families that have been living in Germany for generations considered nationality as the most important criterion, the most religious (= Orthodox) and least religious (= secular) speakers perceived the community as structured by religiosity. This perception by the very religious is no surprise, as religiosity, which for the speakers in this study is Orthodoxy, determines their way of life in almost every aspect. It is the integral component of their Jewishness, and as a result, it is the lens of religiosity, or more precisely, religious denominations within Judaism, through which they perceive the Jewish community in Berlin. For speakers who consider themselves secular and have Russian as their L1, however, religiosity is also the community's structuring criterion. Even if they are not religious, religiosity is what determines their access to and participation within the community, whether this means that they are an active member of the community participating mainly in non-religious events, or do not participate in the community at all.

Those speakers whose families have been living in Germany for generations perceive nationality as the most important criterion when subdividing the community. The reason seems to be that the arrival of migrants from two different countries (while the countries of the former Soviet Union are perceived as one single entity) has challenged their exclusive and central position within the community. The two groups are probably perceived separately due to the different periods of arrival, but also due to the different languages they speak, namely Russian and Hebrew. Here again, the former is perceived as one single language, as differences are ignored or erased. The equation of nationality and language can be explained by the one-nation-one-language ideology that still has a significant impact within Germany. Even though both groups, Israelis and "Russians", are perceived as quantitively overwhelming, the "local Jews" in this study mainly debate their position within the community in relation to the "Russians". The reasons for this might be that the Israelis are often not members of the unity-community and are as a result absent from activities and events under its aegis. In contrast, this is where "local Jews" and Russians get in contact regularly. In addition, the Hebrew language enjoys a high prestige not only among all Jewish speakers from my study, which I prove in my larger research project (in preparation), but also for Jewish speakers in general and throughout history (see Peltz 2010: 141; Myhill 2004). It might therefore be a strategy for the "local Jews" in this study to debate their central place within the community by emphasising their knowledge and use of Hebrew, as well as Yiddish elements from the repertoire and via their knowledge of Jewish religion. This would distinguish them from the group that outnumbers them in quantitative terms.

However, regarding the use of the distinctive Jewish linguistic repertoire, i.e. the integration of lexical items from Hebrew and Yiddish into German, the linguistic variation that is perceived by the speakers from this study is much more complex than the perceived very broad and allegedly clear-cut boundaries between subgroups of the community. Only to some of the perceived groups could some of the tested lexical items from the repertoire be deemed shibboleths. In addition, not all of these items can be considered shibboleths, as they were mentioned as typical for speakers of other groups as well. Moreover, additional groups emerged when the informants were discussing the tested lexical items.

A question for further research that therefore arises, which I am investigating in my larger project, is what are the additional factors that affect the linguistic choices of Jewish speakers in Berlin if the perceived groups can explain only part of the inter- and intraspeaker variation within the community.

References

a. Research literature

Aptroot, Marion/Gruschka, Roland (2010): *Jiddisch. Geschichte und Kultur einer Weltsprache*). München: Beck.

Belkin, Dmitrij (2017): „Positive jüdische Geschichte: Babel 21. Ein Diaspora-Update". In: Dmitrij Belkin (ed.): *#Babel 21: Migration und jüdische Gemeinschaft*. Berlin: Hentrich und Hentrich Verlag.

Benor, Sarah B. (2008): "Towards a New Understanding of Jewish Language in the Twenty-First Century". In: *Religion Compass* 2, 1062–1080.

Benor, Sarah B. (2011): "Mensch, bentsh, and balagan: Variation in the American Jewish linguistic repertoire". In: *Language & Communication* 31, 141–154.

Blommaert, Jan/Verschueren, Jef (2010): "The Role of Language in European Nationalist Ideologies". In: Bambi B. Schieffelin/Kathryn A. Woolard/Paul V. Kroskrity (eds.): *Language ideologies. Practice and theory*. New York: Oxford University Press, 189–210.

Eckert, Penelope (2008): "Variation and the indexical field". In: *Journal of Sociolinguistics* 12 (4), 453–476.

Eckert, Penelope (2012): "Three Waves of Variation Study. The Emergence of Meaning in the Study of Sociolinguistic Variation". In: *Annual Review of Anthropology* 41, 87–100.

Gold, David L. (1981): "Jewish Intralinguistics as a Field of Study". In: *International Journal of the Sociology of Language* (30), 31–46.

Hary, Benjamin H./Benor, Sarah B. (eds.) (2017): *Language in Jewish Communities, Past and Present*. Berlin: de Gruyter Mouton.

Irvine, Judith T. (2001): "'Style' as distinctiveness. The culture and ideology of linguistic differentiation". In: Penelope Eckert/John R. Rickford (eds.): *Style and sociolinguistic variation*. Cambridge: Cambridge University Press, 21–43.

Irvine, Judith T./Gal, Susan (2000): "Language Ideology and Linguistic Differentiation". In: Paul V. Kroskrity (ed.): *Regimes of language: Ideologies, polities, and identities*. Santa Fe: School of American Research Press, 35–84.

Jacobs, Neil G. (2005): *Yiddish. A linguistic introduction*. Cambridge: Cambridge University Press.

Jahns, Esther (2021): *Language ideologies and linguistic choices of German-speaking Jews in Berlin – A qualitative analysis*. Doctoral thesis. Universität Potsdam.

Johnstone, Barbara/Andrus, Jennifer/Danielson, Andrew E. (2006): "Mobility, Indexicality and the Enregisterment of 'Pittsburghese'". In: *Journal of English Linguistics* 34, 77–104.

Klagsbrun Lebenswerd, Patric J. (2016): "Jewish Swedish". In: Lily Kahn/Aaron D. Rubin (eds.): *Handbook of Jewish languages*. Leiden, Boston: Brill, 431–452.

Kranz, Dani (2015). *Israelis in Berlin: Wieviele sind es und was zieht sie nach Berlin?* Bertelsmann Stiftung.

Kranz, Dani (2016): "forget Israel – The Future is in Berlin! Local Jews, Russian Immigrants, and Israeli Jews in Berlin and across Germany". In: *Shofar* 34 (4), 5–28.

Meuser, Michael/Nagel, Ulrike (1991): "ExpertInneninterviews – vielfach erprobt, wenig bedacht". In: Garz, Detlev/Kraimer, Klaus (eds.): *Qualitativ-empirische Sozialforschung*. Wiesbaden: Verlag für Sozialwissenschaften, 441–471.

Myhill, John (2004): *Language in Jewish society. Towards a new understanding*. Clevedon: Multilingual Matters.

Peltz, Rakhmiel (2010): "Diasporic Languages: The Jewish World" In: Joshua A. Fishman/ Ofelia García (eds.): *Handbook of language and ethnic identity*. Oxford, New York: Oxford University Press, 135–152.

Rickford, John R./Eckert, Penelope (2001). "Introduction". In: Eckert, Penelope/Rickford, John R. (eds.): *Style and sociolinguistic variation*. Cambridge: Cambridge University Press, 1–18.

Spieß, Constanze (2018): "'Deutschland muss Deutschland bleiben' – Sprachliche Selbst- und Fremdpositionierungsaktivitäten im Kontext politischer Äußerungen über Migration am Beispiel des Ausdrucks Leitkultur". In: *Kulturwissenschaftliche Zeitschrift* 3, 35–55.

Spolsky, Bernard (1983): "Triglossia and literacy in Jewish Palestine of the first century". In: *International Journal of the Sociology of Language* (42), 95–109.

Spolsky, Bernard/Benor, Sarah B. (2006): Entry »Jewish Languages« In: Keith Brown (ed.): *Encyclopedia of language & linguistics*. Amsterdam: Elsevier, 120–124.

Weinberg, Werner (1969): *Die Reste des Jüdischdeutschen*. Stuttgart: Kohlhammer.

Weinberg, Werner (1994): *Lexikon zum religiösen Wortschatz und Brauchtum der deutschen Juden*. Stuttgart-Bad Cannstatt: Frommann-Holzboog.

Wexler, Paul (1981): "Jewish Interlinguistics. Facts and Conceptual Framework". In: *Language* 57 (1), 99–149.

b. Empirical sources

Interviews conducted and transcribed by myself (not accessible).

c. Online references

Kessler, Judith (2003): *Umfrage 2002*. http://www.jg-berlin.org/beitraege/details/umfrage-2002-i31d-2003-06-01.html (accessed 30 July 2021).

Kranz, Dani (2019): *The Israeli "Diaspora" in Germany: One of a Kind*. https://www.pij.org/articles/1978/the-israeli-diaspora-in-germany-one-of-a-kind (accessed 30 July 2021).

Strack, Christoph (2018): *Berlin, die Stadt, in der Juden leben wollen*. https://www.dw.com/de/berlin-die-stadt-in-der-juden-leben-wollen/a-46179033 (accessed 30 July 2021).

ZWST – Zentrale Wolfahrtsstelle der Juden in Deutschland (2021): Mitgliederstatistik https://zwst.org/de/service/mitgliederstatistik/ (accessed 30 July 2021).

Mercédesz Czimbalmos
Masculine Disposition and Cantonist Ancestry
Symbolic Capital within the Jewish Community of Helsinki

1 Introduction

Currently, there are three Jewish congregations in Finland: the Jewish communities of Helsinki and Turku and a recently established Reform Jewish community.[1] In neither congregation does the membership exceed 1500 individuals. The membership of the Jewish Community of Helsinki, being 10 times larger than the one in Turku, is the country's largest operating Jewish congregation. The roots of these congregations, and of Finnish Jewry in general, go back to when Finland was part of the Russian Empire. The first Jews who arrived in Finland and who were allowed to settle in the territory without converting to Christianity were soldiers who had served in the Russian military. The "Cantonists" were young Jewish boys who were educated in "canton schools" for the purpose of later serving in the military (for further reading, see: Torvinen 1989; Illman/Harviainen 2002). Today, individuals whose families arrived in Finland "via" the Cantonist system are still very often referred to as "Cantonists".

While descendants of Cantonist families dominated the Finnish-Jewish scene in the first half of the 20th century, the community went through several changes and often attempted to redefine its notions of social, cultural and religious boundaries with the outside world. This included the identity and practices of the community itself.

Members of the community perceive themselves, and are perceived by other congregants, in a variety of different ways. This has affected both their ritual and non-ritual lives over the course of the past century. Some of these ways have recently been studied in my own doctoral dissertation (see Czimbalmos 2021a), which utilised the framework of vernacular religion (see Primiano 1995; Bowman 2004; Bowman/Valk 2012) to analyse the practices and traditions of intermarried congregants. As the study pointed out, the interplay between the three main

---

[1] This contribution was finalised before the Reform Jewish community was established.

aspects of vernacular religion, between the "official", "folk", and "individual" (Bowman 2004: 6), were present at all levels of congregational practice. "Official" religion, as the *halakhah* or Jewish law that the congregations followed, "folk" religion, in the form of commonly accepted views and procedures, and "individual" religion, in the personal interpretations that certain congregants supported with regard to what constitutes Jewishness (see Czimbalmos 2021a: 63). The study results showed remarkable differences between the practices of male and female congregants: female congregants often employ creativity when "doing Judaism", as opposed to their male counterparts, who often refrain from such practices and rely on their cultural heritage. Moreover, as the study also concluded, certain congregational practices were established in the community so that male congregants could regain power (see Czimbalmos 2021a: 85–86).

Scholars of various academic fields have used the conceptualisations of French sociologist Pierre Bourdieu to understand how institutions and organisations function in a given environment (e.g. DiMaggio/Powel 1983; Embirmayer/Johnson 2008). In the Finnish context, Helena Kupari (2016) utilised the Bourdieuan concept of *habitus* (which I will return to later in this article) when studying intermarriages among displaced Karelian women (see Kupari 2016). As Kupari highlights, however, Bourdieu's social theory has not gained the kind of status within religious studies that it holds in many other fields of study. A central reason for this is that his work concerning religion has often been deemed lacking in sophistication (e.g. Hervieu-Léger 2000: 110–111; Kupari 2016: 14). As Kupari points out, this is despite the fact that Bourdieu's corpus includes a few texts that explicitly address religion. In these, he primarily argues that the division of labour promoted by urbanisation established the necessary condition for the emergence of an independent religious field. This field is divided up among different religious specialists who control religious knowledge and who compete for religious capital (see Bourdieu 1991; Kupari 2016:13). David Swartz suggests that Bourdieu's field framework may not be the most suitable for studying congregations, as the analytical perspective calls for situating particular entities within a broader framework with respect to the struggle over the significance of religion (Swartz 1996: 83). Nevertheless, various studies have used Bourdieu's body of work for analysing how religion specialists accumulate power and frame various contexts (Kupari 2016: 14).

As recent research on the two existing Jewish congregations in Finland points out, the globalisation of Finnish society and the demographic changes that the local Jewish congregations underwent affected their practices significantly over the past century (see, e.g., Weintraub 2017; Illman 2019; Czimbalmos 2021a). The changes – especially within the Jewish Community of Helsinki – indicate specific underlying dispositions and power structures within these two institutions. The definitions of Judaism and Jewishness are rather complex: Jewish identity and what constitutes Jewishness has been analysed and argued by academics and representatives of Jewish communities worldwide. In the case of the informants for the current study, these definitions vary. For this reason, the study will not attempt to define either of these concepts and aims to present Jewish community as an organisation, which, due to its nature, operates with specific rules that are mainly tied to religious convictions and localised traditions.

I argue that the lines along which the congregational practices were redefined – or intentionally left "untouched" – signal the presence of certain forms of symbolic capital. These forms support the reproduction of power both in the practices and the perceptions of the congregational membership. By mainly drawing on the Minhag Finland project's empirical material (to be discussed at a later point in this article), while also utilising Pierre Bourdieu's concept of symbolic capital, this study analyses the underlying disposition and power structures within these communities.

2 From the Russian military to the Finnish-Jewish *Smörgåsbord*

The Jewish Community of Helsinki – and Finnish Jewry in general – has its roots in the Imperial Russian Army.[2] The first Jews who were allowed to settle in Finland without converting to Christianity were soldiers in this military, including those who had been trained in the Cantonist school system. They arrived in Finland from a variety of locations within the Russian Empire, and as such, mainly had Jewish roots in Litvak (Lithuanian) congregations with *Ashkenazi*[3] traditions (see Torvinen 1989; Czimbalmos/Pataricza 2019; Muir/Tuori 2019). In a recent historiographical contribution, Simo Muir and Riikka Tuori conclude that those who founded the community had decided that they would create an Orthodox Jewish congregation

---

2 *Smörgåsbord* is a Swedish term, used to describe a buffet-style luncheon. I use it metaphorically in order to represent the diversity of local Jewry.
3 Ashkenazi Jews, that is, those Jews of Central and Eastern European origin. *Sephardic Jews*, by contrast, are from the areas around the Mediterranean Sea, including Portugal, Spain, the Middle East and Northern Africa. *Mizrachi Jews* are the descendants of local Jewish communities that had existed in the Middle East or North Africa.

in Finland. As this form of Judaism was the only one that they were familiar with in their youth, they may have lacked other options (see Muir/Tuori 2019: 12).

After Finland became independent, its Jewish minority gained the right of Finnish citizenship in 1917, and in 1918 the Jewish Community of Helsinki was added to the register of Jewish communities in Finland (see Muir/Tuori 2019: 18). Regardless of the favourable legal conditions, however, the congregation started to face various challenges that primarily concerned administrative matters. In addition to granting citizenship to Finnish Jews in 1917, the Finnish Parliament passed the Civil Marriage Act (CMA), which went into effect in 1918. The CMA allowed Finnish Jews to marry people of other faiths without any obligation to convert to Christianity (see Czimbalmos 2019). Having been granted this freedom, the number of intermarriages between Jewish and non-Jewish citizens started to increase, and intermarriages became part of the everyday lives of Finnish Jews. In addition to the CMA, the Freedom of Religion Act (FRA) was also passed by the Finnish parliament, which caused further complications within the community. According to the Orthodox Jewish law that the Jewish Community of Helsinki followed, a child with a Jewish mother or a person who had converted to Judaism was considered to be Jewish. The FRA, however, defined one's religious denomination based on that of the father: a child was to be a member of the religious community that their father belonged to unless their parents expressly agreed otherwise in a written contract. To create a solution for this problematic situation, the community issued a protocol in which they stated that a child of one Jewish parent is to be registered in the congregation's books. Children, however, whose mothers were not Jewish were not considered Jewish until they underwent conversion as a child. In addition, boys were required to be circumcised even if they were halakhically Jewish, which remained the congregation's practice until March 2018 (see Czimbalmos 2019, 2020a, 2020b, 2021a).

These developments affected the lives of the individuals and families involved, and influenced congregational traditions as well. The rise in intermarriages first resulted in a growing number of childhood conversions, followed later on by a growing number of adulthood conversions within the congregations (see Czimbalmos 2021a, 2021b). Individuals who married non-Jewish women often faced rejection and discrimination, as was also the case for their converted spouses. Naturally, when Finnish society as a whole started to become more international, the demographics of the Jewish Community of Helsinki were also transformed: foreign Jews started to join the community from a variety of backgrounds (see Weintraub 2017; Czimbalmos 2021a) and often shared very similar experiences to the earlier excluded, often marginalised intermarried congregants or converted spouses. Today, the congregation is rather diverse, with members coming from a large variety of religious backgrounds (see Czimbalmos 2021a). This often results in conflicting opinions about religious practices as well as creative solutions to these issues.[4]

3 Methods and material

The core sources of this study are qualitative interviews (n=101) conducted by Minhag Finland team members[5] with members of the Jewish communities of Helsinki and Turku – all members being older than 18 years of age – between February 2019 and February 2020 as part of the "Boundaries of Jewish Identities in Contemporary Finland" (Minhag Finland) project. Depending on the preferences of the informants, the interviews were conducted in several languages, including English, Swedish and Finnish[6]. The quotations derived from the interviews that were not conducted in English were translated by me. To make it easier to comprehend the quotations – in the case of grammatical errors, for example – I decided to edit them without changing the overall meaning or content of the quotation itself.

The outline of the interview was semi-structured and mainly reflected on the aspects of Finnish-Jewish everyday life among the congregational membership, while also touching upon their rituals. At the time of our interviews, all informants who took part in the study identified with one of the gender binaries. Among them, there were fifty-four women, and forty-seven men. The interview structure was designed in accordance with the framework for vernacular religion (see Primiano 1995; Bowman 2004; Bowman/Valk 2012). As a result, most interviews were centred around topics such as the congregations' *minhagim*[7], or those related to dietary habits, family lives, conversions, and relations with society in general.

---

[4] A detailed historical account, as well as an analysis of certain matters mentioned in here can be found in a recent contribution titled *Intermarriage, Conversion, and Jewish Identity in Contemporary Finland: A study of vernacular religion in the Finnish Jewish communities* (see Czimbalmos 2021a).
[5] The members of the Minhag Finland team: docent Ruth Illman, docent Simo Muir, PhD Dóra Pataricza, PhD Riikka Tuori and the author of this contribution.
[6] Other languages were also used when interviewing the members of the respective congregations. However, these are languages that have such a minority position within the communities that they would potentially disclose the identity of the informants. They will therefore not be mentioned.
[7] Plural form of *minhag*: traditions, customs.

In addition to the qualitative interviews conducted within the Minhag Finland project, information derived from a large body of archival materials (such as board meeting minutes, membership and marriage registries, rabbinical correspondence, and other administrative documents) about and belonging to the Jewish Community of Helsinki were included in the study's empirical material. Due to the diverse body of data, thematic analysis (see Braun/Clarke 2006; Braun/Clarke/Terry 2015) was chosen as an analysis method. Previous research has pointed to the existence of various power dynamics within the congregation, which resulted in different approaches to religious practices among the male and female congregants (see for example Czimbalmos 2020b, 2021a). Taking these results into consideration, the analysis was implemented based on preconceived themes that proved to be very much present – both overtly and covertly – in the data set. The key themes that arose from the analysis were *masculine disposition as symbolic capital* and *Cantonist ancestry as symbolic capital*.

4 Ethical considerations

The material analysed in the current study involves sensitive data concerning the informants of the study as well as their immediate kin and close-knit community. Participation in the Minhag Finland research was voluntary, and the informed consent of the informants was obtained before proceeding. As agreed upon before the collection began, the data use and storage will be overseen by *Suomen Kirjallisuuden Seura* (Finnish Literature Society), whose office will also serve as the data storage site.[8] The Jewish Community of Helsinki granted access to their archival sources. In order to protect the identity of the informants, pseudonyms were used to refer to them. Certain interviews from the general Minhag Finland data set have previously been analysed and quoted from.[9]

---

[8] The same ethical guidelines were followed by everyone involved in the Minhag Finland project.
[9] In addition, the pseudonyms are not associated directly with the interview quotes among the list of references. This was to avoid the possibility of revealing the identity of the informants in the event that there were interviews that had been used in previous research.

5 The concept of symbolic capital

Pierre Bourdieu's approach can be summarised through the main concepts in his theoretical apparatus – *habitus*, *capital*, and *field* – that he established to facilitate a relational analysis of social phenomena (see Grenfell 2008: 220–222; Kupari 2016: 13). These essential tools can be used to uncover the mechanics of superiority and inequality in particular social spaces.

According to Bourdieu, the social world can be conceptualised as a series of relatively autonomous but structurally homologous scenes or *field*s where various forms of cultural and material resources or *capital* are produced, consumed and circulated. Naturally, agents and their social positions are located within a given field, which is a space of both conflict and competition (see Bourdieu 1984; Wacquant 1992: 17–18; Navarro 2006: 14; Kupari 2016). The boundaries and parameters of a given field will reflect the field's history of struggles for particular forms of capital (see Swartz 1996). The structure of a field is essentially the product of its history, which is where previous struggles resulted in not only the particular constitution of that field but also in establishing the value of particular kinds of capital (see McKinnon/Trzebiatowska/Brittain 2011: 357). In the Bourdieuan understanding, "capital denotes the different kinds of resources, values, and wealth around which crystallise the power relations in any field" (Kupari 2016: 13). Throughout their lives, individuals strive to maintain capital. Capital can take various forms, and these are essentially determined by the field in which capital is used (see Bourdieu 1986: 252–253). Capital is therefore "a resource, effective in a given social arena that enables one to appropriate the specific profits arising out of participation and contest in it" (Wacquant 1998: 223). As sports players on a field, individuals are in a constant struggle to maintain their capital. Their positions are influenced by the capitals that they can mobilise on the field, though capital cannot be evenly distributed among all individuals. For this reason, they are positioned hierarchically (see McKinnon/Trzebiatowska/Brittain 2011: 357).

Symbolic capital is perhaps one of Bourdieu's most ambiguous and significant concepts (see Steinmetz 2006: 449). In his own definition (1994: 8) he states that "Symbolic capital is any property (any form of capital whether physical, economic, cultural or social) when it is perceived by social agents endowed with categories of perception which cause them to know it and recognise it, to give it value".

Similar to all forms of capital, symbolic capital is more or less equivalent to power – whether material or symbolic. They often reinforce one another, and in doing so, maintain the *status quo*. Making capital is an instrument of both "domination and its reproduction in human society" (Rey 2014: 52). Symbolic capital is not mere wealth that can be gathered and piled up; it is instead "a self-reproducing form of wealth, a kind of 'accumulated labor' that gives its owner 'credit' or the ability to appropriate the labor and products of others" (Urban 2003: 360). Symbolic capital – like economic capital – is transferable to social networks. It is a form of prestige or honour that is attached to a family (see Bourdieu 1977: 177–179). When individuals or families convert certain goods to symbolic capital, they can successfully expand their power.

When an activity's domain gains autonomy from social, political, or economic constraints, the autonomisation generates elites who are the holders of a type of relevant capital, and responsible for the specific activity's legitimate interpretation of representations and practices. The elites' capital – regardless of its nature – is always a capital of recognition (see Hilgerz and Mangez 2014: 6). This is the case when the field becomes more and more autonomised, and the practical knowledge connected to the field's specific history or heritage is objectified, celebrated and guarded by the "guardians of legitimate knowledge" (Hilgerz/Mangez 2014: 7).

Religion scholar Terry Rey suggests that *symbolic violence* is also a central concept in Bourdieu's theory, and thus adds it to the apparatus mentioned above (see Rey 2014). When explaining his suggestion, Rey draws on Loïc Wacquant's argument that "the whole of Bourdieu's work may be interpreted as a materialist anthropology of the specific contribution that various forms of symbolic violence make to the reproduction and transformation of structures of domination" (Wacquant 1992: 14–15). The convertibility of different forms of capital is realised through implicit conversion rules that structure and are structured by the various fields of power operating within society, which are processes and rules of distinction (see Gilleard 2020: 3). Dominant groups generally succeed in legitimising their own culture, and as a result, based on subjective perceptions of taste, remain superior to those they consider inferior, (see Bourdieu 1984: 245). Essentially, they exercise symbolic violence and use their legitimate culture to monopolise privileges, exclude individuals from high-status positions, or, to the contrary, assign them these same positions (see Bourdieu/Passeron 1977). The legitimate culture marked and defined by these groups is used to assume privileges and mark cultural proximity (see Bourdieu/Passeron 1977: 31).

Bourdieu's field theory (see Bourdieu 1993a) is fundamentally about power relations, symbolic struggles and inequalities in resources and capital (see Miller 2016: 351). Bourdieu always considered class to be gendered, and for this reason class and gender are intimately connected. Nevertheless, he continued to pay little attention to the relationship between gender and different forms of capital. Moreover, he also considered capital to be gender-neutral (see Huppatz 2009: 46;

McCall 1992: 842). According to Diana Miller, Bourdieu's theorisation on how gender relates to symbolic capital remains – as Miller puts it – "underdeveloped" in his body of work (Miller 2014: 464). Furthermore, Miller describes how in *Masculine Domination* (Bourdieu 2001), Bourdieu theorises gender relations – solely along the binary – within the dichotomy of a dominant-dominated relationship (see Miller 2014: 464). By ignoring certain gender relations, field theorists tend to ignore an axis of power and inequality (see Adkins/Skeggs 2004; Miller 2016: 351). According to Kate Huppatz, gendered dispositions function as embodied forms of capital. For this reason, she differentiates between "masculine capital" and "feminine capital" (Huppatz 2009). Due to the importance of reputation, honour and esteem from the perspective of symbolic capital, gendering capital is of special importance. As Miller (2014: 563) argues: "A gender-free view of symbolic capital risks overlooking an important dynamic underlying this key form of currency in fields of cultural production".

In the current study, I argue that the Jewish Community of Helsinki utilises "masculine disposition" as a form of symbolic capital and that in the current case, male and masculine capitals continue to dominate the feminine and female capitals.[10] Furthermore, I argue that when lacking this particular form of capital, congregants accumulate another form of symbolic capital (*Cantonist ancestry as symbolic capital*), which essentially occurs via the utilisation of kinship connections.

6 Analysis

6.1 Masculine disposition as symbolic capital

Since the passage of the CMA and FRA by the Finnish Parliament, the gradual rise in intermarriage rates (see Czimbalmos 2019; Czimbalmos 2021a) has had an effect on the community. Intermarriage is generally not supported by Orthodox Jewish religious authorities (see Hirt/Mintz/Stern 2015), which was also visible in the congregational attitudes at the time. This will be discussed later in this article.

---

10 In the current context, masculine capital or masculine disposition equals identifying as a man, and being assigned the male gender at birth. Similarly, feminine or female disposition equals identifying as a woman and being assigned the female gender at birth. The reason behind the binary division is that none of the interview informants identified themselves as not belonging to the binary.

During his rabbinical term, Rabbi Simon Federbusch[11] issued a *taqqanah* – a rabbinical statute – which confined the rights of intermarried men and denied them the right to be granted an *aliyah*[12] (see Czimbalmos 2019: 49–50). This resulted in a significant loss of their religious and social capital within the congregation. The decision was essentially the first example of using symbolic violence to exert power (see Bourdieu/Passeron 1977: 20) within the community. As the growing number of intermarriages affected more and more men (and consequentially, their rights to rise to the Torah), there was an attempt to change this "tradition". However, it remained in practice until the 1970s (see Czimbalmos 2019: 51). Even when men were denied the right to rise to the Torah, their presence was expected and necessary in the community for performing ritual obligations, which require a *minyan* – that is, a quorum of 10 adult Jewish men. Naturally, intermarried women faced social exclusion often and were subject to various degrees of marginalisation within the community. These aren't as well-documented, however there are examples of women who lost their capital within the community and who were expelled from it by their families (see Czimbalmos 2019; Kieding Banik/Ekholm 2018). There is also proof that they withdrew their membership from the congregation (see Czimbalmos 2019; HrJFH; Ak; NA Bmm; NA Hpl), which may have partially been the result of their social rejection (see Czimbalmos 2021a).

Orthodox Judaism is a gender-traditional branch of Judaism (see Avishai 2008; Avishai 2016). In (non-egalitarian) Orthodox Jewish communities – like the present one – men have certain ritual obligations in the synagogue, some of which do not concern women. In such communities, the official markers of symbolic capital lie in the Jewish law that the congregation seeks to follow, and can be exemplified by the status of children within the community: the status of children as halakhically Jewish is only "secured" if they convert to Judaism, or if their mother is Jewish. In such contexts or, in other words, fields, it is perhaps not very surprising that women often have devalued capital and live on the margins of their communities. Interestingly, however, the Minhag Finland informants prove that although this congregation may be nominally Orthodox, the majority of its membership does not identify themselves as Orthodox Jewish, but rather as traditional Jewish, or secular. Nevertheless, in the current narratives, the congregation is officially Orthodox but welcomes Jews from all denominations.

---

[11] The rabbi of the congregation until 1940.
[12] Granting an *aliyah* is calling on a member of a Jewish congregation to read a segment of the Torah. Receiving an *aliyah* is considered to be a great honour.

When the FRA of 1922 defined a child's religious affiliation according to the father's religion – against the requirements of the Orthodox Jewish law – the congregational membership faced a variety of administrative challenges. They were obliged to list the children in the congregational membership books – without acknowledging them as Jewish. The administrative difficulties and the growing number of halakhically non-Jewish children – who were nevertheless listed in the congregational membership books – led the congregation to establish the practice of childhood conversions as early as the 1950s (see Czimbalmos 2019). In order to maintain an Orthodox Jewish community (that is, a community that accepts matrilineal descent or conversion as a basis of membership), the members of the congregation were essentially forced to reproduce the social order so that it would be consistent with the transformed "practical taxonomies" (Bourdieu 1977: 97) of the period – as was already highlighted in previous research (see Czimbalmos 2021a).

The *taqqanah* of Federbusch lost its validity in the 1970s (see Czimbalmos 2019), and even though male congregants often described being pressured into marrying Jewish women, the examples of the congregational archives prove that they very often did not opt to do so (NA). With very few exceptions, it appears that female congregants experienced much harsher exclusion and consequences for their intermarriages than their male counterparts. Nevertheless, two male congregants from Cantonist families remember some negative consequences that male congregants faced when they got married or contemplated marrying someone of a different faith: Itzak recalls being told – before he got married – that he was not allowed to marry anyone else but a Jew, whereas Moishe, who decided to get married to a non-Jewish woman during that same period, faced the rejection of his own family when his mother said *kaddish* after him.[13] Due to the high number of intermarriages in the 1970s, Mordechai Lanxner[14] organised the community's first large adulthood conversion group in 1977 (see Czimbalmos 2021a: 58). The participants at the conversion that spring were mainly women who were married to male Cantonist congregants, or underage woman who were in a relationship with a male Cantonist.

In theory, when the FRA was changed in 1970 and made conform with the *halakhah*, the congregation earned a certain amount of additional autonomy. This was because they were no longer obliged to register children of non-Jewish

---

13 The term specifically refers to the "The Mourner's Kaddish" – a part of the mourning rituals in Judaism in all prayer services, including funerals. "Saying Kaddish" unambiguously refers to the rituals of mourning.
14 The deputy rabbi (1968–1973), then rabbi (1973–1982) for the Jewish Community of Helsinki.

mothers in their membership books, and the traditions they had established continued to exist (see Czimbalmos 2021a: 63; Czimbalmos 2021b). In *Genesis and Structure of the Religious Field* (1991) Bourdieu states that "the autonomy of the religious field asserts itself in the tendency of specialists to lock themselves up in autarchic reference, to already accumulated religious knowledge in the esotericism of a quasi-cumulative production, destined first of all for its producers" (Bourdieu 1991: 9). In the field that is currently being studied, this translates to establishing – and institutionalising – a system where due to the small size of the Jewish marriage market, intermarriages became acceptable – if not encouraged – and intermarried men could remain legitimate members of the congregations. This was in contrast to their female counterparts, who within the community faced social rejection or exclusion, or various forms of symbolic violence. Up until March 2018, the circumcision of male children – regardless of whether or not they are halakhically Jewish – was a prerequisite for accepting children into the Jewish school or congregation. Eva, a mother of two, explicitly commented on this matter when discussing circumcision, which she perceived to be unnecessary, since "if the mother is Jewish, the child is Jewish". Leia, a young woman of Cantonist ancestry, talked about the requirement of circumcision, for which she said she "doesn't see any reason why she would do that" other than to make her child a member of the congregation. Maya, another female informant, talked about issues of certain individuals exercising "power". She illustrated her point by talking about two examples that were particularly hurtful for her. One was her son's *bar mitzvah*[15], where she was initially told to sit at the threshold of the door to the congregation's *minyen room* – the place where the event took place. Eventually, she did not comply with the request and decided to sit inside the room. The other one was at the funeral of her mother, where a member of Chevra Kadisha[16] wanted to forbid her from shovelling soil onto the coffin, which she eventually did do by holding the shovel with her son. The examples of these women show that the congregation's male members continue to hold a very specific symbolic capital within the community, one that is predominantly connected to their gender.

Undeniably, in an Orthodox Jewish community, its religious law or traditions may be used as tools for justifying or denying women the right to specific actions – as was the case with intermarried men after the *taqqanah*. In the case of women's involvement in services and many other matters related to "Orthodox Jewish practice", there is room for discussion about Jewish law and its

---

15 Coming of age ceremony.
16 Lit. "Holy Society". A group of Jewish men and women who are responsible for preparing the deceased for their burial.

interpretations. In the current case, for example, even though the Orthodox understandings of the Jewish law are applied, particular importance is attributed to patrilineal ancestry. One example that illustrates this can be seen in certain liturgical interpretations, the most intriguing of these perhaps being the one connected to the process of calling male congregants to the Torah. For this, Jews are traditionally "divided" into three main tribes: *Cohanim*, *Leviim* and *Yehudim*.[17] From the liturgical perspective, this is especially relevant, as in Orthodox congregations, Cohanim, Leviim and Yehudim are called up to the Torah in this particular order. The statuses of Cohanim and Levi'im are inherited via patrilineal ancestry. Therefore, if a Cohen or Levi marries a non-Jewish woman, their future (male) child will lose his father's status as a Cohen or Levi, and as such, will even fall into the tribe of Yehudim following conversion to Judaism. Regardless of this perception of the halakhah, children of Leviim from halakhically non-Jewish mothers are being called up to the Torah as Levi'im, which is proof that masculine disposition is a form of symbolic capital within the community.

Therefore, the struggle that started with the growing number of intermarriages, and thus, the growing number of halakhically non-Jewish children in the congregation, resulted in certain rules that essentially allow individuals of masculine disposition to dominate the field – regardless of whether or not those rules are in accordance with Orthodox Jewish law. Specific authority, a "characteristic of the field in question" (Bourdieu 1993b: 73), has been successfully monopolised by those who possess masculine disposition – the congregation's symbolic capital.

6.2 Cantonist ancestry as symbolic capital

The gender-traditional nature of Judaism and the domination of those who possessed a particular kind of symbolic capital – in this case masculine disposition

---

17 According to the Jewish tradition, Jacob had twelve sons: their descendants grew into the Twelve Tribes of Israel, among whom the Land of Israel was divided when Joshua conquered it. After the death of King Solomon, this land was divided into the kingdoms of Israel and Judah. Ten of twelve tribes were lost, and the remaining ones became known as "Jews" as an indication of the fact that they descended from the tribe of Judah. Many other Jews from the other tribes also lived in Judah, but over the years, their own separate identity seemed to have ceased, with one exception: the tribe of Levi, within which there were descendants of the High Priest (Aharon), who are today known as Cohanim. Thus, today there are three groups within the Jews: those descending from Aharon (Cohanim), those from the tribe of Levi (Levi'im) and the others, with no particular ancestry connected with either of these, to that of Yehudim. In many non-Orthodox denominations of Judaism, the ties to these tribes have essentially little or no importance in practice.

– was a key and defining theme in the interview and archival materials. Another key theme was identified through the analytical process. Masculine disposition in itself may be "enough" for upholding certain positions or practicing certain traditions in the congregation, but there is another kind of symbolic capital that enables one to exercise power among its members. This form of capital is rooted in the "unique history" of the congregation. As such, it pertains to its founders, "the Cantonists", and is therefore referred to as *Cantonist ancestry as symbolic capital* in the current study.

A male informant, Shimon, who joined the congregation after converting to Judaism, described this phenomenon as the following: "...these Cantonist [men] do not call their children converts, even if they, by all means, are converts. They have this kind of a matter of honour [issue]". Solely by having male relatives of Cantonist ancestry can individuals accumulate symbolic capital, a "capital of recognition" (Hilgerz/Mangez 2014: 6) within the communities. Various examples derived from both the archival and interview materials indicate that the capital accumulated via ancestral ties started to become present in the congregation as a form of symbolic capital, in addition masculine disposition. This capital could be accumulated not only via inheriting it (that is, being born in a family with Cantonist roots), but also via acquired kinship relationships, such as marriage. This is exemplified by the gradual social acceptance of women who converted, for example, in the 1970s. Prior to this period, conversions were not frequently practiced in the community.

One informant, Chaya, recalls not feeling included in the community and even being referred to as a "mistress" up until her son's *bar mitzvah*. At the event, she impressed the older male community members in powerful positions with her reproduction of traditional "Finnish-Jewish dishes", and as such re-created one of the embodiments of Finnish-Jewish "Cantonist culture". With this action, she became in a sense a carrier of symbolic capital. Another informant, who joined the congregation in similar circumstances, talked in her interview about how her peers and their husbands were often not greeted, in the latter case because they were married to converted women. Both women talked about a lengthy learning process that proceeded their conversions, which entailed studying the Jewish law and local traditions, the latter including recipes and dietary customs specific to the Helsinki community. With their learning came a form of symbolic capital and an embodied, particular disposition that confirmed their adherence to the – to use Bourdieu's analogy – "rules of the game". Through the "practical mastery of the specific heritage" (Hilgerz/Mangez 2014: 7) – even without identifying as a man – they were therefore able to accumulate the other kind of symbolic capital.

A couple of years after the first local adulthood conversions in the 1980s, immigrants started to arrive in Finland as the country became more global. Some of them described the Jewish Community of Helsinki as a rather, – in their view – hostile environment. Various informants and congregants reported that the local families and individuals accumulated cultural items and regarded their traditions as the only legitimate ones. Even after the influx of new congregants at the end of the 1970s, it was still somewhat unusual for non-Finnish born Jews to arrive in the congregation. For this reason, when a new person appeared, the congregants' reception was rather cold, as they were "not used to" having "outsiders" in the community.

One woman, Sarah, who in the 1980s came the community from another Askhenazi community, recalled being corrected when she used the Southern Yiddish dialect to pronounce certain words, whereas the dialect spoken in Helsinki was Northeastern Yiddish.[18] As Schwartz describes, "privilege and prestige can be transmitted intergenerationally through forms of cultural capital" (Swartz 1996: 76), which is essentially what Sarah and the earlier quoted Shimon observed among certain Cantonist families who produced the "elite". They were (and are) the honourable, prestigious ones who remained in influential positions within the congregation, either in an official or non-official capacity. Sarah referred to this as a "fallacy", where locals claimed to have represented the "old-line, traditional religious Finnish Jews", overpowering other congregants whose Jewish ancestry originated outside of Finland. In her view symbolic capital has also been accumulated by congregants who joined the community at a later stage –in 1977, for example – after becoming romantically involved with a Finnish Jew of Cantonist ancestry.

In a similar vein, many informants mentioned the case of Jews who arrived in Finland from the former Soviet Union, or congregants who arrived later from other countries (such as Israel) as expats, and how they had similar experiences. Regardless of whether or not they were in theory Jewish according to halakhah, they were not recognised as legitimate (enough) congregants as they did not possess the other form of symbolic capital – in other words, the symbolic capital of Cantonist ancestry. Adam, a member who joined the community after arriving in Finland from abroad, remembers that shortly after he and his family joined the congregation, he often heard congregants talking about the Israelis, asking "Why

---

[18] In a personal conversation, the expert of the topic, Simo Muir, clarified that the Yiddish spoken in Helsinki was in fact a variety of sub-dialects of North-Eastern Yiddish. I would like to thank Muir for this important remark. For further reading, see: Muir, Simo (2004): *Yiddish in Helsinki. Study of a Colonial Yiddish Dialect and Culture*. Helsinki: Finnish Oriental Society.

did they come here?" or "Why did they leave Israel? They should be living in Israel". Moishe, a congregant of Cantonist ancestry, also reflected on this issue:

> [...] but then there have been like immigrants, who then have brought in something new and different. With all the respect, when you give your pinky finger, it doesn't take long that your whole hand is gone. I am not a believer. I am not a believer in any way, but traditions and old things are so important to me! And I think about my children: what kind of a community will they get? It's different from what I had, or what kind of a congregation I lived in. And that's not what I want. I want those traditions in the synagogue, and those traditions connected to [the community], to be the same.

Further in our discussion, he said that he understands the change and is in favour of it in general, but new melodies and liturgical traditions are not "changing the community for the better", since they do not affect the everyday life of the community. He also highlighted that he does not attend the synagogue's services very often. Nevertheless, he found it important to preserve the "old things" that he had been used to since childhood. Many of the Israeli immigrants arriving in Finland have Mizrahi or Sephardi backgrounds. This means that the liturgical traditions that they are familiar with – if they are familiar with any at all – are significantly different from the Ashkenazi ones that the community adheres to: they lack the previously mentioned "practical mastery of the specific heritage" (Hilgerz/Mangez 2014: 7) that the possessors of Cantonist symbolic capital require. A young woman, Chaya, who was raised in this congregation but does not have Cantonist ancestry, talked in detail about how, as a child, Cantonist ancestry was referred to as superior. She was judgemental of the practice of belonging to certain traditions without re-evaluating them, or without having sufficient understanding of them. She concluded her interview by saying that "tradition is peer pressure from dead people", suggesting that the congregational membership has changed considerably, and thus certain traditions could also be subjected to modification. Undeniably, members who had Cantonist roots, such as the informant Moishe – and perhaps others who have similar feelings about adjusting or adapting these traditions to the congregational membership's requirements – have not recognised that individuals who were raised in other communities may have equally sentimental feelings about their own local traditions, and by not being allowed to practice them, feel that they are at the margins of the Helsinki community. Consistent with Bourdieu's theory on religion, congregants who hold Cantonist ancestry as a form of symbolic capital often appear to be striving to legitimise their own culture (that is, their own traditions) based on their subjective perceptions of what they consider right or wrong. This is informed by their own experiences (see Bourdieu 1984: 245). Of course, not all informants addressed the topic with such negative views. Isaac, who is from a Cantonist family, talked about the Israeli "influx" in a somewhat positive manner, which according to many, is not a common perspective amongst congregation members with Cantonist ancestry.

> [...] most of the Israelis who moved to Finland had a Sephardic background, and many of them came from very traditional religious homes. So, one thing that was a very positive contribution to the community's religious life was that we got people to go to the synagogue who could read the Torah and so on. But of course, the way they read the Torah, and the way they sang the traditional songs, were a little bit different from our Ashkenazi tradition. And that brought about some discussion and maybe also some problems and so on. And it also brought some changes to some traditions...

One of the early "Israeli arrivers", Samuel, said that many of his peers who were brought up in Sephardic communities considered the synagogue "too Askhenazi". In his opinion, many of them were married to non-Jews and were "afraid to join" the community, knowing that they will be marginalised cultural producers without any ancestral ties to local families. This was regardless of whether or not they have more liturgical knowledge than their Cantonist counterparts. He was traditionally from an Askhenazi environment and did not feel uncomfortable in the congregation, but was nonetheless aware of the importance of Cantonist ancestry. Hanna, who has Mizrachi roots and joined a community years after the first "influx" of foreigners, remembered a case from recent years where a community member was not even allowed to read the Torah according to his tradition, and was thus denied the prestige associated with this practice:

> The community could be more open and not so Ashkenazi. [...] It will not hurt if once there would be a prayer in a Sephardi way, and if it was allowed to read the Torah, for example, the Yemen[ite] way. [...] Because it's still reading the Torah, it's not about how you read it. And some want to read it according to their own traditions. So it should not be "not as good" as the Ashkenazi way and not allowed in here.

People in the congregation with Mizrachi or Sephardi backgrounds have been attempting to organise "non-Askhenazi" services, but they are rarely, if ever, allowed to hold them. Even with a certain form of capital – the capital of masculine disposition – they are still left on the margins. They can fulfil certain ritual obligations, but only in ways that are accepted by those in positions of power. Denying these possibilities to the congregants seems to stem from the idealised and unique Finnish-Jewish identity rooted in the traditions of – as one young informant named Levi put it – "the forefathers". That is to say, in the traditions of the Cantonist men who founded the congregation over 100 years ago.

Interestingly, however, certain traditions of Sephardi origin were eventually accepted in the community. One example of this the *Ne'ila* at *Yom Kippur*, which was introduced by a male congregant and involves singing *El Nora Alila*[19]. Despite the initial reluctance and the perhaps not so positive initial reception of *gerim*[20] in the community, today converts form a big part of the congregational membership. Benyamin, a member of Cantonist ancestry, explicitly referred to the growing number of converts who did not have any familial or ancestral affiliation to Judaism: "Of course, when you go to the synagogue nowadays, you notice right away that there are only five-six Cantonist families around. The rest are Israelis, or Finnish converts, even downstairs among the men".

"Even downstairs among the men" is an explicit reference to the men who convert to Judaism without having been affiliated with a Jewish woman – which was and is still a relatively rare phenomenon in the congregation (see Czimbalmos 2021b). By "Finnish converts", he is referring to those women who converted to Judaism after meeting their local Jewish spouses. As such, he – perhaps unintentionally – distinguishes between the converts (both men and women) who accumulate symbolic capital through their family relations – either via marriage or via patrilineal ancestry. David, whose Jewish ancestry is non-Cantonist, is reflecting on the prestigious position of the elite families when he says:

> [...] [the congregation] in Helsinki has been a very closed community. [...] here, there is this very special situation, that if someone comes from a – so to say – "Cantonist" family, then he is automatically Jewish if he keeps his surname [...] in Helsinki, the cultural aspects of Judaism [Jewishness] are emphasised.

Along with David, Abraham mentioned that the capital valued in the congregation is not strictly connected to any sense of liturgical knowledge that they would consider important within the community. According to Abraham, congregants of Cantonist ancestry attempt to "preserve their culture" without sufficient liturgical or halakhic knowledge and solely based on their kinship connections to the community's founders:

> [...] if someone tells, "My grandfather was a fiddler", the same person cannot say that he is also a fiddler – unless he is able to play the violin. Like, if you want to be a fiddler, it is not enough that your grandfather was a fiddler. If you can't play the violin, you can't say that you are a fiddler!

---

19 A liturgical poem, that begins the Ne'ilah service at the conclusion of Yom Kippur, the day of atonement. Though it is mainly recited as part of the Sephardi and Mizrachi liturgy, it has also been adopted into Ashkenazi services.
20 Converts.

Essentially, his fiddler metaphor not only touches upon the often-debated question of "what constitutes Jewishness" (see, e.g., Illman/Czimbalmos 2020), it also reflects on the issue of capital and the "practical mastery of the specific heritage" (Hilgerz/Mangez 2014: 7) that is objectified in the congregation. This aspect was and is frequently addressed, especially by those who joined at a later stage in their lives – either because they arrived in Finland as adults or because they decided to convert to Judaism, which in many cases means that they had to complete rather intensive studies before the *giyur*. Deborah, a young convert, explicitly addressed the current congregational membership division and talked about "certain groups" within the community. She also addressed the issue of converts who have no kinship relations with these groups and who end up at the margins of the community as a result. In response, they establish their own circles, which then results in the congregation having three different groups: "the Cantonists", "the Israelis" or the "converts". In practice – she said – "you become a member of the Cantonist or Israeli group if you marry someone from the group" – which is in line with the earlier experiences of women who married Cantonist men in the 1970s, and thus accumulated the valued capital by putting up with the traditions of their spouses' families.

7 Conclusion

In this paper, I argued that two particular kinds of capital had been accumulated in the Jewish Community of Helsinki over the course of the past century: masculine disposition and Cantonist ancestry as symbolic capital.

Members of the Jewish Community of Helsinki strove to maintain these two distinct forms of symbolic capital. The result, as Bourdieu also concluded, is that they are by and large determined by the field and context in which they are used (see Bourdieu 1986: 252–253).

Due to the controversies that arose from the Finnish law and the Jewish law at the beginning of the 20th century, intermarried Jewish women and men alike suffered from a loss of power and exclusion within their community (see Czimbalmos 2019; Czimbalmos 2021a). The congregation's leadership, along with the guidelines they received from certain rabbinical authorities, established a system that ensured that Jewish men regained their power within their congregation (see Czimbalmos 2021a: 65–66), which established their gender as a form of symbolic capital within their communities. As the examples in this study show, the Jewish Community of Helsinki utilises masculine disposition as a form of symbolic capital, and in the current case, male or masculine capital continues to dominate the feminine or female capital. Furthermore, when lacking the necessary masculine disposition, congregants can accumulate another form of symbolic capital, Cantonist ancestry, by utilising kinship connections and acquiring the "practical mastery of the specific heritage" (Hilgerz/Mangez 2014: 7). These forms of capital allowed male congregants and those who joined their families via kinship relations (such as marriage) to maintain the *status quo* and reproduce their domination within their congregation.

Via the reproduction of these two forms of symbolic capital, certain members of the different congregations reproduce "structures of domination" (Wacquant 1992: 14) within their community. The dominant groups, that is, Cantonist men, or those who can acquire Cantonist capital through marriage, for example, have succeeded in legitimising their power within their congregation through the subjective perceptions that they attributed to their ancestry. As such, by denying certain individuals the ability to change certain traditions or the "rules of the game", for example, they are able to keep their power and legitimacy while also exercising symbolic violence within the Jewish community. By applying specific "conservation strategies" (Bourdieu 1993b: 73) as a means of monopolising capital, they are the ones who determine the power relations within the field.

Naturally, the examples only represent one part of the bigger picture and are based on the experiences of individuals who volunteered to take part in a broader research project. For these reasons, they cannot be considered universal. Nevertheless, they can indicate an underlying phenomenon or narrative in the congregation that may result in certain members leaving the community altogether or not attending its events frequently. As the examples I've given point out, the two main types of symbolic capital that are accumulated in the Jewish Community of Helsinki are also connected to experiences of social exclusion. Both forms of symbolic capital are shared by certain members of the congregation and are considered culturally superior. The symbolic profit gained through the transmission of these forms of capital is the ability to maintain the boundaries of the community and its unique identity, where the form of desired symbolic capital essentially stems from masculine dispositions and the accumulation of Cantonist ancestry. Through the production of these forms of symbolic capital – and as a result, symbolic boundaries – inequalities are produced (Lamont/Pendergrass/Pachucki 2015: 851) within the community.

The textual sources of the current study, as well as the individual narratives of the informants, echo the experiences of exclusion and marginalisation of those who failed to accumulate the Jewish Community of Helsinki's two kinds of symbolic capital.

References

a. Research literature

Adkins, Lisa/Skeggs, Beverley (eds.) (2004): *Feminism After Bourdieu*. Oxford: Blackwell.

Avishai, Orit (2008): "'Doing Religion' in a Secular World: Women in Conservative Religions and the Question of Agency." In: *Gender & Society 22* (4), 409–433. https://doi.org/10.1177/0891243208321019 (accessed 13 March 2021).

Avishai, Orit (2016): "Theorizing Gender from Religion Cases: Agency, Feminist Activism, and Masculinity." In: *Sociology of Religion 77* (3), 261–279. https://doi.org/10.1093/socrel/srw020 (accessed 13 March 2021).

Bourdieu, Pierre (1977): *Outline of a Theory of Practice*. Cambridge: Cambridge University Press.

Bourdieu, Pierre (1984): *Distinction: A social critique of the judgement of taste*. Cambridge, MA: Harvard University Press.

Bourdieu, Pierre (1990): *The Logic of Practice*. Cambridge: Polity Press.

Bourdieu, Pierre (1991): "Genesis and Structure of the Religious Field of the religious field." In: *Comparative Social Research* 13, 1–43.

Bourdieu, Pierre (1993a): *The Field of Cultural Production*. New York: Columbia University Press.

Bourdieu, Pierre (1993b): *Sociology in Question*. New York: Sage.

Bourdieu, Pierre (2001): *Masculine Domination*. Cambridge: Polity Press.

Bourdieu, Pierre/Passeron, Jean-Claude (1977): *Reproduction in Education, Society, and Culture*. Beverly Hills: Sage.

Bourdieu, Pierre (1986): "The forms of capital." In: J. Richardson, ed. *Handbook of Theory and Research for the Sociology of Education*. Westport, CT: Greenwood: 241–58.

Bourdieu, Pierre (1994): "Rethinking the State: Genesis and Structure of the Bureaucratic Field." In: *Sociological Theory, 12* (1), 1–18. https://doi.org/10.2307/202032 (accessed 30 July 2021).

Bourdieu, Pierre 1991: "Genesis and Structure of the Religious Field." In *Comparative Social Research* (13) 1–44.

Bowman, Marion (2004): "Taking Stories Seriously: Vernacular Religion, Contemporary Spirituality and the Myth of Jesus in Glastonbury." *Temenos* 39–40, 125–142. https://doi.org/10.33356/temenos.4821 (accessed 10 January 2021).

Bowman, Marion/Valk, Ülo (2012): "Introduction: Vernacular religion, generic expressions and the dynamics of belief." In: Marion Bowman/Ülo Valk (eds.): *Vernacular Religion in Everyday Life: Expressions of Belief*. Sheffield: Equinox Publishing, 1–22.

Braun, Virginia/Clarke, Victoria (2006): "Using thematic analysis in psychology." *Qualitative Research in Psychology* 3 (2): 77–101, https://doi.org/10.1191/1478088706qp063oa (accessed 19 March 2021).

Braun, Virginia/Clarke, Victoria/Terry, Gareth (2015): "Thematic Analysis." In: Poul Rohleder/Antonia C. Lyons (eds): *Qualitative research in clinical and health psychology*. Basingstoke: Palgrave MacMillan, 95–114.

Czimbalmos, Mercédesz (2019): "Laws, doctrines and practice: a study of intermarriages and the ways they challenged the Jewish Community of Helsinki from 1930 to 1970." In:

Nordisk judaistik/Scandinavian Jewish Studies 30 (1), 35–54. https://doi.org/10.30752/nj.77260 (accessed 5 January 2020).

Czimbalmos, Mercédesz (2020a): "'Everyone does Jewish in their own way': Vernacular practices of intermarried Finnish Jewish women." *Approaching Religion* 10 (2), 53–72. https://doi.org/10.30664/ar.91381 (accessed 12 March 2021).

Czimbalmos, Mercédesz (2020b): "Yidishe tates forming Jewish families: Experiences of intermarried Finnish Jewish men." *Nordisk judaistik/Scandinavian Jewish Studies* 31 (2), 21–40. https://doi.org/10.30752/nj.97558. (accessed 30 July 2021)

Czimbalmos, Mercédesz (2021a): *Intermarriage, Conversion, and Jewish Identity in Contemporary Finland: A Study of Vernacular Religion in the Finnish Jewish Communities*. Doctoral dissertation. Åbo Akademi University.

Czimbalmos, Mercédesz (2021b): "Rites of Passage: Conversionary In-Marriages in the Finnish Jewish Communities." In: *Journal of Religion in Europe* 14 (1–2), 1-27. https://doi.org/10.1163/18748929-20211502 (accessed 26 november 2021).

Czimbalmos, Mercédesz/Pataricza, Dóra (2019): "Boundaries of Jewish Identities in Contemporary Finland." [Editorial]. *Nordisk judaistik/Scandinavian Jewish Studies* 30 (1), 1–7. https://doi.org/10.30752/nj.80214 (accessed 5 January 2020).

DiMaggio Paul J./Powell, Walter W. (1983): "The Iron Cage Revisited: Institutional Isomorphism and Collective Rationality in Organizational Fields." In: *American Sociological Review* 48 (2), 147–160.

Embirmayer, Mustafa/Johnson, Victoria (2008): "Bourdieu and Organizational Analysis." In: *Theory and Society* 37 (1), 1–44.

Gilleard, Chris (2020): "Bourdieu's forms of capital and the stratification of later life." In: *Journal of aging studies 53* 100851. https://doi.org/10.1016/j.jaging.2020.100851 (accessed 30 July 2021).

Grenfell, Michael (2008): "Postscript: Methodological Principles." In: Michael Grenfell (ed.): *Pierre Bourdieu: Key Concepts*. Stocksfield: Acumen, 219–227.

Hervieu-Léger, Daniele (2000): *Religion as a Chain of Memory*. New Brunswick: Rutgers University Press.

Hilgerz, Mathieu/Mangez, Eric (2014): "Introduction to Pierre Bourdieu's theory of social fields" In: Mathieu Hilgerz/Eric Mangez (eds): *Bourdieu's Theory of Social Fields. Concepts and Applications*. London: Routledge, 1–36.

Hirt, S. Robert/Mintz, Adam/Stern, Marc D. (eds.) (2015): *Conversion, Intermarriage, and Jewish Identity*. New York, NY: The Michael Scharf Publication Trust of the Yeshiva University Press.

Huppatz, Kate (2009): "Reworking Bourdieu's 'Capital': Feminine and Female Capitals in the Field of Paid Caring Work." In: *Sociology (Oxford)* 43 (1), 45–66. https://doi.org/10.1177/0038038508099097 (accessed 26 July 2021).

Illman, Karl-Johan/Harviainen, Tapani (2002): *Judisk Historia* [Jewish History]. Åbo: Åbo Akademi.

Illman, Ruth (2019): "Researching vernacular Judaism: Reflections on theory and method." In: *Nordisk judaistik/Scandinavian Jewish Studies 30* (1), 91–108. https://doi.org/10.30752/nj.77287 (accessed 21 January 2020).

Illman, Ruth/Czimbalmos, Mercédesz (2020): "Knowing, Being, and Doing Religion." In: *Temenos* 56 (2), 170–199. https://doi.org/10.33356/temenos.97275 (accessed 18 March 2021).

Kieding Banik, Viebeke/Ekholm, Laura (2018): "Culture, Context and Family Networks: Values and Knowledge Transfers Among Eastern European Jews in the Nordic Countries 1880–1940." In: Ulla Aatsinki/Johanna Annola/Mervi Kaarninen (eds.): *Families, Values, and Transfer of Knowledge in Northern Societies 1500–2000*. New York: Routledge, 120–142.

Kupari, Helena (2016): *Lifelong Religion as Habitus: Religious Practice among Displaced Karelian Orthodox Women in Finland*. Leiden/Boston: Brill.

Lamont, Michèle/Pendergrass, Sabrina/Pachucki, Mark (2015): "Symbolic Boundaries." In: James D. Wright (ed.): *International Encyclopedia of Social and Behavioral Sciences*. Oxford: Elsevier, 850–855.

McCall, Leslie (1992): "Does Gender Fit? Bourdieu, Feminism, and Conceptions of Social Order," In: *Theory and Society* 21 (6), 837–867.

McKinnon, Andrew M./Trzebiatowska, Marta/Brittain, Christopher Craig (2011): "Bourdieu, Capital, and Conflict in a Religious Field: The Case of the 'Homosexuality' Conflict in the Anglican Communion." In: *Journal of Contemporary Religion* 26 (3), 355–370. https://dx.doi.org/10.1080/13537903.2011.616033 (accessed 30 July 2021).

Miller, Diana L. (2014): "Symbolic Capital and Gender: Evidence from Two Cultural Fields." *Cultural Sociology* 8 (4), 462–482. https://doi.org/10.1177/1749975514539800 (accessed 30 July 2021)

Miller, Diana L. (2016): Gender, Field, and Habitus: How Gendered Dispositions Reproduce Fields of Cultural Production. *Sociological forum (Randolph, N.J.)* 31(2), 330–353. https://doi.org/10.1111/socf.12247 (accessed 30 July 2021)

Muir, Simo (2004): *Yiddish in Helsinki. Study of a Colonial Yiddish Dialect and Culture*. Helsinki: Finnish Oriental Society.

Muir, Simo/Tuori, Riikka (2019): "'The Golden Chain of Pious Rabbis': the origin and development of Finnish Jewish Orthodoxy." In: *Nordisk judaistik/Scandinavian Jewish Studies* 30 (1), 8–34. https://doi.org/10.30752/nj.77253 (accessed 9 January 2020).

Navarro, Zander (2006): "In search of a cultural interpretation of power: The contribution of Pierre Bourdieu." In: *IDS Bulletin* 37 (6), 11–22. https://doi.org/10.1111/j.1759-5436.2006.tb00319.x. (accessed 30 July 2021)

Primiano, Leonard N. (1995): "Vernacular religion and the search for method in religious folklife." In: *Western Folklore*, 54 (1): 37–56.

Rey, Terry (2014): *Bourdieu on Religion: Imposing Faith and Legitimacy*. New York: Routledge.

Steinmetz, George (2006): "Bourdieu's Disavowal of Lacan: Psychoanalytic Theory and the Concepts of 'Habitus' and 'Symbolic Capital.'" *Constellations (Oxford)*, 13 (4), 445–464. https://doi.org/10.1111/j.1467-8675.2006.00415.x (accessed 19 October 2020).

Swartz, David (1996): "Bridging the Study of Culture and Religion: Pierre Bourdieu's Political Economy of Symbolic Power." In: *Sociology of Religion* 57 (1), 71–85.

Torvinen, Taimi (1989): *Kadimah. Suomen juutalaisten historia* [Kadimah. The history of Finnish Jews]. Helsinki: Otava.

Urban, Hugh B. (2003): "Sacred Capital: Pierre Bourdieu and the Study of Religion." In: *Method & Theory in the Study of Religion* 15 (4), 354–389.

Wacquant, Loïc J. D. (1992): "Toward a Social Praxeology: The Structure and Logic of Bourdieu's Sociology." In: Pierre Bourdieu/Loïc J. D. Wacquant (eds.): *An Invitation to Reflexive Sociology*. Cambridge: Polity Press, 1–47.

Wacquant, Loïc J. D. (1998): "Pierre Bourdieu." In: Rob Stones (ed.): *Key sociological thinkers*. London: Palgrave, 215–229.

Weintraub, Daniel (2017): "Juutalaiset ja juutalaisuus Suomessa [Jews and Jewishness in Finland]." In: Ruth Illman/Kimmo Ketola/Jussi Sohlberg (eds.): *Monien uskontojen ja katsomusten Suomi* [The various religions and beliefs of Finland]. Tampere: Kirkontutkimuskeskus, 116–126.

b. Empirical sources

Archival sources

National Archives of Finland (NA) Finnish Jewish Archives, Archives of the Jewish Community of Helsinki.
Bmm. Board minutes 1919–29, box 39: 22.4.1924; 1930–4, box 40: 5.12.1933, 2.1.1934; 1935–9, box.
41: 18.11.1937, 1940–9, box 42: 1950–4, box 43; 1955–59, box 44: 1968–77: box 45.
Hpl. Appendices to the board minutes: 1967, 1968, 1969, 1970.
Kii. Controversy concerning registering children born to non-Jewish mothers: 1946–73, box 163.
On-site Archives of the Jewish Community of Helsinki (JCH).
HrJFH. Hufvud-Register *öfver* medlemmar Judiska Församlingen I Helsingfors [Main Register over the members of the Jewish Community of Helsinki], 1919–.
Ak. Asiakirjat 1946–80.

Interview material

Minhag Finland Interviews.
The interviews will be preserved in the archives of the Finnish Literature Society (SKS).

c. Online sources

Boundaries of Jewish Identities in Contemporary Finland project: https://polininstitutet.fi/en/boundaries-of-jewish-identities-in-contemporary-finland-minhag-finland/ (accessed 17 July 2021).

Maya Hadar
Together we Stand?

Exploring National Identification Among Israeli Arabs, Jews and Immigrants Following Israeli Military Successes

1 Introduction

Notwithstanding differences between social subgroups in contemporary Israeli society, a majority of both Jewish and Arab Israelis have proclaimed their pride over the past decade in being Israeli and have done so despite the fact that they have frequently experienced political violence. This interesting data illustrates the complex nature of group identification, as Israeli Arabs constitute a national minority that has little connection with the State of Israel's core Zionist ethos. Additionally, Israeli Arabs suffer from ongoing discrimination (even in the eyes of the majority of the Jewish public, see Hermann et al. 2016), and are in a "tight spot" where the ongoing Israeli-Palestinian conflict is concerned.

Group identification is regarded as an important phenomenon by social scientists, especially as it pertains to national identification. The importance of one's sense of national identification was previously researched as part of nation-building processes (see Bendix 1980) and was more recently addressed with regard to the European refugee crisis, Brexit and the resurgence of right-wing political parties across the globe (see Bekhuis et al. 2013; Gusterson 2017; Kaufmann 2016; Osborne et al. 2017). While identity salience[1] changes over time and in

---

[1] Scholarship emphasises the multidimensionality of the self and conceptualises the self in terms of multiple role-based concepts (e.g., McCall/Simmons 1978, Rosenberg 1979). Social psychologists and sociologists tend to "conceive important parts of self as identities, or internalized role designations … thus the organization attributed to self often pertains to the way in which discrete identities relate to each other" (Stryker/Serpe 1994: 17). Parts of the self, also referred to as *identities*, are organized hierarchically according to salience or psychological centrality (Stryker/Serpe 1994). According to Brenner, Serpe, and Stryker "… the likelihood of a given identity being played out in social interaction will be significantly impacted by the salience of the identity relative to the salience of other identities the person holds" (2014: 232). Identity Salience refers to "the probability that a given identity will be invoked in social interaction" (Stryker 1968, [1980] 2003) or, alternatively, as a substantial propensity to define a situation in a way that

Open Access. © 2023 the author(s), published by De Gruyter. This work is licensed under the Creative Commons Attribution 4.0 International License.
https://doi.org/10.1515/9783111039633-007

relation to broader societal perceptions (see Gilroy 1997: 305), violent conflicts pose a threat to national identification and, as a result, profoundly affect it. Whereas threats to identity were found to enhance identity salience, their effects vis à vis group identification remain insufficiently understood.

How resilient is the national identity of individuals in the face of persistent political violence? Whereas the relevant literature considers political violence a unitary phenomenon and primarily focuses on the effects of exposure to the violence itself, it consistently overlooks the impact of its outcome. Do distinct outcomes of political violence (such as wars and military operations) affect national identification in different ways? Does group performance (success vs failure) or membership in an ethnic group (ethnic minority vs minority) influence the impact?

According to social identity theory, one of the most comprehensive theories of group relations (see Abrams/Hogg 1990; Emler/Hopkins 1990; Tajfel 1974; Tajfel/Turner 1979; Turner 1975), a prime motive for individuals to identify with a specific group is that it enhances their esteem, both in their own eyes and in the eyes of others. Whereas individuals are motivated to proclaim their association with a successful group, this may have negative social consequences for members with a low status or who belong to a losing group. It is thus to be expected that victories and defeats will have distinct impacts where group identification is concerned. Therefore, this paper aims to explore the impact of the aftermath of political violence (based on group performance framed by the local media) on national identification across social groups in Israeli society (Jews, Arabs, and Immigrants). Bearing in mind the multi-layered nature of individual identities, mechanisms of inclusion and exclusion within national and religious communities, and Israel's political history, the various social groups are expected to illustrate distinct impacts.

2 Theoretical framework and hypotheses

In the past, most countries were assumed to be nation-states that mainly encompassed a single dominant ethnic group (see Smith/Jarkko 1998). However, minorities seeking self-determination, along with immigration and modern politics, led to the prevalence of multi-ethnic, heterogenic states (such as the UK, Canada and Spain) (see Gurr 2000).

---

provides an opportunity to perform that identity (Stryker/Serpe 1982; Brenner/Serpe/Stryker 2014: 232).

National identity is considered "the cohesive force that holds nation-states together" (Smith/Jarkko, 1998: 1). Affinity with the state or a sense of patriotism has not only been associated with government effectiveness (see Ahlerup/Hansson 2011), tax compliance (see Konrad/Qari 2012), pro-trade preferences (see Mayda/Rodrik 2005), support for a united European community (see Risse 2015), and life satisfaction at an individual level (see Morrison et al. 2011; Reeskens/Wright 2011), but also with nationalist attitudes (see Smith/Jarkko 1998; Wagner et al. 2012). In this study, *national pride* is used as a proxy for Israeli national identification. This operationalisation is appropriate given Smith/Kim's definition of "national pride" as "the positive effect that the public feels towards their country, resulting from their national identity" (2006: 127). National pride is both the sense of esteem that a person has for one's nation as well as the self-esteem[2] that one derives from their national identity (see Smith/Kim 2006).

Whereas individuals strive to maintain or enhance their self-esteem and achieve a positive self-concept, social identity theory posits that an essential part of an individual's sense of self is derived from membership in social groups (i.e. social identity) (see Emler/Hopkins 1990; Tajfel 1959; Tajfel/Turner 1979). In other words, the self-esteem of individuals was found to be associated with their group's status/value (see Tajfel 1981). Values connotations associated with groups are the result of social comparisons between one's in-group and a relevant out-group. Consequently, groups compete not just for material resources, but for anything that can enhance their self-definition: i.e. positive social identity (see Abrams/Hogg 1990; Oakes/Turner 1980; Turner 1981). Consequently, individuals are motivated to Bask in Reflected Glory (BIRGing) and proclaim their associations with a successful group, and to Cut Off Reflected Failure (CORFing), which, in other words, means to dissociate oneself from a losing group.

BIRGing is a strategic impression management technique that enables individuals to raise their esteem in the eyes of others by publicising their connection with a successful other (see Hirt et al. 1992) without having been instrumental to that success. BIRGing involves a process of unit formation between the individual and the successful group (see Cialdini et al. 1976) and is considered an essential means by which individuals maintain a positive self-concept (see Tesser 1988). The tendency to BIRG explains the "fair weather" fandom that is observed when sports teams are successful (see Becker/Suls 1983; Cratty 1983; Hirt et al. 1992) and, following a positively evaluated group performance (e.g. victory in a war, or

---

[2] Self-esteem was explicitly referred to as a motivation behind intergroup behaviour. (Tajfel/Turner 1979: 40).

the successful completion of a military operation - H1), contributes to an expected increase in in-group identification among the general population.

While identifying with a group may affirm an individual's sense of self-worth, a group's debacle may lead to negative and unavoidable consequences (see Edwards 1973; Roberts 1976). Accordingly, an important corollary to BIRGing is **CORFing**, an image protection tactic that enables individuals to avoid being associated with an unsuccessful other and to distance themselves from them (see Snyder et al. 1983). A classic example of the tendency to CORF is the "killing/shooting the messenger" metaphor, which describes peoples' reluctance to deliver bad news as a means to avoid association with the message and the negative evaluations that follow (see Manis et al. 1974).

Whereas the general Israeli population is expected to follow H1, relevant scholarship identified asymmetric attitudes towards one's country within minority and majority groups. According to Staerklé et al. (2010), ethnic, linguistic and religious majorities tend to identify more with the nation and are more inclined to strongly endorse a nationalist ideology than minorities do. Staerklé et al. also found that the most considerable difference between minorities and majorities exists in ethnically diverse countries (see 2010: 491). Dowley & Silver (2000) obtained a similar finding and attributed it to a cohort effect (see Smith/Jarkko 1998). Consequently, and against the backdrop of the aforementioned academic literature, members of distinct minority groups are not expected to follow the general relationship between group identification and group performance (which in this case corresponds to increased national identification following Israeli military successes) (The "Minority Hypothesis": H2).

2.1 Israeli society in context

Israeli society, with its high heterogeneity of various groups representing class, religious, national, ethnic and cultural differences, is often seen as the ultimate "laboratory conducive to the study of the development of negative political attitudes towards various minority groups" (Canetti-Nisim et al. 2008: 91). The main ethnic groups, Jewish and Arab Israelis[3], split into subgroups with distinct identities. Jews divide according to levels of religiosity, ethnic background[4] and time

---

[3] According to current reports by the Central Bureau of Statistics (2020c), Jews constitute 73.9% of Israel's population, Arabs/Palestinians constitute 21.1%.
[4] Ashkenazi Jews exiled to Europe and Sephardic/Mizrachi Jews exiled to Spain, North Africa and Middle Eastern countries.

of immigration (new immigrants and old-timers). Non-Jews mainly split into Christian Arabs, Muslim Arabs, Druze and Bedouin.

External threats are known to function as cohesive factors. Consequently, Israel's security situation and past wars have served to entrench a deep sense of shared destiny (e.g., Bar-Tal, 2013). However, studies on the aftermath of political violence also point to negative attitudes and fragmentation among various social groups in Israel (cf. Sullivan et al., 1985; Pedahzur & Yishai, 1999; Canetti-Nisim & Pedahzur, 2003).

Two notable minority groups in contemporary Israeli society are Arab Israelis and immigrants. The former constitutes an ethnic minority[5] in a country widely perceived as the "Jewish state" and the homeland of the Jewish people (see Herzl 1896). The latter are distinguished from the native population due to their foreign origin and, at times, religion[6]. Members of both groups often report a sense of social exclusion and marginalisation alongside a feeling of being treated as second-class citizens (see Ghanem 2016; Raijman 2010, Raz 2004).

One can hypothesise that due to processes of marginalisation and social and political exclusion, these minority group members may not perceive the states' victory as "their own". With this being the case, an increase in national identification following Israeli victories is unlikely to manifest itself among members of the two observed minority groups. The more segregated and discriminated against the members of these groups perceive themselves to be, the more likely that they will experience a **decrease** in national identification following Israeli victories. Due to the context of the warfare being analysed (the Israeli-Palestinian conflict), this is especially true for Arab Israelis.

2.2 The use of emphasis and equivalence framing in shaping individual opinion

This research is predicated on the fact that national identification within Israel (operationalised as national pride) fluctuates following discrepant outcomes of political violence that Israel participated in. Assessments of outcomes that were

---

[5] As such, the overall level of national identification among Arab Israelis is expected to be lower than that of the (predominantly Jewish) general population and of Jewish Israelis.
[6] While FSU immigrants to Israel are predominantly Jewish, according to the Israeli Ministry of the Interior, 61.5% of Russians (about 34,552 persons) and 66% of Ukrainian (26,256 persons) immigrants that arrived in Israel between 2012 and 2019 are not Jewish (as they are decedents/partners of Jews, they were granted Israeli citizenship according to the Law of Return (Nahshoni 2019). See further discussion under the "Discussion" section).

conducted by individuals are rarely based on the measurement of objectives (military achievements, deaths inflicted by each party, etc.). Politicians, interest groups and media outlets strive to shape the preferences of ordinary individuals, whose opinions affect electoral outcomes and often guide day-to-day policy decisions (e.g. Erikson/MacKuen/Stimson 2002). They often do so by employing specific communication frames (see Druckman 2011; Gitlin 2003; Iyengar 1990).

"'Framing' refers to 'the way the story is written or produced', including the orienting headlines, specific word choices, rhetorical devices employed, narrative form, etc." (Jamieson/Cappella, 1997: 39). As highlighted by Druckman, "the frame leads to alternative representations of the problem and can result in distinct evaluations and preferences" (2011: 6). A competition over which many substantively distinct values or considerations should carry the day results in a *strategic* political environment of *competing* information (see Berelson et al. 1986; Schattschneider 1960). Two common frames include emphasis framing and equivalence framing.

Emphasis framing is a persuasion technique that draws attention to specific aspects that encourage certain interpretations of the relevant context and discourage others (see Schutz 2013a). It applies to a broad range of decisions where no "correct answer" exists. Politicians, interest groups and media outlets strive to shape the preferences of ordinary individuals whose opinions affect electoral outcomes and often guide day-to-day policy decisions (e.g., Erikson/MacKuen/Stimson 2002).

Equivalence framing is defined as purposely stating or logically portraying equivalent information in a way that encourages specific interpretations and discourages others. This is in order to alter our preferences. Whereas emphasis framing focuses on different information, equivalence framing focuses on the same information while attempting to phrase it in the most compelling way (see Schutz, 2013b). For example, Nelson, Clawson and Oxley (1997) studied people's willingness to allow hate groups to conduct a rally. They found that specific framing was significant in affecting an individual's views of the opposing arguments (free speech vs public safety) and caused them to adjust their preferences accordingly.

In the current research, both frames were employed by the Israeli press in communicating the aftermath of each episode of political violence (either successful or unsuccessful from the Israeli point of view), which affected each Israeli's national identification.

3 Data, measures, method

To test the effect of discrepant outcomes of political violence on individual national identification at the micro level, it was necessary to focus on one particular country. Due to theoretical and methodological considerations, the study was restricted to Israel. As the theory that formed the basis of this study required group members to respond to various outcomes of political violence, it was necessary to identify a country that experienced recurrent violence with diverse outcomes. Israel has experienced chronic and persistent political violence that has been characterised by periods of fighting, such as wars and military operations. During the years that the study was conducted, from 2003 to 2013, Israel endured nine periods of political violence, which thereby fulfilled the aforementioned prerequisite.

Furthermore, political violence has a salient presence in the lives of Israelis, as the country is only 22,072 km², and the relevant fighting periods concerned both its southern ("Pillar of Defence" and "Protective Edge") and northern borders ("Second Lebanon War"). Given the high levels of exposure to political violence, both in scale and in frequency, along with the availability of micro-level survey data, the case of Israel is particularly suitable for studying the relationship between discrepancy and national identification in the aftermath of political violence. In addition, until recently national identification in Europe had largely declined across generations. This was in reaction to the extreme nationalism that led to World War II, and to globalisation and political integration (see Smith/Kim 2006). In this regard, Israel is an exception.

Whereas Judaism is a cohesive element for most of the country's residents and a core element in Israel's existence as a Jewish nation-state (despite undeniable religious-secular disputes, Levy et al. 2002), Israeli society is characterised by high heterogeneity, with class, religious, national, ethnic and cultural differences separating the various groups that it is comprised of.

In its early years of nationhood, Israel's cohesive value was establishing pioneer settlements (see Eisenstadt 2019), and it based its new Israeli-Jewish identity on the concept of Zionism (see Sachar 2013). However, during the last several decades, the consensus surrounding the question "what does it mean to be Israeli?" has been subject to extensive scrutiny. Nowadays, this meaning is defined differently by each of the social subgroups. Recent trends in Israeli social and academic discourse even include "post-Zionism" or "anti-Zionism", casting doubt on the need for Israel to be defined as "the Jewish state" (see Arian et al. 2007).

Despite its high heterogeneity, one observes many signs that there are high levels of national identification, both in ordinary times and during periods of national crises (see Arian et al. 2010). Lastly, the methodological considerations for using Israel as a case study include the availability of high-quality survey data and the ability to control for country-specific characteristics.

3.1 The selection of episodes of political violence

Following Schneider et al. (2017), the episodes of political violence used in the current research were identified by the Penn State Event Data Project (PSEDP) based on a temporal criterion. The PSEDP uses automated coding of news reports in order to generate political event data that has the Middle East, the Balkans and West Africa as its focus. The project researchers coded Reuters and Agence France Presse (AFP) articles using two different coding schemes: World Event Interaction Survey (WEIS) and Conflict & Mediation Event Observations (CAMEO). As in Schneider et al. 2017, the CAMEO scheme was chosen over the WEIS scheme, as the former is available until 2015. The AFP CAMEO Levant data set includes 246,382 events (after duplicate filtering) and covers April 1979 to March 2015. After removing events in which Israel was not involved and events that did not occur within the study's timeframe, the project researchers selected events coded as "fight[7]".

Nine episodes of political violence were identified following the cross-referencing of events that were coded as "fight" with data from secondary sources (the Israeli Defense Forces spokesperson unit's website, the IDF's news archive search engine, the Al Jazeera website). A manual check was also conducted in order to validate that the events were not incorrectly coded. The list was also checked for consistency with events coded as "ceasefires", as several of the chosen fighting episodes were concluded with a ceasefire. Due to data availability, five of the nine episodes of political violence (four military operations and one war) were analysed in the current research[8] (see tab. 1).

---

[7] The AFP CAMEO dataset uses seven codes for conflict-related events: "Use conventional military force", "Impose blockade & restrict movement", "Occupy territory", "Fight with small arms and light weapons", "Fight with artillery and tanks", and "Employ aerial weapons".

[8] Other operations ('Rainbow', 'Summer Rains', 'Autumn Clouds', 'Hot Winter', and 'Returning Echo', aka March 2012 Gaza–Israel clashes) took place during this period. However, given that their outcomes were undetermined due to insufficient media coverage, they were excluded from the analysis.

Tab. 1: Episodes of Political Violence Used in the Research 2004–2013

ID	Name Given by the IDF	Short Background	Start Date	End Date	Actors Involved	Outcome Perceived by Israelis[9]
1	Operation "Days of Penitence/Repentance"	Most substantial IDF incursion into Gaza since the start of the Al-Aqsa intifada in September 2000, launched following the death of two Israeli children from a rocket launched by militants in the strip.	29/09/ 2004	16/10/ 2004	IDF & Palestinian terror organisations, primarily Hamas	Favourable
2	Operation "First Rain"	Israeli Air Force week-long offensive launched against Hamas and Islamic Jihad targets in Gaza following the extensive firing of rockets at Israeli communities in southern Israel.	23/09/ 2005	01/10/ 2005	IDF, Hamas & Islamic Jihad	Favourable
3	Second Lebanon War	Israeli joint airstrike and ground invasion of southern Lebanon precipitated by the firing of rockets from Lebanon at Israeli border towns and the abduction of two IDF soldiers by Hezbollah.	12/07/ 2006	14/08/ 2006	IDF & Hezbollah	Unfavourable
4	Operation "Cast Led:"/Gaza War	A vast three-week military operation by Israeli air, naval, artillery and ground forces in the Gaza Strip. Resulted in a high casualty rate.	27/12/ 2008	18/01/ 2009	IDF & Hamas	Favourable

---

9 Constructed by the author based on a manual evaluative assertion analysis – a type of content analysis used to "extract from a message the evaluations being made of significant concepts" (Osgood et al, 1956: 47).

ID	Name Given by the IDF	Short Background	Start Date	End Date	Actors Involved	Outcome Perceived by Israelis[9]
5	Operation "Pillar of Defense"	An eight-day IDF operation in the Hamas-governed Gaza Strip. Commenced in response to the killing of the chief of the Gaza military wing of Hamas and the launch of over 100 rockets towards Israel for 24 hours.	14/11/2012	21/11/2012	IDF, PRC, Al-Aqsa Martyrs, Hamas,	Unfavourable

3.2 Survey measures

The data concerning Israeli national identification originates from five social surveys that were administered between 2005 and 2013 as part of the Israeli Democracy Index (IDI). The data was collected by the Guttman Center for Public Opinion and Policy Research, a branch of the Israeli Democracy Institute (see Arian et al. 2009), which holds the most comprehensive database on public opinion in Israel. IDI surveys evaluate the quality and functioning of Israeli democracy by collecting quantified and comparable information regarding three main aspects: institutions, rights & stability and social cohesion (see Arian et al. 2003). Annual interviews were conducted with representative samples (about 1,200 individuals) of the adult population in Israel in Hebrew, Arabic and Russian. While 12 surveys were conducted during the specified timeframe, only those that took place following the conclusion of each episode of political violence were analysed.

3.3 National identification

The dependent variable in the empirical analysis is national identification, proxied by national pride, the positive feeling that individuals have about their country as a result of their national identity (see Smith/Kim 2006). National pride was found to be a function of a variety of individual-specific characteristics (see Evans/Kelley 2002) such as national identification (see Dimitrova-Grajzl et al. 2016), market conditions (see Lan/Li 2015) and contemporary events (see Kavetsos 2012). *National Pride* was operationalised through respondents' answers to the question "*How proud are you to be Israeli?*[10]". Responses ranged from "not proud at all" to "very proud".

3.4 Perceived aftermath of political violence

The independent variable was constructed based on a manual evaluative assertion analysis (see Schneider et al. 2017) of relevant articles and commentaries that originated in the three daily newspapers with the largest total readership in Israel (see Mana 2015): *Yediot Aharonot, Ma'ariv* and *Ha'aretz*. Since the research examines changes in national pride levels among Israelis, objective measurements that may reflect "success", if they even exist, are unbeknownst to Israelis. Consequently, they are less likely to shape public opinion than the media frames that Israelis are exposed to. *Perceived outcome* was operationalised as the perceived aftermath of each episode of political violence (according to table 1) from the Israeli point of view: favourable/victory (1) and unfavourable/defeat (0).

3.5 Control variables

Since no relevant panel data is available in Israel, it was deemed necessary to control for those respondent personal characteristics that were likely to affect national identification (see Coenders/Scheepers 2003; Stubager 2009). Consequently, *religiosity, education, age, gender* and *social class* are also included in the analysis. Assessing respondents' membership in social and ethnic groups was based on the *social group* variable, which refers to the social group that respondents chose to associate themselves with (Jews/Arabs/Immigrants).

Whereas in the past, anti-nationalist arguments for nationhood were wielded mainly by the political left, and arguments ranging from anti-universalist premises to positive national values usually originated in the political right, left-wing liberals and social democrats now deploy a nation-affirming set of arguments as often as conservatives (see Benner 1997). Consequently, political affiliation was expected to play a pivotal role in determining the impact of Israeli military operations on national pride. Political orientation was measured on a 5-point scale, ranging from right to left. Two macro-economic indicators of the performance of

---

[10] One should take into consideration the problematic nature of using social surveys to collect this type of data. The usage of vague concepts such as "pride" leaves room for various interpretations, thus creating the problems of interpersonal incomparability (Bauer et al. 2014; King et al. 2003) or measurement inequivalence (e.g. Davidov et al. 2014; Freitag/Bauer 2013).

Israel's economy were also added as controls; *economic growth* and *inflation* rate[11]. While the former can elevate national pride levels, the latter might depress it.

4 Findings

Being comprised of different ethnic and religious minorities, contemporary Israeli society is highly diverse. The Israeli public chronically and persistently experienced political violence: between 2004 and 2013, Israel experienced nine periods of fighting, each lasting from a few days to up to several months.

In order to get a preliminary sense of the fluctuation of national pride within the relevant timeframe, Figure 1 charts the perceived outcomes of this violence and the mean values of national pride across various social groups in Israel. As answers to the relevant question ranged from (1) very proud to (4) not at all proud, it is important to note that a lower mean marks a higher level of national pride.

Jewish Israelis demonstrate the highest levels of national identification, whereas Arab Israelis demonstrate the lowest levels when compared with Jewish Israelis and the general population. National identification levels among Israeli immigrants are similar to those observed by the overall population: low compared with the majority group (native Jewish Israelis), and high compared with the largest ethnic minority group (Arab Israelis). The existence of fluctuations in national identification across social and ethnic groups is also apparent.

When considering the difference in mean values following Israeli victories and defeats among the broader Israeli society, these appear to be relatively small. An increase in overall national pride levels is apparent after the successful completion of operations "First Rain" and "Days of Penitence" in 2004–2005 (-.11). A sharp decrease is observed following the unsuccessful cessation of the Second Lebanon War (in which the Israeli Defense Forces failed to secure the return of Israeli soldier Gilad Shalit[12]) in 2006[13] (+0.22). The successful termination of operation "Cast Lead" (aka the Gaza war) seems to bring about a slight increase in

---

[11] The measures are based on annual World Development Indicators for Israel for the year of the surveys. *Economic growth* is Israel's real GDP growth per survey year and *inflation* is the rate of inflation in consumer prices.
[12] Shalit was captured by Hamas militants on 25/06/2006 in a cross-border raid via tunnels near the Israeli border with the Gaza strip. He was eventually released on 18/10/2011 in a prisoner exchange deal (see Bergman 2011).
[13] As this war was fought in the summer of 2006, the following survey, which took place in 2007, was utilised (thus appearing under 2007 in Figure 1).

national pride (-.8). Finally, a very mild increase in national pride (-.5) appears in 2013, following the unsuccessful completion of operation "Pillar of Defense".

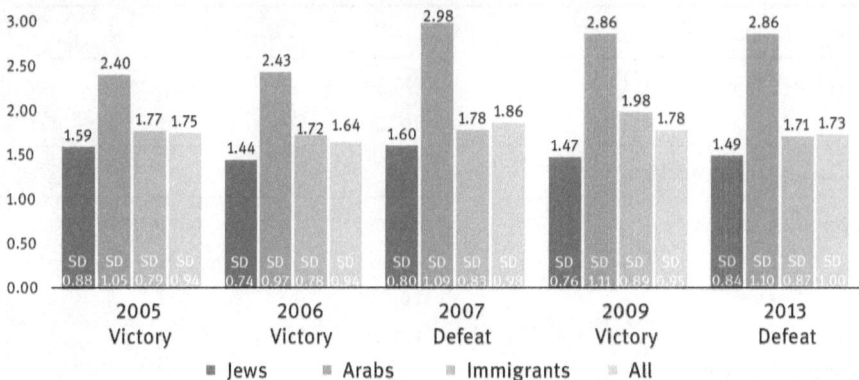

Fig. 1: Mean Values of National Pride Levels Across Social Groups in Israel Following Various Victories and Defeats.

Apart from the latter[14], fluctuations in national identification appear to align with predictions based on social identity theory: the successful completion of Israeli military operations are associated with increased national identification among the general population and vice versa.

When considering the fluctuations in national identification among minority groups, the data appears to be only partially consistent with the "minority hypothesis". Among Israeli immigrants, an increase in national pride was registered following the victory in 2005 (-0.05), but not following the successes in 2006 (+0.06) and 2009 (+0.2). Moreover, whereas the defeat in the Second Lebanon War was associated with decreased national pride (+0.06), the unsuccessful completion of operation "Pillar of Defense" in 2013 is associated with increased pride (-0.27).

Among Arab Israelis, an opposite tendency is observed: among members of this ethnic minority, a decreased national pride level was associated with Israeli victories (+0.3 in 2005 and +0.55 in 2006). In contrast, the defeat in the Second Lebanon War in 2006 was associated with increased pride (-0.12). No change in national pride was registered following the Israeli loss in 2013.

---

14 This may be the result of using a smaller sample size for the 2013 survey (1,000 respondents compared with 1,200 in previous years) and a larger maximum sampling error (3.2 compared with 2.8 in previous surveys).

Tab. 2: The Effects of Outcomes of Episodes of Political Violence on Israeli National Pride

	Model 1	Model 2
National pride		
Victories (-defeats)	-0.303***	-0.177***
	(-5.97)	(-3.46)
Individual-Level Variables		
Observing tradition	-0.092***	-0.094***
	(-3.31)	(-3.43)
Social class	0.009	0.011
	(0.22)	(0.30)
Social group: Arabs	1.946***	1.963***
	(9.80)	(9.47)
Social group: Immigrants	0.772***	0.760***
	(3.57)	(3.67)
Education	0.055**	0.054**
	(2.93)	(2.84)
Gender	0.036	0.037
	(0.99)	(1.00)
Age	-0.009***	-0.009***
	(-6.40)	(-6.12)
Political identity	0.196***	0.190***
	(4.83)	(4.78)
Country-Level Variables		
Economic growth		0.016
		(1.16)
Inflation		0.067***
		(8.41)
cut1_cons	1.062***	1.380***
	(9.05)	(5.74)
cut2_cons	2.593***	2.912***
	(18.61)	(11.93)
cut3_cons	3.858***	4.178***
	(34.38)	(20.22)
AIC	10184.02	10178.48

	Model 1	Model 2
BIC[15]	10203.5	10197.96
LogL (model)	-5089.009	-5086.24
N	4,886	4,886

Note: The estimations are the result of ordinal logit regression (STATA 14). The table reports coefficients, and t statistics can be found in parentheses. Clustering according to survey year. * p<0.05 ** p<0.01 *** p<0.001.

As is apparent from the preliminary findings (which are descriptive and do not assume causation), discrepant political violence outcomes (whether favourable or unfavourable from the Israeli point of view) seem to be influenced by membership in a social/ethnic group. I now turn to the statistical analysis of these relationships.

Table 2 depicts the results of two ordinal logistic regression models[16]. In Model 1, I examine the effects of individual-level predictors and the outcomes of episodes of political violence on national pride levels among Israelis. In Model 2, country-level predictors are added to the analysis. Military results (victories versus defeats) achieve a high level of significance in both models. As is the case with the preliminary findings, a decrease in value marks an increase in pride. This is due to the utilisation of the dependent variable.

5 Discussion

With its communities of various origins, Israel is a multi-ethnic, deeply divided society that is split along social, ethnic, cultural, religious and political lines.

The results of the statistical analysis of the different models point to a positive effect that victories have on the national pride of the general Israeli population – this was highly associated with an increased national identification. As such, it supported the prevailing hypothesis based on social identity theory (H1).

Membership in minority groups, both ethnic (Arab Israelis) and social (Immigrants), was found to be highly significant insofar as decreased national pride is

---

15 Akaike and Bayesian Information Criterion (AIC, BIC) are probabilistic statistical measures meant to quantify the performance of the model on the dataset (log-likelihood), alongside the complexity of the model (see Browniee 2020).
16 Due to lower BIC and AIC values, the ordinal logistic models are superior to the multilevel mixed-effects ordered logistic models. Consequently, results from the former model are reported in the text.

concerned. In other words, Israeli victories were not associated with increased national pride for Arab Israelis and Immigrants. Quite to the contrary: military operations that ended favourably (from the Israeli point of view) were associated with decreased national pride among members of these two minority groups. Consequently, this supported the "minority hypothesis".

5.1 What can account for the observed decrease in national pride following Israeli victories among members of the examined minority groups?

As a homeland of the Jewish people that was founded on a Zionist-Jewish narrative, no plurality of ethnic discourse existed in Israel for over 50 years (see Hadar 2019: 21). Yet Israel is home to a large Arab population (constituting one-fifth of the country's population), most of whom self-identify as Palestinians. Consequently, both Palestinian nationalism and Israeli citizenship shape the collective identity of the Arab community in Israel (see Peleg/Waxman 2011: 31). Exploring identity shifts among Arab Israel in the 21st century, Peleg & Waxman (2011) point to a process of "Palestinisation'" – a gradual transition from an Arab Israeli identity (a result of "Israelisation" – integration into Israel's Jewish society) to a more entrenched Palestinian identity (see Peleg/Waxman 2011, 27).

As the largest ethnic minority, Arab Israelis have full citizenship and are guaranteed equal protection under Israeli law. However, as non-Jews, Arab Israelis are, by definition, excluded from the national Jewish narrative and full participation in society (see Tessler 1977: 313). According to Abu-Saad (2006): "The centrality of the notion of 'Jewishness' to Israel's national identity has been translated, in practical terms, into the subordination of the indigenous Palestinian Arab minority [...] to the Jewish majority" (Abu-Saad, 2004, Lewin-Epstein and Semyonov, 2019).

Israeli exclusionism and discriminatory practices against its largest outgroup – Arab Israelis – include interpersonal and institutional ethnic discrimination (e.g., Daoud et al. 2018, Enos et al. 2018), ethnic segregation, income inequality (e.g., Lewin-Epstein/Semyonov 1992, Semyonov/Lewin-Epstein 2011) and limitation of citizenship rights (see Alcott 2018, Saïd 2020). Persistent ethnic intolerance and racist incidents against Arab Israelis were also documented by reports produced outside of the academy (see Hermann et al. 2012, Adalah 2016, Amnesty International 2021).

While Judaism, the Holocaust and the Israeli–Palestinian conflict were instrumentalised in creating a cohesive Israeli (Jewish) society during Israel's first decades of nationhood, Arabs were villainised (see Hadar et al. 2022). This further contributed to the exclusion of Arab Israelis from Israeli society.

When it comes to the Israeli-Palestinian Conflict, Arab Israelis are caught between a rock and a hard place. On the one hand, Arab Israelis are loyal to their Palestinian brothers and sisters and support their quest for self-determination (see Russell 2021). On the other hand, Arab Israelis have personal and economic interests that are equally and existentially threatened when Israel experiences political violence with a negative outcome.

Immigrants are an example of another large minority group in Israeli society[17]. Israel's active encouragement of Jewish immigration since its very inception (1948) resulted in a constant flow of immigrants arriving from various countries. Over 3.3 million immigrants made Israel their home, about 44.3% of whom immigrated from 1990 onwards (see Central Bureau of Statistics 2020a). In the two and a half years that followed Israeli statehood, approximately 687,000 Jewish immigrants entered the state, mainly from Europe. This was followed by 1.6 million Immigrants from Arabic-speaking Middle Eastern countries and North Africa. The collapse of the Soviet Union (1989–1991) marked the beginning of yet another massive immigration wave to Israel.

Over a million citizens of the former Soviet Union (FSU) have arrived in Israel since 1989 (see Galili 2020), 80% of whom immigrated between 1990 and 2001. As the Israeli population in 1988 was roughly 4.4 million, it is no wonder that the tension between native Israelis and immigrants became one of the prevalent social rifts in Israeli society (see Al Haj 2004). Immigration from the FSU continues to this day, but at a much slower pace[18] (see Central Bureau of Statistics 2019). While they are predominantly Jewish, and thus belong to the majority ethnic group, FSU immigrants constitute a distinct cultural and linguistic group in Israeli society (see Galili/Bronfman 2013).

Jewish immigration to Israel was established in the "Law of Return" enacted in 1950, which stated the right of every Jew to immigrate to Israel. As discrepancies[19] exist between the definition of "Jewish' according to the Law of Return and

---

[17] In 2019, immigrants constituted 21% of the Israeli population. The main countries of origin are FSU (49%), Morocco (7%) and the United States (5%) (OECD 2021).
[18] Even in recent years, the vast majority of immigrants to Israel arrive from the FSU (Central Bureau of Statistics 2020a). In 2015, immigration from France peaked (6,628 immigrants arrived in Israel). However, a decrease in the number of immigrants from France is apparent in recent years (Central Bureau of Statistics 2020a). At the end of 2019, approximately 87,500 Ethiopian-born persons lived in Israel (Central Bureau of Statistics 2020b).
[19] The "Law of Return" utilises a wide definition of the term for citizenship purposes. According to the law, a person that had, or was married to a person who had one Jewish grandparent

the Rabbinical Law (Jewish religious law), more than 340,000 Russian-speaking Israeli citizens are not considered Jewish from a religious perspective (see Haskin 2016, Tolts 2017). The results of this discrepancy are not insignificant, especially since the Chief Rabbinate of Israel has sole jurisdiction over many aspects of Jewish life, including personal status issues (marriages, divorce, burial, etc.) (see Tartakovsky 2012). As such, "the gap between the strict religious definition of 'kosher Jewishness' and a broader view of proper 'Israeliness' has remained a high-profile social issue for Russian *olim* (immigrants)" (Remennick/Prashizky 2012: 61).

National consensus regarding the constant threat to Israel's survival and the compulsory army service for the majority of the Israeli population (Jewish men and women[20]) secured the role of the Israeli Defence Force (IDF) as *a* key to Israeli-Jewish identity (see Herzog 1998). As the defender of the Jewish nation-state and the country's most universal social institution (see Perko 2003), the IDF was crucial in cultivating national consciousness and patriotism among Israelis during Israel's first decades of statehood (see Hadar/Häkkinen 2022). While the depiction of the IDF as "a people's army" has lost some of its strength[21], the IDF remains an instrument of conveying a sense of national identity among Jewish Israelis[22]. Arab Israelis are exempt from mandatory service in the IDF, whereas Jewish immigrants are either exempt from service or serve a shorter time than native Israeli Jews (depending on their age). As such, it is no surprise that members of these minority groups exhibit lower levels of national identification in comparison with the Jewish native population. Moreover, the fact that these populations were not directly instrumental in favourable military outcomes supports the findings of this study.

Consistent with the academic literature, most of the control variables reached significant levels. Whereas both age and level of religiosity (observance of tradition) have a strong and positive effect on national pride, education has a negative effect, but is less significant. Interestingly, political affiliation was found to be highly significant in decreasing national pride. While social class and economic growth yielded insignificant results in this regard, inflation appears to profoundly and negatively affect national pride.

---

qualifies for Israeli citizenship. As per Rabbinical law, Jewishness passes through the maternal line only, and only Orthodox conversion to Judaism is acknowledged.

20 Religious women and ultra-orthodox men and women are exempted. Non-Jews (Muslims, Bedouins, Druze, etc.) may choose to volunteer for service, but are not legally obliged to serve.

21 Due to the growing segments of the Jewish population that are being excused from duty.

22 Even nowadays, serving in the IDF is regarded by many Israelis as a rite of passage to full citizenship where immigrants are concerned (see Hadar/Häkkinen 2022).

5.2 A vicious cycle of exclusionism and violence

The analysis of the impact of Israeli warfare on national identification among social groups revealed that the impact is highly influenced by the perceived outcome of the warfare (from the Israeli point of view) and by subgroup membership (minority vs majority). It was argued that the marginalisation of minority groups might account for the discrepancy in outcomes, as members of such groups may not view Israeli military success as their own. Yet we should also note that increased social exclusion was found to be a long-term effect of exposure to political violence.

Scholarship exploring the relationship between threat perceptions, political extremism and exclusionism points to the impact of these factors on social identity and, consequently, group identity (e.g., Canetti-Nisim et al. 2009; Canetti et al. 2008; Canetti et al. 2017; Shamir/Sagiv-Schifter 2006).

Threat perception[23] has been considered by many as the "single best predictor of hostile intergroup attitudes" (Canetti-Nisim et al., 2008: 90 citing Sullivan, 1985; Quilliam 1985; Stephan & Stephan 2000). While much research focuses on the relationship between the views of the Jewish communities towards Arab Israelis, Riek et al. (2006) and Stephan et al. (2009) highlighted that threats could also promote animosity towards out-groups not directly related to the threats.

Immigrants, for example, are often seen as both real threats to the political and economic power of the in-group and symbolic threats, as they may differ in values, beliefs and attitudes (see Stephan/Stephan 2000; Esses et al. 2001; Stephan et al. 2005). As such, studies also pointed to the relationship between threat perceptions and different types of anti-immigrant exclusionism (e.g., Sniderman et al. 2004; Stephan et al. 2005; Halperin et al. 2009). Consequently, according to social identity theory, recurring instances of warfare seem to solidify social fragmentation and the derogation of out-groups (see Tajfel/Turner 1986). At the same time, exclusionism and marginalisation of minority groups reinforce their self-perception as out-groups, which may account for why they exhibit decreased national identification (even following Israeli victories).

---

[23] Alongside the impact of emotions triggered as a result of exposure to violence (e.g. fear, hatred and anger, Halperin 2008).

6 Conclusion

In this paper, I raise several important yet neglected questions: what is the impact of discrepant political violence outcomes on group identification? Is the impact influenced by group performance (success/failure from the Israeli point of view) and does it vary across social groups (minority vs majority) within Israeli society? These questions are critical when the longevity of national identification is concerned and when a country is faced with recurring episodes of political violence. Due to its diverse society, multiple episodes of political violence with various aftermaths, and available data, Israel has proven to be an excellent case for examining the aforementioned questions.

The experience of being subject to persistent political violence, framed as successfully or unsuccessfully completed by the local media, had an interesting effect on the Israeli public. The study demonstrates that different outcomes of political violence significantly affect group identification. Consistent with social identity theory and the self-esteem protection/enhancement strategies derived from it (BIRGing and CORFing), the general Israeli population experienced an increase in national pride following Israeli victories.

Upon disaggregating Israeli society, a clear difference emerged between the three largest communities in Israel: Arab Israelis, native Jewish Israelis and immigrants. Compared with native Jewish Israelis, members of minority groups (both ethnic Arab Israelis and social/cultural immigrants) did not exhibit increased national pride following Israeli military victories. Quite to the contrary: Israeli victories were associated with decreased national pride among members of both groups. This finding is consistent with academic literature exploring minority groups. One may attribute this the well-documented marginalisation of these groups, which underpinned their view and self-perception as "out-groups" (whereas native Jewish Israelis are perceived as an "in-group").

Israeli Arabs, the largest minority group in Israel, shares neither the country's Jewish narrative nor its Zionist ethos. Immigrants, predominantly from the FSU, experience marginalisation along cultural and religious lines. The latter can be attributed to the discrepancy between the civic and religious definition of "Jewish". Additionally, as both groups are not directly instrumental to favourable military outcomes, group members do not perceive Israeli military successes as "their own". Decreased national pride among Arab Israelis following Israeli victories can also be attributed to the ethnic nature of the warfare, the Israeli-Palestinian conflict and the fact that Arab Israelis often identify as Palestinians.

The erosion of national identification among marginalised minority groups is a worrying phenomenon not only for Israel, but for any highly heterogenous society experiencing recurring political violence, even if it has a successful outcome.

References

a. Research literature

Abrams, Dominic Ed/Hogg, Michael A. (1990): *Social identity theory: Constructive and critical advances*. Springer-Verlag Publishing.

Abu-Saad, Ismael (2004): "Separate and unequal: The consequences of racism and discrimination against Palestinian Arabs in the educational system in Israel". In: *Social Identities* 10 (2), 101–127.

Abu-Saad, Ismael. (2006): "State Educational Policy and Curriculum: The Case of Palestinian Arabs in Israel". In: *International Education Journal* 7 (5), 709–720.

Ahlerup, Pelle/Hansson, Gustav (2011): "Nationalism and government effectiveness". In: *Journal of Comparative Economics* 39 (3), 431–451.

Al Haj, Majid (2004): *Immigration and ethnic formation in a deeply divided society: The case of the 1990s immigrants from the Former Soviet Union in Israel*. Leiden/Boston: Brill.

Alcott, Blake (2018): "Palestine's Legitimate Citizenry". In: *Global Jurist* 18 (3), 23–46.

Bar, Revital/Zussman, Asaf (2017): "Customer discrimination: evidence from Israel". In: *Journal of Labor Economics* 35 (4), 1031–1059.

Bar-Tal, Daniel (2013): *Intractable conflicts: Socio-psychological foundations and dynamics*. Cambridge University Press.

Bauer, Paul C./Barbera, Pablo/Ackermann, Kathrin/Venetz, Aaron (2014): "Vague concepts in survey questions: A general problem illustrated with the left-right scale". In: *EPSA Conference*.

Becker, Michael A./Suls, Jerry (1983): "Take me out to the ballgame: The effects of objective, social, and temporal performance information on attendance at major league baseball games". In: *Journal of Sport Psychology* 5, 302–313.

Bekhuis, Hidde/Lubbers, Marchel/Verkuyten, Maykel (2013): "How education moderates the relation between globalisation and nationalist attitudes". In: *International Journal of Public Opinion Research* 26, 487–500.

Bendix, Reinhard (1980): *Kings or people: Power and the mandate to rule*. University of California Press.

Benner, Erica (1997): "Nationality Without Nationalism". In: *Journal of Political Ideology* 2, 189–206.

Berelson, Bernard R./Lazarsfeld, Paul F./McPhee, William N. (1986): *Voting: A study of opinion formation in a presidential campaign*. University of Chicago Press.

Brenner, Phillip S./Serpe, Richard T./Stryker, Sheldon (2014): "The causal ordering of prominence and salience in identity theory: An empirical examination". In: *Social psychology quarterly* 77 (3), 231–252.

Canetti-Nisim, Daphna/Pedahzur, Ami. (2003): "Contributory factors to Political Xenophobia in a multi-cultural society: the case of Israel". In: *International Journal of Intercultural Relations* 27 (3), 307–333.

Canetti-Nisim, Daphna/Ariely, Guy/Halperin, Eran (2008): "Life, pocketbook, or culture: The role of perceived security threats in promoting exclusionist political attitudes toward minorities in Israel". In: *Political Research Quarterly* 61 (1), 90–103.
Canetti-Nisim, Daphna/Halperin, Eran/Sharvit, Keren/Hobfoll, Stevan E. (2009): "A new stress-based model of political extremism: Personal exposure to terrorism, psychological distress, and exclusionist political attitudes". In: *Journal of Conflict Resolution* 53 (3), 363–389.
Canetti, Daphna/Elad-Strenger, Julia/Lavi, Iris/Guy, Dana/Bar-Tal, Daniel (2017): "Exposure to violence, ethos of conflict, and support for compromise: Surveys in Israel, East Jerusalem, West Bank, and Gaza". In: *Journal of conflict resolution* 61 (1), 84–113.
Cialdini, Robert B./Borden, Richard J./Thorne, Avril/Walker, Marcus R./Freeman, Stephen/Sloan, Leynold R. (1976): "Basking in reflected glory: Three (football) field studies". In: *Journal of personality and social psychology* 34 (3), 366–375.
Coenders, Marcel/Scheepers, Peer (2003): "The effect of education on nationalism and ethnic exclusionism: An international comparison". In: *Political Psychology* 24, 313–343.
Cratty, Bryant J (1983): *Psychology in contemporary sport: guidelines for coaches and athletes*. Englewood Cliffs: Prentice-Hall.
Daoud, Nihaya/Gao, Meiyin/Osman, Amira/Muntaner, Carles (2018): "Interpersonal and institutional ethnic discrimination, and mental health in a random sample of Palestinian minority men smokers in Israel". In: *Social psychiatry and psychiatric epidemiology* 53 (10), 1111–1122.
Davidov, Eldad/Meuleman, Bart/Cieciuch, Jan/Schmidt, Peter/Billiet, Jaak (2014): "Measurement equivalence in cross-national research". In: *Annual Review of Sociology* 40, 55–75.
Dimitrova-Grajzl, Valentina/Eastwood, Jonathan/Grajzl, Peter (2016): "The longevity of national identity and national pride: Evidence from wider Europe". In: *Research & Politics* 3 (2), 1–9.
Dowley, Kathleen M./Silver, Brian D. (2000): "Subnational and national loyalty: Cross-national comparisons". In: *International Journal of Public Opinion Research* 12, 357–371.
Druckman, James N. (2011): "What's it all about? Framing in political science". In: Keren, Gideon (ed.), *Perspectives on Framing*. New York: Psychology Press, 279–302.
Eisenstadt, Shmuel Noah (2019): *The transformation of Israeli society: An essay in interpretation*. New York: Routledge.
Emler, Nicholas/Hopkins, Nicholas (1990): "Reputation, social identity, and the self". In: Dominic Abrams/Michael A. Hogg (eds.): *Social Identity Theory: Constructive and Critical Advances*. New York: Springer-Verlag.
Enos, Ryan D./Gidron, Noam (2018): "Exclusion and cooperation in diverse societies: Experimental evidence from Israel". In: *American Political Science Review* 112 (4), 742–757.
Erikson, Robert S./MacKuen, Michael B./Stimson, James A. (2002): *The macro polity*. Cambridge University Press.
Esses, Victoria M./John F. Dovidio/Lynne M. Jackson/Tamara L. Armstrong. (2001): "The immigration dilemma: The role of perceived group competition, ethnic prejudice, and national identity". In: *Journal of Social Issues* 57 (3), 389–412.
Evans, Mariah D./Kelley, Jonathan (2002): "National pride in the developed world: Survey data from 24 nations". In: *International Journal of Public Opinion Research* 14, 303–338.
Freitag, Markus/Bauer, Paul C. (2013): "Testing for measurement equivalence in surveys: Dimensions of social trust across cultural contexts". In: *Public Opinion Quarterly* 77, 24–44.
Galili, Lily/Bronfman, Roman (2013): *The Million That Changed the Middle East: Soviet Immigration to Israel* [in Hebrew]. Tel Aviv: Matar.

Ghanem, As'as (2016): "Israel's second-class citizens: Arabs in Israel and the struggle for equal rights". In: *Foreign Affairs* 95, 37–42.

Gilroy, Paul (1997): "Diaspora and the detours of identity". In: Kathryn Woodward (ed.) *Identity and Difference*. London: Sage Publications, 299–343.

Gitlin, Todd (2003): "The whole world is watching: Mass media in the making & unmaking of the new left". University of California Press.

Golan-Agnon, Daphna (2006): Separate but not equal: Discrimination against Palestinian Arab students in Israel. In: *American Behavioral Science* 49 (8), 1075–1084.

Gurr, Ted Robert, 2000. *Peoples versus states: Minorities at risk in the new century*. US Institute of Peace Press.

Gusterson, Hugh (2017): "From Brexit to Trump: Anthropology and the rise of nationalist populism". In: *American Ethnologist* 44 (2), 209–214.

Hadar, Maya (2019): "Renegotiating Israeli Identities, Collective Victimhood and Social Exclusion of Arab Israelis in a Changing Social Reality". In: *Psychology and Developing Societies* 31 (1), 7–30.

Hadar, Maya/Häkkinen Teemu (forthcoming 2021): "Conscription and Willingness to Defend as Cornerstones of National Defence in Israel and Finland". In: *Journal of Political and Military Sociology*.

Hadar, Maya/Miesch, Regula/Segev, Elad (2022): "Politicising the Holocaust: A comparative analysis of Israeli and German speeches". In: Elad Segev (ed.): *Semantic Network Analysis in Social Sciences*. New York: Routledge, 94–111.

Halperin, Eran (2008): "Group-based hatred in intractable conflict in Israel". In: *Journal of Conflict Resolution* 52 (5), 713–736.

Halperin, Eran/Canetti-Nisim, Daphna/Hirsch-Hoefler, Sivan (2009): "The Central Role of Group-Based Hatred as an Emotional Antecedent of Political Intolerance: Evidence from Israel". In: *Political Psychology* 30 (1), 93–123.

Haskin, Arie (2016): "Non-jewish Immigrants from the FSU." In: Tudor Parfitt/Netanel Fisher (eds.): *Becoming Jewish: New Jews and emerging Jewish communities in a globalised world*. Cambridge Scholars Publishing, 243–258.

Herzl, Theodor (1896): *The Jewish State (trans. Sylvie d'Avigdor)*. London: NuttPress.

Herzog, Hanna (1998): "Women's status in the shadow of security". In: Daniel Bar Tal/Dan Jacobson/Aharon S. Klieman (eds.): *Security concerns: Insights from the Israeli experience* Stamford, CT: JAI Press.

Hirt, Edward R./Zillmann, Dolf/Erickson, Grant A./Kennedy, Chris (1992): "Costs and benefits of allegiance: Changes in fans' self-ascribed competencies after team victory versus defeat". In: *Journal of personality and social psychology* 63 (5), 724–738.

Iyengar, Shanto (1990): "The accessibility bias in politics: Television news and public opinion". In: *International Journal of Public Opinion Research*. 2, 1–15.

Jamieson, Kathleen H./Cappella, Joseph N. (1997): "Setting the record straight: Do ad watches help or hurt?". In: *Harvard International Journal of Press/Politics* 2 (1), 13–22.

Johnson, Elmer H. (1973): *Social problems of urban man*. Homewood: Dorsey press.

Kavetsos, Georgios (2012): "National pride: War minus the shooting". In: *Social indicators research* 106 (1), 173–185.

King, Gary/Murray, Christopher J./Salomon, Joshua A./Tandon, Ajay (2003): "Enhancing the validity and cross-cultural comparability of measurement in survey research". In: *American political science review* 98 (1), 567–583.

Konrad, Kai A./Qari, Salma (2012): "The last refuge of a scoundrel? Patriotism and tax compliance". In: *Economica* 79, 516–533.

Lan, Xiaouan/Li, Ben G. (2015): "The economics of nationalism". In: *American Economic Journal: Economic Policy* 7 (2), 294–325.

Lewin-Epstein Noah/Semyonov Moshe (1992): "Local-Labor markets, ethnic segregation, and income inequality". In: *Social Forces* 70 (4), 1101–1119.

Lewin-Epstein, Noah/Semyonov, Moshe (2019): *The Arab minority in Israel's economy: Patterns of ethnic inequality.* Routledge.

Manis, Melvin S./Cornell, Douglas/Moore, Jeffrey C. (1974): "Transmission of attitude relevant information through a communication chain". In: *Journal of Personality and Social Psychology* 30 (1), 81–94.

Mayda, Anna M./Rodrik, Dani (2005): "Why are some people (and countries) more protectionist than others?". In: *European Economic Review* 49 (6), 1393–1430.

McCall, George J./Simmons, Jerry L. (1978): *Identities and Interaction.* New York: Free Press.

Morrison, Mike/Tay, Louis/Diener, Ed (2011): "Subjective well-being and national satisfaction: Findings from a worldwide survey". In: *Psychological science* 22 (2), 166–171.

Nelson, Thomas E./Clawson, Rosalee A./Oxley, Zoe M. (1997): "Media framing of a civil liberties conflict and its effect on tolerance". In: *American Political Science Review* 91 (3), 567–583.

Oakes, Penelope J./Turner, John C. (1980): "Social categorisation and intergroup behaviour: Does minimal intergroup discrimination make social identity more positive?". In: *European Journal of Social Psychology* 10, 295–301.

Okun, Barbara S./Friedlander, Dov (2005): "Educational stratification among Arabs and Jews in Israel: Historical disadvantage, discrimination, and opportunity". In: *Popululation Studies* 59 (2), 163–180.

Osborne, Danny/Milojev, Petar/Sibley, Chris G. (2017): "Authoritarianism and national identity: Examining the longitudinal effects of SDO and RWA on nationalism and patriotism". In: *Personality and Social Psychology Bulletin* 43 (8), 1086–1099.

Osgood, Charles/Saporta, Sol/Nunnally, Jum (1956): "Evaluative assertion analysis". In: *Litera* 3, 47–102.

Pedahzur, Ami/Yishai, Yael (1999): "Hatred by hated people: Xenophobia in Israel". In: *Studies in Conflict and Terrorism* 22, 101–17.

Peleg, Ilan/Waxman, Dov (2011): *Israel's Palestinians: the conflict within.* Cambridge University Press.

Perko, F. Michael (2003): "Education, Socialization, and Development of National Identity: The American Common School and Israel Defense Forces in Transnational Perspective." In: *Shofar* 21 (2), 101–119.

Raijman, Rebeca (2010): "Citizenship status, ethno-national origin and entitlement to rights: Majority attitudes towards minorities and immigrants in Israel". In: *Journal of Ethnic and Migration Studies* 36 (1), 87–106.

Raz, Avi (2004): "The stand tall generation: The Palestinian citizens of Israel today". In: *Israel Studies Forum* 19 (2), 136–138.

Reeskens, Tim/Wright, Matthew (2011): "Subjective well-being and national satisfaction: taking seriously the 'proud of what?' question". In: *Psychological Science*, 22 (11), 1460–1462.

Remennick, Larissa/Prashizky, Anna (2012): "Russian Israelis and Religion: What Has Changed after Twenty Years in Israel?". In: *Israel Studies Review* 27 (1), 55–77.

Riek, Blake M./Mania, Eric W./Gaertner, Samuel L. (2006): "Intergroup threat and outgroup attitudes: A meta-analytic review". In: *Personality and Social Psychology Review* 10 (4), 336–353.

Risse, Thomas (2015): *A community of Europeans? Transnational identities and public spheres*. Cornell University Press.

Roberts, Michael (1976): *Fans! How we go crazy over sports*. Washington: New Republic Book Company.

Rosenberg, Morris (1979): *Conceiving the self*. New York: Basic.

Russell, Micah (2021): "Diverging Identities: The Juxtaposition of Palestinians in Israel and the Occupied Territories". In: *Sigma: Journal of Political and International Studies* 38 (1), 2.

Sachar, Howard Morley (2013): *A history of Israel: From the rise of Zionism to our time*. New York: Knopf.

Saïd, Ibrahim L. (2020): "Some are more equal than others: Palestinian citizens in the settler colonial Jewish State". In: *Settler Colonial Studies* 10 (4), 481–507.

Schattschneider, Elmer Eric (1960): "The Semisovereign People". New York: Holt, Rinehart and Winston.

Schneider, Gerald/Hadar, Maya/Bosler, Naomi (2017): "The oracle or the crowd? Experts versus the stock market in forecasting ceasefire success in the Levant". In: *Journal of Peace Research* 54 (2), 231–242.

Semyonov, Moshe/Lewin-Epstein, Noah (2011): "Wealth inequality: ethnic disparities in israeli society". In: *Social Forces* 89 (3), 935–959.

Shamir, Michal/Sagiv-Schifter, Tammy (2006): "Conflict, Identity, and Tolerance: Israel in the Al-Aqsa Intifada". In: *Political Psychology* 27 (4), 569–595.

Smith, Tom William/Jarkko, Lars (1998): *National pride: A cross-national analysis*. Chicago: National Opinion Research Center, University of Chicago.

Smith, Tom William/Kim, Seokho (2006): "National pride in cross-national and temporal perspective". In: *International Journal of Public Opinion Research* 18 (1), 127–136.

Sniderman, Paul M./Theriault, Sean M. (2004): "The structure of political argument and the logic of issue framing." In: Willem E. Saris/Paul M. Sniderman (eds): *Studies in public opinion: Attitudes, nonattitudes, measurement error, and change*. Princeton: Princeton University Press, 133–65.

Snyder, Charles R./Higgins, Raymond L./Stucky, Rita J. (1983): *Excuses: Masquerades in search of grace*. John Wiley & Sons.

Staerklé, Christian/Sidanius, Jim/Green, Eva G./Ludwin, Molina E. (2010): "Ethnic minority-majority asymmetry in national attitudes around the world: A multilevel analysis". In: *Political Psychology* 31(4), 491–519.

Stephan, Walter G./Renfro, Lausanne C./Esses, Victoria M./Stephan, Cookie W./Martin, Tim (2005): "The effects of feeling threatened on attitudes toward immigrants". In: *International Journal of Intercultural Relations* 29 (1), 1–19.

Stephan, Walter G./Ybarra, Oscar/Rios, Kimberly (2009): "Intergroup Threat Theory". In: Nelson Todd D. (eds.): *Handbook of Prejudice, Stereotyping, and Discrimination*. New York: Psychology Press, 43–59.

Stephan, Walter G./Stephan, Cookie W. (2000): "An integrated threat theory of prejudice". In: Stuart Oskamp (ed.): *Reducing prejudice and discrimination*. New York: Psychology Press, 23–45.

Stryker, Sheldon (1968): "Identity salience and role performance: The relevance of symbolic interaction theory for family research". In: *Journal of Marriage and the Family* 30 (4), 558–564.

Stryker, Sheldon (2001): "Traditional symbolic interactionism, role theory, and structural symbolic interactionism: The road to identity theory". In: Jonathan H. Turner (ed.): *Handbook of sociological theory*. Boston: Springer, 211–231.

Stryker, Sheldon/Serpe, Richard T. (1982): "Commitment, identity salience, and role behavior: Theory and research example". In: William Ickes/Eric S. Knowles (eds.): *Personality, roles, and social behavior*. New York: Springer.

Stryker, Sheldon/Serpe, Richard T. (1994): "Identity salience and psychological centrality: Equivalent, overlapping, or complementary concepts?" In: *Social psychology quarterly* 57 (1), 16–35.

Stubager, Rune (2009): "Education-based group identity and consciousness in the authoritarian-libertarian value conflict". In: *European Journal of Political Research* 48 (2), 204–233.

Sullivan, John L./Shamir Michal/Walsh Patrick/Roberts Nigel S. (1985): *Political tolerance in context: Support for unpopular minorities in Israel, New Zealand and the United States*. Boulder, CO: Westview.

Tajfel, Henri (1959): "Quantitative judgement in social perception". In: *British journal of psychology* 50 (1), 16–29.

Tajfel, Henri (1981): *Human groups and social categories: Studies in social psychology*. Cambridge University Press Archive.

Tajfel, Henri (1974): "Social identity and intergroup behaviour". In: *Information (International Social Science Council)* 13 (2), 65–93.

Tajfel, Henri/Turner, John C. (1979): "An integrative theory of intergroup conflict". In: William G. Austin/Stephen Worchel (eds.): *The social psychology of intergroup relations*. Monterey, CA: Brooks/Cole, 33–37.

Tartakovsky, Eugene (2012): "The Israeli Immigration Policy: Some Lessons from the Last Wave of Mass Immigration from the Former Soviet Union". In: *Current Politics and Economics of the Middle East* 3 (3), 353–371.

Tesser, Abraham (1988): "Toward a self-evaluation maintenance model of social behavior". In: *Advances in experimental social psychology* 21, 181–227.

Tessler, Mark A. (1977): "Israel's Arabs and the Palestinian Problem". In: *Middle East Journal* 31 (3), 313–329.

Tolts, Mark (2017): "Mixed marriage and post-Soviet aliyah." In: Reinharz, Shulamit/DellaPergola Sergio (eds.): *Jewish intermarriage around the world*. London: Routledge, 89–104.

Turner, John C. (1981): "Towards a cognitive redefinition of the social group". In: *Cahiers de Psychologie Cognitive/Current Psychology of Cognition* 1 (2), 93–118.

Turner, John C. (1975): "Social comparison and social identity: Some prospects for intergroup behaviour". In: *European journal of social psychology* 5 (1), 1–34.

Wagner, Ulrich/Becker, Julia C./Christ, Oliver/Pettigrew, Thomas F./Schmidt, Peter (2012): "A longitudinal test of the relation between German nationalism, patriotism, and out-group derogation". In: *European sociological review* 28 (3), 319–332.

b. Empirical sources

Arian, Asher/Atmor, Nir/Hadar, Yael (2007): The 2007 Israeli democracy index: Auditing Israeli democracy cohesion in a divided society. Israel Democracy Institute. Jerusalem.

Arian, Asher/Philippov, Michael/Knafelman, Anna (2009): Auditing Israeli Democracy–2009: Twenty Years of Immigration from the Soviet Union. Israeli Democracy Institute. Jerusalem

Arian, Asher/Hermann, Tamar/Lebel, Yuval/Philippov, Michael/Zaban, Hila/Knafelman, Anna (2010): Auditing Israeli Democracy–2010. Israel Democracy Institute. Jerusalem.

Arian, Asher/Nachmias, David/Navot, Doron/Shani, Danielle (2003): The 2003 Israeli Democracy Index: Measuring Israeli Democracy. Israel Democracy Institute. Jerusalem.

Hermann, Tamar/Heller, Ella/Cohen, Chanan/Bublil, Dana/Omar, Fadi (2016): The 2016 Israeli democracy index. The Israel Democracy Institute. Jerusalem.

Hermann, Tamar/Atmor, Nir/Heller, Ella/Lebel, Yuval (2012): The Israeli democracy index 2012. The Israeli Democracy Institute, Jerusalem.

Central Bureau of Statistics, State of Israel. (2020a): Immigration to Israel 2019 [Media release]. https://www.cbs.gov.il/he/mediarelease/DocLib/2020/223/21_20_223e.pdf (accessed 2 July 2021).

Central Bureau of Statistics, State of Israel. (2020b): The Population of Ethiopian Origin in Israel: Selected Data Published on the Occasion of the Sigd Festival [Media release]. https://www.cbs.gov.il/he/mediarelease/DocLib/2020/358/11_20_358e.pdf (accessed 2 July 2021).

Central Bureau of Statistics, State of Israel. (2020c): Population of Israel on the Eve of 2021 [Media release]. https://www.cbs.gov.il/he/mediarelease/DocLib/2020/438/11_20_438e.pdf (accessed 2 July 2021).

Levy, Shlomit/Levinsohn, Hanna/Katz, Elihu (2002): Israeli Jews—A portrait: Beliefs, values, and observance of the Jews in Israel. The Israeli Democracy Institute, Jerusalem.

Mana, Mia (2015): TGI survey 2015, Readership in Israel. http://b.walla.co.il/item/2875015 (accessed 30 January 2016).

OECD (2020): Recent changes in migration movements and policies – Key figures on immigration and emigration – Israel. https://stat.link/fx4gv2 (accessed 3 July 2021).

c. Online references

Adalah – The Legal Center or Arab Minority Rights in Israel (2016): Israel: new discriminatory and anti-democratic legislation. https://www.adalah.org/en/content/view/9344 (accessed 1 July 2021).

Amnesty International (2021): Amnesty International report 2020/21: the state of the world's human rights. https://www.amnesty.org/download/Documents/POL1032022021ENGLISH.PDF (accessed 1 July 2021).

Bergman, Ronen (2011): Gilad Shalit and the Rising Price of an Israeli Life. *The New York Times*. https://www.nytimes.com/2011/11/13/magazine/gilad-shalit-and-the-cost-of-an-israeli-life.html (accessed 1 July 2021).

Browniee, Jason (2020): Probabilistic Model Selection with AIC, BIC, and MDL. Machine Learning Mastery. https://machinelearningmastery.com/probabilistic-model-selection-measures/ (accessed 2 July 2021).

Galili, Lily (2020): The Other Tribe: Israel's Russian-speaking Community and how it is Changing the Country. https://www.brookings.edu/wp-content/uploads/2020/09/FP_20200921_other_tribe_galili.pdf (accessed 02 July 2021).

Kaufmann, Eric (2016): "It's NOT the economy, stupid: Brexit as a story of personal values". In: *British Politics and Policy at LSE* 7. https://blogs.lse.ac.uk/politicsandpolicy/personal-values-brexit-vote/ (accessed 02 July 2021).

Nahshoni, Kobi (2019): Mnistry of Interior corrects: Most Russian and Ukrainian immigrants aren't Jewish; Most immigrants from the US and France are Jewish. https://www.ynet.co.il/articles/0,7340,L-5648100,00.html [Hebrew] (accessed 02 July 2021).

Schutz, Bart (2013a): Emphasis Framing. Wheel Persuas. https://www.wheelofpersuasion.com/technique/emphasis-framing/ (accessed 02 July 2021).

Schutz, Bart (2013b): Equivalence Framing. Wheel Persuas. https://www.wheelofpersuasion.com/technique/equivalence-framing/ (accessed 02 July 2021).

Herbert Rostand Ngouo
Religion Weaponised

An Analysis of the Deployment of Religious Themes in the Discourse of Anglophone Nationalist and Secessionist Leaders and Activists in Cameroon

1 Introduction

Populism, separatism and nationalism are spreading in countries around the world. While many separatist or secessionist propensities are connected to ethnic nationalism or the quest for economic fulfilment, others are fuelled by religion, as has been the case in Northern Ireland, Central African Republic, Pakistan and India.[1]

Politics and religion are an odd couple that have maintained or sustained fragile connections due to the centrality of religion in people's relationships with one other and in the construction of a common space. Religion, whether African Traditional, Christian or Islamic, is a fundamental or most important element in the lives of Africans (see Awolalu 1976; Mbiti 1999; Pawlikova-Vilhanova 2020; Wariboko 2017; Ngom/Kurfi/Falola 2020), and as a result permeates all aspects of individual lives and group identities. It is all too normal that it is becoming pervasive. In addressing a problem that concerns their daily lives and futures, Africans do sometimes unconsciously or consciously invoke divine intervention (see Awolalu 1976; Wariboko 2017; Pew Forum on Religion & Public Life 2010). In politics, religious discourse is used to push an agenda, and the misuse of religion may have devastating consequences (see P. Marshall 2018). There are few studies on the issue (see P. Marshall 2018; Campbell 2020).

Religion has been found to be the central reason for conflicts and civil wars in some communities and countries around the globe, in particular when it has some ethnic components. This creates social divisions among the populations

---

1 My sincere gratitude goes first to Hanna Acke for her immense patience, warmth and scientific leadership. I also thank, through her, Åbo Akademi University in Turku, Finland, for funding my trip to Turku to attend the BTWS2 conference during which the preliminary findings of this paper were presented. I thank all the reviewers for their insightful comments which were very helpful in the revision of this paper. This article would not have been possible if not for all your support.

Open Access. © 2023 the author(s), published by De Gruyter. This work is licensed under the Creative Commons Attribution 4.0 International License.
https://doi.org/10.1515/9783111039633-008

within a territory. Moreover, in recent years, a great number of terrorist attacks have been associated and/or attributed to religion and religious groups. Since the 9/11 attacks on the World Trade Center (WTC), radical or extremist Muslim groups have been blamed for terrorist attacks around the world. But there have been very few attacks attributed to Christian groups. More recently, some religious-induced conflicts have been reported in Sub-Saharan Africa (see Basedau 2017): there was a heavy religious overtone in the 2011 post-electoral crisis in Côte d'Ivoire. More recently (in 2014), in the Central African Republic (CAR) (see Lado Tonlieu 2021), religion was instrumentalised in the divide between the country's North and South, which caused two communities that had long lived together peacefully and harmoniously to initiate a bloody and deadly confrontation. With regard to the case of Côte d'Ivoire, Vüllers (2011) notes that the crisis took on religious connotations due to the fact that the roles of President Gbagbo and his wife Simone were construed as divine (see Raynal 2005; Miran 2006: 88; Vüllers 2011).

Syncretic religiosity also remains a central element in defining the lives of Africans, even in the postcolonial era. Christianity and Islam are quickly expanding their domains in the social life of communities that were initially Traditional (see Wariboko 2017); African Traditional Religion predates and prevailed over every other religion on the continent throughout its history. While holy war introduced Islam in Africa, Christianity was diffused through colonisation. At present, Christianity keeps spreading and Islam continues to permeate the dominion of African Traditional Religion. While Catholicism and Protestantism have become deeply established in the Cameroonian populations, Pentecostal (Evangelical) movements are quickly spreading, winning more converts and exerting more and more influence on society as a whole (see Pawlikova-Vilhanova 2020; Wariboko 2017; Ngom/Kurfi/Falola 2020; Pew Forum on Religion & Public Life 2010). The growth of the number of Pentecostals (Renewalists) among the total population is particularly noteworthy. In 2015, it accounted for 35.32 of the continent's Christian population of 574.52 million and 17.11 percent of the continent's total population of 1.19 billion (see Wariboko 2017).

1.1 Research problem and research questions

Religion is one of the most dividing social elements, and has been the cause of many conflicts. The politicisation of religion is therefore worth studying in the postmodern era, when it was expected that religion would be relegated to the private sphere. It is important to study the new ways in which it is used in society, not only in relation to social media, but also in its political deployment in developing nations. While examining people's comments about the ongoing Anglophone crisis

in Cameroon, I noticed some religious allusions, and was pushed to dig deeper in order to see how these allusions have been used within the framework of the secessionist conflict. The following research questions guide my inquiry.
- RQ1. What is the nature of the allusion or reference to sacred texts in Anglophone nationalist and secessionist social media discourse in Cameroon?
- RQ2. What is the function and effect of deploying religious themes in the secessionist discourse?
- RQ3. What religious ideology can be identified?
- RQ4. What reasons account for the deployment of religious themes in the rhetoric used by Anglophone leaders on Facebook?

1.2 Aim of the study

This paper sets out to analyse the nature and function of religious discourse, as well as the ideological implications of the use of Biblical allusions and references, such as phraseologies, speech acts and biblical metaphors as a persuasive and manipulative strategy in the Anglophone armed secessionist crisis in Cameroon. Anglophone pro-secession activists placed religion at the centre of their nationalist struggle, while Cameroonian identity was repudiated and placed at the margin.

In this article, we push the boundaries in our analysis of religious language and the deployment of religion in political discourse in order to propose that the imbuement of discourse with Bible-like expressions, the militarisation of prayer and recourse to the God strategy (see Domke and Coe 2011: 7) in a socio-political crisis constitute the weaponisation of religion. In the case of the armed conflict between secessionist insurgents and the Cameroonian army, we argue that religion is used by the secessionists as an instrument for legitimising a controversial option – armed rebellion – in order to ultimately resolve the longstanding Anglophone problem. In fact, the conflict is not a religious one. In principle, religion has never constituted a dividing factor between Anglophones and Francophones in Cameroon. Therefore, the conflict does not have the religious motives that the insurgents are trying to give it. Vüllers (2011) notes that literature makes a distinction between "religious civil wars" and "religious violence". In this view, a civil war is "religious" if the parties of the conflict should differ in their religious affiliations, and/or if religious ideas are an issue in the conflict (see Svensson 2007: 936–937; Toft 2007: 97; Basedau et al. 2011).

1.3 Background of Anglophone nationalism in Cameroon and the deployment of religious themes in violent secessionist conflict

Cameroon is by constitution a secular (lay) country, which means that there is no state religion. Freedom of religion is guaranteed. The Cameroonian people, just like most Africans, are deeply religious. While the majority of the population practices the traditional religion, most of these people would also claim some association with Christianity. Christianity and Islam are the dominant "civil religions" (Wald 2003; Toolin 1983)[2]. It is only during Christian and Moslem celebrations that a public holiday is observed in Cameroon. The religious landscape would suggest that Cameroon is a predominantly Christian country. Sources like Pew Forum on Religion & Public Life (2010) and the 2005 population census in Cameroon (BUCREP 2010) reveal that more than 60% of the population self-identifies as Christians, whether it is Catholicism, Protestantism or Pentecostalism. Cameroonians seem to associate Christianity with modernity, while their ancestral religion is what constitutes their roots. Although the traditional religion is ostracised in the public sphere, it remains the matrix of their world view, the soul of the people. The Government of Cameroon regularly calls for ecumenical religious celebrations in order to pray for peace or for any issues of national significance. Pentecostal churches have always organised long periods of fasting and prayers each time Cameroon has been confronted with aggression from external forces, or with internal political upheaval and troubles. Unarguably, Christian traditions prevail over all other religious practices in the public space, to an extent that goes beyond what Torpey (2010) calls "latent religiosity".[3]

While there is no major religion-induced conflict, Cameroon has been affected by a enduring socio-political dispute between the Anglophone minority and the

---

[2] Wald (2003) and Toolin (1983): Wald defines civil religion as "the idea that a nation tries to understand its historical experience and national purpose in religious terms […] Civil religion reflects an attempt by citizens to imbue their nation with a transcendent value. The nation is recognized as a secular institution, yet one that is somehow touched by the hand of God." (Wald 2003: 55). Toolin (1983: 41) defines civil religion as "a self-congratulatory relationship between politics and religion".

[3] Latent religiosity can be observed and deduced from public life. The Christian Calendar of events (just like any religious Christian celebration such as Christmas, Easter, Pentecost, Ascension and Assumption) are adopted, and public holidays are decreed accordingly. Moreover, Sundays are days of rest. On the other hand, we have seen official events, office and business working hours being adjusted to accommodate religious demands, such as during Ramadan, or Muslim prayer time.

Francophone dominant majority – i.e. the Anglophone problem – that led to a secession crisis in 2016. The Anglophone problem (see Konings/Nyamnjoh 1997) in Cameroon has its roots in the colonial period, as Cameroon, which was a German protectorate from 1884 to 1916, was divided between France and England after World War II. After about 50 years of separate administration by the French and the English under the trusteeship of the League of Nations and the United Nations, the two territories were reunited on 1st October 1961 to form a federal state. However, the reunification negotiation, and later on the 1972 unification process, are said to have been marred by deceit.

The Anglophone Problem (see Konings/Nyamnjoh 1997) refers to the long-standing tension between the Cameroonian government and the Anglophone minority with regard to the "socio-political marginalisation" and linguistic assimilation of the latter. Anglophones have always expressed their malaise and disputed the intention of the Francophones to francophonise (culturally assimilate) them. The awareness among various strata of the Anglophone Cameroonians that all is not well and that nothing is done about their plight is the cause of their participation in separatist movements, which are growing in popularity among young and old members of the Anglophone community. In a nutshell, the Anglophone Problem is nurtured by: (a) the inability and failure of successive governments of Cameroon, since 1961, to respect and implement the articles of the Constitution that uphold and safeguard what British Southern Cameroons brought to the Union in 1961. After reunification between French-speaking Cameroon and (English-speaking) Southern Cameroons, Cameroon became via constitution the Federal Republic of Cameroon with two states (three quarters French-speaking and one quarter English speaking) and two official languages: French and English. (b) The violation of the Constitution, demonstrated by the dissolution of political parties and the formation of one political party in 1966, and other such acts judged by West Cameroonians to be unconstitutional and undemocratic; and (c) the cavalier management of the 1972 Referendum that took the foundational element (Federalism) out of the 1961 Constitution. In 1972, following a referendum, the political system evolved from a federal state to a unitary state with one government. The British Southern Cameroons became two administrative provinces called the "North-West" and "South-West" regions. (d) The 1984 law amending the Constitution, which gave the country the original East Cameroon name (The Republic of Cameroon) and thereby erased the identity of the West Cameroonians from the original union. West Cameroon, which had entered the union as an equal partner, effectively ceased to exist. (e) The deliberate and systematic erosion of the West Cameroon cultural identity that the 1961 Constitution sought to preserve and protect by providing a bi-cultural federation. The Anglophone communities have expressed their dissatisfaction about the union on several occasions, some of which were institutionalised. This is the case with the 1993 and 1994 All Anglophone Conferences (AAC 1 and AAC 2).

Cameroonian Anglophones kept complaining that their recommendations to the Cameroonian government had fallen in deaf ears. Since November 2016, they have vehemently expressed their outrage throughout Cameroon's two English-speaking regions through civil disobedience, arson, scorched land, mass protest, slaughtering of civilians as well as bloody armed conflict to obtain secession. The Government of Cameroon attempted negotiation with the civil society organisation consortium. The leaders of the consortium who negotiated with the Government from December 2016 to January 2017 were Dr Fontem Neba, a university lecturer, Agbor Balla and Bobga Harmony, both lawyers, and Tassang Wilfred, a teachers' union leader. As the negotiations failed, the Government dissolved the consortium. The first two leaders were arrested and jailed, while the others were smuggled out of the country. As a result, some leaders based abroad took over the revolution and became radicalised. As the Anglophone leaders did not have access to the mainstream media, social media became their main means of communication between web activists and the population. Their potential for enhancing enfranchisement, emancipating the masses and engaging with civilians was fully deployed, so as a result, the Government suspended the Internet in the restive regions for three months.

Social media was used to diffuse separatist propaganda without any risk of censorship. Ngouo (2020) discussed web activism among Anglophones, demonstrating how they repudiate the Pan-Cameroonian identity and assert Anglophone nationalism. This is done through carefully avoiding the use of the English translation of Cameroon's official name, "The Republic of Cameroon". They instead use the French "La République du Cameroun". Furthermore, the North-West and South-West regions are two of the country's 10 regional entities, but the separatists assert their rejection of the Pan-Cameroonian nationality by calling them 'Southern Cameroons', 'Ambazonia' or the 'Federal Republic of Ambazonia'. Anglophone Cameroonians are referred to as Ambazonians or Southern Cameroonians (see Ngouo 2020).

The presentation of the socio-political context and of some of the stakeholders shows that religion was not the root cause of the crisis. Most Anglophones in Cameroon are characterised as being very religious with Christianity (both nominal and devout) being the most visibly dominant major religion. When the crisis broke out, many churches located in the Anglophone regions, and even Anglophones living in and outside of the regions, supported subversion and secession, on grounds that they have always felt marginalised. Individuals prayed for unrest, hoping that God would intervene in favour of Anglophones. The Ambazonian leaders seem to have taken advantage of this religiosity. In fact, some of the diasporic secessionist leaders who had instigated secession and masterminded the bloody armed confrontation were either pastors or religious affiliates based in the USA, Norway, UK, or South Africa, where they were out of the Government's reach. Some of the prominent leaders are:

Sisiku Ayuk Tabe is the first affirmed leader of the Ambazonian Government Council (AGC). He strutted around in foreign cities until he was arrested in Nigeria alongside nine other leaders in January 2018 and extradited (deported). They were eventually judged and sentenced by a military court in Yaoundé.

Ayaba Cho Lucas, a hardliner among the secessionists, is a proclaimed commander of the Ambazonian Defence Forces (ADF). He was granted the Norwegian citizenship a few years ago.

Samuel Sako Ikome (former pastor of Deeper Life in Cameroon) is the current interim president of the Ambazonian Government Council (AGC).

Chris Anu, a US-based pastor, originates from the Lebialem Division of the South-West Region of Cameroon (one of the contested territories). He is the brother of Lekeakeh Oliver, alias Field Marshall, one of the most dreaded leaders of the Red Dragons (Anglophone militia) of Fontem. The latter proclaimed himself King of Fontem on 1st October 2019. Others include Mark Bareta, Ebenezert Akwanga and Boh Herbert.

2 Literature review and theoretical consideration

The connection between religion, (civil) war and armed conflict has regained the interest of researchers since 1980, and Rapoport (1984: 659) has argued that the medieval conflicts were instilled by religious interests. It was not until the 1970s/beginning of the 1980s that there was a resurgence of religious justifications for political violence. In the conflict between Northern Ireland and Southern Ireland, Catholicism and Protestantism were at the centre of contention. Religion-related or religion-instigated conflicts have occurred in Africa and throughout the world (see Basedau/Schaefer-Kehnert 2019; Basedau 2017; Basedau/Pfeifer/Vüllers 2016; Basedau et al. 2011). In most Islamist jihads, religion is always the professed and asserted motive or the legitimating instrument of political violence, extremism and terrorism, as non-Muslims are considered non-believers or unfaithful (see Hide 2014, Paterson 2019). As Hide (2014) comments, religiously (Christianity as well as Islam) motivated violence and political violence, or religious discrimination, occurred regularly as a number of nationalist movements on nearly all continents, in an effort to build their national identities, used religion as an inalienable part of their self-determination and self-definition during the late 19th century and the beginning of 20th. However, the politicisation of religion (see P. Marshall 2018) does not occur without its share of conflict.

2.1 Conceptual approaches to the study of the politicisation of religion, religious language and discourse in politics

Language is at the centre of communication. In political discourse, it is a powerful tool for mediating between leaders and the people, and for this reason, the choice of words is part of the discursive strategy that aims to determine meaning. From a functional systemic perspective (see Halliday 1992), linguistic analysis of political discourse may look at linguistic elements such as lexical sets, conceptual metaphors, phraseologies and the idioms of allusions and references. Religious language is also used in discourse. Du Bois (1986) identified some of the features of religious language as including: (i) use of rituals, (ii) archaic elements, (iii) euphemism and metaphor, (iv) semantic opacity, (v) unusual fluency, and (vi) magic words. Furthermore, to identify if a speech contains religious (Christian) rhetoric, a preliminary list of religious keywords must be made that includes other religious phraseology. These would be words that directly refer to religion ("religion", "religious", "spiritual", "faith", "Christian", "God", "Lord", "Almighty", "heaven") and religious practices ("pray", "worship", "bless", "church", "Bible", "scripture").

In politics, the Bible has been a familiar and useful literary source (see Dreisbach 2007, 2017; Roche 2015). Indeed, the Scripture has been employed for literary, rhetorical and political purposes. The study of the use of Christian or Bible-like language as a discursive strategy to rally Christian communities in politics also examines phrases, figures of speech, and rhythms that resemble, imitate, or evoke the familiar scriptural (Bible) texts. In addition to allusions, there are many reasons why authoritative texts, including sacred writings, are referred to and cited in political discourse. A study of the Bible's use in political rhetoric has focussed on how and for what purposes the Scripture is used, as not all uses of the Bible in political discourse have been for strictly spiritual ends. Fornieri (2003) analyses 19th century U.S. president Abraham Lincoln's use of the Bible and demonstrates that it was part of his accent. Lincoln's recourse to Biblical text was not cynical or manipulative, unlike many other political figures who do so in bad faith (see Dreisbach 2007, 2017) or, even, as non-Christians. Lincoln used it in at least five different ways (a) theologically, (b) civil theologically, (c) evocatively, (d) allegorically, (e) and existentially (see Fornieri 2003). Dreisbach (2017) summarises some functions of biblical allusions in political discourse. These include: (1) to enrich a common language and cultural vocabulary through distinctively Biblical phrases, figures of speech, proverbs, aphorisms and the like; (2) to enhance the power and weight of rhetoric through its identification with a venerated, authoritative sacred text; (3) to identify and define normative standards and transcendent rules for ordering and judging public life; and (4) to gain insights on the character and designs of God, especially as they pertain to his dealings with men and nations.

The study of the function of Biblical allusion and reference also focuses on how metaphors and speech acts with religious connotations are used to imbue discourse with sanctity. Keane (2004) emphasised the place of speech acts in general and performatives in particular as well as metaphors in religious language, as metaphors are used to activate ideology. This is in line with Halliday and Hasan (1985: 20), who argue that there are two different kinds of considerations in language, not only the linguistic clues, but also the situational ones. They claim that "The linguistic concerns relations within the language, patterns of meaning realised by grammar and vocabulary, and the other, situational, concerns the relations between the language and the features of the speaker's and hearer's material, social and ideological environment".

The approaches to the analysis of the deployment of religious rhetoric in political discourse presented above do not always contribute to the understanding of religion's impact on society. There are studies on religion and conflict, on religion and politics, and on the weaponisation of religion. There are also studies on biblical allusions in political speeches, but there are no studies on the weaponisation of religion from a discursive perspective that this paper is investigating, especially with regard to social media. Studies on how religion is weaponised in discourse (and in social media) are rare, if they even exist at all.

Studies about conflict induced by conflicting Christian factions in politics are rare. A few include Chitando (2005), Miran (2005) and Vüllers (2011). Other researchers have also examined religion and politics, looking at how political leaders and politicians make reference to the Bible in their speeches (see Dreisbach 2007, 2017; Roche 2015). More recently, new studies have gone further to question new forms of religious language, as well as new ways in which religion is deployed in politics. Van der Veer's book (2017) brings together case studies of the political salience of prayer in Nigeria, France, India, Russia and the United States. Ruth Marshall (2016) discusses the centrality of prayer conceived as a form of political praxis; McAllister (2015, 2017) elaborates on the militarisation of prayer in the deployment of spiritual warfare in pro-dominionism politics. Campbell (2020) discusses how politicising religion may have negative effects. Paul Marshall

(2018) opines that the religionisation of politics or the politicisation of religion leads to conflicts.

2.2 The conceptual framework of the weaponisation of religion in social media discourse

As already noted, this study examines how secessionists use religious (Christian) ideology, through biblical references and allusions in social media discourse, to legitimate their fight for secession in Cameroon. It proposes that the deployment of religious political discourse is done "cynically and manipulatively", which is the weaponisation of religion in discourse. This study is even more important due to the fact that it addresses the weaponisation of religious discourse in new media, which has the potential to disenfranchise voices.

In recent years, the digitalisation of social life with the advent of social media communication, as well as the emergence of electronically mediated communication across all platforms, spaces, sites and technologies (see KhosraviNik 2018) that is enhanced by digital connectivity, has not only enabled social mobilisation with regard to political revolution (see Bardici 2012), but also a proliferation of negative content, such as disinformation. New and social media are viewed as a way to overcome state-controlled media and content, especially in the developing world. However, social media platforms are also increasingly being used as a means of empowering disruptive voices, messages and ideologies (see Bartlett/Birdwell/Littler 2011; Olaniran /Williams 2020). As such, social media has contributed to both the rise of weaponisation in general, and to the weaponisation of religion (see P. Marshall 2018) in the political sphere. It exacerbates the effect of disinformation and can facilitate its use as a political tool to "weaponize" religious intolerance (see Paterson 2019). According to Paul Marshall (2018: 3) "A value is 'weaponised' when it is invoked in bad faith, in an effort to peddle insincere political talking points".

In this light, Paterson (2019) discusses the rise of religion-driven cyber terrorism through the weaponisation of religious intolerance in Indonesian cyberspace. He comments that the impact of these technologies in enabling an extremist Islamic "hacktivist" group called "Muslim Cyber Army" (MCA) to access a much larger audience as a means to propagate religious intolerance in a far more pervasive manner. In the same vein, Brooking and Singer (2016) discuss in *The Atlantic* how social media was weaponised by jihadists of the Islamic State. It helped ISIS to become "the first terrorist group to hold both physical and digital territory", according to Jared Cohen, a former State Department staffer who is now the director of Jigsaw. Through social media, ISIS saturated cyberspace with hashtags – using armies of Twitter bots – and created and redesigned one-sided skirmishes so that they appeared to be significant battlefield victories.

Weaponisation is becoming a widespread strategy in activism and politics. Just like social media, the body and race, religion is being weaponised. While it is a powerful tool for social and political mobilisation, it is latent unless activated. To use religion's potential political power, activists can invoke it in their political rhetoric. The weaponisation of religion is decried when religion is associated with something that is not in itself religious. P. Marshall (2018) emphasises that religion can only be politically manipulated if it is both present and significant enough to be manipulated.

As proposed in this study, the weaponisation of religion in discourse is enacted through a number of principles:

(1) Saturating discourse with religious allusions and references in order to attract support from the target religious group (use of citation, intertextuality, idiom, phraseologies, lexis, etc.). This strategy helps to imbue the discourse with sanctity or a religious overtone.
(2) The deployment of "the God for us" or "God on our side" rhetoric. It consists in:
    (a) Adjudging or arrogating God's approval: God approves of what we are doing; even in the case of religious conflict, once one of the parties, in good or bad faith, ascribes and arrogates God's approval by rejecting the validity of the other party and, labelling it as evil.
    (b) Victimhood discourse: God is on the side of the oppressed – we are oppressed, so God is on our side.
    (c) Demonising the other party: those who are attacking us are evil, they are demonic.
(3) Diffusion of religious ideology in discourse through the use of religious metaphors: metaphoric reference to biblical imagery and characters, attributing the character (messianic) of Bible heroes to living personages, and associating biblical elements with the current situation.
(4) The deployment of the rhetoric of spiritual warfare (see R. Marshall 2016) and the militarisation of prayer (see McAlister 2016a, 2016b) in a dominionist project: this consists of using military and warfare metaphors in religious discourse; using words, expressions and phraseologies as spiritual weapons to attack, destroy and enact violence; using spiritual violence to legitimate physical violence. Spiritual warfare consists in exerting spiritual power to liberate society from evil spiritual beings. To that end, God's supernatural interaction with the natural realm is solicited.

3 Methodology, data collection and analysis: Data sources

The rise of digital technology, and especially of social media, is giving rise to multiple approaches to the study of social phenomena, as their spread has fostered a spontaneous and uncontrolled mobilisation of the masses. As we argue in this paper, the use of social media in a separatist insurgency in Cameroon has facilitated the deployment of religion in discourse. While conducting digital ethnography in order to understand the problem, my attention was attracted to the recurrent use of religious (biblical) and Bible-like expressions in the posts and comments on the Facebook pages of Anglophone activists. This incursion of religion into a violent conflict where there is no religious divide between Cameroonian Anglophones and Francophones prompted me to start scrutinising the overall discourse of secessionist leaders and their followers. I started browsing through the Facebook pages of Anglophone activists, observing and tracking all discourse and expressions that pointed to religion in general and to the Bible or Christianity in particular. Most of the Facebook pages were dedicated to the Anglophone problem. The most obvious ones are the following:

- Ambazonian Defence Forces
- British Southern Cameroons Resistance Forces
- English Cameroon for a United Cameroon (EC4UC) https://www.facebook.com/OneCameroonPeaceUnityCommonsense
- Southern Cameroons Ambazonia Consortium United Front (SCACUF): https://fr-fr.facebook.com/SCACUF

Social media (primarily Facebook) have played a very crucial role in the Anglophone crisis. Most secession leaders reside in the diaspora, and the only means for them to stay connected with the population and armed groups is the Internet. Facebook enabled activists as well as common users to communicate both privately and publicly with peers and the target population within their network, who live either within the confines of Cameroon's Anglophone area or beyond it. In Cameroon, there are 17 million telephone subscribers, with Internet access having soared from 6% to 35% within four years (2016–2020).

Even the moderate activists living in Cameroon preferred to voice their opinion using pseudo account names on social media. As their appearance in the mainstream media was restricted or censored, social media guaranteed them a platform for freedom of speech. Moreover, the social medium played a double role: that of information channel and mediumistic[4] instrument.

I compiled a corpus of religious, Bible-like expressions, references and phraseologies that were produced by activists. They were made up of all expressions (appearing in posts and comments, or in responses to a post) that point to the Bible or Christian ideology and practices. Some posts are regarded as prompting posts (by the leaders) while other posts and comments (by followers) are reactions prompted by the posts of some leaders. In some cases, some followers posted comments with a religious overtone under a post that had no connection to religion. Therefore, a lexical item may occur in isolation in some discourse string, or be included in a sequence of discourse where there was an abundant use of biblical jargon. The content was selected because it was imbued with religious ideology.

Below are some samples of prompting messages that were posted by secessionists leaders:

> President Federal Republic of Ambazonia: [...] I Am Convicted Deep Down In My Spirit That, Keeping The HOPE of Ambazonia ALIVE, And Trusting the Almighty Is The Only SHIELD We Have Against The Raging Darkness Of Occupation.
> On Going Battle in Njinikom. Keep the fighters in Prayer. Fund The Resistance
> Tingoh VILLAGE UNDER ATTACK BY LRC, HOUSES ONFIRE. CIVILIANS ARE ADVISED TO STAY AWAY. PUT CIVILIANS & SOLDIERS IN PRAYERS.
> Your Defence Forces are battling Cameroon's occupational military in Nkambe. Pray for them.
> ONGOING BATTLE IN THE NJINIKOM/FUNDONG AXES! KEEP THE FIGHTERS IN PRAYER.

These religious signs are in the form of lexical words and expressions, idiomatic expressions, phraseologies and speech acts. At the discourse level, we have biblical phraseologies being used as speech acts, and some metaphorical allusion to biblical characters.

---

4 Medium: a means or instrumentality for storing or communicating information/someone who serves as an intermediary between the living and the dead; a spiritualist. Mediumistic is used in this context to capture the fact that social media seems to have acquired another role, a telepathic one through which secessionist leaders communicated to the subconscious mind of the people. Social media was the spiritual interface between the source and the receiver.

4 Data analysis

The study of the deployment of religious rhetorical themes in the discourse – and eventually their weaponisation – by Anglophone secessionists in the armed conflict between them and the Cameroonian Anglophone government is conducted at three levels of analysis: intertextuality, which looks at the nature (lexis [jargon] and citations, phraseologies and idioms) and type of allusion as well as the function of allusions and references to the Bible/Christianity, the pragmatic function (speech acts) of biblical and Christian phraseologies and idioms, and the ideological implication of the references (enacted through metaphor) that result in weaponisation.

4.1 Biblical and religious intertextual figures in Anglophone secessionist discourse

Intertextuality consists of creating meaning in a text (hypotext) by using part of another text (hypertext). In the Anglophone secessionist discourse, religion is activated through intertextual figures that may include allusions, references, quotations and calques that are primarily lexicosemantic. The analysis of the utterances (posts) shows a use of words and lexical expressions that were borrowed from the biblical and Christian lexicon or jargon. There are different categories of allusions:

(a) Lexical-semantic expressions referring to biblical lexis and concepts

These include expressions and words associated with divinity, Christian rituals, Bible characters, references to religious institutions and rituals as well as direct citation and/or paraphrasing of Bible scripture. The posts below illustrate this:

(1) No amount of diplomacy would ever work with LRC[5]. LRC is a devil, and the only way to reform the devil is to kill the devil

(2) The **evil** regime will soon beg to be our peaceful neighbor

(3) Pa Tassang is an honourable man fighting to liberate his people. Your **satanic** francophone Beti Ewondo regime tried to corrupt but this incorruptible man stood on the side of his oppressed Ambazonian **brethrens**. No amount of insults will dampen his resolve so go

---

5 La République du Cameroun.

tell your **evil demon** in Yaounde that he will one day pay for his crimes against the Ambazonian people. **We shall be free in Jesus name amen.**

(4) Dr Ben, You have constantly call our fellows brothers and sisters to be wise, to remain patriotic and focused on promoting values such as peace, education, God Luck, Our Almighty GOD is watching each and every one of us.

(5) The person who writes this is an idiot..not different from this bad government..anyone supporting this government must go to hell..idiot

A Christian reading the above posts is struck by the presence of the words that he or she is familiar with. There is reference to religious rituals like prayer and praying; to biblical lexis and concepts like "hell", wickedness, evil (referring to negative entities); to biblical figures like "Jehovah" (a variant of God's biblical names), "Jesus" (the messiah or saviour), "Almighty God" (the supreme being), "King Nebuchadnezzar" (a Bible character who is assumed to be one of the first great world emperors), "Judas" (the Jesus disciple who betrayed him), the "devil" and "satan" (allusions to the biblical figure who is antagonistic to God and humans).

(b) Reference to Biblical characters

In other instances of allusions to Christianity, we observe allusions to biblical figures such as "God", "Jesus", "Judas", "Satan" and "King Nebuchadnezzar", as in the following examples:

(6) Pls be conscious and stop disturbing our peace and united country by the will of GOD. So stay where u are quiet and enjoy what **Satan** have provide.

(7) We are not biafra, but copying wrong styles of Biafra that failed them and will continue to failed until they gain back their senses as King Nebuchadnezzar did, plead for mercy and worship God and acknowledged Him as the only one who has power on earth and beneath and also above.

(8) Judas played his role for mankind to be free. The Judas(es) in our midst will also play their roles for Ambazonia to be free.

(c) Biblical citations and paraphrases

In some of the comments provided by the followers, whether in response to promptings or not, the activists make verbatim or partial citations of the Bible. In others, they paraphrase the scriptures.

(9) My eyes are fixed on the prize, until we reach Buea. For one who holds the plough and keeps looking back is unfit for Ambaland 😊
(10) No peace for the wicked
(11) General as a pastor I say NO Weapon form against you shall prosper go ahead liberate your land
(12) Well spoken General RK. The God of Abraham, Isaac and Jacob will certainly protect you till Buea 🙏🙏

In the above utterances, the propositions "NO Weapon form against you shall prosper" and "No peace for the wicked" are verbatim citations of Isaiah 48:22 and Isaiah 54:17, respectively; the story of Daniel 4 is also paraphrased when King Nebuchadnezzar is evoked. Furthermore, just like in the many instances of the Bible (Exodus 3:6/ 3:15/ 4:5) where God refers to himself as "the God of Abraham, Isaac and Jacob", the activists use the same expression in their post (12). We also have partial quotations of the Bible with excerpts from Philippians 3:14 ("My eyes are fixed on the prize") and Luke 9:62 ("who holds the plough and keeps looking back").

(d) Biblical/Christian phraseologies and idioms

Anglophone secessionist discourse abounds in biblical phraseologies and idioms that imbue it with sanctity. As will be shown in the following section, some of those expressions have performative force.

4.2 Pragmatic analysis: speech acts and Christian phraseologies (incantation, blessing, curses, swear words, invocation)

Christianity has inherited many rituals from Jewish traditions, including religious mysticism. Dennis (2007) states that both the Bible and Jewish mysticism emphasise that God created the universe by means of a series of "speech acts", "the power to use words to construct and to destroy under certain conditions". He premises that some special mystical power is enacted through the pronouncement of God's names, through words and phrases that God speaks, and the Hebrew alphabet.

Anglophone separatist leaders and their followers use a variety of pragmatic artifices as a rhetoric tool were inspired by biblical and Christian ideology. Some phraseologies, idioms and propositions are used as swear words, blessings and judgemental proclamations (imprecation) with performative effect. They are classified according to their effects and their functional intent within the discourse. Their use may be for incantations, blessing and well-wishing, cursing and swear words. They are classified as expressive (thanking), declarations (cursing and blessing), directives (prayer requests) and other categorisations.

(1) Assertive (representative) speech acts

These describe the situation and commit the speaker to the truth of the expressed proposition, e. g. assertions, claims and reports.

In (13) and (14), the speaker asserts that "The lord is your strength" and "through the grace of god both the living and the dead shall get to Buea". By making those statements, the Anglophone activists assert the way that they represent the future, their position in relation to God and their secessionist project.

(13) Thanks you General Rk. The lord is your strength.
(14) Gen. Ivo remain our inspiration in spirit and Gen R K .our inspiration in the physical. Whether dead or alive and through the grace of god both the living and the dead shall get to Buea

(2) Expressive speech acts

These express the speaker's attitudes and feelings towards the proposition (excuses, complaints, thanks and congratulations)

In (15) we have a prompting post that was followed by comments in the form of expressive speech acts. The ones with religious language are highlighted.

(15) British Southern Cameroons Resistance Forces:
LRC attacked lower Bafut today. Left THREE LRC terrorist demons six feet deep!
All BSCRF soldiers safely back in base. No civilian casualties noted.
Property damage to be assessed during daylight.
No Retreat, No Surrender! #FundGroundAction #AmbazoniaMustBeFree
Comments
Brave warriors 👍
We thank God and you our valiant warriors.
Until we reach Buea.
Congrats comrades
Amen we thank God for that protection

(3) Declarations

Declarations are speech acts that alter the reality in accordance with the proposition of the declaration using "In Jesus name" and "Amen". Both are adjacency pairs in Christian liturgy.

In (16), "in Jesus name" is used as a declaration. In (15) above, one of the followers responds to a statement with "Amen we thank God for that protection". In (17) and (18), another concludes their own statement with "Amen."

(16) Nfor Vivian shut up pa I pray God will deliver u **in Jesus name**
(17) We shall be free in Jesus name Amen
(18) May God c u an de people Ambazonia through.. Amen !!

"In Jesus name" is a phraseology that is used as a declaration in Christian circles. According to Geoffrey Dennis, the use of names of power is a pervasive aspect of all religious spells and is considered critical to lending efficacy to an incantation. These may include God's names, angels, the righteous dead, even one's mother. In Christian circles, "In Jesus name" is used to claim divine backing of the request. In secessionist discourse, it is used to claim God's validation of the stated declaration. It is usually followed by the utterance "Amen".

"Amen," which means "so be it", is used in Christian rhetoric or discourse to express agreement with something that has been said, or to affirm that what one has said is right. Its use is widespread among Pentecostal evangelicals (see Wharry 2003). In church services, it is uttered repeatedly in response to speakers' declarations, as a Gospel truth marker (see Ndzotom Mbakop 2018) or spiritual well-being statement, and as a rhythmic marker (see Wharry 2003). In this study, followers of the separatists say them in response to declarations or sentential statements uttered by their leaders as a way of expressing their consent and approval.

(4) Directives and declarations that use formulaic words for blessing and well-wishing

In religion, a blessing (also used to refer to the bestowing of such) consists of the infusion of something with holiness, spiritual redemption or divine will. In the context of Ambazonian discourse, blessings are usually pronounced by followers of the leaders who want to wish them well. They are also given in the form of requests to God that favour the territory and its future leaders. In the context of our study, the concept of blessing contributes to understanding the concept of weaponisation in that the blessings are invoked for the secessionists, while curses are rained down upon their opponents. The following posts illustrate this point.

(19) May Jehovah bless you abundantly in Jesus name amen
(20) God bless Ambazonia thank you H. E DR SAMUEL SAKO IKOME Ambazonian president #draft draft drafts till freedom
(21) May God strengthen you brave General RK long live Ambazonia and shot live the strogle
(22) Commander Ayaba! God bless you! Long live Ambazonia!
(23) Dr. Ayaba Cho. You are a great fighter but Unification will help us complete this winning struggle. God bless and protect you. Senior software Engineer Germany
(24): Thank you our Revolutionary Leader for the great Sacrifice. We trust your know-how in such an unprecedented moment. May God continue to grant you wisdom and protect you.
(24) Thank you our Revolutionary Leader for the great Sacrifice. We trust your know-how in such an unprecedented moment. May God continue to grant you wisdom and protect you.
(25) God is in control as we remember fallen heros, God's will shall be done the word of God is power can see you reading it that is why you are different keep up our General God is watching your back
(26) A great lost from Batibo we the mothers we honor our son thanks for your sacrifices RIP and we honor the rest of heroes. **You guys are cover with the blood of Jesus Christ**

(5) Use of formulaic and magic words for incantation, cursing, swear-words and spells

"An incantation or spell is a spoken word, phrase, or formula of power, often recited as part of a larger ritual, which is recited in order to effect a magical result" (Dennis 2007). It is also the act of using words in order to induce enchantment, charm or cast a spell on somebody or something. In religion, incantation is done through the utterance of magic spells and the use of opaque language. Some phraseologies that are stated and often repeated carry charming powers. In the Pentecostal charismatic circles (see R. Marshall 2016), it is assumed that the invocation of God through the pronouncement of the name of Jesus has power to change the order of things, first in the invisible world, then in the visible one. When pronounced with the will of God, these phrases are expected to have performative effects in the invisible and visible realm. In saying them, the speakers are actually asking for divine intervention or for malefic powers to enter into battle on their behalf. In most instances, some of the swear words are used to cast a curse on someone, or bless them.

Cursing is mostly associated with negative emotions such as sadness and anger, which is why people in the online world mainly use curse words to express their anger towards those who do not support the separatist agenda. In the Ambazonian discourse, we have noticed curse-like invectives. By using these "theurgic" spells (see Dennis 2007), the speakers assume that God has in some way delegated that power/authority to them in order to act or to reverse a situation. The examples below illustrate this point.

(27) The Lord God! The Lion of the tribe of Judah, and the Mighty Man in battle will fight for you, brave warriors!!! I cover all of you with the blood of Jesus Christ, and I blind the eyes of the enemy, paralyze their hands and weapons in the matchless name of Jesus Christ!!!

(28) Any spirit of power struggle and lies telling in Tassang Wilfred, out-out, out, out in Jesus name

(29) God punish devil may EC4UC go to hell.in order to get your own position you are being against your brothers and sisters right. That position you'll never get. God punish devil idiot!!!

(30) And sheep will attempt to follow his deadly order. That fake president is a dangerous cultist terrorist looking for innocent souls to devour. But the God that we serve has given us authority to trample over him. That's exactly what we are doing. God punish the devil.

In (27), there is an imprecation which reads "I blind the eyes of the enemy, paralyze their hands and weapons".

(6) Prayer and Invocation

In many instances within the discourse, directives are used for prayers and invoking God, to seek his direct intervention and interference in the conflict on behalf of Ambazonian fighters. The prayers also invoke divine help and assistance for the people.

(31) Amen, and may the hands of God continue to upheld and strengthen you as you lead Ambazonians to freedom from LRC.

(32) General Rk the most loving in the land we thank you so so much may God empire you the more to take us to Buea in Jesus name Amen

(33) Lord open the eyes of Ambas to know that we are just beginning the revolution. Help Ambas that they will not faint in this race till we reach our destination.

(34) Ooh God listing to the cry of our general Rk ,Big number and the rest may u continued to strength them until will we are free my uncle general Ivo we shall continued to cry ,and pray for your loving spirit to rest in peace and also protect the other general u left behind to continued the struggle (water and water with God everything is possible)

4.3 Functions of religious deployment in Anglophone separatist discourse

Activating religious themes in an armed conflict situation in the Anglophone regions of Cameroon is a means of imbuing the crisis with religious meanings and significance, as there is otherwise no religious divide between Cameroonian Anglophones and Francophones. In this situation, the secessionists use a plethora of metaphors and images borrowed from the Bible to rally Christians to their plight and objective: liberation from the francophone yoke.

The use of a specific type of religious rhetoric by Ambazonian leaders, divine ordained rhetoric, is a manipulative discourse strategy aimed at increasing Anglophone expectations for victory over the Cameroonian military.

In this regard, the Amba war draft posted on the Facebook wall of Sako Ikome (the interim president of the Ambazonia defence council) clearly portrays the leaders' decision to place religion as a central issue in the armed conflict to liberate Ambazonia. It reads:

(35) I Am Convicted Deep Down In My Spirit That Keeping The Hope Of Ambazonia Alive, And Trusting The Almighty Is The Only SHIELD We Have Against The Raging Darkness Of Occupation.

In the discourse of Anglophone activists, there are many metaphors that reference biblical scriptures. These include: the journey of Israel from Egypt to the Promised Land; the assignation of messianic characteristics to Ambazonian leaders and fallen heroes; and the transfer of this characterisation into the spiritual realm as a form of spiritual warfare.

(a) The metaphor of the Hebrew exodus and journey to the promise land

As represented in the following post, the Cameroonian Government is Egypt, the Ambazonians are the Jews leaving Egypt and Ambazonia is their promised land.

(36) When we picked up Arms to defend our homeland we knew we might not make it to **the Promised Land.**
(37) This words breaks my heart courage great fighter u will make it to the promise land for God is with u
(38) Let the God of king Solomon continue to renew your wisdom as you lead us to the promise land president we are behind you

Through evoking this metaphor of the journey of the children of Israel from Egypt to the promised land, the secessionists align the circumstances of the Anglophones with those referred to in the corresponding scriptures and use the analogies of the Judeo-Christian Bible to support their secessionist campaigns.

(b) Assigning messianic characteristics to some Anglophone leaders and fallen armed fighters

The assignation of messianic characteristics to the Anglophone leaders is a consistent discursive strategy used by Ambazonians. They presume that their move to secede is "God ordained", with leaders and fighters seen as sent by God to help their cause. In some statements, a leader is characterised and qualified as a "chosen one", as shown in the following posts.

(39) Dr you are the chosen one to lead this struggle. **God** is Not a Man. CIC Ayaba Cho Lucas, Was Born For This Course

When some fighters died in the battle fields, the tributes paid to them depict the role that has been assigned to them: that of the Messiah, in the likeness of Jesus Christ, who shed his blood and died to save humanity from doom.
   Tribute to a fallen fighter:

(40) Gen Ivo. You gave ur life so that we may be free!!
Just like Jesus Christ, you bled and died [...]. for our motherland Ambazonia. God sent you as his son, but once again the people rejected their own saviour. I am 100% convinced that you had to die for us to move ahead. Ambazonia will be free.
(41) [...] No mortal can stop the freedom you died for. Miss you My General, shake glad hands with the Man of War, the Ancient of days, Jesus Christ!
(42) Legends to the heros who bought the land with their blood...

(c) Militarisation of prayer and the metaphor of spiritual warfare

From the Charismatic Pentecostal perspective, secessionists comprehend their struggle from a spiritual warfare perspective that "[...] is a collection of rituals, practices and discourses that aim to do battle with (typically) invisible supernatural threats" (Marshall/Prichard 2020: 4). In the biblical ideology, God is the Lord of hosts who leads his people to battle. Biblical stories provide a variety of conflicts between the Chosen People and their enemies, whereby God always stood on the side of the Chosen People to help them thrive. This is exemplified by a passage from Exodus in the Bible, Chapter 17, verses 8 to 11. Here, Moses asked Joshua to go to the battlefield, while he (Moses) was to go to the mountain to pray. The outcome of the battle was determined by Moses having his hands lifted up. It is also inferred from Biblical ideology that beyond the visible realm, there is an invisible realm where spiritual beings wage war, and humans can influence the outcome through their prayers. The warfare ideology or paradigm is a biblical construct that shows that there is demonic and satanic opposition to the believer achieving felicity. As such, the believer has to wage war against these forces to reach their desired end.

By regarding the Ambazonians as fighting the raging forces of occupation, the Ambazonia leader implies that God is on their side as "a shield", and is going to help them prevail over the "darkness of occupation". This statement helps one infer that a spiritual dimension is given to the armed conflict between the Ambazonian militia and the Government of Cameroon's military forces. From this perspective, the Government of Cameroon, the oppressor, has assumed the role of Satan and the Ambazonians are fighting to free themselves from bondage. In the corpus we have expressions such as "satanic francophone", "evil demon" and "satanic", which are used to characterise the Government of Cameroon or the political entity "La Republique to Cameroun". Furthermore, "the devil" is used metaphorically to refer to Cameroon, which is assumed the role of oppressor of Ambazonians. Cameroonian political entities and figures are associated with negative biblical entities such as "Lucifer, Devil, satanic (..) regime, your evil demon, bondage, yoke, Hell", and the secessionists or Ambazonians are assigned positive characterisations. From the point of view of the secessionists it is valid to assume that the conflict is first and foremost a spiritual war. This helps to legitimate the armed confrontation.

The following prompting post and responses to it illustrate this point.

(43) TINGOH VILLAGE UNDER ATTACK BY LRC. HOUSES ON FIRE. CIVILIANS ARE ADVISED TO STAY AWAY. PUT OUR CIVILIANS & SOLDIERS IN PRAYERS.
It is well our ancestors will cover you all [...] the intruders will be put to shame...fear not our brave warriors
We are in prayer for now hence thanks our head man for your ideas
God will protect u all in Jesus name
God protect wuna
It shall be well with you people in Jesus name I pray
The Lord God! The Lion of the tribe of Judah, and the Mighty Man in battle will fight for you, brave warriors!!! I cover all of you with the blood of Jesus Christ, and I blind the eyes of the enemy, paralyze their hands and weapons in the matchless name of Jesus Christ!!!

We also see warfare vocabulary like "battle", "fight", "brave warrior", "enemy", and "weapon" in utterances like "[...] Mighty Man in battle will fight for you, brave warriors!!!", "cover all of you with the blood of Jesus Christ, and I blind the eyes of the enemy, paralyze their hands and weapons". As illustrated by the above posts, God is invited to participate in the armed conflict in order to give the impression that the Ambazonians are "fighting for the Kingdom of God" (Vüllers 2011).

(d) Adjudging or arrogating divine backing of the insurgency

One of the secessionists' discursive strategies consists of adjudging or arrogating God's support of the insurgency based on the victims' discourse (see Chilton 2004), which states the syllogism that "God is on the side of the oppressed". Since Anglophones are victims of the oppressor or aggressor – in this case, *La Republique* – God is on their side.

(44) [...] Thanks Cho, keep on. God is on the side of the oppressed
(45) [...] Lord open the eyes of Ambas to know that we are just beginning the revolution. Help Ambas that they will not faint in this race till we reach our destination.
(46) hat do u have to tell us today big man and before u say anything remember with u or without u we will have our restoration because God almighty has already ordained that. At the point when we feel we are at the end of the rope, we are not at the end of hope. God is seeing us through.

(e) God for us rhetoric

Anglophone secession leaders resorted to the "God for us" rhetoric to legitimise their decision to pursue armed confrontation against the Government of Cameroon and its military. The God-for-us or God's-on-our-side rhetoric is one manipulative tool used by political leaders. Establishing a relationship between God and politics is what Domke/Coe (2010), quoted in Roche (2015: 7), called "The God Strategy". It consists of claiming that one's cause is supported or backed by God, inspired by God; or of invoking God for the purposes of partisan politics. We see a number of statements and propositions that suggest that the activists presume that God is on their side. Phrases and expressions like "into sustainable peace-flavored independence of a God-ordained richly progressive nation in varying ramifications", "[...] the battle is almost over. Christ is on the throne and we are on the winning side", "God is on our sides because we stand for justice", "God given opportunity", "God has spoken already and freedom is around the Conner" clearly reveal that the secessionists presume that God supports their cause. As such, this assumption contributes to the legitimation and validation of their controversial campaign. The statements and claims also presume that God does not support the Cameroonian Government and the military – just the Anglophones.

The posts below illustrate this analysis.

(47) A lot of heat will be produced in this process and thank God, we have a formidable cooling system, "corporate prayers" for peaceful exit from bondage in the yoke of La République du Cameroun into sustainable peace-flavored independence of a God-ordained richly progressive nation in varying ramifications.

(48) It's a no vote simply rigging of election. The regime is accursed but at the appointed time the Almighty God will straighten up things for the good of the weak. Paul Biya who made himself equal to God killing human randomly - it's a pity. Maranatha and Shalom

(49) God is on our sides because we stand for justice. evil can never prevail over good. The LA republic government fail to understand that one with God is majority. my fellow southern Cameroonians prayer is a sure key to success. So let's keep praying God while protesting peacefully hoping that Jehovah will fight for us in Jesus name

(50) Nobody can stop this God given opportunity to regain our statehood. The struggle continues.

(51) God has spoken already and freedom is around the Conner. The pressure is mounting because the battle is almost over. Christ is on the throne and we are on the winning side

(52) You shall reach Buea and help build the nascent Ambazonia Army. God will see you through

In the above posts, there are constant and consistent references to God, and in every instance the secessionists claim that God is on their side. We have a diversity of expressions and utterances, which include "peace-flavoured independence of a God-ordained", "God is on the side of the oppressed", "God is on our sides because we stand for justice", "God has spoken already and freedom is around the Conner", "God is with us", and "God is seeing us through". Knowing that most Anglophones are religious, the secessionist activists (leaders and followers) use Bible metaphors and imagery to build a storyline for baiting the anglophones into armed conflict, which would enable them to obtain independence from the satanic and oppressive regime of *La Republique du Cameroun*.

The historical case studies attest to the fact that more often than not, leaders and politicians resort to religious rhetoric when they are desperate in the middle of a crisis (see Day/Adam 2018; Dreisbach 2014). During times of crisis, the deployment of religious language and the invocation of God appear to be ways of either expressing one's impotence or rallying the followers of a religion to one's cause. The functions of the God strategy or allusions to the Bible in political discourse have mainly been studied in the USA, where the focus has been on the use of biblical imagery to rally Christian communities. In fact, the use of biblical metaphor in discourse helps one to construct their ideology. In the case that is the focus of this article, it is used to legitimise secession.

5 Discussion

Without a doubt, religion is a very divisive element within society. Our analysis of the Anglophone pro-secession discourse data has shown that the socio-political crisis has assumed a religious overtone and that social media has been an empowering tool in this regard. This study has provided data that show that separatists tactfully use language to diffuse the belief that Ambazonia, the territory which they are fighting to recover or to establish is in fact their promised land, just as the armed conflict has been ordained by God. It was assumed by Anglophone activists that Ambazonia, their new nation, is a Christian one, in contrast to *La République du Cameroun*, which is characterised as an evil entity.

In addition to allusions and references to the Bible, Anglophone web activists used biblical phraseologies and other speech acts to perform invocations, curses and blessings. We have suggested that there is actually no religious divide between Anglophone and Francophone Cameroonians. There are therefore no grounds to claim that Francophone Cameroon is a devilish occupational force and that the would-be Federal Republic of Ambazonia has a biblical and Christian foundation with God's backing. Imbuing the secession discourse with Christian themes is therefore a form of weaponising religion. Religion is instrumentalised to rally more mass support to the separatist cause. As Roche (2015) notes, Domke and Coe's (2010) "God strategy" or Ericson's (1980) "God-centered or/biblical rhetoric" is a strategic and carefully executed political act, not necessarily a genuine belief in or reliance on God. As the activists seem to have made the fight for secession from Cameroon a continuation of the Jews' Exodus from Egypt to the Promised Land, their invocations and prayers aim at calling on God to intervene and free them from their oppressor. Or, in other words, they are fighting a spiritual battle to witness God's Kingdom to come and restore the freedom taken from them by LRC.

Prayer is perceived and employed as a weapon of warfare in order to carry out spiritual violence. It is also a central means of redemption praxis within the Pentecostal milieu (see Tarusarira 2020; McAlister 2016a, 2016b, R. Marshall (2016). Anglophones use it in their quest to secede. The instrumentalisation of religion for political aims has also been posted on social media in other cases of conflict in Africa (see Basedau 2017; Basedau/Schaefer-Kehnert 2019). In Côte d'Ivoire (see N'Guessan 2015, Vüllers 2011), a cross-section of Christian peoples likened the role of Gbagbo to that of a Messiah who had come to liberate their nation from the Oppressor, the French. In the current Anglophone crisis, abduction, arson attacks and the butchering of so called "traitors" have been perpetrated by Ambazonian fighters in order to advance their cause, which has led to forceful condemnations from the national and international community. Their claim that God would support barbaric violence is more than questionable. However, the secessionists still claim to have God's support, as they see the Anglophones as the elect people at the centre of God's attention, even as they are also marginalised as refugees. The politicisation of religion (see P. Marshall 2018) is an issue of debate, just like the militarisation of prayer (see McAlister 2016a, 2016b) in (socio-)political struggles; the more extreme of the two being the weaponisation of religion. Morris-Chapman (2019) discusses an Ambazonian theology of liberation that examines the question of self-defence in relation to acts of state-sponsored violence. He explores the question of resistance to the State as a reaction to the postcolonial marginalisation that Anglophone Cameroonians experienced. Resorting to Christianity as a means to validate violence is comparable to Islamist terrorism, where jihad is the driver of barbaric and violent acts. Islamic religious arguments are sometimes used to legitimise violent terrorism as they claim that governments and political entities that have no respect for Islamic laws must be fought. They also refuse to acknowledge those leaders as they claim to only acknowledge a higher divine law whose application is binding for them. According to Paterson (2019), most Islamic terrorists in Indonesia consider all those who do not condone their actions as infidels. The members of these groups consider themselves to be engaged in a struggle between good and evil, where every outgroup entity embodies evil (see Juergensmeyer 1997). Religion is therefore instrumentalised to legitimate terrorism, and this misuse is a form of weaponisation.

6 Conclusion

This study aimed to investigate the religious discourse deployed by Anglophone secessionists engaged in armed conflict with the Cameroonian government and military. We found that Biblical allusions and Christian phraseologies were used to imbue the discourse with Christian ideology. This study claims that this discursive strategy amounts to weaponisation, that is, involving God in an armed conflict as a means to rally support from a large quantity of gullible Christians in Cameroon's Anglophone regions. This armed conflict has become violent, as the Ambazonian fighters and government forces have resorted to gruesome killings.

Ambazonians fighters claim to be doing it in the name of God, who has ordained this struggle. Vüllers (2011: 6) warned that the politicisation of religious identities can result in believers committing violent acts at specific times and locations. Religious extremism should not only be viewed from the perspective of an isolated group carrying out violent attacks in the name of religion, it also encapsulates those social struggles in which religion is used as a weapon. It includes using religious beliefs to justify violent acts or invoking God's assistance while committing these same acts. Weaponising religion is very common in the political discourse of liberal democracies where religion is central to the public life. For instance, in the USA, where Americans have long been committed to a series of beliefs that attribute a special, God-given role to America on the global stage (see Roche 2015). Consequently, in times of crisis, their leaders use allusions to the Bible to rally the support of Christians for their projects.

This study shows that religion is gaining ground and has become a controversial and problematic aspect of the public and political sphere. It has highlighted how much religion is still a powerful force in the Cameroonian socio-cognitive environment, thereby contributing to the debate regarding secularisation in democracies. This tends to contradict post-modern discourse's prediction that religion would lose its authority.

References

a. Research literature

Awolalu, Jospeh Omosade (1975): "What is African Traditional Religion?" In: *Studies in Comparative Religion* 9 (1), http://www.studiesincomparativereligion.com/Public/articles/What_is_African_Traditional_Religion-by_Joseph_Omosade_Awolalu.aspx (accessed 02 August 2021).

Bardici, Minavere Vera (2012): *A Discourse Analysis of the Media Representation of Social Media for Social Change – The Case of Egyptian Revolution and Political Change*. MA thesis. Malmö University. https://www.diva-portal.org/smash/get/diva2:1482748/FULLTEXT01.pdf (accessed 02 August 2021).

Bartlett, Jamie/Birdwell, Jonathan/Littler, Mark (2011): *The new face of digital populism*. London: Demos.

Basedau, Matthias (2017): "The Rise of Religious Armed Conflicts in Sub-Saharan Africa. No Simple Answers". In: *GIGA Focus Africa* (4), https://www.giga-hamburg.de/en/publications/giga-focus/rise-religious-armed-conflicts-sub-saharan-africa-simple-answers (accessed 02 August 2021).

Basedau, Matthias et al. (2011): "Do Religious Factors Impact Armed Conflict? Empirical Evidence from Sub-Saharan Africa". In: *Terrorism and Political Violence* 23 (5), 752–779. DOI: 10.1080/09546553.2011.619240 (accessed 02 August 2021).

Basedau, Matthias/Pfeiffer, Birte/Vüllers, Johannes (2016): "Bad Religion? Religion, Collective Action, and the Onset of Armed Conflict in Developing Countries". In: *Journal of Conflict Resolution* 60 (2), 226–255. DOI: 10.1177/0022002714541853 (accessed 02 August 2021).

Basedau, Matthias/Schaefer-Kehnert, Johanna (2019): "Religious discrimination and religious armed conflict in sub-Saharan Africa: an obvious relationship?" In: *Religion, State & Society* 47 (1), 30-47, DOI: 10.1080/09637494.2018.1531617 (accessed 02 August 2021).

BUCREP (2010): *3ème RGPH, The Population of Cameroon in 2010*, Yaoundé.

Campbell, David E. (2020): "The Perils of Politicized Religion". In: Daedalus 149 (3): 87–104, DOI: https://doi.org/10.1162/DAED_a_01805 (accessed 02 August 2021).

Chilton, Paul (2004): *Analysing Political Discourse, Theory and Practice*. London: Routledge.

Chitando, Ezra (2005): "'In the beginning was the land': The appropriation of religious themes in political discourses in Zimbabwe". In: *Africa* 75 (2), 220–239. DOI: https://doi.org/10.3366/afr.2005.75.2.220 (accessed 02 August 2021).

Domke, David/Coe, Kevin (2010): *The God Strategy. How Religion Became a Political Weapon in America*. Oxford: Oxford University Press.

Dreisbach, Daniel L. (2014): "The Bible in the Political Culture of the American Founding". In: Daniel L. Dreisbach/Mark David Hall (eds.): *Faith and the Founders of the American Republic*, New York: Oxford University Press, 144–173.

Du Bois, John W. (1986): "Self-evidence and ritual speech". In: Wallace L. Chafe/Johanna Nichols (eds.): *Evidentiality. The Linguistic Coding of Epistemology*. Ablex.

Ericson, David F. (1997): "Presidential inaugural addresses and American political culture". In: *Presidential Studies Quarterly* 27 (4), 727–744.

Fornieri, Joseph R. (2003): *Abraham Lincoln's Political Faith*. DeKalb: Northern Illinois University Press.

Halliday, M. A. K. (1992): "Systemic Grammar and the Concept of a 'Science of Language'". In: M. A. K. Halliday: *On Language and Linguistics*, Vol. 3 in *The Collected Works of M.A.K. Halliday edited by Jonathan J. Webster*. London: Continuum, 199–212.

Halliday, M. A. K./Hasan, Ruqaiya (1985): *Language, Context and Text. Aspects of Language in a Social-Semiotic Perspective*. Geelong: Deakin University Press.

Hide, Enri (2014): "Religion as a Legitimizing Instrument of Political Violence in Mediterranean". In: *Journal of Social Sciences* 5 (13), 184–190. DOI:10.5901/mjss.2014.v5n13p184 (accessed 12 August 2021).

Juergensmeyer, Mark (1997). "Terror Mandated by God". In: *Terrorism and Political Violence* 9 (2), 16–23. DOI: 10.1080/09546559708427400 (accessed 12 August 2021).

Keane, Webb (2003): "Religious Language". In: *Annual Review of Anthropology* 26 (1), 47–71. DOI:10.1146/annurev.anthro.26.1.47 (accessed 12 August 2021).

Keane, Webb (2004): "Language and religion". In: Alessandro Duranti (ed.): *A Companion to Linguistic Anthropology*. Malden, MA: Blackwell, 431–448.

KhosraviNik, Majid (2018): "Social Media Critical Discourse Studies (SM-CDS)". In: John Flowerdew/John E. Richardson (eds.): *The Routledge Handbook of Critical Discourse Studies*. New York: Routledge, 582–596.

Konings, Piet/Nyamnjoh, Francis B. (1997): "The Anglophone Problem in Cameroon". In: *Journal of Modern African Studies* 35 (2): 207–229. DOI: https://doi.org/10.1017/S0022278X97002401 (accessed 12 August 2021).

Lakoff, George/Johnson, Mark (1980): *Metaphors We Live by*. Chicago: University of Chicago Press.

Ludovic, S. J., Lado Tonlieu (2021): "Religion and Peacebuilding in Sub-Saharan Africa". In: Terence McNamee/Monde Muyangwa (eds.): *The State of Peacebuilding in Africa. Lessons Learned for Policymakers and Practitioners*. Cham: Palgrave Macmillan, 47–64. DOI: https://doi.org/10.1007/978-3-030-46636-7_4 (accessed 12 August 2021).

Marshall, Kimberly/Prichard, Andreana (2020): "Spiritual Warfare in Circulation". In: *Religions* 11 (7), 327. DOI: https://doi.org/10.3390/rel11070327 (accessed 12 August 2021).

Marshall, Ruth (2016): "Destroying arguments and captivating thoughts. Spiritual warfare prayer as global praxis". In: *Journal of Religious and Political Practice* 2 (1), 92–113, DOI: 10.1080/20566093.2016.1085243 (accessed 24 June 2021).

Mbiti, John S. (1999): *African Religions and Philosophy*. 2nd edn. Oxford: Heinemann.

McAlister, Elizabeth (2016a): "The militarization of prayer in America. White and Native American spiritual warfare". In: *Journal of Religious and Political Practice* 2 (1), 114–130, DOI: 10.1080/20566093.2016.1085239 (accessed 12 August 2021).

Miran, Marie (2005): "D'Abidjan à Porto Novo. Associations islamiques et culture religieuse réformiste sur la Côte de Guinée". In: Laurent Fourchard/André Mary/René Otayek (eds.): *Entreprises religieuses transnationales en Afrique de l'Ouest*, Paris: Ibadan, 43–72.

Miran, Marie (2006): "The Political Economy of Civil Islam in Côte d'Ivoire". In: Michael Bröning/Holger Weiss (eds.): *Politischer Islam in Westafrika. Eine Bestandsaufnahme*. Berlin: Friedrich Ebert Stiftung, 82–113.

Morris-Chapman, Daniel Pratt (2019): "An Ambazonian theology? A theological approach to the Anglophone crisis in Cameroon". In: *HTS Teologiese Studies/Theological Studies* 75 (4), a5371. DOI: https://doi.org/10.4102/hts.v75i4.5371 (accessed 12 August 2021).

N'Guessan, Konstanze (2015): "Côte d'Ivoire. Pentecostalism, Politics, and Performances of the Past". In: *Nova Religio* 18 (3), 80–100. DOI: https://doi.org/10.1525/nr.2015.18.3.80 (accessed 12 August 2021).

Ndzotom Mbakop, Antoine Willy (2018): "Comparative Analysis of the Pragmatic Functions of 'Amen' in Mainstream Protestant and Pentecostal Churches in Cameroon". In: *Corpus Pragmatics* 2 (4), 333–349. DOI: https://doi.org/10.1007/s41701-018-0032-4 (accessed 12 August 2021).

Ngom, Fallou/Kurfi, Mustapha H./Falola, Toyin (eds.) (2020): *The Palgrave Handbook of Islam in Africa*. Cham: Palgrave Macmillan. DOI: https://doi.org/10.1007/978-3-030-45759-4 (accessed 12 August 2021).

Ngouo, Herbert Rostand (2020): "Polarized Facebook Discourse on Anglophone Nationalism in Cameroon". In: *Studies in Pragmatics and Discourse Analysis* 1 (1), 58–76. DOI: https://doi.org/10.48185/spda.v1i1.77 (accessed 12 August 2021).

Olaniran, Bolane/Williams, Indi (2020): "Social Media Effects. Hijacking Democracy and Civility in Civic Engagement". In: John Jones/Michael Trice (eds.): *Platforms, Protests, and the Challenge of Networked Democracy. Rhetoric, Politics and Society*. Cham: Palgrave Macmillan, 77–94. DOI: https://doi.org/10.1007/978-3-030-36525-7_5 (accessed 12 August 2021).

Paterson, Thomas (2019): "The Indonesian Cyberspace Expansion. A double edge sword". In: *Journal of Cyber Policy* 4 (2), 216–234. 4, DOI: 10.1080/23738871.2019.1627476 (accessed 12 May 2021).

Pawlikova-Vilhanova, Viera (2020): "Islam and Christianity in Africa". In: Fallou Ngom/Mustapha H. Kurfi/Toyin Falola (eds.): *The Palgrave Handbook of Islam in Africa*. Cham: Palgrave Macmillan, 233–251. DOI: https://doi.org/10.1007/978-3-030-45759-4_13 (accessed 12 May 2021).

Rapoport, David C. (1984): "Fear and Trembling: Terrorism in Three Religions Traditions". In: *The American Political Science Review* 78 (3), 658–677. DOI: https://doi.org/10.2307/1961835 (accessed 12 August 2021).

Raynal, Sandrine (2005): "En Côte-d'Ivoire, 'les forces du bien contre les forces du mal'". In: *Hérodote* 119 (4), 111–128. https://www.herodote.org/spip.php?article193 (accessed 20 July 2022).

Roche, Megan, Alexandria (2015): *Rhetoric, Religion, and Representatives. The Use of God in Presidential Inaugural Addresses from 1933-2009 as Reflections of Trends in American Religiosity.* MA Thesis. Florida State University. http://purl.flvc.org/fsu/fd/FSU_migr_etd-9456 (accessed 20 July 2022).

Svensson, Isak (2007): "Fighting with Faith. Religion and Conflict Resolution in Civil Wars". In: *Journal of Conflict Resolution*, 51 (6), 930–949.

Tarusarira, Joram (2020): "Religious Politics in Africa. Fasting for Politics, or Political Fasting in Zimbabwe?" In: *Exchange* 49 (1), 31–52. DOI: https://doi.org/10.1163/1572543X-12341548 (accessed 20 July 2022).

The Bible (2010). Authorized King James Version, National Publishing.

Toft, Monica Duffy (2007): "Getting Religion? The Puzzling Case of Islam and Civil War". In: *International Security* 31 (4), 97–131.

Toolin, Cynthia (1983): "American civil religion from 1789 to 1981. A content analysis of Presidential Inaugural Addresses". In: *Review of Religious Research* 25 (1), 39–48.

Torpey, John (2010): "A (Post-) Secular Age?" In: *Social Research* 77 (1): 269–296.

Veer, Peter van der (eds.) (2017): *Prayer and Politics*. London: Routledge.

Vüllers, Johannes (2011): "Fighting for a Kingdom of God? The Role of Religion in the Ivorian Crisis". In: *GIGA Working Papers* (178). https://pure.giga-hamburg.de/ws/files/21244673/wp178_vuellers.pdf (accessed 20 July 2022).

Wald, Kenneth D. (2003): *Religion and Politics in the United States*. 4th edn. Lanham: Rowman and Littlefield.

Wariboko, Nimi (2017): "Pentecostalism in Africa". In: Oxford Research Encyclopaedia of African History. DOI: https://doi.org/10.1093/acrefore/9780190277734.013.120 (accessed 12 April 2021).

Wharry, Cheryl (2003): "Amen and Hallelujah preaching: Discourse functions in African American sermons". In: *Language in Society*, 32 (2), 203–225. DOI: https://doi.org/10.1017/S0047404503322031 (accessed 24 June 2021).

b. Online sources

Brooking, Emerson T./Singer, P. W. (2016): "War Goes Viral. How social media are weaponized". In: *The Atlantic*. https://www.theatlantic.com/magazine/archive/2016/11/war-goes-viral/501125/ (accessed 02 August 2021).

Dennis, Geoffrey W. (2007): "Incantations, Spells and Adjurations. Some traditional Jewish sources indicate belief in the efficacy of spells." https://www.myjewishlearning.com/article/incantations-spells-adjurations/ (accessed 02 August 2021).

Dreisbach, Daniel L. (2015): "Sacred Rhetoric and political discourse". In: *Law & Liberty*. https://lawliberty.org/sacred-rhetoric-and-political-discourse/ (accessed 02 August 2021).

Dreisbach, Daniel, L. (2017): "The Promises and Perils of Using the Bible in Political Discourse". In: Mark Elliott/Patricia Landy (eds.): *The Bible and Interpretation*. https://bibleinterp.arizona.edu/articles/2017/02/dre418022 (accessed 02 August 2021).

Marshall, Paul (2018): "Politicizing Religion. Politics, not Religion?" In: *Hudson Institute*. https://www.hudson.org/research/14598-politicizing-religion (accessed 12 August 2021).

McAlister, Elizabeth (2016b): "The Militarization of Prayer and Evangelical Spiritual Warfare in Haiti". A lecture by Elizabeth McAlister, Professor of Religion at Wesleyan University, as part of the Spring Colloquium 2016 series 'Political Imaginaries Across Latin America and the Caribbean'. https://as.nyu.edu/content/nyu-as/as/research-centers/clacs/events/spring-2016/the-militarization-of-prayer-and-evangelical-spiritual-warfare-i.html (accessed 12 August 2021).

Pew Research Center (2010): *Tolerance and Tension: Islam and Christianity in Sub-Saharan Africa*, www.pewforum.org/2010/04/15/executive-summary-islam-and-christianity-in-sub-saharan-africa/ (accessed 15 June 2021).

Part III: **Contradictory Operations of Marginalisation and Centralisation**

Christopher M. Schmidt
Shaping Identity through the Use of Language
The Finland Swedish Paradox

1 Introduction

The relationship between language and identity is manifold. According to Berger/Luckman (1993), identity can be understood as a form of primary socialisation. The relationship between language and identity can also be seen as the use of linguistic register in order to differentiate other users of the same language for the purposes of marking group identity (see Joseph 2004). In the present article, linguistic behaviour is examined from a social psychological perspective while asking in which ways the use of language can be a denominator for building language-based group identity. This has also been referred to as shaping identity through language (see Thim-Mabrey 2003: 2). In this article we will go a step further and ask in what way belonging to a linguistic minority, using the language of that minority and experiencing a vital threat to that minority language can be central to maintaining subjective minority identity. This phenomenon could be likened to two opposite sides of a coin that are facing two different directions while still completing each other, thus constituting a paradoxical whole. The present article examines this in the context of the Finland Swedish discourse surrounding linguistic behaviour in relation to the country's two national languages – Finnish and Swedish, where the Swedish-speaking Finns represent the country's minority. The term "Finland Swedish" is used throughout the article to refer to this minority.[1]

Research focusing on the Finland Swedish minority has partly dealt with examining the use of the minority language – often with respect to local variations

---

[1] The term was mainly introduced in Finnish official debate from 1910 to 1914, when the Swedish-speaking minority was searching for a suitable linguistic denominator for its national status. By 1945 it had gained semi-official status (see Mustelin 1983). There is an underlying duality in terms of identity, as Finland Swedes at the same time are part of the Finnish nationality, which makes it rather artificial to separate Finland Swedish history from Finnish history, even though attempts are made (see Stenius 1983).

Open Access. © 2023 the author(s), published by De Gruyter. This work is licensed under the Creative Commons Attribution 4.0 International License.
https://doi.org/10.1515/9783111039633-009

– as a sign of lived identity (see Ståhlberg 1995; Allardt 1984; Lönnqvist 1984), whether from a historical perspective, as part of a developing Finnish State (see Sundberg 1985; Fewster 2000; Klinkmann 2011), or from a more culturally analytical perspective (see Åström/Lönnqvist/Lindqvist 2001), to name a few. Most of these works have their scientific starting point in ethnological and folkloristic research, both being well-established research domains in Finland.[2] Klinkmann points out that despite the many publications on the topic, the historical description of Finland Swedes has presented difficulties for identifying what exactly "being Finland Swedish" means (see Klinkmann 2017: 31). According to Allardt (1983: 36), the categories of "periphery" and "minority" are problematic for applying in a traditional sense to the Finland Swedes. In terms of location, they live in both urban centres and in rural areas, mostly in the southern and western parts of the country, and at a local level mostly mixed together with the Finnish-speaking majority. Historically, they have played a central role in shaping the governmental and administrative foundations of the 19th Century that in the 20th century led to the emergence of the independent state. Still, in terms of population, they form a minority in the country, and their membership in that minority is defined more by language than by geographic location. According to Sundberg (1985: 2), possessing Swedish-language skills as a denominator for belonging to this minority group differentiates it from most European minorities. It is a specific aspect of Finnish society that the individuals themselves can decide on which group they belong to. This means that the categorisation of belonging to the minority or majority is a personal decision and not up to government authorities. In this sense, it is a self-categorisation. As a consequence, that decision, if the individual wants to make it, can be changed by them through language registration. Based on her empirical studies of the Finland Swedish minority, Sundback (2015: 35) points out that an individual's decision to change their language registration might also reflect an unwillingness to be categorised as solely belonging to one of the two language groups. According to Allardt/Starck (1981: 42–46), in addition to self-categorisation, the other main individual classification categories are family descent, cultural traits and those social organisations that can serve as communication platforms for Finnish society's Swedish-speaking minority.

---

2 For a wider overview of research on Finland Swedish culture, history and language, see the introduction in Klinkmann/Henriksson/Häger (2017); from a historical perspective, see Engman/Stenius (1984); under the concept of social capital, see Sundback/Nyqvist (2010).

Regarding the question of self-assessment in terms of belonging to a group,[3] it is interesting to see how the role of language and culture affects the way Finland Swedes view themselves. In a Gallup poll conducted in 2019, 88% of the respondents (n = 1154) claimed that it is very important to care about the Swedish language in Finland (in addition, 9% are somewhat of the same opinion) and 87% stated that it is very important to care about the Finland Swedish culture in Finland (in addition, 11% are somewhat of the same opinion). When asked how significant this culture is to them, only 80% said that it was very important (see Herberts 2019). This poll hints at the factor that linguistic consciousness is stronger among Finland Swedes than their awareness of their culture as a group. The fact that they belong to a minority is crucial for shaping identity in the case of Finland Swedes, which the research institute *e2* found after it conducted a survey in 2018 on the identity domains among this group (n = 6746). In the same study, generic values such as childhood, family, education, work life and friends played an insignificant role in shaping the identity of the Finnish-speaking majority (see Bäck 2018).

If values related to way of life are of less relevance than language in shaping the identity of Finland Swedes, then at this point one can raise the question of the different ways that the language factor can be so important to Finland Swedish minority identity. Before delving into this question, it is worth looking at the historical context in which the Finland Swedish minority became established in Finland. Finland Swedish identity cannot be fully grasped without first taking into account the historical development of the Swedish language's role within the country. Following Finland's independence in 1917, Swedish was granted second official language status (see Finlex 2003). This development has a long history, as Finland had been part of the Swedish Empire since the 13th Century, up until it became part of Russia in 1809 following the Swedish-Russian war. During the 19th Century, there were Finland Swedes who were highly active in promoting Finnish national identity in areas such as administration, education, culture and economics (see Ekberg 2000: 18–23).

According to the magistrate's self-registration records, the amount of Finland Swedes in the country has decreased since the 1950s. From the perspective of linguistic identity, this development is not without significance. From 1950 to 2000, the number of Finland Swedes has decreased from 348,000 to 291,000. After a short rise from 2008 to 2012, the number has been in steady decline. Today the registered number is around 289,000, which corresponds to about 5.2 % of the total

---

[3] In this article, the term "self-categorisation" is used to describe group belonging in terms of language registration. The term "self-assessment" denotes group belonging in terms of minority versus majority group in a broader sense.

population (see Saarela 2021: 13). Most Finland Swedes live in bilingual towns or areas and are thus in constant contact with speakers of the majority language.

2 Intersectionality and double bind theory

Due to the constantly changing numbers for registered members among the minority, the ongoing migration in and out of the country, and the tendency towards bilingual marriages in some parts of the country, the number of individuals who belong to the minority is in constant flux. It is important to notice right now that the Finland Swedish minority is not to be understood as a national minority in the conventional sense (see Klinkmann/Henriksson/Häger 2017: 12), but rather as a minority that is defined through its use of Swedish as means of communication, and therefore through its constant quest to safeguard Swedish at the institutional level (see Sundback 2006: 408). This is a crucial aspect because it is also the starting point for an identity dichotomy that is characteristic of this minority, which this article will investigate further. As the distinction from the Finnish-speaking majority is always in flux – mainly due to ethnic self-assessment and bilingual marriages, the language as such cannot automatically serve as an ethnic criterion. However, it is nonetheless this minority's central group criterion (see Sundback 2010: 58). This paradoxical situation shapes the relationship and attitudes that the Finland Swedish minority has towards the Finnish-speaking majority, and in terms of identity, the whole concept of minority becomes very complex when the language has a central function. This is especially the case when the legal right to use the Swedish mother tongue at an institutional level is not always made possible. With regard to this kind of a situation, Klinkmann/Henriksson/Häger (2017: 12) refer to a "experienced minority". Should one use the language of the majority due to convenience (and thereby weaken the "experienced minority" identity) or should one insist on their legal right? This is not an easy question to answer as it is not merely an issue of language use as such. The scenario of being torn between different choices that influence subjective minority identity also exists at other levels, such as the choice between emigrating to Sweden (and thereby giving up the "minority experience" as an identity marker) or staying in the home country, which is as much a part of their national identity as it is for the Finnish-speaking majority. For this reason, belonging to the Swedish-speaking minority should not to be confounded with having separatist beliefs (see Sundback 2006: 410).

Under the concept of intersectionality, people have also tried to understand the different dichotomies in everyday minority life and its possible consequences for the assessment of one's identity (see Klinkmann 2017; Strandén-Backa/Backa 2017; Henriksson/Häger 2017). Intersectionality as introduced by Crenshaw (1989; 1991) is the idea that power and social ranking can have different functions when examining the position of women within society. To better understand the social positioning of Black women, Crenshaw (1991) pointed out that it is not enough to only address the issue from a gender-related perspective, but to combine (intersect) this perspective with the dimension of race. This is because white women – even when they are weaker positioned than white men – still have a higher-ranking position than women of other races when it comes to social class. Intersectional categories are not only added, but also seen as intensifying one other. Knudsen (2005) uses the term to analyse Norwegian minority cultures and identities in textbooks. Lykke (2007) discusses implicit intersectionality based on Scandinavian research in the specialty of feminist Marxism, and, more specifically, in that of queer feminism. She widens the theoretical aspect of intersectionality and differentiates between explicit and implicit forms. Here the former term is used to examine explicit use of intersectionality, while the latter is used to examine power systems and identity categories as intersections without naming them as such. In the case of the Finland Swedish minority, intersectionality can be a central aspect when examining the relationship between social position and identity, where self-assessment can be influenced through many factors that can interact and reinforce each other. Klinkmann (2017) discusses intersectionality in the case of the Finland Swedes from a social historical point of view. Henriksson/Häger (2017) discuss the intersectional perspective utilising newspaper debates about regional politics in the healthcare sector as their bases, while only partly touching on the role that language can have. Strandén-Backa/Backa (2017) treat the question of intersectionality from the perspective of subjective minority self-assessment. According to Klinkmann/Henriksson/Häger (2017: 15), intersectionality factors can be manifold in the case of the Finland Swedish minority, which can include such examples as language, social class, individual preferences and living in a certain area. The crucial question for shaping identity is how individuals are coping with different forms of intersectional identity positioning when identity is placed under stress by external factors, such as a perceived penetration of the majority language into areas of daily life where one was previously able to use the minority mother tongue. A more thorough investigation of how language (both as a means of communication and as an identity criterion) can be tied to intersectional identity strategies is still missing in the case of the Finland Swedes, which is why this article will try to shed some light on this question.

The paradoxical role that language can have as a criterion for the Finland Swedish minority becomes evident when one considers that, on the one hand, a growing number of bilingual individuals feel like they belong to both the Swedish-speaking minority and the Finnish-speaking majority, which in turn can lead to a greater acceptance of using Finnish in daily life. But at the same time, this tendency is also seen as a threat coming from the "outside" that undermines the traditional tendency to use Swedish and weakens the Swedish-speaking way of life (see Sundback 2010: 55). As the Swedish language has gradually had a less prominent role as an identity criterion at the individual level, at a collective level it has nevertheless kept its central role as a minority criterion (see Sundback 2010: 59). It is on the collective level that the concept of a language-based "threat" against the minority is kept alive through different narratives, of which the Moomin narrative is central (see Rönnholm 2001; Ruusuvuori 2005; Henriksson 2010; Klinkmann 2011). Here, the fictional characters of (the Finland Swedish author) Tove Jansson's tales from Moominvalley are viewed as communal points of identification at a collective level. According to this narrative, the Finland Swedish community inside the imagined Moominvalley is under a constant threat from the outside. Interestingly enough, the ingroup/outgroup dichotomy implies a paradoxical relationship between both categories, which Klinkmann describes as the double bind phenomenon: in order to be able to criticise the Finland Swedish way of life from the outside, one needs to be part of it from the inside, to be part of the conceived group identity that Klinkmann in turn refers to as the "mental landscape" of the inside group (see Klinkmann 2011: 284).[4]

Klinkmann uses the concept of *double bind* as introduced by Gregory Bateson in order to describe a fundamental communication dilemma where an answer to a question can serve as a double bind that simultaneously points in different directions, thus forming a paradox (see Klinkmann 2011: 284). The Finland Swedish minority status already entails a double bind, as this group forms both part of a different national culture as well as an ethnic-cultural minority. This dilemma for identity self-assessment gets even more complicated when one considers that the Finland Swedish minority is not a homogeneous group, as there are considerable local cultural differences between the Finnish-language Swedish-language population areas (see Sundberg 1985: 19–22). In the case of the Finland Swedish minority, one can assume that both intersectional factors (such as national belonging, language identity, minority group, minority culture, language skills, regional identity, perceived threats of exercising mother tongue) and the potential double bind between these factors entail possible contradictions at a psychological level when the minority tries to cope with these factors in everyday life.

---

[4] Klinkmann is not alone with this view. For an overview of other authors on this matter, see Klinkmann 2011: 283–285.

This potential implicit contradiction for self-assessment crystallises most clearly in the narratives about the usage of the group's mother tongue. It arises out of the dichotomies involved in Finland Swedish self-assessment for language proficiency: Swedish-speaking as being non-Finnish; being non-bilingual versus being bilingual; living a language register as a dialect or sociolect as opposed to academic Swedish (see Strandén-Backa/Backa 2017: 90). Even if these dichotomies do not necessarily and automatically have to entail contradictions for minority identity, they might still lead to paradoxes in the search for identity self-assessments. The problems with language-based identity might even be imposed from the "outside" through narratives in society of the kind that "Finland is Finnish, not Finnish and Swedish, and there is the idea of a nation state that is more or less predominant when it comes to language: one country and one language" (Strandén-Backa/Backa 2017: 92). The present article will show the psychological implications that this can have for minority identity and the strategies that are employed to cope with it.

Both intersectionality and double bind are aspects that can serve to understand the paradoxical situation in which a language-based minority can find itself. In the case of the Finland Swedish minority, this article will examine different kinds of materials in order to elucidate the interconnectedness between intersectional aspects and possible double binds linked to these aspects when examining the role of language for the dimensions of Finland Swedish identity. In order to do so, different types of documentation will be used; both Finland Swedish experience-based media comments (as primary sources) and results from other investigations on language attitudes. I will also take a look at the ways in which they are interpreted within a Finland Swedish perspective. By combining primary as well as evaluated material from "inside" the Finland Swedish perspective (see Klinkmann 2011), a more complex qualitative picture can be drawn with regard to the role that language has with respect to Finland Swedish minority self-assessment. In order to also preserve the inside perspective in the empirical data evaluations, the article will take into account the ways in which Finland Swedish scholars have evaluated empirical data on the subject matter dealt with in this article.

3 Linguistic self-assertion and its realisation

The media coverage of issues having to do with the Finland Swedish minority always focuses on linguistic aspects, which in itself shows the importance of language for this minority. Since the advent of new media, these experiences have also been documented and are accessible in a variety of media. In this section I present quotations from the media discourse that have been translated from the original Swedish.[5]

As shown in the introduction, when one considers the consequences that can arise out of possible double bind situations that speakers from the minority group can find themselves in, there is a very high level of awareness of the minority's mother tongue advocacy. The inside perspective refers to phenomena that arise from the inner scope of the minority and that are defined by minority-related criteria or can be triggered by their own minority-induced logic. This means that they can be explained from this perspective.

All the more astonishing is a phenomenon that comes from daily experience, one that runs counter to this awareness in concrete linguistic action. This is the change from the minority mother tongue to the national majority language, although – and this is the main reason for a paradoxical situation against the backdrop of documented language awareness – there need not be any external reason for changing one's language:

(1) When a Finnish speaking person joins a group that consists of Finland Swedes, many Finland Swedes change the language into Finnish. In Southern Finland in particular, this is an everyday experience. (Berg 2018)

This behaviour is all the more astonishing, as the relationship between minority and majority in these kinds of groups is the opposite of what is normally found at the national level. The paradoxical dimension of this kind of behaviour, which arises from its double bind implications (a gesture meant to be nice is at the same time perceived to be its opposite), is even more evident, as the representatives of the Finnish majority do not necessarily consider this to be something positive. This can be seen in the case of the Finnish speaker quoted below:

(2) It is a typically Finland Swedish thing, at least in the region of the capital, to switch the language into Finnish, when a Finnish speaking person joins a group. The gesture that was meant to be nice quickly gets the opposite effect for the Finnish speaking person. (Berg 2018)

---

[5] In order to render the original conceptual ways of expression so that they are discernible to the reader, the quotations do not use idiomatic translation into English or orthographically corrected modes of writing. This is important for grasping the kind of underlying conceptual and/or emotional dimension attached to the utterances. All translations from Swedish in this article are mine.

The tendency to abandon one's own Finland Swedish mother tongue not only occurs in group dynamic settings as shown above, but also in those cases where a representative from each language group is present. However, this language behaviour is not always to the liking of the Finland Swedish speakers themselves. One respondent (woman, anonymous) in a survey of 1000 participants documented in Herberts 2019 expresses the intersectionality between the moral implications of this action and the subject's physical condition as follows:

(3) I speak fluent Finnish and by that I get the errand quicklier done. That is wrong of me but the health condition is sometimes bad and you can't cope with it. (Herberts 2019: 49)

Still, Finland Swedes do make the effort to have conversations in Swedish. Although guaranteed by the country's Basic Law, this is seen as especially problematic in the healthcare sector, as the following answers from different respondents in Herberts' documentation show:

(4) The nurse at the reception told me off, because I was speaking Swedish. I complained about it and her boss phoned me later and reprimanded me, because I did not appreciate their "best nurse". (Herberts 2019: 34)
(5) I have also experienced to be directly laughed at when I had asked a nurse something in Swedish. (Herberts 2019: 34)
(6) In the hospital at Seinäjoki a young male nurse said that we in Finland speak Finnish. I got angry, but still answered him calmly in Finnish that Finland is a bilingual country and you can also learn Swedish! (Herberts 2019: 37)

Quotations 4–6 are examples of the different types of double binds that are involved. In (4) the basic legal right to use the mother tongue leads to its sanctioning; in (5) it leads to one being ridiculed and in (6) the arbitrary suppression of this right leads to mental stress in spite of the calmness of the speaker's outside appearance. As can be seen in the above quotations from different respondents, they all refer to their mother tongue as "Swedish". An implicit intersectional dilemma might occur when speaking about Swedish as the language of the Finland Swedes, as the Finland Swedes speak regional variants of Swedish that dominate their linguistic landscape. Reuter et al. group the Finland Swedish language somewhat unspecifically next to dialects, slang and sub-variants as a sub-form of standard Swedish (see Reuter/Hällström-Reijonen/Tandefelt 2017: 18). The classification of Finland Swedish in the grey area between dialect and standard language pushes the subliminal dilemma regarding the formation of a Finland Swedish linguistic identity to the extreme. It is little surprising then that Wikner

(2019) comes to the following conclusion in her survey on Finland Swedish linguistic behaviour in the capital region:

(7) A general finding regarding the respondents' views on Swedish in Helsingfors is that it is difficult to describe. Many of the respondents could not find a name for their language. They say they don't know what it is: it's not a dialect, it's not standard Swedish – so what is it then? (Wikner 2019: 50)

The results expressed in Wikner (2019) show that the language status that the mother tongue can give its speakers (according to (7) above) can imply a possible double bind between being a "language" in form of a mother tongue ("standard Swedish") and a language that is only viewed as a dialect. This can potentially imply that it is a paradoxical linguistic identity.

And yet it is nonetheless necessary to regard Finland Swedish as a linguistic means of identification. When the Finland Swedish daily newspaper Östnyland (ÖN) asked its readers what it means to be Finland Swedish, they got 250 answers. The paper quotes from these to demonstrate that for its readers, language and identity are interconnected:

(8) It is important to support the Swedish language and culture so that it can continue to live. It means a beloved mother tongue in a bilingual country. (Kurri, 5th of November 2018)

The different kinds of double binds in which Finland Swedes live as a minority within the framework of their own linguistic identity give rise to different dimensions of paradox that I will discuss in the following chapter.

4 Paradoxes of identity

Based on the previous remarks on the role of the Finland Swedish mother tongue as an identity-forming characteristic of the minority, and on the simultaneous tendency to avoid using the mother tongue in bilingual interactions with representatives of the majority, one form of paradox can be discerned. Characteristic of this paradox is that linguistic self-confidence and pride in one's own language both seem to remain intact, as can be seen in the reader comments of the daily Finland Swedish newspaper Östnyland:

(9) My identity and my [Finland Swedish] business card.
That's the best, I mean Finland Swedish with its wonderful words and dialects. (Kurri 2018; reader comments)

The crucial role of this language awareness for the Finland Swedish minority was also made clear during an opinion survey (carried out by Aula Research Oy) on the role of language and culture among Finland Swedish speakers, as mentioned in the above introduction:

(10) The survey engaged Finland Swedes in a rare way and aroused enormous interest. It was felt that the topic was extremely interesting, topical and important. Several interviewees contacted Aula and wanted to discuss the position of Swedish in today's Finland. The survey also encouraged respondents to provide a record number of comments on their own experiences of the language climate. (Herberts 2019: 13)

However, this linguistic interest and awareness does not necessarily translate to linguistic behaviour. The following remarks are symptomatic of the latent need to speak one's own mother tongue, yet also show that one sometimes chooses not to speak it:

(11) I often speak Finnish, but I'm glad if someone speaks Swedish. (Herberts 2019: 34)
(12) I stopped speaking Swedish, but sometimes I get surprised, for example by pharmacists, when they suggest to speak Swedish. (Herberts 2019: 36)

The paradox resulting from the contradiction between the needs of a mother-tongue life in the public sphere and its simultaneous non-realisation in interactions with speakers of the majority language reflects the nature of the Finland Swedish paradox as a whole. Although it cannot be assumed that this paradox applies unilaterally to all representatives of this minority, the mental strain that results from it are obvious in the respondents' answers to the survey documented in Herberts (2019):

(13) Although I'm bilingual, I do suffer from the fact that I cannot exercise my right to use my mother tongue, which is enshrined in the Basic Law. (Herberts 2019: 37)
(14) I speak fluent Finnish and by that I get the errand quicklier done. That is wrong of me but the health condition is sometimes bad and you can't cope with it. (Herberts 2019: 49)
(15) Not directly discrimination, but many people have an incredible negative attitude towards Swedish speakers and I am completely fed up with it. (Herberts 2019: 65)
(16) The Finland Swedes feel a collective sadness and disappointment about a bad or deteriorating language climate. (Herberts 2019: 82)

A second form of paradoxical linguistic behaviour is rooted in a special kind of intense feeling about oneself. When people try to learn Finnish, they may feel hatred or shame, or both at the same time:

(17) Learning Finnish is still a big burden. I want to, but it's difficult and veeery [sic!] inflamed with all the hatred and shame. (Öhman 2012; reader comment, signed Hannasvirrvarr)

(18) It's almost like I'm ashamed that I don't speak Finnish "like everyone else"; I don't really know where that feeling comes from. Sure, I'd rather speak more Swedish out there in town. (Öhman 2012, reader comment, signed Anonymous)

A third form of paradox concerning the self-perception of Finland Swedes is based on a socially conditioned intersectionality brought on by attitudes within this minority. In this case, regionally rooted cultural differences are combined with the language-based view of other representatives of this minority, which can lead to a paradoxical attitude. This refers to unpleasant avoidances or even harassment by other Finland Swedes that some Finland Swedes have experienced because of their linguistic behaviour. From the perspective of group identity, it becomes paradoxical if the representatives of the minority group express dislike of other members of the same minority or harass them, or if group members experience a feeling of shame among one other because of their linguistic behaviour:

(19) The most unpleasant harassment regarding my own linguistic identity I have experienced was by Swedish-speaking Finns. They believe that bilingual or inhabitants of Helsinki are no genuine "Finland Swedes". (Öhman 3 October 2012; reader comment, signed Smilla)

(20) I really believe that the category "I'm ashamed of my fellow Finland Swedes" occurs more often than the situations when a Finnish speaking person would have said something negative about me (Öhman 3 October 2012; reader comment, signed Anonymous)

5 The role of language in the Finland Swedish paradox

While paradoxes of Finland Swedish linguistic behaviour and reactions to it have so far been primarily presented via a logic that can be classified as subjective or a group-internal self-perception (endogenous perspective), the paradoxical role of language with respect to group identity is now widened with an exogenous dimension. The terms endogenous and exogenous are understood here from a group-specific perspective where endogenous phenomena are induced by the group's internal perception of the minority and an often contradictory logic, as Chapter 4 has shown. Conceptually, the term exogenous in this context aims at the identity-forming behaviour of the minority, which in turn is influenced by events or attitudes that are induced by representatives of other linguistic groups.

In order to fully understand the logic of the intersections of daily life that can be involved in the behaviour relevant to the Finland Swedish minority's group identity, we shall now look at an exogenously triggered event that has led to chain reactions. Using an event in Finnish politics from recent years as an example, the significance of the exogenously anchored intersectionality variables for the question of minority identity can be illustrated further. This event was triggered by political power that conflicted with the needs of the minority.

The example to be discussed here was triggered during the 2015–2019 government term in Finland, when the then head of the Finnish government, Juha Sipilä, initiated a healthcare reform plan that was hotly debated in everyday political life. The idea was to unite the existing healthcare responsibilities of 309 municipalities into a network of 12 larger supra-regional districts in order to be able to have a more centralised state healthcare mandate. This plan was motivated by financial savings, since various areas of medical expertise could thus be more centralised in a given network. As the reform aimed at combining cost saving and bigger health units, it at first glance seemed to be a logical proposal.

However, the undertaking was planned in such a way that the regional distribution of the Swedish-speaking minority was deprioritised. Among other things, the district hospital for the bilingual town of Vasa (Region of Ostrobothnia), including its surrounding predominantly Swedish-speaking regions, was to be transferred to the Finnish-speaking town of Seinäjoki, which in itself forms part of a predominantly Finnish-speaking region. This would have had corresponding consequences for the service offering, which was linguistically geared toward Finnish speakers. It was feared that Swedish as a daily language at the hospital would suffer greatly from this. As healthcare is a pillar of modern societies, this plan led to strong backlash in the (mainly Swedish-speaking) population. The political explosiveness of these plans was above all made clear by the fact that there were also parliamentarians in the governing parties who found the Prime Minister's decision to be incomprehensible (cf. Suominen 2017: 13–14). From the minority perspective, the intersectional dimensions that emerged in this case were (among others) the creation of bigger administrative units, the need to save expenses, the regional demographic differences among the population, the securement of health services and the need for services in one's mother tongue. Among these five intersectional dimensions, only the last one was linguistic.

When examining the discourse that followed, it was the last dimension that dominated it. The extent to which the question of regional reorganisation as part of healthcare reform was also a question of language existence is clear from the reactions that came from the heads of both Finland Swedish circles within the Finland Swedish Party (Svenska Folkpartiet SFP), but also from other parties and officials. At the same time as the Vasa case there was another case on the agenda that pertained to the Finland Swedish language. This concerned the closure of a Swedish-speaking school in another town in the Vasa region (Ostrobothnian town of Pedersöre), but these plans were put on hold in light of the situation around Vasa; allegedly in order not to give too much weight during that period to the debate about the Swedish language's position. Thus, healthcare reform, and with it the relocation of hospitals, was to be carried out in an accelerated procedure:

(21) Malicious tongues claim that one reason for the fast timetable is to delay the debate about the position of the Swedish language for a longer period of time (Suominen 2017: 10)

The extent to which the Vasa case was foremost an existential language issue and only secondarily a logistical healthcare issue is shown by the further reactions across language and party boundaries over the course of these events:[6]

(22) The right to use one's own language, Finnish or Swedish, is a right guaranteed by the Basic Law (President Sauli Niinistö, 29/12/2016 in connection with the municipal reform and the relocation of the emergency hospital from Vasa to Seinäjoki)
(23) How can the basic linguistic rights be secured if the Swedish-speaking inhabitants of Ostrobothnia in the future can no longer rely on receiving such services in their mother tongue that they really need?
It concerns the principles of rule of law and fundamental human rights, but it also concerns good administrative tradition and political culture (Ville Niinistö, leader of the political party the Greens)
(24) The basic language rights require that national languages are equal, both formally and in practice. This has not been taken seriously by the government. (Peter Östman, spokesman for the Christian Democratic Party KD)
(25) Fundamental rights, including basic language rights, are not a matter of opinion. Either fundamental rights do exist or they do not exist (...) Now we are talking about life and death and the right of a person to receive nursing care in his or her mother tongue (Maarit Feldt-Ranta, member of the Social Democratic Party)

The reform decision also impacted a wide range of individuals within the population at an emotional level. A survey of the population includes their reactions to it:

---

[6] All of the following four quotations are documented in Suominen 2017: 9–13.

(26) A personal insult and hurtful. A wet rag right in the face. Indifference to the Finland Swedish situation against better knowledge. An attitude that hurts. (Suominen 2017: 5)

The extent to which this reform issue was perceived as part of a long historical process of weakening the cause for Finland Swedish language was also made clear by reactions from prominent Swedish-speaking figures. The existential need for self-realisation in everyday life and an identity shaped by language use go hand-in-hand here:

(27) The decision on the emergency hospital became a symbolic question for Swedish in Finland. It became the drop that broke the camel's back. (sociologist Kjell Herberts; quote taken from Suominen 2017: 5)

In the party-political lobby of the Swedish-speaking minority, a statement made by member of parliament Mats Nylund to the government during a parliamentary session reflected the outrage at the Vasa decision. The rhetoric, formulated at a purely emotional level, dispenses with factual arguments and instead expresses the painful emotions that the plan had caused for the Swedish-speaking. It became a viral hit for this very reason, which also demonstrates his statement's symbolic relevance for the Finland Swedish side:

(28) How can you have this impudence? How on earth can you? And yes, you can! (Mats Nylund 2006; quoted from Suominen 2017: 86)

The healthcare reform plan, which had become a language-based existential question for the Finland Swedes at the national level, beyond Ostrobothnia, also drew reactions from the Finnish-speaking population. In addition to the statements across certain party lines (see above), there were also (unexpected) signals from the Finnish side regarding the impairment of language identity in the Finland Swedish areas:

(29) I meet Swedish speaking children who are afraid to use their mother tongue in public places. The government knows about it. What does it do? (tweet from the children's ombudsman Tuomas Kurttila one week after the Vasa decision; documented in Suominen 2017: 6)

The broad spectrum of reactions found in the discourse on the closure of the hospital in Vasa made it clear in this case how the language aspect served as a combining factor for the five dimensions of intersectionality summarised above. Due to its central function as a denominator of identity, the language factor even started to "emigrate" into other societal domains, such as the life and behaviour of children in public places – as the quotation above shows. This emigration enlarged the dimensions of explicit intersectionality so that it took on implicit dimensions.

The real political tragedy and short-sightedness of the Sipilä government was that it failed to recognise the special interdependence between basic healthcare needs and basic language rights, although that link became obvious in the discourses that followed. In the spring of 2019, the government wanted to legitimise its political decisions through a new election, but lost the election by a significant margin.[7]

Based on the interconnectedness between language and everyday life demonstrated so far, and due to earlier experiences with shut down hospitals in the country's Finland Swedish regions, the Vasa case and its reactions are to be understood as more than just historical coincidences in light of previous hospital shutdowns. A birth hospital was closed down in Ekenäs (2010) and in Borgå (2016), respectively; both of them having been situated in the country's Swedish-speaking regions and having mainly served as popular hospitals for Swedish-speaking mothers. This was due to their innovative methods, their local proximity and their comparably small sizes in terms of average number of patients. The closing down of these (and other) institutions in Swedish-speaking regions has contributed to a growing awareness of possible intersections with other dimensions of daily life, mostly in terms of the interconnectedness of language and identity, which is why it is of no surprise that the linguistic dimension of the Vasa case was brought forward in the debate regarding the hospital closure.

At this stage one can ask whether linguistic identity as such can imply a double bind in the Finland Swedish case, and if this double bind can be resolved? This question is all the more relevant because it influences the overall situation of the Finland Swedes in terms of the logic behind their identity. Here, two dimensions of alienation seem to emerge in the Finland Swedish case. One of these dimensions refers to the endogenous self-perception on the question of identity-determining factors. In this context, the writer Tove Jansson's Moomin characters can be mentioned. According to a common Finland Swedish self-stereotype, the

---

7 After some significant changes in the tasks and composition of the healthcare reform plan under the newly elected Prime Minister Sanna Marin in 2019, the reform was finally passed through Parliament with a significant majority on 23 June 2021. It widened the final number of healthcare regions to 22 (see Merikanto 2021). For the district of Vasa, the final law meant a decisive change, as it retained the existing healthcare system within its own region, with Vasa as the administrative centre. However, this final development was by no means predictable during the innumerable societal and political debates on the subject that occurred during the Sipilä government.

situation of being a minority is often likened in a self-reflective way to that of a Moomin family (see Nikolajeva 2000; Rönnholm 2001; Klinkmann 2011). This is also the case in an evaluation by sociologist Kjell Herberts of the experiences with healthcare reform described above:

(30) When the sociologist Kjell Herberts was asked to choose the most typical Finland Swedish person of all time, he chose Tove Jansson. This took place during the plenary assembly of the young Finland Swedish Social Democrats, who had gathered in December 2017 due to the threat against the Swedish language. Tove Jansson gave us a picture of ourselves: *"The Moomin family lives on their island and Moomin dad goes and waits for the great catastrophe, which is a very Finland Swedish thing: to wait for a catastrophe that never comes."* (Suominen 2019: 84; emphasis in the original)

The fact that these kinds of experiences are palpable existential questions is repeatedly made clear in the comments about the healthcare reform campaign:

(31) The dispute over the central hospital in Vasa is rapidly becoming a symbol of the government's attitude to issues that affect the Swedish [language and identity], and drama is in the air as the reform proposal reaches the boardroom. "We are talking about life and death", Maarit Feldt-Ranta (SDP) explains when the question is put to the vote in Autumn 2016. (Suominen 2019: 85)

The double bind and the implicit "drama" (see quotation above) in this case is that the structural healthcare reform cannot be addressed through population statistics alone (which had previously been attempted), as it led to identity issues of the most serious kind. Regarding the possible dissolution of the underlying contradiction between securing basic health needs and jeopardising language rights, one could now think that the Spring 2019 elections would prevent the healthcare reform plan from being put into action and that the contradiction between exercising political power and securing the minority identity of Finland Swedes would be overcome. However, the way in which the healthcare debate took place shows that the Vasa case was treated as just one episode in a constant struggle for language-based identity. Also, if one applies the Moomin quote mentioned above to the discussion about the experiences of earlier hospital shutdowns, the fact that the Moomin dad is waiting for catastrophe (event though it seemingly "never comes") emphasises the perceived ongoing existence of the problematic situation as a whole. The irrevocability of the contradiction expressed here is presented as symptomatic of the case of the Finland Swedish minority, which seems to shrink over time due to the constant flux in language self-registration (see part 1). This thereby possibly endangers its right to exercise its mother tongue. In her assessment of the overall situation, the journalist Anne Suominen summarises the perceived situation of the Finland Swedes as follows:

(32) The wolf is coming – but not yet for good. (Suominen 2019: 84)

The feeling of powerlessness and alienation in the debate about linguistic reality (i.e. the constantly diminishing population of the minority and due to that the constantly growing role of the mother tongue as a means of internal and external self-assertion) is also expressed by the following publication on the Finland Swedish side, which characterises the emotive implications for the minority:

(33) About the linguistic climate in Finland: Like riding on an escalator in the wrong direction. (Herberts 2019: 1)

If we look at Finland Swedish language from an alienation point of view, the self-alienation is further reinforced by an exogenous perspective when one's own language, a minority language (which in the Finland Swedish case serves as the central aspect of identity as shown in this article), is denied its mother tongue status in a foreign environment:

(34) The own mother tongue Swedish [Finland Swedish] is not identified as a mother tongue in Sweden.[8]

The Finland Swedish identity dilemma with respect to one's own native language status from a foreign perspective is summarised below from an ethnological point of view:

(35) Having Swedish as one's mother tongue but at the same time being regarded as a foreigner; at least in Sweden ... [A] Finn who has Swedish as his mother tongue is not exotic, he is at most a cousin from the countryside. But for the Finland Swede, it can be considered insulting when he hears that he "speaks Swedish well", i.e. that this question is reduced to language competence instead of language identity. (Åström 2001: 43)

---

8 From an interview with the Finland Swedish professor Markus Jäntti, currently living in Sweden. Quote taken from Jens Berg 2018.

6 Finland Swedish conclusions concerning the paradoxical role of language in the relationship between minority and identity

The above discussion has shown that the Finland Swedish situation as a minority is anything but one-dimensional due to the explicit and implicit intersectionalities involved in the Finland Swedish minority case. As has been shown so far, Finland Swedish identity is fundamentally linked to the question of language/choice of language both in principle and in everyday life. Symptomatic in this context were the paradoxes under which linguistic life is shaped. These paradoxes got expressed through different kinds of double bind, where both sides of the double bind were equally relevant. This was shown in the inter-group choice of language (Quotation 1), in possible social consequences when choosing to use the minority language (Quotations 4–6), and, for example, with regard to the opaque language status of Finland Swedish from either an endogenous (quotation 7) or exogenous (quotations 34–35) perspective. As the Vasa hospital case has shown, the problematic double bind implications for the minority are not limited to the use and role of language as such, but form part of an existential self-assessment where, for example, securing basic health needs and jeopardising one's language rights are in conflict with each other.

In this context, it is interesting to note the positionings among the Finland Swedish minority concerning the discourse on the healthcare reform campaign, as reported in Suominen (2017; 2019). Although the reform's worrying aspects were eventually defeated (see Footnote 7 above), this minority group lives under the constant expectation of renewed attempts to curtail their own linguistic rights. This was expressed by both the Moomin comparison and the wolf metaphor quoted above. Repelling a threat and *at the same time expecting* this threat to arrive represent two poles of an identity-creating double-binding relation that is over time marked by constancy, thus forming two logical identity-marker poles. In the Finland Swedish case, the coherence of this double bind is timeless, a seemingly (!) never-ending story. From this point of view, one understands that the government managed to safeguard the interest of the minority when the healthcare reform legislation was ultimately passed, yet the safeguarding itself was still called into question. It is assumed that the next threat to language-based identity may come at any time. And then perhaps the "great catastrophe" will come as well (see Suominen 2019: 84)?

From a purely logical point of view, there is no indication that the endogenous or even the exogenous dimension of this case's linguistic self-determination paradox could be resolved. This is not just a theoretical dilemma. As it turned out, the Finland Swedes' own linguistic-cultural identity must be lived in order to survive, yet at the same time, it is not consistently being lived, as media discourse and socio-political developments have shown. The special feature of the Finland Swedish paradox is therefore its constancy, which eludes any kind of final dissolution. Therefore, even the withdrawal of plans to close Vasa hospital is not a solution to the problematic implications it had for the minority. However – paradoxically enough – it exemplifies the constant need to deal with the possibility that the "wolf is coming" (Quotation 32).

The Finland Swedish paradox is a paradox shaped by a time continuum. This paradox is anchored in the social discourse by the tension of a linguistic identity that is on the one hand expressed and talked about, and on the other hand lived differently. It lives through and due to the constancy of its own intersectionalities, which results in different double binds. As this article has shown, these double binds contain certain contradictions. Although this kind of situation in a way threatens the minority language status, it also – paradoxically enough – reinforces consciousness of the minority status. Therefore, one can ask whether this minority group does not draw the strength for its identity as a minority from the implicit contradictions that are precisely *due to* its (endogenously as well as exogenously) established language-based paradox?

References

a. Research literature

Allardt, Erik (1983): "De språkliga minoriteterna i Västeuropa och finlandssvenskarna" [The linguistic minorities in Western Europe and the Finland Swedes]. In: Max Engman/Henrik Stenius (eds.): *Svenskt i Finland 1. Studier i språk och nationaliteter efter 1860* [Swedish in Finland 1. Studies in language and nationalities after 1860]. Helsingfors: Svenska litteratursällskapet i Finland, 25–41.

Allardt, Erik (1984): "Om olika sätt att uppfatta språkgränser" [On different ways of understanding language borders]. In: Max Engman/Henrik Stenius (eds.): *Svenskt i Finland 2. Demografiska och socialhistoriska studier* [Swedish in Finland 2. Demographic and social historical studies]. Helsingfors: Svenska litteratursällskapet i Finland, 235–241.

Allardt, Erik/Starck, Christian (1981): *Språkgränser och samhällsstruktur. Finlandssvenskarna i ett jämförande perspektiv* [Language borders and society structures. The Finland Swedes in a comparatistic perspective]. Stockholm: Awe/Gebers.

Åström, Anna-Maria (2001): "Är en dubbelidentitet möjlig?" [Is double identity possible]. In: Anna-Maria Åström/Bo Lönnqvist/Yrsa Lindqvist (eds.): *Gränsfolkets barn. Finlandssvensk marginalitet och självhävdelse i kulturanalytiskt perspektiv.* [Children of border people. Finland Swedish marginality and self-assertion from cultural analytical perspective]. Helsingfors: Svenska litteratursällskapet i Finland, 37–49.

Åström, Anna-Maria/Lönnqvist, Bo/Lindqvist, Yrsa (eds.) (2001): *Gränsfolkets barn. Finlandssvensk marginalitet och självhävdelse i kulturanalytiskt perspektiv* [Children of the border people. Finland Swedish marginality and self-assessment from a cultural analytical perspective]. Helsingfors: Svenska litteratursällskapet i Finland.

Berger, Peter L./Luckmann, Thomas (1993): *Die gesellschaftliche Konstruktion von Wirklichkeit. Eine Theorie der Wissenssoziologie.* Frankfurt/Main: Fischer.

Crenshaw, Kimberlé (1989): "Demarginalizing the Intersection of Race and Sex: A Black Feminist Critique of Antidiscrimination Doctrine, Feminist Theory, and Antiracist Politics". *University of Chicago Legal Forum* 1989 (1), 139–167.

Crenshaw, Kimberlé (1991): "Mapping the Margins: Intersectionality, Identity Politics, and Violence Against Women of Color". In: *Stanford Law Review* 43 (6), 1241–1299.

Ekberg, Henrik (2000): "Die russische Zeit". In: Kristina Beijar et al. (eds.): *Zwei Sprachen, ein Land – das finnische Modell.* Helsinki: Schildts, 15–27.

Engman, Max/Stenius, Henrik (1984): *Svenskt i Finland 2. Demografiska och socialhistoriska studier* [Swedish in Finland 2. Demographic and social historical studies]. Helsingfors: Svenska litteratursällskapet i Finland.

Fewster, Derek (ed.) (2000): *Folket. Studier i olika vetenskapers syn på begreppet folk* [The people. Studies in the way different sciences understand the term people]. Helsingfors: Svenska litteratursällskapet i Finland.

Henriksson, Blanka/Häger, Andreas (2017): "Tidningsdebatt om hot mot den finlandssvenska identiteten" [Newspaper debate about the threat against the Finland Swedish identity]. In: Sven-Erik Klinkmann/Blanka Henriksson/Andreas Häger (eds.): *Föreställda finlandssvenskheter. Intersektionella perspektiv på det svenska i Finland* [Imagined dimensions of being Finland Swedish. Intersectional perspectives on Swedish in Finland]. Helsingfors: Svenska litteratursällskapet i Finland, 57–83.

Henriksson, Linnéa (2010): "Språkgruppernas relation till varandra och till den kommunala offentligheten" [The interrelation between the language groups and their relationship with the municipality]. In: Susan Sundback/Fredrica Nyqvist (eds.): *Det finlandssvenska sociala kapitalet. Fakta och fiktion* [The Finland Swedish social capital. Fact and fiction]. Helsingfors: Svenska litteratursällskapet i Finland, 135–159.

Joseph, John E. (2004): *Language and identity. National, ethical, religious.* Houndsmills: Palgrave.

Klinkmann, Sven-Erik (2011): *I fänrikarnas, martallarnas och dixietigrarnas land. En resa genom det svenska i Finland* [In the country of the lieutenants, pine trees and the dixie tigers. A journey across the Swedish in Finland]. Helsingfors: Svenska litteratursällskapet i Finland.

Klinkmann, Sven-Erik (2017): "Om finlandssvenska identiteter, intersektioner och hanteringsstrategier" [On Finland Swedish identities, intersections and application strategies]. In: Sven-Erik Klinkmann/Blanka Henriksson/Andreas Häger (eds.): *Föreställda finlandssvenskheter. Intersektionella perspektiv på det svenska i Finland* [Imagined dimensions of being Finland Swedish. Intersectional perspectives on Swedish in Finland]. Helsingfors: Svenska litteratursällskapet i Finland, 29–56.

Klinkmann, Sven-Erik/Henriksson, Blanka/Häger, Andreas (eds.) (2017): *Föreställda finlandssvenskheter. Intersektionella perspektiv på det svenska i Finland* [Imagined dimensions of being Finland Swedish. Intersectional perspectives on Swedish in Finland]. Helsingfors: Svenska litteratursällskapet i Finland.

Knudsen, Susanne V. (2005): "Intersectionality – A Theoretical Inspiration in the Analysis of Minority Cultures and Identities in Textbooks". In: Éric Bruillard et al. (eds.): *Caught in the Web or Lost in the Textbook?* 8th IARTEM Conference, 61–76. Online: https://iartemblog.files.wordpress.com/2012/03/8th_iartem_2005-conference.pdf (accessed 2 November 2021)

Lönnqvist, Bo (1984): "Språkgränsen – fiktion eller verklighet" [The language border – fiction or reality]. In: Max Engman/Henrik Stenius (eds.): *Svenskt i Finland 2. Demografiska och socialhistoriska studier* [Swedish in Finland 2. Demographic and social historical studies]. Helsingfors: Svenska litteratursällskapet i Finland, 267–279.

Lykke, Nina (2007): "Intersektionalitet på svenska" [Intersectionality in Swedish]. In: Bodil Axelsson/Johan Fornäs (eds.): *Kulturstudier i Sverige* [Culture studies in Sweden]. Lund: Studentlitteratur, 131–148.

Mustelin, Olof (1983): "'Finlandssvensk' – kring ett begrepps historia" [Finland Swedish – about the history of a term]. In: Max Engman/Henrik Stenius (eds.): *Svenskt i Finland 1. Studier i språk och nationalitet efter 1860* [Swedish in Finland 1. Studies in language and nationalities after 1860]. Helsingfors: Svenska litteratursällskapet i Finland, 50–70.

Nikolajeva, Maria (2000): "Barnlitteraturen efter krigen" [Children's literature after the wars]. In: Clas Zilliacus (ed.): *Finlands svenska litteraturhistoria, andra delen. 1900-talet* [Finland's Swedish literary history, second part. 20th Century]. Helsingfors: Svenska litteratursällskapet i Finland, 303–317.

Reuter, Mikael/Hällström-Reijonen, Charlotta af/Tandefelt, Marika (2017): "Finlandismer i skriven finlandssvenska" [Finlandisms in written Finland Swedish]. In: Marika Tandefelt (ed.): *Språk i prosa och press. Svenskan i Finland – i dag och i går* [Language in prose and press. Swedish in Finland – today and yesterday]. II: I. Helsingfors: Svenska litteratursällskapet i Finland, 16–31.

Rönnholm, Bror (2001): *Muminvärlden som identitet. Strödda dagen efter-tankar om Tove Janssons finlandssvenska roll* [Moomin world as identity. Miscellaneous thoughts the day after about the Finland Swedish role of Tove Jansson]. In: Åbo Underrättelser 29 Juni 2001.

Ruusuvuori, Juha (2005): *Muukalainen Muumilaaksossa, eli, Asutko vieläkin Taalintehtaalla?* [The stranger in the Moomin valley, or, Do you still live in Dalsbruk?] Helsinki: WSOY.

Saarela, Jan (2021): *Finlandssvenskarna 2021 – en statistisk rapport* [The Finland Swedes 2021 – a statistical report]. Svenska Finlands Folkting. Online: https://folktinget.fi/Site/Data/1597/Files/Finlandssvenskarna%202021_statistisk%20rapport_Folktinget_KLAR.pdf (accessed 25 November 2021).

Ståhlberg, Krister (ed.) (1995): *Finlandssvensk idenditet och kultur* [Finland Swedish identity and culture]. Åbo: Åbo Akademis tryckeri.

Stenius, Henrik (1983): "Vad är ett vi i historien?" [What is a we in history]. In: Max Engman/Henrik Stenius (eds.): *Svenskt i Finland 1. Studier i språk och nationalitet efter 1860* [Swedish in Finland 1. Studies in language and nationalities after 1860]. Helsingfors: Svenska litteratursällskapet i Finland, 9–22.

Strandén-Backa, Sofie/Backa, Andreas (2017): "Den kategoriserade forskaren. Om självreflexiv intersektionalitetsanalys och normativ finlandssvenskhet" [The categorised researcher. About self-reflective intersectionality analysis and normative Finland Swedishness]. In: Sven-Erik Klinkmann/Blanka Henriksson/Andreas Häger (eds.): *Föreställda finlandssvenskheter. Intersektionella perspektiv på det svenska i Finland* [Imagined dimensions of being Finland Swedish. Intersectional perspectives on Swedish in Finland]. Helsingfors: Svenska litteratursällskapet i Finland, 84–105.

Sundback, Susan (2006): "'Att krama en finne'. Variationer kring språkgränsen i Finland" [To embrace a Finn. Variations around the language border in Finland]. In: Marianne Junila/Charles Westin (eds.): *Mellan majoriteter och minoriteter. Om migration, makt och mening* [Among majorities and minorities. About migration, power and meaning]. Helsingfors: Svenska litteratursällskapet i Finland, 405–422.

Sundback, Susan (2010): "Nationell minoritet och etnisk identitet" [National minority and ethnic identity]. In: Susan Sundback/Frederica Nyqvist (eds.): *Det finlandssvenska sociala kapitalet. Fakta och fiktion* [The Finland Swedish social capital. Fact and fiction]. Helsingfors: Svenska litteratursällskapet i Finland, 45–63.

Sundback, Susan (2015): *Land, språk och socialt kapital. Sverigefinnar och finlandssvenskar som minoriteter i två grannländer* [Land, language and social capital. Sweden Finns and Finland Swedes as minorities in two neighbouring countries]. Åbo: Abo Akademis förlag.

Sundback, Susan/Nyqvist, Fredrica (2010): *Det finlandssvenska sociala kapitalet. Fakta och fiktion* [The Finland Swedish social capital. Fact and fiction]. Helsingfors: Svenska litteratursällskapet i Finland.

Sundberg, Jan (1985): *Svenskhetens dilemma i Finland. Finlandssvenskarnas samling och splittring under 1900-talet* [The dilemma of Swedishness in Finland. The gathering and dispersal of the Finland Swedes during the 20th Century]. Helsingfors: Societas Scientiarum Fennica.

Thim-Mabrey, Christiane (2003): "Sprachidentität – Identität durch Sprache. Ein Problemaufriss aus sprachwissenschaftlicher Sicht." In: Nina Janich/Christiane Thim-Mabrey (eds.): *Sprachidentität – Identität durch Sprache*. Tübingen: Narr, 1–18.

b. Empirical sources

Bäck, Jenny (2018): Finsk- och svenskspråkiga tänker i stort sett lika – men minoritetsidentitet skiljer grupperna åt [Finnish and Swedish speakers mostly think alike – but the minority identity creates a difference between the groups]. (11.10.2018). Online: https://www.hbl.fi/artikel/finlandssvenskarna-ar-mer-knutpatriotiska-skillnaden-mellan-osterbottningar-och-huvudstadsbor-stor/ (accessed 25 November 2021).

Berg, Jens (2018): *De tio finlandssvenska budorden* [The ten Finland Swedish commandments]. Blog from a series of radio interviews, published 25th of June 2018. https://svenska.yle.fi/kategori/specialtema/de-tio-finlandssvenska-budorden (accessed 15 October 2021).

Herberts, Kjell (2019): *Som att åka rulltrappa åt fel håll – en rapport om språkklimatet i Finland* [Like riding the escalator in the wrong direction – a report on the language climate in Finland]. Helsinki: Agenda. https://www.agenda.fi/Rapport/om-sprakklimatet-i-finland-som-att-aka-rulltrappa-at-fel-hall/ (accessed 5 November 2021).

Kurri, Helen (2018): *I Finland talar man svenska* [In Finland we speak Swedish] In: Daily newspaper Östnyland, Nov. 5th 2018. Online: https://www.ostnyland.fi/artikel/i-finland-talar-man-svenska/ (accessed 10 November 2021).

Merikanto, Tiina (2021): *Analyysi: Kun Marinin hallitus ymmärsi riisua sote-uudistuksen luurangoksi, alkoi tapahtua - mutta todellisuus paljastuu vasta käytännössä* [Analysis: When the Marin government understood to strip the health care reform to its skeleton, things started to happen - but the reality will only reveal itself in practice] In: YLE online: https://yle.fi/uutiset/3-11982186 (accessed 20 February 2022).

Öhman, Jeanette (2012): *I Finland talar man finska!* [In Finland we speak Finnish!] Podcast. https://www.jeanetteohman.com/2012/10/03/i-finland-talar-man-finska/ (accessed 6 November 2021).

Suominen, Anne (2017): *Regeringen Sipilä och svenskan* [The government Sipilä and Swedish]. Helsinki: Agenda https://www.agenda.fi/Rapport/ regeringen-sipila-och-svenskan/ (accessed 15 October 2021).

Suominen, Anne (2019): *"Vargen kommer - men inte riktigt än!"* [The wolf is coming – but not yet!] In: Kjell Herberts: Som att åka rulltrappa åt fel håll. Agenda, 84–90. https://www.agenda.fi/Rapport/om-sprakklimatet-i-finland-som-att-aka-rulltrappa-at-fel-hall/ (accessed 5 November 2021).

Wikner, Sarah (2019): *Svenskan i Helsingfors. Uppfattningar, perception och variation* [Swedish in Helsinki. Opinions, perceptions and variations]. Åbo: Åbo Akademis förlag.

c. Online sources

Finlex (2003): Finnish Basic Law, 423/2003. Language Act. Online: https://www.finlex.fi/en/laki/kaannokset/2003/en20030423 (accessed 24 November 2021).

Diana Hitzke
Contradictory Narratives in Sorbian Literature

The Concept of a 'Sorbian Island' and Discourses of Hybridity

This article reflects on contradictory narratives of Sorbian identity in Sorbian literature. In order to avoid the simple application of concepts that emerged in hegemonic contexts to minority narratives, as well as a view of minorities as incomparable case studies (for a discussion of this problem from a narratological perspective, see Kim 2012), this article seeks to understand the dynamic interplay between hegemonic concepts and specific minority literary works and contexts. In Sorbian literature (for an overview see Joachimsthaler 2011 and Lorenc 2004), for example, the concept of insularity and the image of a Sorbian island in the German sea[1] is much more important and helpful when analysing Sorbian narratives than the concept of the nation, though the nation does of course also appear.[2] This is not to claim that the Sorbian minority generally prefers to use concepts other than the nation, but instead to propose that if we read the narratives carefully (as done by Lorenc 1999) and analyse the cultural discourses in which they emerged (as done by Nedo 1965, Keller 2002 and Tschernokoshewa 2015), insularisation and hybridisation seem to be much more appropriate to the Sorbian situation than the hegemonic concept of the nation.[3]

---

[1] The Sorbian writer and researcher Kito Lorenc speaks of the "traditionellen Bild von der 'slawischen Insel im deutschen Meer'" [traditional image of the "Slavic island in the German sea"; Lorenc 1999: 409, my translation] and depicts the history of this metaphor from the 19th to the end of the 20th century (Lorenc 1999). In literature, this metaphor is especially important in Jakub Lorenc-Zalěski's 1931 work *Kupa zabytych* (The Island of the Forgotten).
[2] The Sorbian professional music and dance ensemble, for example, is known as the "Sorbian National Ensemble". In popular discourse, of course, concepts such as "Sorbian national literature" are also used. Sorbs generally refer to themselves as "serbski lud" (Sorbian people).
[3] Although the concept of hybridity is introduced later in this discussion, mainly via Tschernokoshewa's research and publications (for example: 2015), it should be regarded as the necessary counterpart to the critique of insularity images put forward by Paul Nedo in the 1960s (see Nedo 1965).

1 Insularisation and hybridisation

Minority narratives are not only affected by hegemonic concepts – they are also confronted with a contradiction: on the one hand, they try to emphasise their cultural uniqueness and autonomy, not only as a means of self-empowerment, but also in order to be able to assert legal claims. On the other hand, they want to be recognised as equal members in the society in which they live and to which they largely feel a sense of belonging. The multiple belongings which appear in minority (and migrant) contexts have been convincingly described with the concept of hybridity (see Bhabha 2004; and with a focus on the Sorbs, Tschernokoshewa 2015). In the recent past, both German and global society has developed a much more open attitude to transculturalism and multilingualism. At the same time, however, right-wing movements have grown, and a view of culture reminiscent of monolingualism and monoculturalism has reasserted itself (see Yildiz 2012 and Hitzke 2019: 17–20).

In societies where one language dominates – such as Germany – both members of minorities and migrants have knowledge of an additional language and, unlike the majority, live a multilingual, transcultural life. Even if cultural elements from minority and (post-)migrant communities – for example, traditional customs, food or music – are adopted into the majority culture or used commercially, the accompanying languages (such as Sorbian, Turkish or Russian in Germany) almost never take on a larger societal role. Unlike cultural hybridity, linguistic hybridity is often lived only by migrants and minorities. The important Chamisso Prize, which honours works in German that deal with cultural change or multiple cultural affiliations, speaks volumes in this respect, as it presupposes integration via the language. In general, the multilingualism of German culture is not very visible (see Joachimsthaler 2011 with regard to literature).

However, hegemonic cultures are not the only ones to produce monolingual and homogeneous narratives and constructions. Despite their multilingual, transcultural experience, minoritarian and migrant self-descriptions also refer to such ideas. The insularity narratives (see footnote 1 and the literary text by Jurij Koch discussed below) sometimes try to obscure or erase hybrid and entangled life worlds, raising the question of why multilingual and transcultural communities would present themselves as monolingual and homogeneous.

Because minority discourses are often founded on exclusion – as with the metaphor of an island – it doesn't seem promising to analyse them *either* through a lens influenced by methodological nationalism (which supposes, perhaps unconsciously, that there is a unity of a people, language and history/culture; for the concept see Wimmer/Glick Schiller 2002) *or* a perspective that focuses only on hybridity and entanglement. I attempt to show how processes of insularisation and hybridisation are present in Sorbian literature.

This article does not concern itself with the question of why certain narratives in literature appear at a specific historical moment or in the texts of a specific author. Instead, I take a more systematic and structural approach to show the variety of conceptualisations of Sorbian culture. These range from a very narrow depiction of a Sorbian family on a farm threatened by its German surroundings in Jurij Koch's *Wišnina* (The Cherry Tree) to very open narratives that combine Sorbianness with worldliness, as in Jurij Brězan's *Krabat*, or depict Sorbian life as hybrid, as in the narratives of Angela Stachowa and Lubina Hajduk-Veljkovićowa.

Interestingly, very different images relating to insularity or hybridity can be found in narratives by the same author. The poet Róža Domašcyna, for example, writes both multilingual poems and poems depicting a way of Sorbian life that draw on the tradition of the insularity discourse (see Hitzke 2019: 124–130). Jurij Koch, whom I will later discuss in detail, depicts Sorbs and their way of life in very different ways depending on how much the Sorbs are affected by their German surroundings. A story about a German man who wants to win the affection of a Sorbian woman, even as he aims to destroy her family's land in his professional function as a hydraulic engineer (see Koch 2015, 1984), is treated quite differently than a story about the social problems within a single Sorbian community (see Koch 2008). In the first case, the Sorbian-German relationship is portrayed intimately, while in the second, the Sorbian community only interacts with its German surroundings through the larger, vaguer structures of the German state and economy.

The image of the island plays a key role in scholarship on Sorbian literature and culture. Elka Tschernokoshewa refers to Paul Nedo's 1965 criticism of the notion of Sorbian culture as an island (see Nedo 1965) in order to justify her own research perspective, which is based on concepts of hybridity. Tschernokoshewa summarises Nedo's criticism as follows: "Territoriale Abgeschlossenheit, Dauerhaftigkeit, Stabilität, Homogenität sind Grundparameter der Figur der ethnischen Insel" [Territorial seclusion, permanence, stability, and homogeneity are the basic parameters of the figure of the ethnic island; Tschernokoshewa 2015: 70, my translation]. She refers to Nedo's position against the fixation on language and his critique of German research on linguistic islands as nationalistic, revanchist and Nazi-imperialist (see Tschernokoshewa 2015: 71). Tschernokoshewa herself rejects the attempt to restrict Sorbian culture to an imagined island of linguistic and cultural homogeneity, and instead assumes a hybrid German-Sorbian life world in her own research. She overcomes notions of the island as a "homogenisierende[s] Paradigma" [homogenizing paradigm; Tschernokoshewa 2015: 72, my translation] and investigates in its place the "Frage nach Vermischungen, neuen Konfigurationen oder doppelter Zugehörigkeit" [question of mixtures, new configurations or double affiliation; Tschernokoshewa 2015, my translation]. Although the conception of Sorbian culture as an island was criticised as early as 1965 and has been the subject of controversy ever since (Lorenc 1999 and Keller 2002), references to insularity can be found again and again in literature. Many works of fiction depict a homogenous, secluded rural village population which resembles the island described by Nedo (1965), Keller (2002: 300) and Tschernokoshewa (2015: 70). As I explain below, however, other texts offer a counter-image to the island – for example, Jurij Brězan's *Krabat* (1976).

Recent conceptual work on the image of the island reminds us that island discourses need not be exclusively binary ("earth and water, land and sea, continental and insular, big and small, enclosed and open, close and remote, connected and secluded", Dautel/Schödel 2016: 11). Rather, ideas of "seclusion, separation, self-enclosure, smallness and detachment" (Dautel/Schödel 2016: 11) allow for a certain ambivalence. Dautel and Schödel state: "Alternative concepts of islands [...] understand the sea surrounding an island not as a border but as a momentum of opening the insular space which connects the island into a flexible and open space [...]" (Dautel/Schödel 2016: 14). Other studies have described islands as interactive spaces or networks of exchange (see Goldie 2011: 7–8.). Of course, this re-evaluation of islands and insularity has not gone uncriticised – Elizabeth DeLoughrey, for example, to whom Goldie refers, warns against "unexamined celebrations of deterritorialization" (Goldie 2011: 10) that could lead to a failure to adequately address indigenous claims to land ownership, minority nationalist movements or forced migration (Goldie 2011: 10). In this respect, it is important to give due consideration to the difference between autonomy and belonging, as well as to the ambivalences with which minorities are confronted in their cultural self-descriptions.

2 Insularisation and hybridisation in Sorbian narratives

The questions is whether and how a specificity of Sorbian culture has been constructed in literary texts since the 1970s and which narratives underlie these works. I start from the premise that in hybrid cultures and societies, different positions can be occupied and articulated by the same actors, and that these positions cannot be clearly categorised according to a process-like, open concept of culture. In Sorbian literature, we find both narratives that describe a cultural specificity of the Sorbs and those in which Sorbian life is not described in terms of difference, but rather within the framework of intersectional diversity. The first type can be identified by processes of insularisation, the second by hybridisation.

It is therefore not only those texts in which the Sorbian culture constitutes the subject of the narration or in which it is of central importance that serve as objects of investigation, but also those in which Sorbian culture is not the primary subject. In response to criticism of the essentialising concept of culture, literary and cultural studies have shifted their focus towards identity and discursive positions (Jewishness, Irishness, migrant writing, etc.). This has made it possible to avoid rigid categories such as origin or territorial and national belonging, but it has also meant that narratives of cultural belonging that emphasise cultural specificity and difference have received more attention. Narratives that do not focus on difference, but rather emphasise the common ground in transcultural communities, have consequently faded from view. In order to avoid this trap, Sorbian life worlds should be examined without the presumption of their cultural specificity and difference.

In the following sections, I analyse a selection of texts that produce insular and hybrid life worlds, then juxtapose their contradictory narratives. It is particularly important here to explore the relationship between minority and majority. When does separation occur? At what level are differences identified and how are they justified? In which contexts are ideas of insularisation and hybridisation played against each other? How are the life worlds of minorities presented differently in hybrid (with reference to the majority society) versus homogenous contexts?

3 Hybrid and insular perspectives on Sorbian rural life: Jurij Brězan and Jurij Koch

In Jurij Brězan's novel *Krabat* (1976), the relationship between the Sorbian saga figure Krabat and his antagonist Reissenberg is not primarily explored as a relationship between the Sorbian and the German world, and thus between the minority and the majority. The opening and closing passages can be interpreted as calling into question the centuries-old contrast between the German and the Sorbian through the absence of the island motif and the alternative reference to rivers and the sea.

Monika Blidy points out that Brězan does not "wörtlich auf die traditionelle Insel-Symbolik zurückgreift" [literally refer back to the traditional island symbolism; Blidy 2016: 43, my translation], but that "die räumliche Anordnung der in seinen Texten dargestellten Welt" [the spatial arrangement of the world depicted in his texts; Blidy 2016: 43, my translation] evokes it on several occasions. This shows how strong the influence of the island metaphor is, even in texts that develop a counter-concept. In any case, Brězan's *Krabat* can be seen as a critical approach to the metaphor of an island in the sea as it was used in Sorbian literature (see Lorenc-Zalěski 2002 [1931], Lorenc 2004). In contrast to novels that begin with this metaphor, his begins and ends with the statement that the sea would be different "if it did not also include the water of the Satkula" (my translation, Brězan 2004: 15 and 420; Sorbian version: "njepřiwzało tež wodu rěčki Satkule", Brězan 1976: 5; German version: "nähme es nicht auch das Wasser der Satkula auf", Brězan 2004: 15). Below, I quote the opening and closing sentences of the novel, first in the German version, then in the Sorbian version and finally in my own English translation .

> Genau im Mittelpunkt unseres Kontinents – wie viele hierzulande irrtümlich glauben, also auch der Welt – entspringt die Satkula, ein Bach, der sieben Dörfer durchfließt und dann auf den Fluß trifft, der ihn schluckt. Wie die Atlanten, so kennt auch das Meer den Bach nicht, aber es wäre ein anderes Meer, nähme es nicht auch das Wasser der Satkula auf. (Brězan 2004: 15).
> Dokładnje wosrjedź našeho kontinenta – potajkim tež swěta, kaž mnozy tule mylnje wěrja – žórli so Satkula, rěčka, kotraž sydom wjeskow poji a potom na rěku trjechi, kiž ju srěbnje. Kaž atlasy tak tež morjo rěčku njeznaje, ale wono by było hinaše morjo, hdy by njepřiwzało tež wodu rěčki Satkule. (Brězan 1976: 5).
> [Exactly in the centre of our continent – and as many in this country mistakenly believe, of the world as well – the Satkula, a brook that passes through seven villages to meet the river that swallows it, has its source. Like the atlases, the sea does not know the brook, but it would be a different sea if it did not also include the waters of the Satkula.] (Brězan 2004: 15, my translation).

At the end of the novel, the passage of the brook varies:

> [...] das Wasser der Satkula [...] – eines Bachs, der genau im Mittelpunkt der Welt entspringt, sieben Dörfer durchfließt und dann auf den Fluß trifft, der ihn schluckt. Wie die Atlanten, so kennt auch das Meer den Bach nicht. Aber es wäre ein anderes Meer, nähme es nicht auch das Wasser der Satkula auf. (Brězan 2004: 420)
> [...] do wody Satkule – rěčki, kotraž dokładnje wosrjedź swěta žórli, sydom wjeskow poji a potom na rěku trjechi, kotraž ju srěbnje. Kaž atlasy tak tež morjo rěčku njeznaje. Ale wono by było hinaše morjo, hdy by njepřewzało [sic] tež wodu rěčki Satkule. (Brězan 1976: 453)
> [(...) the waters of the Satkula, a brook that rises in the very centre of the world, flows through seven villages and then meets the river that swallows it. Like the atlases, the sea does not know the brook. But it would be a different sea if it did not also include the waters of the Satkula.] (Brězan 2004: 420, my translation)

The relationship between Sorbian culture and the world is described with the metaphor of water and flow, thus radically undermining the image of the border and unbridgeable disconnect. Krabat's metamorphoses and shapeshifting, as well as his appearance in different times and spaces, can also be described as a "flowing" or "streaming". With its "poetics of flowing" (see Hitzke 2019: 135–144), the novel thus confronts the formative images of Sorbian literature – "the sea, the island, the ship" (see the title of Lorenc' *Das Meer, Die Insel, Das Schiff*, 2004, my translation) – with a surprisingly open alternative.

While the initially predominant phrase "swallowing" refers to the superiority of the sea and the majority, the relation between brook, river and sea is transformed over the course of both passages. Swallowing becomes including. Parallel to this, the geographical relativism (the opening passage speaks of the continent; in both passages, the atlases "do not know the brook") is replaced by a new perspective. The final passage no longer mentions the continent and instead situates the Satkula and the seven villages at the centre of the world. Thus, the brook is no longer talked about as part of a cartographical reality in which it does not exist. Instead, it represents a reality of its own. On the one hand, this valorises the minority's own narrative and position; on the other hand, it also transfers the responsibility for the minority to the world community.

The cultural openness that *Krabat* introduces into Sorbian literature does not consist of exploring the relationship between Sorbian and German culture, but in locating Sorbian culture in the world and mapping the relationship between that world and the region of Lusatia. Brězan is topographically quite unambiguous (the river Satkula, along with Rosenthal and Bautzen, are real places); likewise, *Krabat*'s plot and other elements (like songs or the mythical figure of the Aquarius) are taken from Sorbian culture. At the same time, the regional, cultural and linguistic descriptions are not specifically marked as Sorbian, and many descriptions consciously remain open (for example, the unnamed seven villages, or the protagonist's name, Serbin, which only hints at Sorbian, etc.). The nearly identical passages at the beginning and end of the novel, with their focus on the waters of the Satkula, allow us to read *Krabat* as a novel which opens up new perspectives on the positioning of Sorbian culture within the world, one that is oriented towards openness and interweaving. Fortifications and borders (but also islands and ships) are abandoned in favour of flowing water and its associated hybridity.

In contrast to Brězan's approach, Jurij Koch's novella *Wišnina* (The Cherry Tree; 1984) takes up and reinforces familiar island narratives in a highly symbolic way. The story deals with the relationship between the Sorbian woman Ena and the German engineer Sieghart. The first scene already characterises this relationship as a threatening one: Sieghart drives his Jeep towards a house at night, where Ena sits at a table with her fiancé, Mathias. From the beginning, Sieghart is an intruder in her life. He is portrayed as stereotypically male: he is unafraid, refuses help, constantly measures himself against others, likes technology and believes in progress. The contrasts between the German engineer and the Sorbian residents of the farm are also made apparent by their modes of transportation – Sieghart drives his Jeep, while Ena rides a bicycle, and Mathias, his horse. The contrast between nature and technology, a traditional way of life and modernity or progress, is not only strong, but also coalesces around the binary poles of Sorbian versus German culture.

Sorbian culture is presented as homogenous, close to nature and sustainable. The destruction of nature is closely associated with the decay of values and loss of tradition. For example, Ena's grandfather has to cut off the crown of a cherry tree because someone has driven a poisonous nail into it. He further tells Sieghart that the storks are not coming back this year, but Sieghart does not understand the grandfather's sadness. Sieghart's profession as an engineer stands in contrast to Ena's sustainable perspective. His company examines the soil in the area, practicing "constructive hydraulic engineering" and "settlement management" (both in my translation; German version: "Konstruktuiver Wasserbau" and "Siedlungswirtschaft", Koch 2015: 38; Sorbian version: "Konstruktiwny wodotwar. Sydlerske hospodarstwo", Koch 2005: 36). When Sieghart remarks that his whole family is involved with water, Ena responds:

> "Ich, sagte sie, erschaffe nichts. Nehmen, was vorhanden ist. Weitergeben, was man selbst erhält. Teilen. Arbeit auf dem Feld. Mutter, Großvater, Mathias [...] Sein, wie die Menschen sind. Hier" (Koch 2015: 43).
> "Ja, wona rjekny, ja bóhtónknjeza njehraju. Ja přjimuju a dale dawam. A ja njepytam. Kaž bych hižo namakała. Mać, dźěd, Maćij. Dźěło na polu. A doma. Doma, to je rjane słowo" (Koch 2005: 41).
> ["I [.....] create nothing. Taking what is available. Giving what you receive yourself. Sharing. Working in the fields. Mother, grandfather, Mathias ... Being as people are. Here"] (Koch 2015: 43, my translation).

Sieghart can take little pleasure in this attitude and asks if it isn't boring on the farm (Koch 2015: 44 and Koch 2005: 41). A further contrast arises between Sieghart's rational approach and Sorbian culture, which is depicted as shaped by myths. Traditional mythical figures such as the Aquarius appear in the narrative; their presence also blurs the boundaries between reality and imagination in the narrated world. For Sieghart, the Aquarius is an object of derision:

> Irgendwann hatte er erfahren, dass die Menschen hier an den Wasserman glaubten, an irgend so ein Vieh unterm Wasser, an einen Mann mit Froschaugen und Flossen, an einen Frosch mit männlichen Zügen, weiß der Teufel (Koch 2015: 42).

Něhdźe bě zhonił, zo tu ludźo do wódneho muža wěrja, do někajkeho tajkeho skoćeća pod wodu, do muža ze žabjacymi wočemi a płujadłami, do žaby z muskimi kajkosćemi, čert wě (Koch 2005: 40).
[At some point he learned that people here believed in the Aquarius, some kind of underwater creature, a man with frog's eyes and fins, a frog with male attributes, the devil knows] (Koch 2015: 42, my translation).

From his perspective, the Sorbian myths are a joke, the farm inhabitants backwards. The whole plot serves to confirm the narrative of the Sorbian island in the German sea, which is constantly threatened by destruction. Sieghart intrudes in Ena's Sorbian life world and eventually succeeds in entering into a relationship with her. The relationship has fatal consequences. After Ena and Sieghart have grown closer, Sieghart and his colleagues attend Ena and Mathias's wedding-eve party. As Sieghart finally advances towards Ena, Mathias sees the two of them, drags them into his carriage and drives them wildly through the forest to the pond, where the carriage and horses end up in the water (see Koch 2015: 77 and Koch 2005: 71). Mathias drowns in the process. At first, Ena cannot imagine starting a relationship with Sieghart, but then she does. Their wedding takes place in winter and is depicted in stark contrast to the traditional Sorbian wedding on the farm that Ena would have celebrated with Mathias. Not only is it celebrated in winter instead of summer, in a hotel in the city instead of on the farm (see Koch 2015: 90 and Koch 2005: 84), the whole event is marked by sadness and disappointment, and is viewed as inappropriate by the Sorbian guests. Ena's grandfather says, "Zu Hause hätten alle getanzt. Dann wäre es gewesen, wie eine Hochzeit zu sein hatte" (Koch 2015: 91); "Doma bychu wšitcy rejowali. Tam by kwas był" (Koch 2005: 85) ["At home everybody would have danced. Then it would have been like a wedding should be" (Koch 2015: 91, my translation)], and Ena imagines that she is wearing the traditional Sorbian bridal costume when she looks in the mirror (see Koch 2015: 92). Finally, on the evening of the wedding, Sieghart announces that he is being promoted and the couple is expected to move to Paris. Ena is not excited about this, replying, "Was soll ich dort?" (Koch 2015: 96); "Što ja tam dyrbju?" (Koch 2005: 89) ["What am I going to do there?" (Koch 2015: 96, my translation]. As this scene indicates, Ena is unhappy in Paris. She frequently imagines seeing Mathias, and finally returns to the farm to put it all behind her. In the meantime, her grandfather has died, and another dramatic scene follows: wanting to bid farewell to her memories, she walks with a hunting rifle to the pond, where she believes she will see Mathias. When her vision of her dead lover says that she will never forget him, she shoots him – but in reality, she shoots Sieghart.

The plot structure makes it clear that the contrasts between the Sorbian and German worlds are perceived as being fixed within the framework of Koch's narrative. They are not created performatively through certain scenes or conversations, nor do they develop through concrete conflicts; rather, a number of opposites are presented as given (in this case, nature vs. technology; tradition vs. progress; sustainable living vs. destruction of nature; being tied to the farm vs. mobility). All of Ena's alternatives to the Sorbian wedding and life on the farm – her relationship with Sieghart, the wedding in the city, their departure for Paris – are presented from the beginning as doomed to failure. Due to the rigid distinction between the Sorbian and outside worlds, an encounter does not seem possible without conflict and catastrophe. Beyond the German environment, even France is portrayed as negative, which means that Ena remains bound to the Sorbian island. This however, has been marked by devastation: the area has been destroyed by economic development, and the traditional way of life is gradually being abandoned. Therefore, in this narrative, Sorbian life worlds are almost completely anchored in the past. The present is correspondingly marked by nostalgic projection into the past, and thus by a time that can no longer be retrieved. A conveyance of the Sorbian way of life into the present – by transformation, for example – does not seem possible. A life outside of Lusatia seems unimaginable and not worth living. As if to confirm this logic, the story ends after the deaths of three people.

The positions taken by Brězan and Koch, then, could not be more different: while the former situates Sorbian culture within the world, the latter depicts it as an island threatened by the German environment. Brězan shows hybrid worlds, while Koch presents a binary worldview that amounts to the destruction of a culture. In this respect, Koch's fiction echoes his journalistic work: he has written extensively on the decline of Sorbian villages due to lignite mining, describing its effects on the life of the local human and animal populations.[4] Both narratives are indeed intertwined in his work. In his essay "Die Schmerzen der endenden Art" (The Pain of a Dying Species; Koch 1992), Koch draws parallels between a disappearing bird species and Sorbian culture:

---

4 Peter Barker highlights the link between those processes and the loss of the Sorbian way of life in Koch's view: "In *Die Landvermesser* [...], Koch raised for the first time the question of the relationship between the loss of cultural and spiritual values as a result of the destruction of the Sorbian way of life and the advantages conferred on society in general through industrial progress" (Barker 2006: 100). Furthermore, Barker quite rightly observes: "Koch sees the relationship between Sorbian and German culture as one in which the smaller one is essentially under threat. An insistence on clear frontiers he sees as the only possible defense against total submergence". (Barker 2006: 101).

> Ich bin vom Wahnsinn der Metapher besessen. Ich will wissen, ob die beiden Exemplare der Mandelkrähe noch im Land sind. Es liegt im Urinteresse meiner ethnischen Art, daß ich wissen muß, ob in meiner Zeit, vor meinen Augen [...] etwas zu Ende gekommen ist, was nicht hätte zu Ende kommen sollen. Ich wünsche mir, der schöne Vogel möge noch da sein. So wie ich mir die Welt *nur mit meiner* ethnischen Art vorstellen kann. Sein, ihr Ausbleiben bedeuteten Verlust. Nach und nach wäre die Armut landesweit spürbar. Vielleicht sogar kontinental und planetar (Koch 1992: 42, emphasis in the original).
> [I am obsessed with the madness of the metaphor. I want to know if the two specimens of the European roller still exist in the country. It is in the primal interest of my ethnic species that I know whether in my time, before my eyes [...] something has come to an end that should not have come to an end. I wish the beautiful bird was still there. Just as I can only imagine the world with my ethnicity. Its absence would mean loss. Little by little, the poverty would be felt nationwide. Perhaps even continental and planetary] (Koch 1992: 42, my translation).

According to the text's logic, the European roller is either in the country or it has disappeared; the text is not interested in its actual whereabouts. The same applies to Ena: she is either on the Sorbian farm or has disappeared from it; her life in Paris seems meaningless. Thus, we find here – in contrast to *Krabat* – a conception of Sorbian culture that remains separated from the world. Koch and Brězan thus provide extremely contradictory conceptions of what it means to belong to the Sorbian minority.

4 Non-binary perspectives and depictions of Sorbian city life: Angela Stachowa and Lubina Hajduk-Veljkovićowa

While the narratives by Jurij Brězan and Jurij Koch discussed above can be considered representative of Sorbian prose, Sorbian literature also offers alternatives to the homogeneous peasant image of the Sorbs. While Koch adopts the island discourse and Brězan develops alternatives to it, the authors Angela Stachowa and Lubina Hajduk-Veljkovićowa, by contrast, depict Sorbian lifestyles in urban environments. Thus, the idea of a Sorbian island that is strongly bound to the structure of the village and the farm is destabilised by the heterogeneous and multilingual space in which the protagonists move. In such a context, Sorbian culture must be represented by something other than village traditions.

The title story in Angela Stachowa's collection *Sobotu wječor doma. Powědančka* (Saturday Evening at Home: Stories, 1978) is about a couple. In a neutral and objective style, the first-person narrator reports on his relationship and everyday life with his wife, Majka. The reader learns that the couple lives in an apartment in the old town centre. She is a teacher, and because he is in Berlin studying to become a teacher, they only see each other on weekends. The narrator makes references to Sorbian culture when he describes their wedding: for him, the traditional wedding was not particularly important, but he mentions its great social significance. The couple's weekends often follow the same pattern: on Friday evening, they tell each other everything that happened during the week, and on Saturday, they rest (see Stachowa 1978: 8–10).

One Saturday, instead of going to their parents' houses as agreed (his mother waits for them with lunch, her parents wait for them with coffee and cake), they stay home and spend the whole day sleeping in; in the evening, they go out. The suspenseful structure of the story suggests that something is going to happen. Since the story is mainly about everyday life and the couple's relationship, however, the reader is likely to assume that this will take the form of a complicated conversation, perhaps a quarrel. The narrator and his wife go to a restaurant and drink champagne. Then the incident occurs: they are approached by some drunken men and asked why they are speaking Sorbian. The situation escalates. The other diners in the restaurant do nothing to defend the Sorbian couple, who are not even allowed to call the police.

This episode of discrimination is shocking partly because, until now, the couple's Sorbianness has not been particularly marked. The narrator's simple, direct language and his casual discussion of the traditional elements of his wedding – embedded between breakfast and washing up – serve to downplay its distinctness. Rather, it becomes clear that while some traditions have continued, there is also a certain scepticism or indifference towards them. Traditional customs are presented as variable and transformable, and their meaning is questioned – quite in contrast to Koch's *Wišnina*. Here, Sorbian everyday life is described in relation to neither insularisation nor hybridisation. Nevertheless, the couple's life and relationship are disturbed by the discrimination in the restaurant. The experience is jarring for both the characters and the reader because it appears in the narrative without any prior construction of cultural difference.

One representation of hybrid Sorbian-German culture that avoids the trope of Sorbian culture as threatened or endangered can be found in Lubina Hajduk-Veljkovićowa's contemporary crime novel *Módry buny* (Blue Beans, 2018). The story takes place in the Sorbian-German community in Lusatia and provides insight into the everyday life of the Sorbian commissioner and her family. Janka Žurowa is portrayed as a woman who, in addition to her demanding work, acts as caregiver to both her child and her parents. She lives with her Bulgarian husband Manuš and her son Stanij in the old town of Bautzen and has an extended

Sorbian family. The Sorbian world is not portrayed as contrasting with the contemporary world, but rather as being part of it. The rumour mill from her Sorbian extended family helps Janka Žurowa to solve her criminal case, for example, and she has a productive working relationship with her German colleague. The Sorbian environment is described without clichés and, as a contrast to the traditional depiction of Sorbs, her husband Manuš, while preparing for the traditional fair, stands in the kitchen wearing a T-shirt with "fuck you all" emblazoned on it. Furthermore, Hajduk-Veljkovićowa modernises the Sorbian language and adapts it to the present.

5 Conclusion

As can be observed in Koch's and Brězan's narratives, the island motif is central, although different in the depiction of Sorbian culture. In the former case, it is confirmed; in the latter, it is questioned by the metaphor of flow. Processes of insularisation and hybridisation are characteristic of both narratives. An entirely different perspective that is partly due to the shift in action from the village to the urban space can be found in Angela Stachowa's story – which, written in 1978, has a date of origin falling between those of Brězan's (1976) and Koch's (1984) narratives – as well as in the work of the present-day writer Lubina Hajduk-Veljkovićowa.

References

a. Research literature

Barker, Peter (2006): "'The Pain of a Dying Species' or the 'New Waters' of a Bicultural Literature: Sorbian Literature since 1990". In: *Neohelicon XXXIII* (2), 91–103.
Bhabha, Homi K. (2004): *The Location of Culture*. London/New York: Routledge.
Blidy, Monika (2016): *Das Hügelchen, fünf Kornhalme hoch. Realität – Fiktion – Imagination in Jurij Brězans reifer Schaffensphase*. Dresden: Neisse Verlag.
Dautel, Katrin/Schödel, Kathrin (2016): "Introduction –Insularity, Islands and Insular Spaces". In: Katrin Dautel/Kathrin Schödel (eds.): *Insularity. Representations and Constructions of Small Worlds*. Würzburg: Königshausen & Neumann, 11–28.
Goldie, Matthew Boyd (2011): "Island Theory. The Antipodes". In: Maeve McCusker/Anthony Soares (eds.): *Islanded Identities. Constructions of Postcolonial Cultural Insularity*. Amsterdam, New York: Rodopi, 1–40.
Hitzke, Diana (2019): *Nach der Einsprachigkeit. Slavisch-deutsche Texte transkulturell*. Berlin et al.: Peter Lang Verlag (https://doi.org/10.3726/b16372).

Joachimsthaler, Jürgen (2011): *Text-Ränder. Die kulturelle Vielfalt in Mitteleuropa als Darstellungsproblem deutscher Literatur*. Heidelberg: Winter.
Keller, Ines (2002): "Sorbische Volkskunde als Inselforschung? Überlegungen zu einem ‚alten' Thema". In: Michael Simon/Monika Kania-Schütz/Sönke Löden (eds.): *Zur Geschichte der Volkskunde: Personen – Programme – Positionen*. Dresden: Thelem, 291–300.
Kim, Sue. J. (2012): "Introduction: Decolonizing Narrative Theory". In: *Journal of Narrative Theory* 42 (3), 233–247.
Lorenc, Kito (1999): "Die Insel schluckt das Meer". In: *Zeitschrift für Slavische Philologie* 58 (2), 409–422.
Lorenc, Kito (2004): *Das Meer, Die Insel, Das Schiff. Sorbische Dichtung von den Anfängen bis zur Gegenwart*. Heidelberg: Wunderhorn.
Nedo, Paul (1965): "Sorbische Volkskunde als Inselforschung". In: *Lětopis C* (8), 98–115.
Tschernokoshewa, Elka (2015): "Die Hybridität von Minderheiten. Vom Störfaktor zum Trendsetter". In: Erol Yildiz/Marc Hill (eds.): *Nach der Migration. Postmigrantische Perspektiven jenseits der Parallelgesellschaft*. Bielefeld: Transcript, 65–87.
Wimmer, Andreas/Glick Schiller, Nina (2002): "Methodological Nationalism and Beyond: Nation-State Building, Migration and the Social Sciences". In: *Global Networks* 2 (4), 301–334.
Yildiz, Yasemin (2012): *Beyond the Mother Tongue: The Postmonolingual Condition*. New York: Fordham University Press.

b. Empirical sources

Brězan, Jurij 1976: *Krabat*, Zhromadźene spisy w jednotliwych wudaćach 8 [Krabat, collected works in single editions]. Bautzen: Domowina-Verlag.
Brězan, Jurij 2004: *Krabat oder Die Verwandlung der Welt*. Frankfurt am Main: Suhrkamp.
Hajduk-Veljkovićowa, Lubina (2018): *Módry buny* [Blue Beans]. Bautzen: Domowina-Verlag.
Koch, Jurij (2015 [1984]): *Der Kirschbaum*. Bautzen: Domowina-Verlag.
Koch, Jurij (2008): *Na kóncu dnja. Powědančko* [At the End of the Day. A Story]. Bautzen: Domowina-Verlag.
Koch, Jurij (2005 [1984]): *Wišnina* [The Cherry Tree]. Bautzen: Domowina-Verlag.
Koch, Jurij (1992): *Jubel und Schmerz der Mandelkrähe*. Bautzen: Domowina-Verlag.
Lorenc-Zalěski, Jakub (2002 [1931]): *Kupa zabytych* [The Island of the Forgotten]. Bautzen: Domowina-Verlag.
Stachowa, Angela (1978): *Sobotu wječor doma. Powědančka* [Saturday Evening at Home. Stories]. Bautzen: Domowina-Verlag.

Katharina Bock
The Pressure to Convert

Literary Perspectives on Jewishness in the Era of Jewish Emancipation in Denmark

In the 1820s and 1830s numerous Jewish characters seem to suddenly surface in Danish fiction. During these and the following years, almost all Danish authors wrote at least one narrative text in which one or more Jewish characters appear and play a leading role. These narratives include *Den gamle Rabbin* (1827; The Old Rabbi) by Bernhard Severin Ingemann (1798–1862), *Jøderne paa Hald* (1828; The Jews at Hald) by Steen Steensen Blicher (1782–1848), *Jøden* (1836; The Jew) by Thomasine Gyllembourg-Ehrensvärd (1773–1856) and *Jødepigen* (1855; The Jewish Maiden) by Hans Christian Andersen (1805–1875) as well as the novels *Guldmageren* (1836/1851; The Gold Maker) by Carsten Hauch, *Udaf Gabrielis's Breve til og fra Hjemmet* (1850; From Gabrielis's Letters To and From Home) by Frederik Christian Sibbern, *Kun en Spillemand* (1837; Just a Fiddler) by H.C. Andersen and *At være eller ikke være* (1857; To be, or Not to Be) also by Andersen. Despite being big names in Danish literature at the time, today the majority of these authors are unknown outside of Denmark. Andersen is the only one who is currently known beyond Denmark's borders. Although mostly recognised because of his fairy tales, it was his novels which first made him popular. He is also the only one who wrote repeatedly about Jewish characters and topoi, in different phases of his life and in different literary genres; three of these texts will be discussed in this essay.[1]

---

[1] There are two further novels, which cannot be taken into consideration here, but should at least be mentioned: His first comical-experimental novel *Fodreise fra Holmens Canal til Østpynten af Amager i Aarene 1828 og 1829* [A Journey on Foot from Holmen's Canal to the Eastern Point of Amager 1828 and 1829] from 1829, in which the character of the 'eternal Jew', Ahasverus, appears as an eerie-fantastical inspiration for the searching poet on his journey through the recent history of literature. Also in his last novel *Lykke-Peer* [Lucky Peer] from 1870 an important Jewish supporting character appears, who plays a significant role as a companion of the non-Jewish main character. Here too, the focus is on creative self-expression and not questions of religion.

Note: Translated from German into English by Rett Rossi.

Open Access. © 2023 the author(s), published by De Gruyter. This work is licensed under the Creative Commons Attribution 4.0 International License.
https://doi.org/10.1515/9783111039633-011

Compared to the literature being written in its neighbouring countries, Danish literature proves to be a noteworthy exception. Whereas Jewish characters barely appear in Swedish and Norwegian narrative texts during the first half of the 19th century (see Bock 2021: 22–13; Räthel/Schnurbein 2020; Rohlén-Wohlgemuth 1995; Rothlauf 2009), the representation of Jewish characters in German fiction – with the exception of a few – is marked by anti-Jewish stereotypes (see Massey 2000). In contrast, the Jewish characters appearing in Danish narratives are rarely encoded with anti-Jewish sentiments, rather they tend to be characterised positively and idealised. This essay is meant to provide an overview of these texts and to introduce the context of their origin. The first part of the essay focusses briefly on some of the most important content-related and structural features of texts in which Jews are narrated from a Christian perspective. It thus represents a synopsis of my dissertation (Bock 2021). In the second half, I take a closer look at the first novel written by the Danish-Jewish author Meïr Aron Goldschmidt (1819–1887), *En Jøde* (1847; A Jew). This text is all the more remarkable because it is one of the first literary representations in Europe of the emancipation process from a Jewish perspective. In juxtaposing these texts which look at Jews from Jewish and Christian narrative perspectives, it becomes clear how formative the viewpoint of the Christian majority is for the self-understanding and emancipation process of the Jewish minority.

Though none of the characters described in the texts by Christian authors are free from stereotypes and ambivalent attributions, it is noticeable that the narrative voices are consistently sympathetic to the Jewish characters. They consistently take a position of admiration for the Jewish characters and are thus able to generate similar feelings in readers. While the representations of Jews are predominately positive – or better "positive" – they are not unproblematic. The term 'philosemitism' has proven fruitful for the labelling of this at times irritating ambivalence, even though or specifically because the history of the term is itself ambivalent (see Grimm 2013; Kinzig 2009; Rensmann/Faber 2009; Thurn 2015: 38–47; Zuckermann 2009; Theisohn/Braungart 2012; Theisohn/Braungart 2017). I use it here as a heuristic tool to name and make visible the duplicity of the texts (see Bock 2021: 29–35). Since philosemitism is a decidedly Christian discourse (see Bock 2021: 230–232; Theisohn/Braungart 2017), the first part of this essay is only concerned with texts by Christian authors. Using a selected novella as an example, some fundamental motives will be outlined, especially that of conversion, but also anti-Jewish violence and the question of who or what is actually Jewish or is understood as Jewish.² First however, I will provide an outline of the historical context within which these novels and novellas arose.

1 Jews and Jewish emancipation in Denmark

The literary texts which I will be addressing here were all written during an era of cultural flourish but economical and political crisis. In 1807, during the Napoleonic Wars, Copenhagen was bombed by English naval forces and was for the most part destroyed. Thousands of civilians died and the Danish fleet was completely lost to England. Subsequent to the wars, in 1813, Denmark declared national bankruptcy. The Treaty of Kiel from 1814 also forced the Danish King Frederick VI, to cede the Norwegian region, which had been under the Danish crown for 400 years, to Sweden. Within a few short years, Denmark had therefore dramatically lost political power and size as well as economic stability. Amidst this, a rich cultural life developed which was to become known in Danish history as *Guldalderen* [the Golden Age] and lasted up until the mid-19th century. At the same time, as in many other European countries, the debate about the Jewish population's legal equality gained momentum. The first Jews had already arrived via the Netherlands in Denmark at the start of the 17th century, with the first Jewish community being established in Copenhagen in 1684. In the 17th and 18th century, Jewish life in Denmark was subject to similar restrictions as Jews in other European countries. Although, these were significantly less rigorous than for example in Prussia, there were extensive missionary efforts and anti-Jewish violence. At the end of the 18th century, the Danish Crown Prince and later King Frederick VI began implementing reforms for the equality of Jews. This set off discussions in both Christian and Jewish populations about the possibilities, conditions and consequences of equality.

When Denmark declared national bankruptcy in 1813, it was "the Jews", who, as so often, were scapegoated and considered a threat to Denmark. An inflamed public debate ensued about the question of whether Danish Jews should, may or must be rendered legally equal with non-Jewish Danes. Over a course of months, Danish intellectuals argued publicly for and against the equality of Jews, a fight which became known as the "literary Jewish feud." Finally at the start of 1814,

---

2 All of the texts from non-Jewish authors mentioned here have be extensively analysed in my dissertation "Philosemitische Schwärmereien. Jüdische Figuren in der dänischen Erzählliteratur des 19. Jahrhunderts" (Bock 2021). The second part of this essay, which focuses on Meïr Aron Goldschmidt's novel *En Jøde* is based on a talk I gave at my defence.

Frederick VI granted Danish Jews civil rights, making them for the most part equals with Christian Danes. They continued however to be excluded from certain public offices and positions. As Jews they were not permitted to serve the state, that means, male Jews were allowed to vote, but were not allowed to stand for election. They were not allowed to be civil servants nor could they have a military career. Thus the legal situation of Jews was clearly improved, but they were not yet completely equal. And antisemitism and discrimination were far from extinct. In the autumn of 1819, the Hep-Hep riots which started in Germany spread to Denmark. The situation settled until 1830, when the heated mood following the July Revolution sparked renewed debates about the equality of Jews and anti-Jewish violence. Ultimately in 1849, Denmark created a new constitution in which religious freedom was anchored. Jewish Danes were therefore finally, completely legally equal to their non-Jewish compatriots (see Albertsen 1984; Blüdnikow/Jørgensen 1984; Haxen 2001; Schwarz Lausten 2015: 89–172). The literary texts analysed here thus originated against the background of national uncertainty, Jewish emancipation and anti-Jewish violence. They serve as commentaries on the political and social processes of their time while simultaneously constituting the discourse. The narrative literature more clearly distances itself from a tradition of anti-Jewish representation than dramatic literature does. As philosemitic texts, they reflect and criticise anti-Jewish tendencies and plots, taking an opposing position, thus shaping and changing the discourse which originally produced them.

2 The old Jew, the young Jewess and their Christian saviour

The first Danish narration about Jewish characters is the novella *Den gamle Rabbin* [The Old Rabbi] by Bernhard Severin Ingemann (2007), which was published in 1827. From today's perspective, the novella seems anything but progressive, since it presents its Jewish characters in a very coarse and simplistic manner. The novella is noteworthy nonetheless. The old rabbi, who is the first Jewish character to enter the field of Danish narrative literature, is a 'noble Jew', a far cry from the anti-Jewish representations that had dominated European literature up until this point (see Achinger 2007; Gubser 1998; Gutsche 2014; Hartwich 2005; Klüger 2007; Krobb 2007; Nirenberg 2015). *Den gamle Rabbin* lay the basic schema of philosemitic literature. This pattern returns frequently in

Danish literature up until the end of the 1850s, although with abundant and manifold variations. We will thus take a closer look at this foundational text.

With the growing secularisation and to some degree complete assimilation of Jews in their Hamburg community, an old Jew, the deeply religious Rabbi Philip Moses, and his beautiful, pious, tolerant and caring granddaughter Benjamine, no longer have a home. Benjamine's parents are dead, thus she alternately lives with the two sons of the old rabbi. Nonetheless, she is more tolerated than welcomed by them, since the old rabbi judges their pursuance of assimilation and worldly prosperity, and causes rifts with the sons and their families through his prophetic words of admonition. The novella begins with a speech from the rabbi, immediately tuning the reader into the fact that the one who is speaking is a dignified patriarch:

> "Er din Forfølgelsesdag nu kommen igjen? fortabte, ulykkelige Israel!" – sagde den gamle Rabbin Philip Moses og rystede sit hvide graaskæggede Hoved, da en Efteraarsaften 1819 Stenene fløi ind ad Vinduerne til ham, medens den hamborgske Pøbel raabte: "Hep! Hep!" [...]
> "Ere I Israels Børn endnu" – svarede den Gamle rolig – "saa folder eders Hænder og bøier eders Knæ! vender Eders Aasyn mod Østen, mod Gruset af Guds hellige Stad og beder til Jehova, eders Fædres Gud!" (Ingemann 2007: 99).
> ["Has the day of your persecution returned? lost, unhappy Israel!" – the old Rabbi Philip Moses said and shook his white, grey-bearded head, as, on an autumn evening in 1819, the stones flew through the window at him, while the Hamburgerian mob cried "Hep! Hep!" [...]
> "Are you still the children of Israel" – the old man calmly replied – "then fold your hands and bend your knees! turn your face towards the east, towards the dawn of God's holy city and pray to Jehovah, the God of your fathers!"][3]

Already, these first sentences outline the rabbi's fundamental traits. His manner of speaking characterises him as religious, while the white hair and grey beard trigger associations with the traditional visual representation of the biblical forefathers. Both his speech and his appearance make it clear that he is a symbol of a religion that is as venerable as it is outdated. Paradoxically, the religiosity of the rabbi is emphasised by of all things, his use of "Jehovah", God's alleged name. In doing so, the text overlooks not only the belief that devout Jews do not speak the name of God, but also that the name is *per se* unspeakable. The name "Jehovah" is a Christian invention that ignores precisely this unspeakability and attempts to bypass it (see Becking 2006). At the same time, these first lines insert

---

[3] Unless otherwise noted, the Danish quotes have been translated into German by me. From there, they have been translated into English by Rett Rossi.

the novella into the historical context of the "Hep-Hep" riots and position it on the side of the persecuted. In this situation, the fight between the old Jew and his sons who want to assimilate escalates and the rabbi along with Benjamine leaves the house of the first son and after a brief intermezzo also the house of the other.

The rabbi's granddaughter, the beautiful Benjamine, is introduced in the novella as a "ung sorthaaret Pige [young black-haired girl]", who "skjælvende af Kulde, ved en gammel Jødes Side [gikk] og syntes at trøste ham med en venlig deeltagende Stemme [trembling with cold, walked alongside an old Jew and seemed to comfort him with a sympathetic voice]". In the moonlight, the old rabbi sees "Taarerne glindse i de lange sorte Øienhaar [the tears shimmering in the long black eyelashes]" (Ingemann 2007: 106). Although this is the first time a female character such as this appears in Danish literature, it can be assumed that a large part of the reading audience was already familiar with her. Beginning in the 17th century, the character of the 'fair Jewess' developed into a topos in European literature, which reached its peak popularity at the start of the 19th century, but which is still effective today (see Krobb 1993).

After the break with their family, the old Jew and the beautiful granddaughter are wandering homeless through the cold night, when they are threatened by a violent mob. In this moment, the young Christian artist Veit, rushes to their rescue, saving them from further anti-Jewish attacks. He takes the exhausted pair to his home, where the old rabbi immediately collapses into a kind of coma. Benjamine, who henceforth tirelessly maintains watch at the bedside of the sick, reads from the bible to her restlessly sleeping grandfather. However, she reads not from the Hebrew bible, but from Veit's Christian bible, in fact, from the New Testament. The inner emotion and ultimately the baptism of the soul that she experiences by reading is in turn captured on canvas by Veit, the painter, as is the elder's peaceful, resting face as she reads. As an artist, Veit makes the internal process of divine permeation externally visible. Yet, the old rabbi wants nothing to do with Christianity when he wakes and recovers from his illness. In the meantime, the Christian and the Jewess have fallen in love and ask for the rabbi's blessing to marry. He refuses to give the two young people his blessing though and feels deeply aggrieved by Benjamine's wish. After all, it is the Christians who have pursued the Jews for centuries. For him, his granddaughter's love of a Christian man feels like a betrayal. Out of loyalty and love for her grandfather, Benjamine returns with him to their community and at the side of the elder, only awaits her own death. Veit too, who is impressed by the rabbi's deep and earnest religiosity and Benjamine's loyalty, accepts this decision. However, when the old rabbi once again falls ill and finally dies, he too is saved by the Holy Spirit's baptism of the soul, through the open window. With his dying breath, he gives Benjamine his blessing to marry the Christian and even calls Veit her "Frelser [saviour]" (Ingemann 2007: 122). At the cemetery, Veit approaches Benjamine with a shining mother-of-pearl cross in his hand and their hands meet, literally and metaphorically, over the grave of the dead Jew. A year later, the two of them, now a married couple, once again stand there and below them in the grave, the rabbi stands upright, facing east, looking towards the rising sun and eternal life.

3 Eschatological fantasies of salvation

The three characters symbolise an eschatological conceptualisation of salvation, in which Judaism plays the role of Christianity's renewer (see Heinrichs 2009). In an increasingly areligious world, the young artist Veit represents an exception among secularised Christians and becomes himself, a quasi-religious saviour. His religiosity is characterised precisely by his respect for Judaism, which in turn is imagined here as the traditional precursor religion to Christianity and which itself exhibits no way into the future. The alienation of the rabbi and his granddaughter from the Jewish community is based on the loss of religiosity also among Jews who adapt to their secularised Christian environment. In comparison, the old rabbi embodies the idealised Jewish past, a type of original religious state. The character of the artist follows the idea of an art-religious renewal, which became popular in the 19th century when Christianity lost significance (see Hartwich 2005: 23–28). Gifted with divine genius, it is the artist's – and thus also the author's – obligation to fill the religious void of the enlightened secularised society. Benjamine represents the perfect vehicle for this fantasy. With her intimate relationship to her grandfather, she embodies the connection to the old "original religion". At the same time, due to her deep connection to Judaism, her conversion attests to Christianity as a superior religion leading the way into the future. The old age of the rabbi and their kinship stand in contrast to the Christian man. A future for Benjamine is only possible with the latter; only they can procreate. And a religious renewal is only possible together, a renewal that requires Judaism, but takes place exclusively within Christianity. The power of renewal thus lies in Christianity and in the Christian man, while Judaism and the Jewish woman attest to this power, making it fruitful for future generations.

In the years and decades that followed, numerous novellas and novels were published in which Jewish characters took on central roles. The subjects, topoi and motives which Ingemann introduced into Danish literature with his novella, were taken up frequently, albeit with modifications or variations. The underlying schema of most of them however resembles the setting described above. Almost

30 years later, in 1855, H.C. Andersen (2007) with his fairy tale *Jødepigen* [The Jewish Maiden] tells the story of a baptism of the soul similar to the one Benjamine experienced when she read from the New Testament. The only difference being that his pious Jewess dies in the end from the lack of a Christian saviour. The Jewess in Andersen's (2001) novel *At være eller ikke være* [To be, or Not to Be] from 1857 also dies, although in doing so she is at least able to help a confused Christian find his way back to his beliefs. St. St. Blicher's (2007) novella *Jøderne paa Hald* [The Jews at Hald] from 1828, begins as a ghost story and ends as a conventional conversion and love story. Here, the entire Jewish family even allows themselves to be convinced into baptism, so that in the end there can be a wedding. In his novel *Guldmageren* [The Gold Maker] from 1836/51, Carsten Hauch (1900) only appears to not tell a conversion story, since his character of a 'fair Jewess' is a Christian right from the start and has never been a Jewess. Yet textually, she is so clearly connected to the topos of the 'fair Jewess' that there is still a sense of a conversion story (see Bock 2021: 136–148). The gold maker, from the title, is a 'noble Jew' and takes on the function of a spiritual father and moral role model for this inauthentic Jewess. He himself does not convert and dies unbaptised, however, a Christian secondary character, who is introduced into the text only for this purpose, confirms that "uagtet han var en Jøde af Fødsel, dog var en Christen i Hjerte og Handlemaade [although he was a Jew from birth, in his heart and his actions he was a Christian.] (Hauch 1900: 365)" F. C. Sibbern's (1927) epistolary novel *Gabrielis's Breve til og fra Hjemmet* [From Gabrielis's Letters To and From Home] from 1850 differs from the previous examples in that the Jew in this text has neither a fair granddaughter or daughter, nor is he a central character. In a key passage, he serves to affirm the Christian first person narrator – who is threatened by a crisis of faith – of his own certainty of the immortal soul and thus implicitly confirms the truth of Christianity (see Bock 2021: 154–156). Shortly after, the Christian characters in the novel find their way back to their own faith and the Jew disappears without commentary from the plot – he is simply no longer required.

4 When is a Jew a Jew?

There are also narrative texts, which focus on other themes and pose questions about emancipation and assimilation as well as the visual recognisability of Jews. Already Blicher in *Jøderne paa Hald* takes up this topic, by leaving the origins of his Christian hero in question, only revealing later that he has a Jewish mother. Thomasine Gyllembourg (1867) even centres her novella *Jøden* [The Jew] from

1836, around the question of origins. In it, a young man puzzles about his biological parents, while his natural father, a Jew, presents him as his Christian foster child in order to protect him from the discrimination and violence that he himself experienced as a Jew. The discourse on biological-ethnic belonging or race is inscribed into both novellas. This results in an apparent paradox: Both Christian men stand out due to their "other" appearance, both however are not recognisable as Jews for the other characters. Since they are not read as Jews, they have not had experiences with violence. Revealing later in the text that they have Jewish parents, serves then as an explanation for their deviating appearances (see Bock 2021: 85, 98–100, 104–111; Schiedermair 2013). Readers, who have already been informed by the titles of the two novellas that Jews will play a decisive role in the plot, can interpret the diffuse signs of the "southern" appearances in view of the unexplained biological kinship much earlier. In the end then, they find their assumptions about the unambiguous recognisability of the Jews confirmed.

An earlier novel by Andersen (1988) treats this subject in a particularly complex way. *Kun en Spillemand* [Just a Fiddler] from 1837 is surprisingly progressive compared to the two other Andersen texts published 20 years later. In this novel, the Jewish woman is first attributed characteristics from the familiar arsenal of stereotypical traits. During a trip to Copenhagen she lands in the middle of the "Hep-Hep riots" and is recognised immediately as a Jewess and attacked (see Andersen 1988: 182–183). In the course of the story though, two opposing movements occur. First, an increasing variety of *otherness* is projected onto the Jewess: self-confidence around sexual desire, a sadomasochistic love relationship with a "gypsy", ambivalent gender, syncretism, human-animal hybridity and demonism (see Bock 2021: 165–208; Detering 2002; Schnurbein 2007: 133–139). Secondly, in the course of the plot, the Jewess loses her Jewish traits, so that she, who was introduced as the 'fair Jewess' in the novel, is no longer recognisable as a Jewess, but rather passes simply as a distinguished Dane (see Bock 2021: 208–213). She is the only Jewish character in this series of texts, who does not affirm Christianity, but rather calls it into question. In this novel, it is the Christian antihero, a failed artist, who dies at the end. The novel does not provide any certainty about the immortality of the soul. Its Christian protagonist lands literally in the ditch. Thus this novel is the only one that can be read as telling about the crisis of Christianity without offering a solution in the form of a pious Jewess willing to be converted or a Jewish Christian at heart. And yet, this Jewess also disappears, in that her being Jewish becomes invisible.

5 Christianity as a way to the future

As different as these novellas and novels are, one commonality stands out: Their Jewish characters are not provided a way into the future within Judaism, either with respect to religion or socially. With few exceptions the texts give the Jewish characters two possibilities: death or baptism, sometimes even both. Judaism is presented as the out-dated mother religion of Christianity. Its function in the texts is to be honoured and respected by the sincere Christian characters. Since it is a Christian imagined Judaism, Judaism itself is barely honoured. Instead, it is the honourability and honesty of the Christian protagonists that is brought into focus. Furthermore, in many of the texts, the Jewish characters are used to negotiate an inter-confessional conflict between Protestantism and Catholicism, always with the result that Protestantism is the better version of Christianity and that Catholicism is essentially to blame for the poor qualities of the "common" Jews. The 'noble Jews' are always an exception. Usually their noble attitude is due to them having been rescued by a noble Christian, which often occurred before the narrated time (see Räthel 2016: 123; Surall 2008: 310–314), but, as in *Den gamle Rabbin*, can also be part of the storyline. The call emanating from these philosemitic texts follows the pattern of an extremely ambivalent tolerance. Although, first made famous by Christian Wilhelm Dohm's (1781) Enlightenment essay *Über die bürgerliche Verbesserung der Juden* [On the Civil Improvement of the Jews], this pattern had already been part of the Protestant discourse on Jews since Martin Luther (see Nirenberg 2015: 253–273): If one treats Jews well, then they will quit being Jewish; if one meets them with Christian charity, or enlightened tolerance, then they will be convinced of Christianity or they will become good enlightened citizens.

How then are Jews and Jewesses written about? What knowledge do the texts convey about Jewish life in Denmark? The answer is sobering. Jewish characters predominantly serve as projection surfaces for philosemitic imaginations and for exoticising external labelling processes; both of which are idealising yet as stereotypical as the well-known anti-Jewish biases. Jewish characters have no language of their own with which they tell of Judaism and being Jewish. They embody a Christian-imagined Judaism, characterised by Christian assumptions, attributions and desires. The texts not only fail to present a living Jewish religiosity, they also lack any representation of Jewish life or emancipation processes from Jewish perspectives. In their debates for or against baptism, the literary Jews always discuss the content and meaning of Christianity, not Judaism. None of these narrative texts refer to any Jewish religious scriptures other than the Hebrew Bible, which is referred to here as a matter of course as the Old Testament, the New Testament is thus always implicitly considered a kind of religious update.

Nevertheless, the novels and novellas, and with them their authors, achieve something that needs to be recognised and which differentiates them from anti-Jewish discourse. The texts do not offer a discussion of Judaism in their time, but do examine the meaning of Judaism for Christianity. They do not offer any insights into Jewish life and the process of emancipation within Jewish communities, but they do reflect and judge verbal and physical violence of Christians against Jews. They draw on stereotypical ideas to mark their Jews as Jews and Jewesses as Jewesses, but – despite all the idealisations and ambivalences – develop positive counter-types to existing anti-Jewish stereotypes.

Yet, in summary it can be said that 'the Jew' as a philosemitic figure of thought, serves above all to assure Christians, the non-Jews of their own identity. Jewish voices remain unheard.

6 Finally a novel from a Jewish perspective

It is this literary context, in which in 1845 the Jewish journalist and author Meïr Aron Goldschmidt (1927) published his debut novel *En Jøde* [A Jew]. Goldschmidt was 25 at the time his novel was released. He was raised in an orthodox Jewish family in Copenhagen but enjoyed both a religious and humanist education. He thus grew up amidst the era of Jewish emancipation (see Gurley 2016: 18–26). At the time of his novel's release, this process was not yet complete; religious freedom was not yet anchored in the constitution. The social process had actually just begun. And it is exactly this, which his novel *En Jøde* tells of. It is not only the first Danish novel that describes Jewish life and the process of emancipation from a Jewish perspective, but also the first one in all of Europe (see Gurley 2016: 8–18). And it is the previously published texts that I discussed above, to which his novel relates – has to relate to. In the following, I want to explore if and how the philosemitic discourse reverberates in Goldschmidt's novel. For an answer, I want to focus on the relation between Judaism and Christianity in the novel, where both meet the most intensely and painfully: In the love relationship between the Jew Jacob Bendixen and his Christian fiancée, whose name Thora carries with it a double entendre (the allusion to the Hebrew Torah and the Nordic god Thor), as well as her family, the Fangels.

First, I would like to provide a – grossly abbreviated – overview of the plot: Jacob Bendixen is born during the Napoleonic Wars, at the start of the 19th century. He grows up in a small town in the Danish province Funen in an orthodox

Jewish family. He is the only Jewish child his age in town and is thus often alone since every contact with the non-Jewish children leads to anti-Jewish abuse and insults aimed at him. Jacob is smart and gifted and in the hope that he would one day return to the Jewish community as a successful doctor and scholar, he is sent to Copenhagen in order to attend grammar school and later study medicine. Jacob absorbs the education and *Bildung* he receives in Copenhagen. He cultivates contacts in bourgeois circles; he falls in love with a Christian; her family gives him a warm welcome, the two even want to marry. However, Jacob is repeatedly thrown back to his Jewishness, again and again, sometimes subtly, sometimes explicitly, he is confronted with being different, being a Jew, and with the need to discard this otherness in order to be accepted. He is thus increasingly insecure and unresolvable misunderstandings occur between him and his fiancée and her family. Ultimately, he and Thora separate. As his love relationship falters so too does his way into Danish bourgeois society. In the end he is broken and returns to the Jewish community as the cliché of a Jewish money lender. Soon after, he dies alone and hated.

With this pessimistic end, Goldschmidt links to the topos that Jews become stereotypical characters because of the poor way they are treated by Christians. Nevertheless, the text questions this very topos through its differentiated representation of Jewish lives and Jewish characters. Moreover, Goldschmidt's novel *En Jøde* reflects the prevailing Christian perspective of Jews and Judaism in Denmark. This dominant perspective is not only shaped by anti-Jewish discourse, but also by the stories of Christian authors, which I briefly discussed above. The Fangels share this perspective. They thus do not know more about Judaism or Jewish life than the Christian reader, to whom the novel is addressed. They have no knowledge of living Jewish religious practice, nor do they question the conversion discourse. They behave "well" and "enlightened" towards Jacob and are quite benevolent. The family of his fiancée initially accepts him as a future son-in-law with apparent openness and consideration of his Jewish origins. However, while the Fangels practice tolerance in order to avoid giving Jacob the feeling that he does not belong, he always reckons that he will be unadmittedly rejected as a Jew. In social situations in which the other guests, Christians like the Fangels, chat with one another carefree and accustomed to conventions, Jacob feels uncomfortable and insecure. A vicious circle starts because he now actually becomes gruff and taciturn, which in turn makes the Fangels suspect the reason for this is his Jewishness and to then question the marriage to Thora. When Thora's aunt moves to Copenhagen, she makes Jacob's baptism her personal project, which should solve all these problems. This confirms for Jacob, what he has always known, that as a Jew he is not accepted by Christians as long as he does not become a Christian.

The difficulties he encounters with the Fangels and their social surroundings however are not due to his denomination. Rather, it is the difference in his education and the consequences of his socially isolated childhood that are evident. And both in turn are related to his Jewish origins, which also have something – but not everything – to do with religion. As a child he is isolated because he is growing up in a small Jewish community, where he has no playmates. He is isolated because he cannot play with the Christian children. Instead of learning to play, he learns it is completely normal to be insulted by other children's anti-Jewish shouts. Thus up until his Bar Mitzvah he does not go to regular school, instead he learns from his father and uncle everything he needs to know as a devout Jew in a Jewish community. At the grammar school, the social isolation and hatred towards Jews continues, but here he encounters humanist education which for him is the part of Christianity he strives for and yearns for.

Jacob thus makes a revealing comment to his (also Jewish) friend Levy: "Mit Blod elsker Jøderne; men min Aand kan ikke leve imellem dem. Det er en kristelig Aand, og den søger med instinktmæssig Heftighed sine Lige. [My blood loves the Jews, but my intellect cannot live amongst them. It is a Christian intellect and it seeks its like with instinctual impetuosity.]" (Goldschmidt 1927: 124)[4] This quote opens various fields of discourse. For one, it introduces a blood discourse, which brings Judaism together with biological-ethnic belonging. It also continues the philosemitic idea of Christianity's superiority, even though Christianity is not understood here religiously. The Jew Jacob covets Christianity, in that he desires the *Bildung* and the intellect, which he decisively understands as Christian. He therefore also seems to succumb to the philosemitic paradigm, according to which a good Jew is one who wants to become Christian. But does Jacob want to become Christian? In response to Levy's reply that he should then let himself be baptised, Jacob counters with indignation: "Levy! Det kan De ikke mene alvorlig. Lade mig døbe! fornægte min Fortid, min Barndom, min hele Tilværelse... [Levy! You cannot be serious! Let myself be baptised! To renounce my past, my childhood, my entire being...]" (Goldschmidt 1927: 124) Here it becomes clear that Jacob does not consider Judaism to be a biological-ethnic parameter either. Incidentally the Fangel family also believes this, even though these categories resonate throughout the text. Instead, it is a parameter that is based on the memories and experiences that he has had as a Jew – both as a Jew among Christians as well as a Jew among Jews.

---

4 English translation cited according to Gurley 2016: 85.

7 Struggle for language and sovereignty of interpretation

While experiences with antisemitism and violence are reflected in the texts by Christian authors as well, up to this point there had not yet been a portrayal of a true, I almost want to say "authentic", Jewish life in literature. Goldschmidt meets his Christian readers' ignorance with the psychological representation of his Jewish protagonist Jacob's inner world. He also inserts extensive footnotes in order to explain to his readers the religious practices, Jewish celebrations, Hebrew terms and Yiddish idioms (see Brandenburg 2014). Even the description of the Jewish community in Jacob's hometown is multi-layered and in no way idealised. The novel tells of friendships and arguments between different members of the community. It tells of rich Jews and poor Jews, of Jewish fraudsters and Jewish benefactors, of Jews, who are often simple and sometimes smart. It tells of the love the family has for the young Jacob and their lack of understanding when he starts to question Jewish orthodoxy. In short: It tells of a little educated, but lively Judaism and it does so with a good portion of satire and a certain distance. One thing it is not though: It is not a stereotypical representation of a dead religion. The text tells of an ambivalent, diverse, contradictory Jewish community, of familial warmth and familial conflicts, which shape Jacob's life and of traditions and religious practices, which beyond their religious content are a permanent source of identity, because they are part of his world of experience.

Faced with Thora and her family however, Jacob fails to find any expression of what makes him Jewish and what ties him to Judaism. The author Goldschmidt however, finds an expression for this speechlessness through literary form. Shortly after Jacob and Thora get to know one another at a ball – a ball, to which Jacob as a Jew was almost not invited to, but then due to partly happy and partly unhappy circumstances, was – the novel's text splinters. Fragments of thoughts and associations end abruptly and begin at another point with an ellipsis. Jacob's thoughts circle around the possibility or impossibility of a relationship between a Christian woman and a Jewish man and struggle to find appropriate words (see Goldschmidt 1927: 150–152).

Only a few pages later, it is Thora whose thoughts fragment in a similar way, only to start again anew (see Goldschmidt 1927: 156–159). Here, it is letters drafted to her girlfriend, whom she wants to inform about meeting and becoming engaged to Jacob. These aborted letters give an impression of the image Thora has made of "the Jew" and how she tries to replace stereotypical ideas with the living image of the real Jew, Jacob. From the Jewish usurer to the noble Oriental, from the Jews of the bible up to the Jews of Sir Walter Scott, her associations represent an overview of antisemitic and philosemitic stereotypes. In the letter that she ultimately sends, and which reports of the happy engagement, she however never mentions a word about her fiancé being Jewish (see Goldschmidt 1927: 159–160). One could think this means it is no longer relevant to her. One could also say though, that she wants it to be no longer relevant. And beyond that, I want to suggest that other than drawing on stereotypes, she lacks the language to say what is Jewish about Jacob.

Thus a little later, Jacob complains to his friend Levy that in his presence the Fangels try so obviously not to mention his being Jewish, that it is torturous. Their supposedly tactful way and aversion of every indication of Jews and Judaism make it so clear to him that at no point can they forget that he is a Jew. Jacob's discomfort grows and finally the misunderstandings are so many and the speechlessness so extensive that the break-up between Jacob and Thora seems unavoidable – if Jacob is not able to make himself understandable. And this is precisely the advice that Levy gives him: "Tal til Pigebarnet, Menneske! [My dear man, speak with the girl!]" (Goldschmidt 1927: 175) The prospect of a conversation with her about what being Jewish means for him, fills Jacob with hope and seems to promise salvation. The conversation though, never takes place, in the meantime the conflict is too great. Jacob thus sees his last chance for recognition and equality in a military career and, since such a career is not possible for Jews in Denmark, he goes first to France, then to Algeria and then to Poland. In his good-bye letter to Thora, he finally formulates his relation to Judaism and the conflict he finds himself in. He writes:

> "Du ved heller ikke, med hvilken Magt jeg er knyttet til Jødedommen, hvorledes den blotte Tanke om at forlade den foraarsager mig Pine og Rædsel. Og dog har jeg i Grunden forladt den; det er ikke Religionen, der holder mig – Din Slægts Gud er dog den Samme som min – det er min Barndom, Mindet om min Slægt, om mine Forældre, utallige skjønne Erindringer. Jeg kan ikke forsage dem, rive mig løs fra dem, jeg kan ikke kaste dem ud af min Sjæl [...]. Tror Du ikke nok, at der er en fælles Kjærlighed til Guddommen, hvori vi kunne leve, hvis blot ikke Verden træder forstyrrende imellem os?" (Goldschmidt 1927: 210) [Emphasis in the original].
> ["You also do not know, how strongly bound to Judaism I feel, how the idea alone that I should leave it torments and tortures me. Yet, I *have* in essence left it. It is not the religion that I love – the God of your ancestors is the same as mine –, it is my childhood, the memory of my tribe, my ancestors... countless, wonderful memories. I cannot disavow that, I cannot tear myself away from it, I cannot expel it from my soul. [...] Do you not believe, there is also a more comprehensive love of God in which we both could live, if only the world would not come between us?"]

Thora, does not believe this. Or rather: She does not believe that the world does not want to disrupt their love. She decides to dissolve the engagement and to marry someone else. In the moment that Jacob explains his Judaism, lays it bare to his Christian fiancée from his Jewish perspective, and she, as we later learn, understands it – she and her entire family, even the aunt with her aggressive missionary aspirations, they understand it and are deeply moved by the letter – in this moment, the love between the Jew and the Christian paradoxically becomes entirely impossible.

8 Closing considerations

What does this mean for my closing considerations? The novel *En Jøde* refers to the philosemitic discourse – not only, in taking up and criticising its ambivalence and one-sided perspective, but also by addressing the paradigm of Christianity's superiority. Jacob yearns for Christianity and turns away from Judaism. However, it is not as a religion that he longs for Christianity, since to him it seems hollow and in decline. It is the intellect and *Bildung*, presented as decidedly Christian in Goldschmidt's novel, that attracts him, while Judaism, associated with a deficient education, remains inferior. Jacob's return to the Jewish community is therefore a failure, he is thrown back into a spiritual and intellectual milieu that he had wanted to leave. The text though, does not try to find the responsibility for this failure in Jacob – at least not alone – but (also) in the Christian majority. In doing so, it also connects to the philosemitic discourse. His unwillingness to be baptised is not the problem, rather that it is expected from him. The Fangels' behaviour towards Jacob is characterised by their efforts to be tolerant and belief in their own tolerance while at the same time expecting complete assimilation, which the baptism should serve as evidence of. They are not interested in Jacob's experiences or perspective, nor are they conscious of how their own behaviour contributes to Jacob's increasing insecurity. His personal, always also specifically Jewish life experiences, remain not only unseen by the Fangels, but in view of the dissolved engagement, one could even say: They remain unwanted and undesired.

Goldschmidt however contrasts Judaism as it had previously been portrayed from a Christian perspective in literature with another, very intimate and complex depiction of Judaism. He recognises childhood experiences and memories, that is cultural and familial characteristics, as categories that are sources of identity. The speechlessness, which exists between Jacob and Thora over long stretches of the novel and which is expressed form-wise in fragmentary passages, can be interpreted as a gap: that is a lack of a common idea of what Jewishness is. As long as Judaism is a Christian phantasm, with all the implications of baptism and assimilation, the connection between Thora and Jacob seems possible. Once Jacob finally gives voice to his understanding of Judaism though in his letter to Thora, that is, lets it transform from a Christian phantasm to a real and powerful parameter, the relationship becomes absolutely impossible. Understanding results in separation. Only the readers now have the possibility to speak about Judaism in a new and different way and the relationship between Jews and Christians and to thus create the connection that was not possible for Jacob and Thora.

References

a. Research literature

Achinger, Christine (2007): Gespaltene Moderne. Gustav Freytags Soll und Haben: Nation, Geschlecht und Judenbild. Würzburg: Königshausen & Neumann.

Albertsen, Leif Ludwig (1984): Engelen Mi. En bog om den danske jødefejde. Med en bibliografi af Bent W. Dahlstrøm. [The Angel Mi. A Book about the Jew Controversy in Denmark. With a Bibliography by Bent W. Dahlstrøm.] København: Privat Print.

Blüdnikow, Bent/Jørgensen, Harald (1984). "Den lange vandring til borgerlig ligestilling." ["The Long Way to Civil Equality."] In: Bent Blüdnikow/Harald Jørgensen (eds.): Indenfor murene. Jødisk liv i Danmark 1684–1984. Udgivet af Selskabet for danskjødisk historie, i anledning af 300-året for grundlæggelsen af Mosaisk Troessamfund. [Behind Walls. Jewish Life in Denmark. Published by the Society for Danish-Jewish History, on the 300th Anniversary of the Jewish Community.] København: C.A. Reitzels Forlag.

Bock, Katharina (2021): Philosemitische Schwärmereien. Jüdische Figuren in der dänischen Erzählliteratur des 19. Jahrhunderts (= Beiträge zur Nordischen Philologie 67). Tübingen: Narr Francke Attempto.

Brandenburg, Florian (2014): "'At Orientaleren skal tale som Orientaler...' ["'That Orientals should speak like Orientals...'"] Zur Problematik von Form und Funktion 'Jüdischen Sprechens' in M. A. Goldschmidts En Jøde (1845/52)." In: European Journal of Scandinavian Studies 44/1, 103–126.

Detering, Heinrich (2002): Das offene Geheimnis. Zur literarischen Produktivität eines Tabus von Winkelmann bis zu Thomas Mann. Durchgesehene und mit einer Nachbemerkung versehene Studienausgabe. Göttingen: Wallstein.

Grimm, Markus (2013): "Die Begriffsgeschichte des Philosemitismus." In: Jahrbuch für Antisemitismusforschung 22, 244–266.

Gubser, Martin (1998): Literarischer Antisemitismus. Untersuchungen zu Gustav Freytag und anderen bürgerlichen Schriftstellern des 19. Jahrhunderts. Göttingen: Wallstein

Gurley, David Gantt (2016): Meïr Aaron Goldschmidt and the Poetics of Jewish Fiction. Syracuse: Syracuse University Press.

Gutsche, Victoria Luise (2014): Zwischen Abgrenzung und Annäherung. Konstruktionen des Jüdischen in der Literatur des 17. Jahrhunderts. Berlin/Boston: de Gruyter.

Hartwich, Wolf-Daniel (2005): Romantischer Antisemitismus. Von Klopstock bis Richard Wagner. Göttingen: Vandenhoeck & Ruprecht.

Haxen, Ulf (2001): "Skandinavien." In: Elke-Vera Kotowski/Julius H. Schoeps/Hiltrud Wallenborn (eds.): Handbuch zur Geschichte der Juden in Europa. Band 1. Länder und Regionen. Darmstadt: Primus Verlag, 487–500.

Heinrichs, Wolfgang E. (2009): "Juden als ideelle Hoffnungs- und Heilsträger im Protestantismus des 18. und 19. Jahrhunderts." In: Irene Diekmann/Elke-Vera Kotowski (eds.): Geliebter Feind – gehasster Freund. Antisemitismus und Philosemitismus in Geschichte und Gegenwart. Berlin: VBB, Verlag für Berlin-Brandenburg, 213–231.

Kinzig, Wolfram (2009): "Philosemitismus – was ist das? Eine kritische Begriffsanalyse." In: Irene Diekmann/Elke-Vera Kotowski (eds.): Geliebter Feind – gehasster Freund. Antisemitismus und Philosemitismus in Geschichte und Gegenwart. Berlin: VBB, Verlag für Berlin-Brandenburg, 25–60.

Klüger, Ruth (2007): "Die Säkularisierung des Judenhasses am Beispiel von Wilhelm Raabes 'Der Hungerpastor'." In: Klaus-Michael Bogdal/Klaus Holz/Matthias N. Lorenz (eds.): Literarischer Antisemitismus nach Auschwitz. Stuttgart: Metzler, 103–110.

Krobb, Florian (1993): Die schöne Jüdin. Jüdische Frauengestalten in der deutschsprachigen Erzählliteratur vom 17. Jahrhundert bis zum Ersten Weltkrieg. Tübingen: Niemeyer.

Krobb, Florian (2007): "Was bedeutet literarischer Antisemitismus im 19. Jahrhundert? Ein Problemaufriss." In: Klaus-Michael Bogdal/Klaus Holz/Matthias N. Lorenz (eds.): Literarischer Antisemitismus nach Auschwitz. Stuttgart: Metzler, 85–101.

Massey, Irving (2000): Philo-semitism in nineteenth-century German literature (= Conditio Judaica 29). Tübingen: Niemeyer.

Nirenberg, David (2015): Anti-Judaismus. Eine andere Geschichte des westlichen Denkens. München: Beck.

Räthel, Clemens (2016): Wie viel Bart darf sein? Jüdische Figuren im skandinavischen Theater. Tübingen: Narr Francke Attempto.

Räthel, Clemens/Schnurbein, Stefanie von (eds.) (2020): Figurationen des Jüdischen. Spurensuchen in der skandinavischen Literatur (= Berliner Beiträge zur Skandinavistik 27). Berlin: Nordeuropa-Institut der Humboldt-Universität zu Berlin.

Rensmann, Lars/Faber, Klaus (2009): "Philosemitismus und Antisemitismus: Reflexionen zu einem ungleichen Begriffspaar." In: Irene Diekmann/Elke-Vera Kotowski (eds.): Geliebter Feind – gehasster Freund. Antisemitismus und Philosemitismus in Geschichte und Gegenwart. Berlin: VBB, Verlag für Berlin-Brandenburg, 73–91.

Rohlén-Wohlgemuth, Hilde (1995): Svensk-judisk litteratur 1775–1994: en litteraturhistorisk översikt. [Swedish-Jewish Literature 1775–1994: A Literary-Historical Overview.] Spånga: Megilla-Förlaget.

Rothlauf, Gertraud (2009): Vom Schtetl zum Polarkreis. Juden und Judentum in der norwegischen Literatur. Doctoral Thesis. Universität Wien.

Schiedermair, Joachim (2013): "Der Kaufmann von Kopenhagen. Geld und Gabe in Thomasine Gyllembourgs Novelle 'Jøden' (1836)." In: Klaus Müller-Wille/Joachim Schiedermair (eds.): Wechselkurse des Vertrauens. Zur Konzeptualisierung von Ökonomie und Vertrauen im nordischen Idealismus (1800–1870) (= Beiträge zur Nordischen Philologie 51). Tübingen und Basel: A. Francke, 51–68.

Schnurbein, Stefanie von (2007): "Hybride Alteritäten. Jüdische Figuren bei H.C. Andersen." In: Wolfgang Behschnitt/Elisabeth Herrmann (eds.): Über Grenzen. Grenzgänge der Skandinavistik. Festschrift zum 65. Geburtstag von Heinrich Anz. Würzburg: Ergon Verlag, 129–150.

Schwarz Lausten, Martin (2015): Jews and Christians in Denmark. From the Middle Ages to Recent Times, ca. 1100–1948. Leiden/Boston: Brill.
Surall, Frank (2008): "Vom Sieg der Vernunft über das Vorurteil. Gotthold Ephraim Lessings Frühwerk 'Die Juden'." In: Zeitschrift für Religions- und Geistesgeschichte ZRGG 60, 310–329.
Theisohn, Philipp/Braungart, Georg (2012): "Philosemitismus als literarischer Diskurs." In: Morgen-Glantz. Zeitschrift der Christian Knorr von Rosenroth-Gesellschaft 22, 9–17.
Theisohn, Philipp/Braungart, Georg (2017): "Die überspringende Rede. Philosemitismus als literarischer Diskurs." In: Philipp Theisohn/Georg Braungart (eds.): Philosemitismus. Rhetorik, Poetik, Diskursgeschichte. Paderborn: Wilhelm Fink Verlag, 9–28.
Thurn, Nike (2015): "Falsche Juden". Performative Identitäten in der Literatur von Lessing bis Walser. Göttingen: Wallstein.
Zuckermann, Moshe (2009): "Aspekte des Philosemitismus." In: Irene Diekmann/Elke-Vera Kotowski (eds.): Geliebter Feind – gehasster Freund. Antisemitismus und Philosemitismus in Geschichte und Gegenwart. Berlin: VBB, Verlag für Berlin-Brandenburg, 61–71.

b. Empirical sources

Andersen, Hans Christian (1986): Fodreise fra Holmens Canal til Østpynten af Amager i Aarene 1828 og 1829. Tekstutgivelse, efterskrift og noter af Johan de Mylius. [A Journey on Foot from Holmen's Canal to the Eastern Point of Amager 1828 and 1829. Edited, Annotated and with an Afterword by Johan de Mylius.] København: Det danske Sprog- og Litteraturselskab Borgen.
Andersen, Hans Christian (1988): Kun en Spillemand. Original Roman i tre Dele. Tekstudgivelse, efterskrift og noter af Mogens Brøndsted. [Just a Fiddler. Original Novel in Three Parts. Edited, Annotated and with an Afterword by Mogens Brøndsted.] København: Borgen.
Andersen, Hans Christian (2000): Lykke-Peer. Tekstudgivelse, efterskrift og noter ved Erik Dal. [Lucky Peer. Edited, Annotated and with an Afterword by Erik Dal.] København: Det Danske Sprog- og Litteraturselskab.
Andersen, Hans Christian (2001): At være eller ikke være. Roman i tre Dele. Tekstudgivelse og noter ved Erik Dal. Efterskrift af Mogens Brøndsted. [To be, or Not to Be. Novel in Three Parts. Edited and Annotated by Erik Dal. With an Afterword by Mogens Brøndsted.] Borgen: Det Danske Sprog- og Litteraturselskab.
Andersen, Hans Christian (2007): "Jødepigen." ["The Jewish Maiden."] In: Mogens Brøndsted (ed.): Ahasverus. Jødiske elementer i dansk litteratur. [Ahasversus. Jewish Elements in Danish Literature.] Odense: Syddansk Universitetsforlag, 123–126.
Blicher, Steen Steensen (2007): "Jøderne paa Hald." ["The Jews at Hald."] In: Mogens Brøndsted (ed.): Ahasverus. Jødiske elementer i dansk litteratur. [Ahasversus. Jewish Elements in Danish Literature.] Odense: Syddansk Universitetsforlag, 67–98.
Dohm, Christian Wilhelm (1781): Ueber die bürgerliche Verbesserung der Juden. Mit Königl. Preußischem Privilegio. Berlin/Stettin: Friedrich Nicolai.
Goldschmidt, Meïr Aron (1927): En Jøde. [A Jew.] København: Gyldendal.
Gyllembourg-Ehrensvärd, Thomasine (1867): "Jøden." ["The Jew."] In: C. A. Reitzels Forlag (ed.): Samlede Skrifter af Forf. til "En Hverdags-Historie", fra Gyllembourg-Ehrensvärd. [Complete Works of the Author of "An Everyday Story", by Gyllembourg-Ehrensvärd.] 2. edn. København: C. A. Reitzel, 1–150.

Hauch, Carsten (1900): Guldmageren. En romantisk Begivenhed fra det forsvundne Aarhundrede. [The Gold Maker. A Romantic Incident from Last Century.] København: Gyldendal.
Ingemann, Bernhard Severin (2007): "Den gamle Rabbin." ["The Old Rabbi."] In: Mogens Brøndsted (ed.): Ahasverus. Jødiske elementer i dansk litteratur. [Ahasversus. Jewish Elements in Danish Literature.] Odense: Syddansk Universitetsforlag, 99–122.
Sibbern, Frederik Christian (1927): "Udaf Gabrielis's Breve til og fra Hjemmet." ["From Gabrielis's Letters To and From Home."] In: Poul Tuxen (ed.): Gabrielis' Breve. [Gabrielis's Letters.] København: Holbergselskabet af 23. September, 147–402.

c. Online references

Becking, Bob (2006): Entry »Jahwe«. In: Deutsche Bibelgesellschaft (ed.): *Das Bibellexikon*. Stuttgart: Deutsche Bibelgesellschaft. https://www.bibelwissenschaft.de/stichwort/22127/ (accessed 26 April 2023).

Index

ability 4
African Traditional Religion 155, 156
age 137
Akció 19, 20, 21, 22, 24, 25
Akwanga, Ebenezert 161
Alans 27
Algeria 241
Americans 91, 97
Amsterdam 38
Andersen, Hans Christian 227, 234, 235
Anderson, Benedict 64
Anglophone 6, 155, 156, 157, 158, 159, 160, 161, 166, 168, 170, 171, 175, 176, 178, 180, 181
antisemitism 19, 228, 230, 240
Antwerp 94
Anu, Chris 161
Arabic 136
Aramaic 83, 84
archaeology 38, 41, 43, 51, 53
Arckenholtz, Johan 49, 50, 51
assimilation 14, 19, 234, 242
Attila, King 17
authenticity 11, 12, 17, 18, 20, 23, 26, 27, 28, 29, 30, 31
Ayaba Cho Lucas 161, 176
Ayuk Tabe, Sisiku 161

Balla, Agbor 160
Bareta, Mark 161
Bautzen 219, 224, 226
Beecroft, Alexander 40, 53
belonging 2, 3, 4, 5, 6, 38, 44, 52, 53, 90, 96, 99, 217
Berger, Peter 59
Berlin 5, 7, 37, 41, 43, 44, 46, 47, 49, 52, 83, 84, 85, 86, 87, 88, 89, 90, 91, 92, 93, 94, 95, 96, 99, 100, 101, 224, 225
Bessière, Jean 38, 41
Bible, the 57, 58, 64, 65, 66, 72, 73, 74, 76, 77, 157, 162, 163, 165, 166, 167, 168, 169, 170, 175, 176, 177, 179, 180, 182, 231, 232, 236, 241
Black women 3, 193
Blicher, Steen Steensen 227, 234
Blidy, Monika 217
Borgå 204
Bourdieu, Pierre 46, 104, 105, 109, 116, 118, 121
Brandenburg 41, 43
Braunschweig 37, 49
Brězan, Jurij 215, 216, 217, 222, 223, 225
Bucharest 15, 21, 26
Budapest 26, 33
Budapesti Hírlap 18

Calvinism 37, 41, 49
Cameroon 6, 64, 155, 157, 158, 159, 160, 161, 164, 166, 167, 175, 177, 178, 180, 181
Cameroonians 158, 159, 160, 179, 180, 181
Cap, Piotr 69
Casanova, Pascale 45
categorisation 1, 2, 61, 69
Catholicism 5, 45, 156, 158, 161, 236
Central African Republic 155, 156
centrality 2, 4, 5, 6, 7, 31, 39, 41, 43, 45, 48, 52, 57, 58, 61, 62, 66, 67, 75, 76, 90
China 5, 59, 60, 61, 63, 65, 66, 67, 68, 69, 70
Christian missions 57, 58, 59, 64, 70, 74, 75, 76
Christianity 4, 5, 11, 49, 57, 63, 69, 70, 71, 72, 73, 74, 103, 105, 106, 131, 155, 156, 158, 160, 161, 166, 168, 169, 170, 181, 228, 232, 233, 234, 235, 236, 237, 239, 242
Church of Sweden 59
Cicio-Pop, Ștefan 20, 21, 23, 24, 25
class 4, 5, 110, 133, 137, 193
Cloșca 17, 28
colonialism 57, 58, 72, 74, 75, 76, 159
Combahee River Collective 3, 4
Commonwealth of Independent States 90, 92, 93

Congo 5, 59, 60, 61, 63, 64, 65, 66, 67, 68, 69, 70, 71, 72
Contradiction Studies 3, 6
contradictions 5, 6, 30, 37, 57, 63, 67, 68, 74, 193, 194, 196, 199, 200, 207, 208, 213, 214, 217, 223, 231, 235, 242
conversions 103, 106, 107, 112, 113, 115, 116, 117, 120, 121, 156, 234, 236
Copenhagen 229, 235, 237, 238
cosmopolitanism 37, 40, 44, 48, 51, 52, 53
Côte d'Ivoire 156, 180
Crișan 17, 28
cultural agents 37, 39, 40, 46, 47, 49, 51, 52

Dacians 11, 17, 27
Dandea, Emil 25
Darwin, Charles 60
Davies, William 1
DeLoughrey, Elizabeth 216
democracy 2, 6, 14, 136, 159, 182
Denmark 6, 227, 229, 236, 238, 241
Densușianu, Ovidiu 27
diaspora 39, 45, 52
Dohm, Christian Wilhelm 236
Domašcyna, Róža 215
Du Bellay, Joachim 44

Edict of Nantes 37, 38, 42
Edict of Potsdam 42
education 16, 19, 22, 25, 30, 45, 103, 137, 237, 238, 239
Egan, Ede 19
Ekenäs 204
England 43, 45, 46, 159, 229
English 90, 96, 159, 160
enlightenment 42, 43, 44, 50, 67, 72, 233, 236, 238
entanglement 11, 12, 20, 22, 23, 26, 27, 31, 214, 215
equality 1, 2, 4, 14, 50, 142, 214, 229, 230, 241
Ethiopia 143
ethnicity 5, 14, 19, 26, 27, 31, 130, 131, 133, 137, 138, 141, 142, 143, 146, 155, 192, 194, 215, 223, 235, 239

Federbusch, Simon 112, 113

Feldt-Ranta, Maarit 202, 205
Finland 2, 6, 103, 104, 105, 106, 107, 108, 112, 117, 118, 119, 121, 124, 125, 126, 189, 190, 191, 195, 196, 197, 199, 201, 203, 206
Finnish 189, 192, 196, 199, 202
forestry 14, 15, 20, 22, 24, 25
Foucault, Michel 38, 58, 63
framing 132
France 5, 37, 38, 39, 42, 44, 45, 46, 47, 53, 143, 159, 163, 222, 241
Francophone 37, 41, 51, 159, 180
Frâncu, Amos 22
Fraser, Nancy 4
Frederick the Great 42, 44, 46
Frederick VI of Denmark 229, 230
Frederick William, Elector of Brandenburg 41, 42
Fredrickson, Clark A. 50
French 37, 38, 39, 41, 42, 44, 46, 47, 49, 51, 52, 53, 159, 160
French Antilles 48
Friedman, Jeffrey 38

Gábor, Áron 28
Gauvin, Lise 41
Gbagbo, Laurent 156, 181
gender 4, 5, 104, 107, 110, 111, 112, 114, 115, 116, 119, 120, 121, 122, 137, 235
genealogy 38, 41, 51
Geneva 38, 44
George William, Elector of Brandenburg 41
German 37, 38, 42, 46, 49, 51, 53, 84, 85, 87, 88, 92, 95, 96, 98, 100
Germany 2, 6, 14, 38, 46, 53, 84, 85, 86, 90, 91, 93, 95, 97, 99, 100, 213, 214, 215, 228, 230
Gobineau, Arthur de 67
Goldschmidt, Meïr Aron 228, 229, 237, 238, 239, 240, 241, 242
Greek 83
group identification 127, 128, 130, 146
Gullestad, Marianne 58, 64
Gustavus II Adolphus 50, 51
Gyllembourg-Ehrensvärd, Thomasine 227, 234

Ha'aretz 137
Hajduk-Veljkovićowa, Lubina 215, 223, 224, 225
Ham 73
Hamburg 231
Hammarstedt, Lars Fredrik 72
Harel, Simon 39
Harmony, Bobga 160
Häseler, Jens 40, 43, 45, 46, 47
Hauch, Carsten 227, 234
Hebrew 83, 84, 85, 87, 88, 92, 95, 96, 97, 98, 100, 136, 240
Hegel, Georg Wilhelm Friedrich 4
Helsinki 5, 103, 104, 105, 106, 107, 117, 118, 120, 121, 122, 123, 125, 126
Hensel, Silke 67
Herbert, Boh 161
Herberts, Kjell 203, 205
Hilda 61
Holm, Albert 63
Holocaust, the 89, 90
Horea 17, 28
Huguenots 37, 39, 42, 43, 44, 47
human trafficking 15
Hungarian 11, 18, 27, 29
Hungarians 11, 17, 18, 20, 27, 28, 29
Hungary 5, 11, 12, 13, 14, 15, 16, 17, 18, 19, 20, 22, 27, 29, 31, 32
Huns 17, 18, 28
hybridity 213, 214, 215, 216, 219, 235

Iancu 17, 28
identity 1, 6, 65, 85, 88, 97, 103, 105, 107, 108, 115, 119, 122, 127, 128, 129, 133, 136, 139, 140, 141, 142, 144, 145, 146, 155, 157, 159, 160, 162, 182, 189, 190, 191, 192, 193, 194, 195, 197, 198, 200, 201, 203, 204, 205, 206, 207, 208, 213, 217, 237, 240, 242
identity politics 3
India 49, 155, 163
inequality 75, 109, 111, 122, 142
Ingemann, Bernhard Severin 227, 230
intersectionality 4, 192, 193, 195, 197, 200, 201, 203, 207, 208, 217
intertextuality 168
Iorga, Nicolae 26, 29, 30

Islam 131, 155, 156, 158, 161, 164
Israel 5, 98, 115, 117, 127, 128, 130, 131, 133, 134, 135, 136, 137, 138, 141, 142, 143, 144, 146, 153
Israelis 89, 90, 91, 92, 93, 95, 96, 100, 117, 119, 120, 121, 127, 130, 131, 133, 135, 137, 138, 139, 141, 142, 143, 144, 145, 146
Italy 14

Jansson, Tove 194, 204, 205
Jerusalem 94
Jesus 57, 68, 70, 71, 72, 73, 75, 169, 172, 173, 174, 176, 177, 178, 179
Jewish communities 5, 83, 84, 85, 86, 87, 89, 90, 91, 92, 93, 94, 95, 97, 98, 99, 103, 104, 105, 106, 107, 112, 229, 233, 238, 239, 242
Jewish emancipation 228, 229, 230, 234, 236, 237
John Sigismund, Elector of Brandenburg 41
Johnson, Mark 73
Jordan, Charles Étienne 37, 40, 43, 44, 45, 46, 47, 48, 49, 51, 52, 53
Judaism 6, 85, 86, 87, 88, 89, 90, 95, 97, 99, 100, 104, 105, 106, 112, 115, 116, 120, 121, 142, 170, 227, 233, 236, 237, 238, 239, 240, 241, 242

Karlsson, Sofi 63
Kassel 37, 49
Koch, Jurij 214, 215, 217, 219, 222, 223, 224, 225
Kupari, Helena 104

La Croze, Mathurin Veyssière 37, 40, 45, 46, 47, 48, 49, 51, 52, 53
Ladino 84
Lakoff, George 73
language ideology 93, 100
legitimisation 58, 59, 64, 68, 69, 73, 74, 75, 110, 118, 157, 161
Lincoln, Abraham 162
linguistic repertoire 83, 84, 85, 86, 87, 88, 95, 96, 100
Luckmann, Thomas 59
Lusatia 219, 222, 224
Luther, Martin 236

Ma'ariv 137
Macedonia 64, 65
Mafuta 61
Magyarisation 14
majority 1, 2, 6, 37, 40, 84, 85, 97, 127, 130, 138, 142, 143, 144, 145, 146, 158, 159, 160, 179, 190, 191, 192, 193, 194, 196, 198, 199, 204, 214, 217, 219, 227, 228, 242
Maniu, Iuliu 21, 25
marginality 2, 4, 5, 6, 7, 11, 12, 26, 30, 31, 38, 52, 57, 58, 62, 67, 68, 70, 74, 76, 106, 112, 117, 119, 121, 122, 131, 145, 146, 157, 159, 160, 181
Maria Theresa 15
Mauvillon, Éléazar de 37, 40, 49, 50, 51, 53
metaphors 1, 3, 4, 5, 6, 68, 70, 72, 73, 74, 121, 130, 157, 162, 163, 165, 168, 175, 176, 177, 179, 180, 207, 218, 219
migration 15, 21, 26, 37, 39, 40, 42, 46, 52, 76, 90, 91, 92, 106, 117, 118, 121, 128, 131, 138, 141, 143, 144, 145, 146, 214, 216
minority 1, 2, 3, 5, 6, 37, 40, 52, 127, 128, 130, 131, 138, 139, 141, 142, 143, 144, 145, 146, 189, 191, 192, 193, 194, 195, 196, 198, 199, 200, 201, 203, 205, 206, 207, 208, 213, 214, 216, 217, 219, 223, 228
Moți 5, 11, 12, 14, 15, 17, 18, 21, 22, 24, 25, 26, 27, 28, 29, 30, 31
Muir, Simo 105, 107, 117
multilingualism 52, 83, 214, 215, 223

Nantes 37, 48
narratives 58, 62, 63, 71, 72, 74, 122, 142, 194, 195, 213, 214, 215, 216, 217, 219, 221, 222, 223, 225, 227
National Liberal Party (in Romania) 21
nationalism 12, 14, 19, 20, 21, 23, 24, 30, 31, 129, 133, 142, 155, 158, 160, 161, 214, 215, 216
nationality 4, 5, 38, 40, 44, 47, 52, 66, 67, 70, 74, 89, 91, 92, 93, 95, 96, 97, 99, 100, 213
nation-building 17, 18, 23, 127
Neba, Fontem 160

Nedo, Paul 213, 215
Netherlands, the 229
New York 94
Nicéron, Jean-Pierre 44
Niederrhein 42
Nigeria 161, 163
Niinistö, Sauli 202
Niinistö, Ville 202
Northern Ireland 155, 161
Norway 64, 161, 228
Nylund, Mats 203

Oliver, Lekeakeh 161
Osterhammel, Jürgen 75
Östman, Peter 202
Oxford 45

Pakistan 155
Palestine 83
Palestinians 130, 142, 143, 146
Paré, Francois 40, 48
Paris 45, 48, 221
Paul the Apostle 64
Pentecostal movements 156, 158, 172, 173, 176, 180
Pestmegyei Hírlap 18
Pietism 42, 43, 59, 71, 74
Piirimäe, Pärtel 51
Poland 241
Polish 87, 91, 97, 98
political violence 127, 128, 131, 132, 133, 134, 136, 137, 138, 141, 143, 145, 146, 147
Pop, Laurențiu 21
portraits 60, 61
postcolonial studies 38, 40
Potsdam 46
poverty 15, 24, 25, 26, 28, 70
power 38, 39, 40, 41, 43, 51, 53, 58, 62, 70, 95, 104, 105, 108, 109, 110, 112, 114, 115, 116, 119, 121, 122, 201, 206, 214, 229, 233
privilege 2, 6, 16, 17, 18, 27, 110, 117
Protestantism 4, 5, 40, 48, 50, 53, 59, 64, 65, 76, 156, 158, 161, 236
Prussia 5, 37, 42, 44, 46, 47, 51, 52, 53, 229

race 1, 4, 5, 24, 28, 62, 66, 67, 68, 70, 74, 75, 235
racism 57, 67, 68, 69, 73, 75, 142
Raj, Kapil 39, 43, 47, 52
recognition 1, 4, 7, 12, 14, 29, 110, 116
redistribution 4
Reichardt, Rolf 72
religion 2, 4, 5, 67, 69, 70, 74, 83, 86, 89, 93, 94, 95, 97, 100, 103, 104, 107, 113, 118, 125, 137, 138, 141, 144, 155, 156, 157, 158, 160, 161, 162, 163, 164, 165, 166, 167, 168, 172, 173, 175, 179, 180, 182, 231, 236
Renaissance 52
Rey, Terry 110
Romania 5, 11, 13, 14, 18, 20, 21, 22, 24, 27, 29, 31, 32
Romanian 11, 27
Romanian National Party 21, 23
Romanians 11, 12, 14, 17, 18, 27, 28, 29, 31
Ronsard, Pierre de 44
Russia 163, 191
Russian 87, 90, 91, 92, 93, 95, 97, 99, 100, 136, 144, 214
Russian Empire, the 103, 105
Russians 90, 92, 93, 96, 97, 98, 99, 100
Ruthenians 19
Ruymbeke, Bertrand Van 39, 45

Sako Ikome, Samuel 161
Saxons 18
Scott, Walter 241
Seinäjoki 197, 201, 202
sexuality 4
Sibbern, Frederik Christian 227
Siguranța 22
Sipilä, Juha 201
Sjöholm, Emma 61
Sjöholm, Wilhelm 61
social identity theory 128, 129, 139, 141, 145, 146
sociolinguistics 85, 93, 95
Sorbian 214
Sorbs 6, 213, 214, 215, 216, 217, 218, 219, 220, 221, 222, 223, 224, 225
South Africa 161
Soviet Union 5, 90, 93, 96, 100, 117, 143

St. Barthélemy 58
Stachowa, Angela 215, 223, 225
Stoeffler, F. Ernest 42
Strohmeier-Wiederanders, Gerlinde 41, 42
Suominen, Anne 206
Svenska Missionsförbundet 59, 60, 62, 64, 65, 66, 67, 71, 73
Swartz, David 104
Sweden 5, 49, 50, 51, 58, 62, 65, 75, 76, 191, 192, 206, 228, 229
Swedish 189, 190, 192, 194, 195, 199, 202, 206
Swedish-speaking Finns 2, 6, 49, 189, 190, 191, 192, 193, 194, 195, 196, 197, 198, 199, 200, 201, 202, 203, 204, 205, 206, 207, 208
Swiss German 87, 95
Switzerland 53
symbolic capital 105, 108, 109, 111, 112, 114, 115, 116, 117, 118, 120, 121, 122
Székely 5, 11, 12, 15, 18, 19, 20, 21, 22, 23, 24, 25, 26, 27, 28, 29, 30, 31
Székely Congress 20, 24, 25

Taylor, Charles 4
Thirty Years' War 42, 51
Tisza, István 20
Trajan, Emperor 27
Transylvania 11, 12, 14, 16, 17, 18, 21, 27, 31
Tschernokoshewa, Elka 215
Tuori, Riikka 105, 107
Turkish 214
Turku 103, 107

Ukrainian 93
United Kingdom 161
USA 161, 163, 179, 182

Vaida Voevod, Alexandru 28
Vasa 201, 202, 203, 204, 205, 207, 208
Vienna 42
Voltaire 45, 46, 48
Vornea, Sandru 24
Voss, Julia 60
Vuorela, Ulla 75

Wacquant, Loïc 110

Wade, Ira 43
Walkowitz, Rebecca L. 52
Walldén, Wilhelm 65, 66, 68
Westphalia 42
Wilfred, Tassang 160, 174
witnessing 62, 63, 69
Wolff, Christian 46

World War II 12, 14, 133, 159
writing practices 38

Yediot Aharonot 137
Yiddish 84, 85, 87, 88, 96, 98, 100, 240

Zionism 127, 133, 146

List of Contributors

Hanna Acke, PhD, works as a university lecturer in German language and literature at Åbo Akademi University in Turku, Finland. Acke's research interests include discourse linguistics, language critique, contradictions as well as pejorative and discriminative language.

Katharina Bock, PhD, received her PhD at the Nordeuropa-Institut at Humboldt-Universität zu Berlin, Germany. Her recent work at Diakonie Deutschland in Berlin centres on promoting awareness for democracy and participation in politics. Bock's research interests include antisemitism, conspiracy thinking, and populism as well as psychodynamic perspectives and approaches.

Silvia Bonacchi is Professor of Applied Linguistics and Intercultural Communication at the University of Warsaw, Poland, and director of the Department for Intercultural Pragmalinguistics and Multimodal Communication of the Institute of Specialised and Intercultural Communication (ISIC). Her research interests cover pragmalinguistics, intercultural communication studies, multimodal communication, conversational and discourse analysis.

Mercédesz Czimbalmos, PhD, works as a postdoctoral researcher at the Inez and Julius Polin Institute for Theological Research within Åbo Akademi University in Turku, Finland as well as a senior researcher at the Finnish Institute for Health and Welfare (THL) in Helsinki, Finland. Czimbalmos' research interests include Jewish studies, gender studies, interreligious encounters, and contemporary antisemitism.

Gábor Egry is a historian, PhD, Doctor of the Hungarian Academy of Sciences, director of the Institute of Political History, Budapest. His research interests include nationalism, everyday ethnicity, state society relations and economic imperialism in modern central and Eastern Europe.

Maya Hadar, PhD, LLM, MA Peace Studies and Conflict Resolution, is an assistant professor of International Relations and European studies at Masaryk University, the Czech Republic and a guest researcher at the Institute for Peace Support and Conflict Management of the Austrian National Defense Academy. Her research interests include nationalism and patriotism, identity politics, memory politics and military-society relations in Israel.

Dr. **Diana Hitzke** has worked as a researcher at Erfurt University, JLU Giessen and TU Dresden. She now works in science management at JLU Giessen. Her areas of research are nomadic writing, world literature, transculturality, multilingualism, and minority studies.

Esther Jahns is a sociolinguist and works as a Postdoc at the Carl von Ossietzky Universität in Oldenburg, Germany. Her research interest's include language ideologies, social meaning of variation, Jewish languages, as well as language contact and multilingualism.

Carsten Junker is Professor of American Studies with a Focus on Diversity Studies at TU Dresden, Germany. A special emphasis in his work lies on how social differentiations and cultural patterns, including discursive struggles, are formalised.

Svante Lindberg, PhD, is Senior University Lecturer and a *Docent* in the Department of French Language and Literature at Åbo Akademi University in Turku, Finland. His research interests include among other things the contemporary francophone novel (in particular in Canada and France), world literature, exile literature in Swedish and French, and literary didactics.

Herbert Rostand Ngouo, PhD, is a lecturer in Linguistics in the Department of Bilingual Letters of the University of Maroua in Cameroon. He did his postgraduate and doctoral research in African Studies with specialisation in linguistics. His research interests are sociolinguistics, applied linguistics, and discourse analysis. In Discourse studies, he is interested in emancipatory, political, and religious discourse in Africa, as well as other forms of emerging online discourse modes. In sociolinguistics, he investigates the sociocultural effects of globalization on the ethnolinguistic vitality of minority indigenous languages, and the impact of language policy (in education) on sustainability and resilience of minority ethnolinguistic communities.

Christopher M. Schmidt is Professor of German language and literature at Åbo Akademi University, Finland. He is the initiator and co-founder of the international research-cooperation Europäische Kulturen in der Wirtschaftskommunikation EUKO. His research interests lie within the interdisciplinary scope of intercultural as well as cross-cultural analysis, multimodal text theory, cognitive linguistics, corporate and brand communication, rhetorics and semiotics.

Charlotta Seiler Brylla is Professor of German at Stockholm University, Sweden. Her research interests are in the areas of political discourse analysis, discourse semantics, lexicology as well as comparative language and culture studies. One of her current projects concerns the semiotics of antisemitism and youth's experiences of antisemitism in contemporary Sweden.

Ingo H. Warnke is Professor of German and Interdisciplinary Linguistics at the University of Bremen, Germany. His research interests include discourse linguistics, language in contradiction, and the legacy of the German colonial archive.

www.ingramcontent.com/pod-product-compliance
Lightning Source LLC
Chambersburg PA
CBHW020226170426
43201CB00007B/333